Artforms

AN INTRODUCTION TO THE VISUAL ARTS
Fourth Edition

Duane and Sarah Preble

1817

HARPER & ROW, PUBLISHERS, New York
Cambridge,
Philadelphia,
San Francisco,
London,
Mexico City,
São Paulo,
Singapore,
Sydney

To all who will come to know
the artist within

Editor-in-Chief: Judith Rothman
Development Editor: Fred Henry
Production Managers: Tom Dorsaneo/San Francisco
  and Willie Lane/New York
Cover and Text Designer: Bruce Kortebein
Copy Editor: Naomi Lucks
Cover Photograph: Elaine Keenan
Typesetting: TBH/Typecast, Inc.
Text Art: Sally Shimizu and Phyllis Rockne
Color Separations: Quality Graphic Services, Inc.
  and Arcata Graphics/Kingsport
Printing and Binding: Arcata Graphics/Kingsport

Artforms, Fourth Edition
© 1989 by Harper & Row, Publishers, Inc.

This book was previously published as *Artforms* © 1978,
1985 and *Man Creates Art Creates Man* © 1973.

Library of Congress Cataloging in Publication Data

Preble, Duane.
    Artforms: an introduction to the visual arts / Duane and Sarah
Preble.—4th ed.
    p. cm.

    Bibliography: p.
    Includes index.
    ISBN 0-06-045211-0
    1. Composition (Art) 2. Visual perception. 3. Art—History.
I. Preble, Sarah. II. Title.
N7430.P69 1989   88-24555
700—dc19   CIP

89 90 91 92 93 10 9 8 7 6 5 4 3 2

ACKNOWLEDGMENTS

It has been an awesome, rewarding, and humbling experience to be part of a cooperative venture as large and complex as the publication of ARTFORMS. A great many people have been directly involved in this group effort, and we regret that space does not allow us to name all those who made significant contributions. We appreciate the help of each and every one.

We are particularly grateful to our editors, Judith Rothman, Tom Dorsaneo, and Fred Henry for making it possible for us to be actively involved in the design and production of this edition. Copy editor Naomi Lucks, designer Bruce Kortebein, and production coordinator Polly Christensen were most patient and helpful as we invaded their territory. The staffs of Quality Graphics and Arcata Graphics/Kingsport Press went way beyond business-as-usual as they helped us meet deadlines, and implemented last minute changes.

Thanks also to our many colleagues at the University of Hawaii who generously shared their knowledge and expertise. Diana Schoenfeld deserves special mention for making detailed comments on the entire manuscript.

We would like to express our appreciation to the following reviewers who contributed many helpful suggestions:

La Monte Anderson, Broward Community College
Wayne M. Anderson, Wayne State College
Karen White Boyd, Murray State University
Leif Brush, University of Minnesoto, Duluth
James M. Butterworth, Western Illinois University
Gary Cawood, University of Arkansas at Little Rock
Brian E. Conley, Golden West College
Richard M. Cooler, Northern Illinois University, DeKalb
Earnest J. Davidson, Jr., University of Arkansas at Pine Bluff
James T. Diehr, Austin Peay State University
Michael A. Dorsey, Mississippi State University
Whitney J. Engeran, Jr., Indiana State University
Edna Garte, University of Minnesota, Duluth
E. Carroll Hale II, Eastern Kentucky University
Philancy N. Holder, Austin Peay State University
E. Max Von Isser, Elgin Community College
Sandra L. Johnson, Pasadena City College
Susan Kattas, Inver Hills Community College
Harry D. Korn, Ventura College
Paul W. Kravagna, California State University, Northridge
Pamela Farris Lawson, Radford University
David LeDoux, Middle Tennessee State University
Ock-Kyung Lee, Towson State University
Walter C. Leedy, Jr., Cleveland State University
Felicia Lewandowski, Radford University
Roger Lintault, California State University, San Bernardino

Anne H. Lisca, Santa Fe Community College
Lynn Mackenzie, Northern Illinois University
Floyd W. Martin, University of Arkansas at Little Rock
Jacquelyn McElroy-Edwards, University of North Dakota
Helen Merritt, Northern Illinois University
Lily R. Minassian, Broward Community College
Joseph Molinaro, Broward Community College
Louis F. Mustari, Northern Illinois University
Peter L. Myer, Brigham Young University
Prithwish Neogy, University of Hawaii
Edward A. Parks, Diablo Valley College
Michael E. Parks, SUNY College at Buffalo
Edward R. Pope, University of Wisconsin, Madison
Jean A. Pratt, American River College
Helen R. Pullen, Towson State University
Lisa W. Rabinowitz, Bloomfield College
Jeffrey Ruda, University of California, Davis
Henry Sayre, Oregon State University
Claire Selkurt, Mankato State University
John J. Shaak, California State University, Long Beach
Molly Kay Singer, University of Colorado, Boulder
Jean Sizemore, University of Arkansas at Little Rock
Stan Sporny, University of Arkansas at Pine Bluff
Michael Stone, Cuyahoga Community College West
Candace Jesse Stout, University of Missouri
Betty Sullivan, Punahou School
James E. Sullivan, Southern Illinois University at Carbondale
Harold Wassell, Colorado State University
Donald E. Widen, Fullerton Community College
Dan D. Wood, Southern Illinois University at Carbondale
Elizabeth A. Yarosz, Midwestern State University
Professor Edward A. Youngman, Wingate College

All of our work was brought to final form by the careful management, generosity, and creative spirit of Tom Dorsaneo. His enthusiasm, patience, practical help, and gentle prodding kept us going, and were essential to the completion of the fourth edition of ARTFORMS.

Contents

About the Cover

If it does its job well, a book cover provides an attractive outer wrapping and tells something about the book's contents. For our fourth edition, we sought a cover that would be visually intriguing and capable of introducing this book about all the visual arts. We also wanted an image that could not easily be identified or categorized. We chose Nance O'Banion's MIRAGE SERIES: TOO for its substantial presence as a graphic image, as well as its ability to invite readers to explore between the covers.

Nance O'Banion's handmade paper constructions defy categorization. Her vibrantly colored pieces combine traditional paint media and craft-related materials. O'Banion's concerns go beyond color, texture, pattern, and composition to ideas and content. In MIRAGE SERIES: TOO, she plays off suggestions of clouds against a richly tactile painted surface. MIRAGE SERIES: TOO reminds us that art is ultimately about perception and seeing, rather than subjects, categories, media, styles, or other labels. Because O'Banion approves of showing or displaying this piece with either side up, we show it one way on the cover, and the other way on page 206.

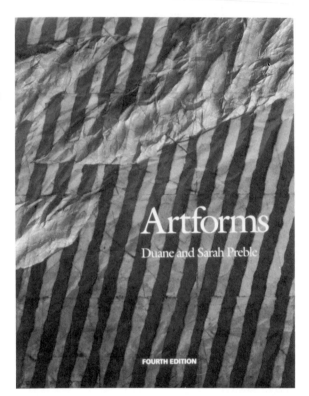

Introduction

Art? Who needs it? Clearly the human race must, for we have continued to invent ways to express our concerns artistically for more than thirty thousand years. In our technological society, which depends so heavily on the scientific method, art enables us to communicate ideas that we cannot express in other ways.

This book grew out of our desire to introduce art through an engaging visual experience, and to help you build an informed foundation for your individual experience and enjoyment of art. By introducing art theory, practice, and history in a single volume, this book is designed to draw you into a new or expanded awareness of the visual arts. We hope ARTFORMS will stimulate you to continue to make discoveries in this vast field of human endeavor, encourage you to develop your own creative abilities, and help you become independent in your continuing experience of the arts.

From the start, we and our editors agreed that ARTFORMS should be as visually exciting as the individual works of art reproduced in it. In this edition, we have written new chapters and added new images, many of which were created in the few brief years since the last edition was published. With these we explore the relationship of today's art to the art of the past, and present some of the new methods and materials available to artists in our rapidly changing world.

Part One introduces the nature of art, aesthetics, creativity, purposes, style, and critical evaluation. Part Two presents the communicative language of vision: form and content, visual elements, and principles of design. This visual and verbal art vocabulary prepares you to sample the broad range of art disciplines, media, and processes presented in Part Three. Parts Four and Five introduce historic world styles and related cultural values. Although Western art history is inevitably given more emphasis, in these chapters we encourage you to become aware of the rich variety of world art. Part Five explores the many ways the art of today has evolved out of the art of the past. The final two chapters discuss art forms of the recent past and contemporary issues.

The domain of the visual arts is extensive. It ranges from drawing and painting to architecture and urban design, from making pots to making films and videos. To limit the length, rather than the scope of ARTFORMS, we have had to be both highly selective and broad in outlook. ARTFORMS goes beyond the appreciation of major artworks. Our primary concern is to open eyes and minds to the richness of the visual arts as unique forms of human experience, and to convey the idea that the arts enrich life best when we experience, understand, and enjoy them as an integral part of the process of living.

1 Saul Steinberg.

PART ONE

Why Art?

Art isn't everything. It's just about everything.

Attributed to Gertrude Stein

1
Barnett Newman.
BROKEN OBELISK.
(See page 22.)

1

The Nature of Art

Art, like life itself, need not be defined or understood to be enjoyed. It must simply be experienced.

Art is not something apart from us. It grows from capacities we all possess. If you have ever experienced something intensely and wanted to share that experience with others, you have been where art begins.

WHAT IS ART?

Art is even harder to define than religion or science. No single definition is big enough. Originally, art meant "skill," but now it means skill and much more. To many, the word *art* refers to something created by an *artist*—who is generally thought to be a painter or sculptor. To others, art also includes anything done so well that it takes on special meaning, as the following dictionary definition suggests:

art (art), n. 1. the quality, production, or expression of what is beautiful, appealing, or of more than ordinary significance.[1]

A *work of art* is the aesthetic expression of an idea or experience, formed with human skills through the use of a medium. A *medium* is any material from which art is made. When a material—or medium—is used in such a way that the work contributes to our understanding or enjoyment of life, we experience the work as art.

When people speak of "the arts," they are referring to music, dance, drama, literature, and the visual arts. The focus of this book is the visual arts—drawing, painting, sculpture, filmmaking, architecture, and so forth. Each of the arts is a unique type of human activity, yet all of the arts grow from a universal human urge to give physical form to ideas, feelings, and experiences. Works of art that add to the experience of many people over a long period of time are considered masterpieces.

There are no absolute standards that can help you appraise the quality of a work of art. If it contributes to *your* experience, then it is probably art for you. This does not mean, however, that you should not consider other interpretations. Although teachers, authors, and art critics can*not* determine your personal likes and dislikes in art, they can offer insights gained from their experience and involvement that provide new dimensions of perception and knowledge for your consideration.

It is best to approach art openly, without bias. Give yourself time to react, and ask yourself questions: How does this work make me feel? Why does it make me feel this way? Did the person who made it have something particular in mind to which I can respond? How was it made? Does it relate to my personal experience in any way?

Many artists say their work is most alive for them when they are in the process of creating it. As a viewer, you share in the creative process when you recreate the work of art as you perceive it. The full pleasure you can experience through participation in the arts results from your curiosity, intuition, and concentration.

2 Charles Schulz.
PEANUTS.
© 1968, United Feature Syndicate, Inc.

Art, for you, cannot exist without your sensitive response.

As Charles Schulz suggests in his PEANUTS comic strip, art is ultimately whatever we think it is. Those who believe that the only "good" art was done in the past are unable to really see and enjoy much of the art of the present. It is human nature to like what you understand or know. Knowing what you like is the beginning; knowing why you respond favorably or unfavorably to certain forms takes you that much further. Ideally, the dialogue between the viewer and work of art can go far beyond likes and dislikes.

Earlier societies, and even some contemporary traditional societies, do not separate art from the rest of life. Some societies do not even have a word for art. The Balinese simply say, "We have no art; we do everything as well as we can." In such traditional societies, the arts document a long heritage of values and give form to spiritual life. In technological societies, however, we tend to think of art as an isolated entity, produced only by uniquely gifted people, most of whom are no longer living. This attitude is reinforced by the fact that we see most works of art in museums, far removed from the life experiences of the people who created them.

Leading artists of the twentieth century have aggressively questioned and expanded art's traditional limits. They have introduced new languages of visual form which have profoundly influenced the material and imaginative life in our time. The entire spectrum of our visible world has been affected—from clothing, utensils, architecture, and automobile design to mass media. In this way, art is very much a part of everyday life. The avalanche of stylishly designed objects and images has itself become both media and

3 SITE Projects, Inc.
GHOST PARKING LOT.
Hamden, Connecticut. 1978.
Used automobiles,
bloc bond, asphalt.

subject for contemporary artists. For example, SITE Projects' use of automobiles and asphalt in GHOST PARKING LOT makes a humorous statement about our pervasive manufactured environment. Here we can see how art has the power to alter our relationship to objects and events outside ourselves, and to help us see them in fresh ways.

Above all, the art of our culture reflects who we are and our relationship to our surroundings. As such, art can give us joy and inspiration and may also lead us to discover disturbing dimensions within ourselves. In the ugliness and distortion of some images, we may recognize some of our own negative or destructive aspects. Yet this very recognition can be an impetus for positive growth.

THE NECESSITY FOR ART

Is it necessary for us to give physical form to things we feel, think, and imagine? Must we gesture, dance, draw, speak, sing, write, carve, paint, and build? To be fully human, it seems we must. The urge to make and enjoy what we now call art has been a driving force throughout human history. Every forward step has been highlighted with the invention of articles and images designed to sustain and celebrate life. Although the forms and functions of art change, humans continue to delight in using perception, thought, feeling, and manual skill to produce and enjoy an infinite variety of forms that extend and enrich experience.

Most of us feel compelled to share experience with others. If an idea or experience is important to us, and we succeed in making it known to another person, we feel confirmed and strengthened by the success. If we fail to get the idea across, we feel frustrated and diminished. Russian novelist and philosopher Leo Tolstoy defined art as a way of communicating feelings:

To evoke in oneself a feeling one has experienced, and having evoked it in oneself, then by means of movement, line, color, sounds or forms expressed in words, so to transmit the same feeling—this is the activity of art.[2]

All societies have produced objects and rituals that extend communication and meet their physical and spiritual needs. Some objects—from simple tools to vast temple complexes—have been designed to meet both physical and spiritual needs simultaneously. Traditional societies seldom distinguish between the practical function of an object and its spiritual and aesthetic significance. Within the context of the NAVAJO SAND PAINTING CEREMONY, healing, spiritual meaning, and aesthetic beauty are inseparable.

In order to understand and work with the elemental forces of nature, to appreciate and explore the mysteries of life, humans developed modes of inquiry and activity. In the West, we separate these into the disciplines of science, religion, philosophy, and art. The arts are but one facet of our attempt to relieve our fears and doubts by integrating the known and the unknown, the material and the spiritual. The finest works of art are a unity of spirit and matter; they remain "alive" regardless of when or where they were created. This is why even ancient art appears timeless, and continues to evoke responses from us today.

Every society values particular areas of human endeavor, and supports them with money and respect. Many earlier cultures we admire today, such as Renaissance Italy, gave support for, and thus had high achievement in, the arts. (During some of the lowest points in human history, such as Nazi Germany, the arts were severely censored.) The arts flourish, and leading figures —seen as cultural heroes—emerge in proportion to the degree of support. In Renaissance Italy, artists were the leading heroes. Leonardo da Vinci, Michelangelo, and Raphael achieved greatness partly because they had early recognition and strong encouragement in the form of education, training, and patronage.

Today's technologically explosive societies need the humanizing rewards of art. Science and the arts serve humanity in complementary ways. Science seeks and finds answers to problems and questions related to our physical world, and forms the basis of our technology; the arts help foster our emotional, spiritual, and imaginative/creative growth, and help give viable, satisfying form to our physical environment.

PERCEPTION AND AWARENESS

Of all our planet's resources, the most precious is human awareness . . .

Don Fabun[3]

Perception and awareness are closely related terms. To be *aware* means to be conscious or heedful, or to know something, either by means of perception or information. To *perceive* is to become aware through the senses, particularly through sight or hearing, and to achieve understanding by means of such awareness.

Surprising as it may seem, much of our sensory awareness is learned. Eyes are blind to what the mind cannot see. As our perception improves, so does our understanding and enjoyment of the world. Art helps us to see, and how we "see" determines how we live. Developing awareness and becoming personally involved in shaping our surroundings can make life more fulfilling.

In learning to live in the world, we learn to conceptualize almost everything we perceive. We place unique elements of our experience into general classes or categories, and give names to such categories so that we can think about them and communicate these ideas to others. The system built up by this process of classification is called a cognitive system. It is shaped by basic cultural values, and provides a framework for perception. We could not get along without such classifications; yet by labeling and categorizing, we often overlook the unique qualities of objects and events, and emphasize those qualities believed to be held in common. Generalized categories, if not balanced by open, unbiased perception, can provide the basis for prejudice of all kinds.

4 NAVAJO SAND PAINTING CEREMONY.
Photograph courtesy of Wheelwright Museum of the American Indian, Santa Fe, New Mexico.

As a group, we have developed "a distinctive way of looking at the world *that is not the way the world actually is* but simply the way our group conventionally looks at our world."[4] Every society's cognitive system keeps it functioning; yet major human problems are caused by the fact that almost any group may believe that its way of seeing things is *reality*—the way the world actually is.

Words and concepts can confuse our sensory impressions. When we look at a subject only in terms of a label or stereotype, we miss the thing itself; we see "tree," "chair," "ugliness," "beauty," rather than *this* tree, this *particular* chair, this *unique* object, person, or situation. We may become aware only to the degree that we are stimulated to develop awareness by other people—our parents, teachers, and friends. The following story provides a graphic illustration.

Joey, a New York City boy with blind parents, had cerebral palsy as a baby. Because of his own and his parents' disabilities, Joey was largely confined to his family's apartment. As he grew older, he learned to get around the apartment in a walker. His mother thought he seemed to have normal intelligence, yet clinical tests showed him to be blind and mentally retarded. At age five, Joey was admitted to a school for children with a variety of disabilities, and for the first time had daily contact with people who could see. Although he bumped into things in his walker and felt for almost everything, as a blind person does, it soon became apparent that Joey was not really blind. *He simply had never learned to use his eyes.* The combined disabilities of Joey and his parents had prevented him from developing normal visual awareness. After working with specialists and playing with sighted children for a year, his visual responses were normal. Those who worked with him concluded that Joey was a bright and alert child. To varying degrees, we are all guided—or limited, as Joey was—in the growth of our awareness by people who influence us.

Degrees of visual awareness can be indicated by the verbs "to look" and "to see." *Looking* implies taking in what is before us in a purely mechanical way; *seeing* is an extension of looking. In the world of function, we must only look at a doorknob in order to grasp and turn it.

When we get excited about the shape and finish of a doorknob, the bright clear quality of a winter day, or the rich color of a sunset, we have gone beyond simple functional looking to the higher level of perception called seeing. Careful observation by sixteenth-century German painter Albrecht Dürer enabled him to reveal the wonder of an ordinary patch of weeds. His watercolor painting appropriately titled THE GREAT PIECE OF TURF shows us a commonplace subject, seen as if for the first time.

Today's urban societies bombard us with stereotyped or "canned" images that may deaden our awareness. Such sensory overload blocks real perception. Even before the development of television, twentieth-century French artist Henri Matisse wrote about the courage it takes to move beyond media stereotypes—to really see:

To see is itself a creative operation, requiring an effort. Everything that we see in our daily life is more or less distorted by acquired habits, and this is perhaps more evident in an age like ours when cinema, posters, and magazines present us every day with a flood of ready-made images which are to the eye what prejudices are to the mind. The effort needed to see things without distortion takes something very like courage.[5]

Sight is more mental than physical. It is mind and eye coordination. For true seeing to occur, the mind must interpret what it encounters visually.

Vision is the means by which we recognize both our physical environment and our inner images of intangibles such as memories and dreams. *Visualization* is the conscious use of imagination and visual memory to preview events or plans before they occur. The character of one's visualization can have a decisive effect on how that event will turn out. The process of visualization enables us to bring together inner and outer realities, and therefore

5 Albrecht Dürer.
THE GREAT PIECE OF TURF. 1503.
Watercolor. 16¼″ × 12⅜″.
Albertina Collection, Vienna.

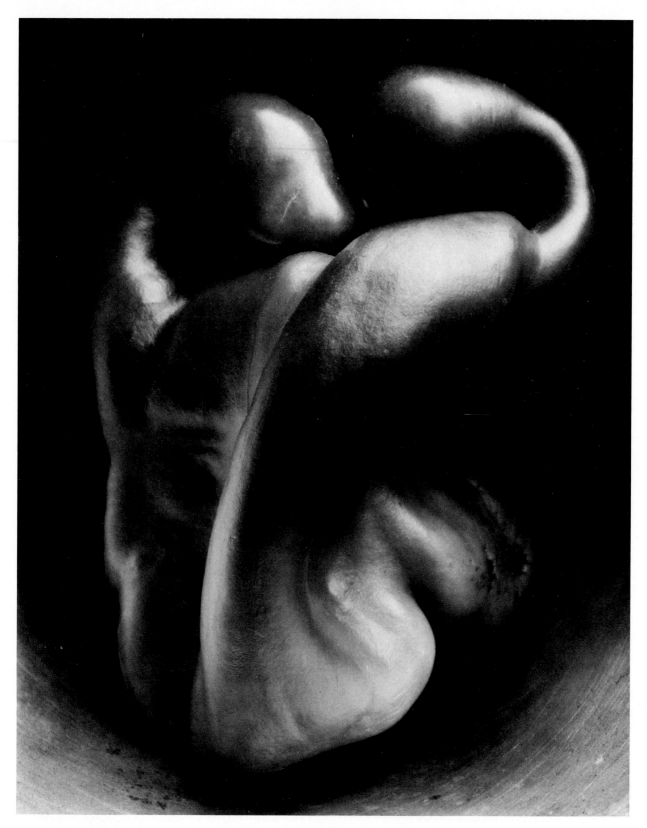

6 Edward Weston.
PEPPER #30. 1930.
Photograph.
© 1981, *Arizona Board of Regents, Center
for Creative Photography.*

provides a means by which ideas and images can be materialized:

A horticulturalist says: "Before you can have beautiful roses on your lawn or in your greenhouse, you have to have beautiful roses in your mind." This is true of many other things. Before a stately building is built it must live in the architect's mind. Before a beautiful picture is painted it must live in the artist's mind. The controlling power of life comes from within.[6]

Experience conditions both inner visualization and outer seeing. The variety of responses to visual stimuli is demonstrated by the enormous breadth of artwork in the world. Some of the differences are cultural, and some are individual. Twelve people depicting the same subject—even from the same vantage point—will make twelve different images based on their different experiences, attitudes, interests, and eyesight. A child and an adult will see the same landscape differently, as will a man and a woman, and a farmer and a developer. Even one individual can have a variety of responses to a given subject. When we look at a photograph of a house, for example, we see enclosed volume; intellectually, we know it contains rooms; and emotionally, we may make associations with "home." A person thinking creatively is aware of these various levels of meaning, and is able to apply the two basic types of human intelligence: rational and intuitive.

As we become aware of our own sensory processes and related aesthetic decisions, we can begin to open up an entirely new world of awareness. Ordinary things become extraordinary when seen in a new way. Is Edward Weston's photograph of a green pepper meaningful to us because we like peppers so much? Probably not. Weston created a significant image on a flat surface with the help of a pepper. A time exposure of over two hours gave the photograph a quality of glowing light—a living presence that resembles an embrace. Through his sensitivity to and expression of form, Weston revealed how this pepper appeared to him. The following notes from his *Daybook* reveal his insights and feelings about this photograph:

August 8, 1930
I could wait no longer to print them—my new peppers, so I put aside several orders, and yesterday afternoon had an exciting time with seven new negatives.

First I printed my favorite, the one made last Saturday, August 2, just as the light was failing—quickly made, but with a week's previous effort back of my immediate, unhesitating decision. A week?—Yes, on this certain pepper,—but twenty-eight years of effort, starting with a youth on a farm in Michigan, armed with a No. 2 Bull's Eye [Kodak] 3½ x 3½, have gone into the making of this pepper, which I consider a peak of achievement.

It is a classic, completely satisfying,—a pepper—but more than a pepper: abstract, in that it is completely outside subject matter . . . this new pepper takes one beyond the world we know in the conscious mind.[7]

April 24, 1930
Clouds, torsos, shells, peppers, trees, rocks, smokestacks are but interdependent, interrelated parts of a whole, which is life.—Life rhythms felt in no matter what, become symbols of the whole.[8]

AESTHETICS

When we are so moved by something that we lose ourselves in the experience, our response may be called an aesthetic experience. *Aesthetic* refers to a sense of the beautiful and, by extension, to sense perception in general. It is interesting to note that the opposite of aesthetic is anesthetic.

Aesthetics is the branch of philosophy that studies the arts and seeks to establish general principles of art and beauty. It also examines intellectual and feeling responses to both the arts and non-art phenomena. In the Western world, aesthetics has focused on the concept of beauty, which is equated with the sublime—something so profoundly affecting that it is associated with the divine.

7   Leonardo da Vinci.
FIVE GROTESQUE HEADS. c. 1490.
Pen and brown ink. 10¼″ × 8½″.
Windsor Castle, Royal Library.
© Her Majesty Queen Elizabeth II.

Other civilizations have also studied the manner in which we are affected by works of art. Asian aesthetic views have remained traditional and stable. In India, philosophers say the aesthetic experience takes place in a transaction between a prepared viewer and a work of art of excellent quality; the aesthetic experience is neither in the beholder nor in the object, but in the interaction of the two. In China, the work of art is expected to express the vitality of the artist, which is consistent with the energy of the universe, in order that viewers may be vitalized through their experience of the art. In Japan, a work of art can provoke awe that cannot be expressed in words.

In the Western world, theories of aesthetics can be categorized as subjective, objective, or a balance of the two. A *subjective* approach holds that judgment is personal, changeable, and unchallengeable, and that all individual responses are equally valid. Here the value of a work is in the response of the viewer rather than the work itself. Conversely, *objective* theories are based on an assumption that there are unchanging standards upon which absolute judgments can be made about all art, regardless of time and place. Nearly any such fixed set of standards results in rejection of the art of many cultures.

Between these extremes are *relativist* theories, which hold that value stems from the interaction between the subjective response of the viewer and the intrinsic qualities of the art object. With this approach, each culture forms its own standards. Many tribal peoples, without the need of a theory, a philosophy, or even a word for art, recognize some works as having greater power than others.

Some people equate the word aesthetic with taste. This view is currently opposed by some artists and art critics, who maintain that art has nothing to do with good taste—that so-called good taste can actually limit an honest response. Recent developments in art can be seen as successive overturnings of what the previous generation considered tasteful. This is why traditional aesthetic theory fails to explain much contemporary art.

In the West, problematic and contradictory views have arisen regarding "art" and "beauty." Beginning with ancient Greece, Westerners have been preoccupied with beauty. Criteria for beauty, and also for art, often consist of culturally accepted standards, rather than individual feelings or personal intuition regarding truth.

Sometimes we use the word "beautiful" to refer to things that are simply pretty. "Pretty" means pleasant or attractive to the eye, whereas "beautiful" means having qualities of a high order, being capable of delighting the eye or engaging the intellectual or moral sense, or doing all these things simultaneously. "Beautiful doesn't necessarily mean good looking."[9]

The ability to be open to possibilities beyond conventional definitions of beauty and ugliness is an important dimension of awareness. If the only function of art were to please the senses, ugliness would have no place in art. We don't expect all works of drama or literature to be pretty or pleasant; why should we have different expectations of the visual arts? Leonardo da Vinci, Shibata Zeshin, and Pablo Picasso—three artists from different times and places—each actively explored dimensions of human "ugliness."

Street life fascinated Italian Renaissance artist Leonardo da Vinci. He was particularly interested in studying people who were striking in appearance, either because they were very beautiful or very ugly. Leonardo found ugliness as worthy of attention as beauty. In fact, he considered ugliness a variation of beauty. In his *Treatise on Painting*, he advised others always to carry a pocket notebook in which to make quick drawings of whatever they observed. He also drew from memory, as sixteenth-century artist and biographer Giorgio Vasari described:

Leonardo used to follow people whose extraordinary appearance took his fancy, sometimes throughout a whole day, until he could draw them as well by memory as though they stood before him.[10]

Elegant lines, charged with energy, depict the garments and frame the ugly head in this detail from nineteenth-century Japanese artist Shibata Zeshin's DANCING RASHOMON. The artist created the terrifying figure from his imagination in order to dramatize a key moment in a story.

The study by twentieth-century Spanish artist Pablo Picasso for his famous painting GUERNICA (see page 411) was part of his personal response to the bombing of a small Spanish town, Guernica, which for him demonstrated the cruelty and brutal ugliness of war. As this study illustrates, even horrible events can provide the basis for constructive communication through art.

8 Shibata Zeshin.
Detail of DANCING RASHOMON. 19th century.
Ink and color on paper. Hanging scroll, 14⅝″ × 20½″.
Honolulu Academy of Arts. Gift of James E. O'Brien.

9 Pablo Picasso.
HEAD (study for GUERNICA). May 24, 1937.
Pencil and gouache. 11⅜″ × 9¼″.
Prado Museum, Madrid.
(See page 411.)

2

Art as Experience

The essence of art is the spark of insight and the thrill of discovery—first experienced by the maker, then built into and carried by the work, and finally experienced by the receptive viewer. In this sense, the art object is a vehicle for the communication of significant experience. The capacity to experience images as art depends on both the quality of the image and the viewer's ability to see.

CREATIVITY

In talking about creativity, let us first consider its two possible meanings: creativity in the sense of creating something new, something which can be seen or heard by others, such as a painting, a sculpture, a symphony, a poem, a novel, etc., or creativity as an attitude, which is the condition of any creation in the former sense but which can exist even though nothing new is created in the world of things. . . .

What is creativity? The best general answer I can give is that creativity is the ability to see (or to be aware) and to respond.

Erich Fromm[1]

Creativity is not limited to those with inborn "talent." We all have the potential to be creative, yet most of us have never been encouraged to develop our creativity. We can do so by becoming open and willing to explore new relationships and insights within ourselves and in the world around us. The source of all art, science, and technology—in fact, all of civilization—is what is called creative imagination, or the creative attitude. As Albert Einstein pointed out: "Imagination is more important than knowledge."[2]

Have you ever been inspired by an idea or faced with a problem? This is where the creative process often begins. Creativity can also be the result of something as simple as playing or "fooling around." During play, we are aware of the possible significance of chance events.

Imaginative visualization is a major part of the creative process. When we form and combine images in the mind's eye, we create a unique experience outside of actual events. One objective of the arts is to make this intangible life of the mind tangible—visible in the visual arts, audible in music, verbal in literature.

Artists—and others in touch with their creativity—must be dreamers, as well as practical realists and skilled workers. The creative process requires the ideas of a receptive, imaginative mind. It also requires the ability to manipulate freely and consciously the elements of perceptual experience—the ability to see beyond what is, to what might be. The creative mind has the ability to see form in apparent formlessness, and to find or make order from apparent chaos.

Studies of creativity have described outstanding characteristics of creative people. These include the abilities to:

□ wonder, be curious

□ be willing to approach new experience with an open mind and to see the familiar from an unfamiliar point of view

□ take advantage of accidental events in order to make desirable but unsought discoveries (called serendipity)

□ make one thing out of another by shifting its functions

□ generalize in order to see universal applications of ideas

□ synthesize and integrate, find order in disorder

□ be in touch with unconscious sources, yet be intensely conscious

□ visualize or imagine new possibilities

□ be analytical and critical

□ know oneself, have the courage to be oneself in the face of opposition, and be willing to take risks

□ be persistent, to work for long periods—perhaps years—in pursuit of a goal, without guaranteed results

Nearly all children have rich, creative imaginations. They naturally reach out to the world around them from birth. They taste, touch, hear, see, and smell their environment, becoming part of it through their senses. All forms of their communication are part of that reaching out. Children who are not supported in such efforts soon cease to be expressive in positive ways.

Most abilities listed as characteristic of creative people are also characteristic of children during the first few years of life. What happens to this extraordinary capacity? According to John Holt, author of *How Children Fail*,

We destroy this capacity above all by making them afraid—afraid of not doing what other people want, of not pleasing, or of making mistakes, of failing, of being wrong. Thus we make them afraid to gamble, afraid to experiment, afraid to try the difficult and unknown.[3]

We tend to encourage or discourage in others what has been encouraged or discouraged in ourselves. Yet to ignore or belittle creative expression is like saying, "Your expression is not valid, therefore you are not valid." For all of us—especially the very young—mental and emotional growth depends on a great deal of encouragement. Opportunities for creative expression are extremely important. They help us achieve an individual sense of identity and self-worth by developing our ability to integrate our experience of the outside world with that of our inner selves.

Many of our basic attitudes about art and our own creativity are shaped during childhood. Artistic efforts are among the most personal kinds of work, and children as well as adults tend to be particularly vulnerable to disparaging remarks about such efforts.

All of us have been children, and many are or will be parents. By examining artistic development in children, adults will be able to encourage the efforts of children, and at the same time come to understand what happened to their own creative development.

Young children depict the world in symbolic rather than realistic ways. Children's art is seen as inferior only when children and others want their work to look like photographs or works produced by trained adult artists. Dissatisfaction usually begins around age nine or ten, and too often results in a lifetime of blocked creativity, of feeling "untalented." Many who succeed in making the shift from child art to adult art bring the art-making process into their later lives either as amateur or professional artists or as enlightened art enthusiasts. Most people make the transition visually, but not artistically. They learn to see the world in terms of adult conventions, but are unable to create corresponding images. They become frustrated because they cannot draw the way they have learned to see.

A universal language exists in children's drawings, paintings, and sculpture. All over the world, drawings by children ages two to six show the same stages of growth—from individualized mark-making or scribbling, through the development of shapes, to recognizable subjects. Although typical motifs recur, their uses and personal variations are infinite.

10 Malia, age 4.
SELF-PORTRAIT.

Self-assurance shows clearly in the smiling SELF-PORTRAIT by a four-year-old girl. The line drawn around the edge of her paper shows an awareness of the whole space. One hand with radiating fingers reaches out, giving strong asymmetrical balance to the composition. Malia accomplished this spontaneously without any adult guidance or conscious knowledge of design.

Young children often demonstrate a fine, intuitive sense of composition. Unfortunately, we lose much of this intuitive sense of balanced composition as we begin to look at the world from a conceptual, self-conscious point of view. We can, however, rediscover our innate sensitivity to design. Picasso is alleged to have said, with some irony, that he could always draw like Michelangelo, but it took him forty years to learn to draw like a child.

At age four or five, children begin to draw things they have seen. This series of drawings shows a four-year-old's struggle to draw an elephant soon after he went to the circus for the first time. Jeff began with the most characteristic part of the elephant—the trunk. He tried several times, impatiently crossing out all but one of his first drawings. (Trial and error is an important part of the creative process.) He not only wanted to draw an elephant, he wanted the elephant to be the right size and in the right place, so that his entire vision of the circus could be complete. When he was satisfied with his elephant, he turned the drawing over and drew the full circus, including an elephant, a lion, a juggler, and a tightrope walker in action. The scene was so real for him that he asked his father to write down the story while he told about his picture.

Jeff's drawing is a record of his wonderful experience at the circus, and evidence of his growing ability to communicate visually—actually to draw what he had in his mind. His own drawing was far more meaningful to him and everyone who saw it than any circus coloring book could have been.

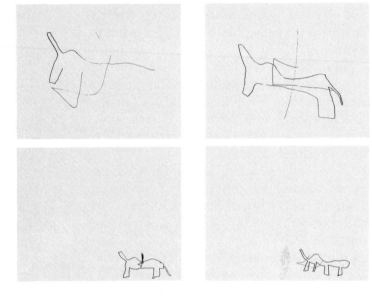

11 Jeff, age 4.
CIRCUS.

Most children who have been given coloring books, workbooks, and predrawn printed single sheets at home and in school become overly dependent on such stereotyped impersonal props. They lose the urge to invent unique images based on their own experience. Without opportunities for personal expression, children lose self-confidence and the urge to be creative.

Pictures grow naturally from personal experience. The Japanese boy who made the painting of the BICYCLE SHOP was working from a subject he knew well. His knowledge and awareness helped him succeed, even though he was at an age when it becomes difficult to draw things as one would like to see them.

For people of all ages, the art-making process provides a way to give form to individual experience, and thereby gain personal satisfaction. Because artistic problems have many equally "correct" solutions, each person—child or adult—has the opportunity to succeed. Discovering the potential for many "right" answers is very healthy; it helps avoid prejudice of all kinds. The arts also stimulate curiosity, which helps expand mental capacity. If presented well, the arts can greatly facilitate all other aspects of education.

The urge to create has nothing to do with art training. The term *folk art* refers to art made by people who have had no art instruction, and often little formal education. It is the skilled but unsophisticated expression of people who care more about simple truths than fashionable trends and historic styles. We tend to think of folk art as pretechnological, yet this form of expression continues to be part of people's lives throughout the world. Imaginative, original art by those who may be considered just plain "folk" has the same fresh, unself-conscious quality we see in the work of children.

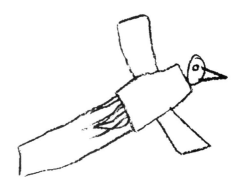

12 Anonymous child.
BIRDS.
a. This picture shows one child's drawing of a bird before exposure to coloring books.

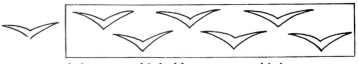

Color seven birds blue.   seven birds

b. Then the child colored a workbook illustration.

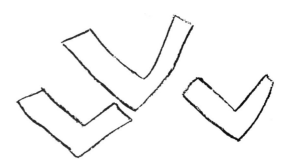

c. After coloring the workbook birds, the child lost creative sensitivity and self-reliance.

13 Anonymous Japanese child.
BICYCLE SHOP.
Ink and watercolor.

Handsome quilted bedcovers are among the most familiar and treasured works of American folk art. The rich colors in Amish quilts are in surprising contrast to the plain and simple lives of the women who make them. The traditional Amish preference for black or subdued hues in clothing has moved toward a greater use of color in the twentieth century, yet it doesn't compare with the free use of color the Amish put into their quilts. Mainstream culture undoubtedly influences the purchase of colorful fabrics for quilts; but some scholars maintain that use of color is an expressive outlet for people who lead

14   AMISH QUILT. "AROUND THE WORLD."
Lancaster County, Pennsylvania. c. 1900
Cotton and wool, 84″ × 84″.
Honolulu Academy of Arts.
Gift in memory of Alice Kamokila Campbell.

what outsiders see as somber lives. The use of geometric shapes and contrasting colors in this quilt is similar to the use of shapes and colors used in prints and paintings by some leading contemporary artists (see page 91).

Many folk artists seem to arise spontaneously, regardless of the surrounding culture. Folk artist Sanford Darling was sixty-three, retired, and a recent widower when he began to paint. Using a three-inch brush and green semigloss enamel, he painted his first picture—on a wall of his house. With additional colors and other brushes, he soon filled the entire wall. Over a period of years, he covered the rest of his house, inside and out, with landscapes and other scenes from his memory. Among Darling's recalled images were things he had seen during a six-month tour of the South Pacific and the Orient, as well as scenes from his youth on a Wisconsin farm. He continued to paint pictures on his furniture and the backs of rugs. His kitchen was eventually dominated by landscapes, including a river which flowed across the refrigerator.

Steve Ashby was a farmhand, waiter, and gardener who enjoyed carving in his spare time. At age fifty-eight, after the death of his wife, he began to work seriously at carving. He made small figures from found objects, wood scraps, and saw-cut plywood, and painted them with model airplane paint. RECEIVING A PACKAGE is a whirligig; the wind turns the propeller, which moves a series of parts and causes the woman's arm to move in and out of the mailbox. The figure's naive charm is enhanced by the addition of motion.

15   SANFORD DARLING IN HIS KITCHEN.
Photograph: Ralph Crane.
Life Magazine. © 1971 Time, Inc.

16   Steve Ashby.
RECEIVING A PACKAGE. c. 1970.
Carved and painted wood. 18″ × 20″ × 7″.
Collection of Chuck and Jan Rosenak.
Photograph: © *Joel Breger.*

17 Sabatino "Simon" Rodia.
a. NUESTRO PUEBLO. Watts, California. 1921–1954.
   Mixed media. Height 100′.
   Photograph: Duane Preble.

The sculptural spires in Watts, California, known commonly as "Watts Towers," were titled NUESTRO PUEBLO (OUR CITY) by folk artist Sabatino Rodia, the Italian tile-setter who built them. Rodia exemplifies the artist who visualizes new possibilities for ordinary materials. He worked on his towers for thirty-three years, making the fantastic structures out of such cast-offs as metal pipes and bed frames held together with steel reinforcing rods, mesh, and mortar. Incredibly, he built the towers without power tools, rivets, welds, or bolts. As they grew up from his tiny triangular backyard like Gothic cathedral spires, he lovingly and methodically covered their surfaces with bits and pieces of broken dishes, tile, melted bottle glass, shells, and other colorful "junk" that he gathered from the vacant lots of his neighborhood. Rodia's towers and the thoughts they represent are a testimony to the creative process. Here is his statement of purpose:

I no have anybody help me out.
I was a poor man.
Had to do a little at a time.
Nobody helped me.
I think if I hire a man
he don't know what to do.

A million times
I don't know what to do myself.
I never had a single helper.
Some of the people say
what was he doing . . .
some of the people
think I was crazy
and some people said
I was going to do something.
I wanted to do something
for the United States
because I was raised here
you understand?
I wanted to do something
for the United States
because there are nice people
in this country.[4]

b. Detail of NUESTRO PUEBLO. Enclosing wall with construction-tool impressions.
Photograph: Jeanne Morgan, Santa Barbara.

18   Edward Hicks.
THE PEACEABLE KINGDOM. c. 1840–1845.
Oil on canvas. 18″ × 24½″.
The Brooklyn Museum, New York.
Dick S. Ramsay Fund.

Edward Hicks—sign painter, Quaker minister, and folk artist—created an extensive pictorial record of Pennsylvania farm life, as well as many paintings of the biblical prophesy of God's peaceable kingdom. In this version of THE PEACEABLE KINGDOM, Hicks revealed his fascination with the shape, color, and character of each animal. The fact that many of the animals in the painting are not native to North America reminds us that the painting is intended to be symbolic rather than documentary. Beyond the detailed animals, we see a seemingly unrelated event—William Penn negotiating his treaty with the Indians. The painting depicts animals and people in harmony with one another, exemplifying the Quaker philosophy of peace.

Many people turn to art making late in life. Anna Mary Robertson Moses, known as "Grandma Moses," began to paint in her seventies when arthritis prevented her from stitching the yarn pictures which were cherished by her family and friends. A self-taught painter, she drew her subject matter from the historic past and the rural area in which her family had lived. In paintings such as THE THUNDERSTORM, Grandma Moses demonstrated a delight in color and pattern, and the ability to communicate depth and distance without the use of pictorial perspective. She painted for over twenty years, and became America's best-known folk painter.

Art provides a means to incorporate individual personalities into lasting and universal expressions. Everyone possesses the potential for an artfull life, but it takes discipline and effort to initiate and sustain this goal.

19   Mary Robertson "Grandma" Moses.
THE THUNDERSTORM. 1948.
Oil on canvas. 20¾″ × 24¾″.
Private collection (K729/M1227).
© 1987 Grandma Moses Properties Co., New York.

PURPOSES AND FUNCTIONS OF ART

The arts arouse our emotions, spark our imaginations, delight our senses, and stimulate our minds. Visual art can advertise, beautify, celebrate, clarify, decorate, educate, enhance, entertain, entice, express, heal, inform, inspire, integrate, intensify, interpret, narrate, persuade, record, reveal, and transform. It can also attack, conceal, deceive, humiliate, incense, obscure, and terrorize.

Communicative functions of art vary according to artists' purposes. A film has more potential for communication than a chair, yet both carry ideas about function and meaning from maker to perceiver.

Without art, we would have little knowledge of past civilizations, or even of the full flavor of life in today's world. Works of art are reliable vehicles for messages from the past because, of all forms of historical evidence, they are the least corrupted by errors and the biased alterations of intervening generations.

The function of most of what we call art from the past was to convey meaning, to give visible form to humanity's hopes, fears, and spiritual concerns. Magical or religious significance is inherent in works such as masks, ritual objects, cave paintings, and cathedrals.

Prior to the modern period, what we now label "art" and "artists" were indistinguishable from the spiritual, moral, and social order of culture. Within traditional societies, people shared the same faith and view of the world; those we now call artists were trained to produce traditional objects and images for agreed-upon purposes and functions. In contrast, the art of modern urban societies is often viewed with confusion and mistrust because it does not have agreed-upon meanings and functions. Longstanding tradition no longer determines all art. Unlike the ancients, we have no clear guidelines to help us respond to and evaluate much contemporary art, or the purposes it serves.

Many works of other cultures or other times were made to serve functions of which we are generally unaware. The CANOE PROW FIGURE from the Solomon Islands (see page 288) employs symbolism meaningful to that culture; it was made to protect travelers. Its present function—to be on view in a museum or reproduced in a book—could be characterized as conveying crosscultural information, while pleasing us with its form and subject.

Functions can overlap within a given work. Art may simultaneously decorate, uplift, convey moral truth, and impart information (see Gauguin's THE VISION AFTER THE SERMON, page 368). Art serves a wide variety of purposes, which we can broadly characterize as personal, social, and utilitarian.

In a general sense, the visual arts include all human creations in which appearance has been a major consideration. When we view art this way, we find that we all have a substantial amount of art in our personal and public lives. We live in buildings, towns, and cities, and use tools and possess objects made with appearance in mind. Our most immediate involvement with the functions of art occurs as we make personal aesthetic decisions on a daily basis: how to style our hair, what to wear, how to furnish and arrange our living spaces, and so on. Such choices make visual statements about who we are, and the kind of world we like to see around us.

We can choose to ignore the artistic aspects of life, making careless choices or leaving aesthetic decisions to others; or we can develop our awareness and our visual participation. Either way, the quality of our lives and the lives of those around us will be affected.

Art also fulfills personal, spiritual needs for many people. The most obvious application of this function can be seen in places of worship, where the architecture itself may create an atmosphere for devotion. However, art does not have to exist in a religious context to move us spiritually. Art can have a magical quality, bringing great joy by evoking a sense of awe, wonder, and appreciation, similar to what has been described as a mystical experience.

20 Barnett Newman.
BROKEN OBELISK. 1963–1967.
Cor-ten steel. 25′5″ × 10′6″.
Rothko Chapel, Houston, Texas.
Photograph: Don Getsug/ TIME *Magazine.*

Barnett Newman, an American painter and sculptor, translated his philosophical and religious concerns into visual form. His BROKEN OBELISK can be seen as a symbol of life in the twentieth century. Newman placed the broken end of an upside-down obelisk on the apex of a pyramid that appears to be floating on light and water. Pyramids and obelisks are known as expressions of an almost unchanging culture; the pyramid is a symbol of timelessness and stability, while the obelisk, when upright, reaches toward the heavens. Newman's obelisk is broken, and appears to be precariously balanced. This dramatic sculpture expresses the instability of life in our rapidly changing times.

Psychological functions of art are closely related to spiritual functions. Living with works of art, participating in art-making processes, and conserving or developing pleasant surroundings are uplifting and satisfying.

Those who want to live with art, but have neither the knowledge nor the money to purchase expensive original works, do well to buy works by artists who are not sufficiently famous to command high prices. The idea is to find or make art you enjoy living with — art that has meaning for you.

Art serves a social function when it goes beyond serving the personal needs of the artist and communicates to more than a few. The visual arts play a central role in the appearances of our homes, urban designs, and public spaces. Some art is made for a particular occasion, such as Mardi Gras, and then discarded when the festivities are over.

Art has long been recognized as a source of power by churches, rulers, and wealthy patrons. Recently, corporations have joined the list. Architecture, painting, sculpture, and now film and television have been used to project and glorify images of deities, political leaders, and heroes. Art commissioned by church and state has inspired, taught, and sometimes intimidated the faithful and the patriotic. Some leaders of the Roman Catholic Church in fifteenth-century Italy supported certain artists, and commissioned works intended to increase their personal power and the power of the Church. In seventeenth-century France, King Louis XIV built an enormous palace and formal garden at Versailles. It has stood for over three hundred years as an impressive symbol of the power of its builder (see page 340).

Today we are surrounded by commercial art in the form of advertisements, most of which are designed to persuade viewers to purchase specific products. Posters, billboards, and television commercials seek to sell us everything from toothpaste to presidential candidates. Not all persuasive art is commercial, however. Art intended to promote social change has been part of many societies (see Margaret Bourke-White's photograph AT THE TIME OF THE LOUISVILLE FLOOD on page 157, and Picasso's GUERNICA on page 411).

Because art can make a strong statement that is clearly understood by a broad spectrum of people, it is often used to impart information in both literate and nonliterate societies. During the Middle Ages in Europe, before there were any printed books, the visual arts provided religious narration. Art continues to serve that function for nonliterate people around the world. The visual arts transcend verbal language to provide a common ground through which people of all nations can increase their understanding and appreciation of each other.

To the degree that the visual arts influence the quality of our surroundings, they are environmental arts. Well-designed utilitarian objects and spaces—from chairs to communities—contribute to the beauty and function of our daily lives. The arts of architecture, furniture design, painting, and sculpture can give comfort and stimulating interest to a home.

GREENACRE PARK provides a place for the public to relax in the middle of New York City. Trees and sounds of water help minimize traffic noise and offer refreshing relief from the harshness of the city. During the lunch hour, the park is so heavily used that people sit on steps and railings rather than go elsewhere, demonstrating the great need for such well-designed and well-maintained urban spaces. Artistic awareness is necessary in order to conserve, restore, design, and build life-enhancing human environments.

21   HOME INTERIOR.

22   Hideo Sasaki, landscape architect.
GREENACRE PARK. 421 East 51st. St., New York City. 1979.
Owned and maintained by the Greenacre Foundation.

STYLE AND THE ARTIST'S PERSONAL POINT OF VIEW

Just as each individual has a unique personality, each artist has a unique style. The word *style* refers to a consistent and characteristic handling of media techniques, elements of form, and principles of design that make a work identifiable as the product of a particular person, group, period, or place. A personal or group style emerges naturally as artists assimilate influences and mature in their expression. Some artists are remarkably consistent in the ways they see the world and view their purposes as artists; their works reflect this in their stylistic continuity. Artists whose attitudes or purposes change may show wide variations in style.

Artists work from their own experience, which includes their absorption of other art. The artist is saying, "This is what is important to me. This is how I see life, or how I want to see it." In this sense, all works of art are self-portraits. In another sense, however, even a representational self-portrait is not merely a self-image, but is also a means to give universal significance to one's personal experience.

When we study a number of works by a given artist, we can begin to recognize that artist's personal expression or style. The works of each of the following four artists demonstrate individually consistent points of view. Each of these artists shows a unity of vision or purpose that is very different from the others. Although they lived during approximately the same time, they came from different countries and held very different attitudes. The first three—Henri Matisse, Käthe Kollwitz, and Werner Bischof—were primarily interested in depicting people. For Louise Nevelson, assembled forms were self-sufficient vehicles of communication.

In 1908, Henri Matisse wrote the following statement about his work:

The purpose of a painter must not be conceived as separate from his pictorial means, and these pictorial means must be the more complete (I do not mean complicated) the deeper is his thought. I am unable to distinguish between the feeling I have for life and my way of expressing it. [5]

Matisse wrote these words a few years before he painted NASTURTIUMS AND THE DANCE. The work illustrates his point. In this painting of a corner of his studio, he shows a chair, a sculpture stand topped with a vase of flowers, and against the wall a section of his large painting called THE DANCE. The human figure had a particular importance for Matisse, who said,

What interests me most is neither still life nor landscape but the human figure. It is through it that I best succeed in expressing the nearly religious feeling that I have towards life. [6]

In NASTURTIUMS AND THE DANCE, Matisse expressed what the French call *la joie de vivre* or "the joy of life." Every line, shape, and color radiates it. And we find such joy in most of his work. Matisse chose to emphasize joyful themes in spite of the fact that during his lifetime (1869–1954), which spanned two World Wars, there was much suffering in the world:

What I dream of is an art of balance, of purity and serenity, devoid of troubling or depressing subject matter, an art which might be for every mental worker, be he businessman or writer, like an appeasing influence, like a mental soother, something like a good armchair in which to rest from physical fatigue. [7]

Matisse was educated as a lawyer, and began his artistic life methodically by becoming thoroughly proficient in the traditional techniques of French art. Throughout his life he worked at adding to both his knowledge and his skills, while being careful to preserve his original naiveté.

For Matisse, a painting was a reality of lines, shapes, and colors before it was a picture of nameable objects. The lyric beauty of his personal style was based on intuition, yet he acknowledged the importance of his years of study. He masterfully assimilated influences from the decorative arts of the Near East, African art, and

23 Henri Matisse.
NASTURTIUMS AND THE DANCE. 1912.
Oil on canvas. 75¾" × 45".
Pushkin Museum of Fine Arts, Moscow.

24 Henri Matisse.
ARTIST AND MODEL REFLECTED IN A MIRROR. 1937.
Pen and ink. 24¹/₁₆″ × 16″.
The Baltimore Museum of Art: The Cone Collection, formed by
Dr. Claribel Cone and Miss Etta Cone of Baltimore, Maryland.
(BMA 1960.12.51).

25 Henri Matisse.
LA NEGRESSE. 1952–1953.
Paper on canvas. 178¾" × 245½".
National Gallery of Art, Washington, D.C.
Alisa Mellon Bruce Fund.

other painters, such as Paul Gauguin, who invented color combinations and forms new to Western and European art. Matisse sought to hide his own struggles in his works, desiring them to look effortless, light, and joyous. He feared, however, that young people would see his work as done with casual facility, even carelessness, and mistakenly conclude that years of study were unnecessary.

In the free and sensuous drawing ARTIST AND MODEL REFLECTED IN A MIRROR, Matisse appears along with the reflected back view of his model. His formal, businesslike image acts as an effective point of contrast to the model, and reminds us that the expressive lines exist because of him.

LA NEGRESSE was inspired by American entertainer Josephine Baker. Matisse cut the huge collage from paper when he was an invalid, less than two years before his death. Despite his failing health, his feeling for life comes across as strongly as ever. In fact, his late works are some of his most powerful and joyous.

26   Käthe Kollwitz.
THE PRISONERS. 1908.
Etching and soft-ground. 12⅞″ × 16⅝″.
Library of Congress, Washington, D.C.

An attitude toward life very different from Matisse's was expressed by Käthe Kollwitz. She lived in Germany during the first half of this century, and was aware that many around her were experiencing anguish and pain. Kollwitz and her husband, a physician, acted as social workers, welcoming troubled people into their home. She revealed her strong identity with the suffering of others in her prints and drawings, many of which appear to be self-portraits. She lost a son in World War I and a grandson in World War II, but her personal grief was secondary to her deep concern for humanity. Kollwitz dreamed of a united world that would elevate human life above the misery she expressed in her art.

Kollwitz was one of the few women whose greatness as an artist was publicly recognized prior to the middle of the twentieth century. The tragic situation in post-World War I Germany led her to use her art as a tool for social change. Believing that art should be for everyone, she chose not to make expensive paintings. Instead, she made inexpensive prints (posters, lithographs, and woodcuts) that ordinary people could afford. (See the discussion of prints, beginning on page 137.) In 1933, Kollwitz was expelled from the Berlin Academy for her anti-Nazi sympathies. She died in 1945, just days before World War II ended.

The three prints reproduced here were made over a period of twenty-six years, yet they are remarkably consistent in mood and graphic quality. THE PRISONERS, done in 1908, was one of a series of prints inspired by Kollwitz's interest in a violent peasant revolution that occurred in southern Germany in 1525.

The lithograph DEATH SEIZING A WOMAN was one of eight prints in Kollwitz's last major print series. Kollwitz achieved the impact of this print by reducing the idea to its essentials: the mother holds her child in a protective grasp and stares ahead in terror as the symbolic figure of death presses down on her from behind. Bold, converging lines focus attention on the mother's expression of fear. The strong sculptural quality in Kollwitz's drawings and prints developed from her study of Rembrandt's use of light, as well as her own experience in making sculpture.

Her SELF-PORTRAIT reveals a kindly, yet monumental face. In addition to being visually strong, Kollwitz's graphic images function as pleas for compassion. By reminding us of the problem of human cruelty, they touch our conscience.

27 Käthe Kollwitz.
DEATH SEIZING A WOMAN. 1934.
Plate IV from the series DEATH (1934–1936).
Lithograph, printed in black. 20″ × 14⁷⁄₁₆″.
Collection, The Museum of Modern Art, New York. Purchase.

28 Käthe Kollwitz.
SELF-PORTRAIT. 1934.
Lithograph. 8¹⁄₁₆″ × 7³⁄₁₆″.
Philadelphia Museum of Art. Given by Dr. and Mrs. William Wolgin.

32 Louise Nevelson.
ROYAL TIDE #1. 1961.
Gilded wood. 8' × 3'.
Collection of Jean and Howard Lipman.

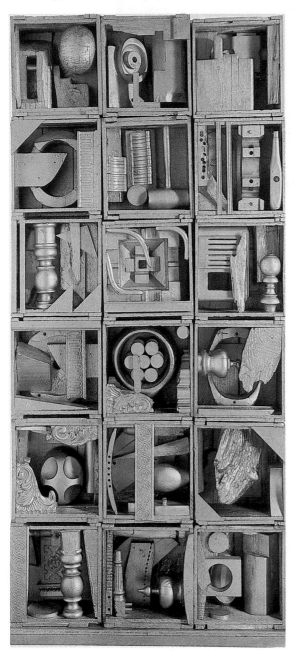

Louise Nevelson came to be recognized as a leading American sculptor in the 1950s. She was born in Russia in 1900, grew up in Maine, and moved to New York City at the age of twenty. There Nevelson energetically pursued her interest in the arts by studying music, drama, poetry, and dance, as well as the visual arts, believing that to be a well-rounded, complete person one must be knowledgeable in all the arts.

Early in her career, Nevelson worked in a variety of styles. She made drawings, prints, and paintings, as well as sculpture in stone, bronze, clay, and wood. It was not until the 1950s that she developed her mature style based on geometric forms. Nevelson's best-known works are large wall constructions made up of numerous boxes filled with found wood fragments. She was an early exponent and leading practitioner of sculpture as environment; her relief walls have been known to extend around entire rooms. In ROYAL TIDE #1, the carefully combined pieces of wood include bits of old furniture and architectural trim. Each compartment is both a composition in itself and part of the total form. Nevelson painted such stacked-box constructions a single unifying color, usually black, white, or gold—which she considered aristocratic colors.

In the late 1960s and 1970s, Nevelson turned from wood to plastic and aluminum, and then to steel, which is most suitable for large outdoor works. SHADOWS AND FLAGS, a group of seven pieces, stands in what is now Louise Nevelson Plaza in New York City.

Nevelson had this to say about the origin and evolution of her constructive style:

I never wanted to make sculpture. I didn't want to make anything like that. I felt my great search was for myself, the inner being of myself, and that was the best way I knew to project how I was feeling about everything in the world. Consequently, it wasn't that I made anything for anybody. Now, we call it "work" and I don't like to call it work at all. It really is a projection of an awareness. People don't understand that when you project from yourself you are really at the height of your awareness, and that means you are at your best.[8]

Toward the end of her life, she returned to wood, making pictorial collages such as VOLCANIC MAGIC X. Nevelson described her sculpture in various media as variations on a theme; her concern with space and shadow carried through all her assemblages, revealing a unity of approach to form.

Different people have different memories. Some have memories for words, some for action—mine happens to be for form.[9]

Nevelson's sculpture demonstrates her belief that it is not what you start out with that counts; it is what you do with it. From scrap, she created elegant, regal structures with an air of timelessness. They are old and new at the same time. They have lived, and they are alive. Nevelson captured the essence of the art process in the following statement:

The joy, if you want to call it that, of creation, is that it opens life to you. . . . It opens and you become more aware and more aware and that is the wonder of it.[10]

33 Louise Nevelson.
Detail of SHADOWS AND FLAGS. Louise Nevelson Plaza, New York. 1977–1978.
One of seven sculptures painted cor-ten steel. Height 72′.
Photograph: © Tom Crane, 1978.

34 Louise Nevelson.
VOLCANIC MAGIC X. 1985.
Wood, paper, and metal. 40″ × 32″ × 6″.
Courtesy of the Pace Gallery, New York.

EVALUATION

Evaluation and selection are important features of the creative process. Direct involvement can be uplifting, as Louise Nevelson suggested. For the artist, the creative experience itself can be more significant than the resulting work. With one's own art, the pleasure continues if the results seem worthwhile. Whether we are experiencing our own work or the work of others, enjoyment comes from a personal sense of quality achieved. It is the determination of quality—the evaluation process—that is hard to describe.

The artist may be the first to question the validity of a work of art. Value judgments in art necessarily involve subjectivity because objective considerations, although valuable, do not go far enough. Factors such as permanence are measurable, but they are meaningless unless the work is worth preserving. Quality in art has little to do with complexity of technique, degree of difficulty, training, or the education of the artist.

Those who seek criteria for determining artistic quality often apply at least some of the principles the ancient Greeks believed art must contain: truth, beauty, order and harmony, and moral goodness. However, in the late twentieth century, there is much less agreement on the meaning of these concepts than there was in ancient Greece.

As the world changes, the arts of past and present are reevaluated. Few famous artists or styles have had unchanging reputations. The impressionist painters of the late nineteenth century (see pages 358–361) are the best-known example of a group of artists who, in their own time, were rejected by critics, museums, and the public because their style differed radically from that of their predecessors. Today, impressionist paintings have an honored place in museums and are well loved by the public.

Standards that may have been useful in the past are difficult, if not impossible, to apply to those examples of today's art in which the artists have intentionally sought to go beyond or deny long-established traditions. The gap between the taste of much of the public and the preferences of practicing artists, patrons, and critics is the result of revolutionary innovation in all the arts during our century of rapid change. There is no gap with popular arts such as television, magazine illustration, and rock music, yet these arts are influenced by the work of avant-garde (leading radical) artists. Contemporary art is as varied, complex, and contradictory as the culture that creates it. If we close our eyes and minds to what may be new and hard to understand, we will miss the opportunity to learn from and enjoy an artist's fresh insights, and the contemporary artist in turn will suffer from our lack of support. Why is it easier to accept the work of pioneering scientists than that of avant-garde artists?

Quality is relative. Determination of value in art, or anything else, changes from person to person, from country to country, and from age to age. Changes in taste are not the same as changes in value. We can recognize aesthetic quality in works we would not want to live with. Our concept of what constitutes "good art" changes as we mature and develop our critical skills.

When we speak of art criticism, it is important to realize that the word "criticism" refers to discriminating judgments, both favorable and unfavorable. Art criticism may include description, formal analysis, interpretation, value judgment, and biographical and historical information. If you were a critic, you might begin by describing what you see in terms of media, size, and nameable aspects of the work. Formal analysis includes a discussion of the way various visual elements and principles are used, while interpretation deals with the meaning or symbolism of the work. What is the artist saying? Biographical or historical information often clarifies or sheds light on the intention of the artist, and provides clues to the reasons a particular work looks the way it does. Criteria upon which many art professionals agree include degree of originality; sensitivity to the character and appropriate use of materials; and consistency of concept, design, and execution.

Professional criticism is based on the educated response and evaluation of the art critic. The professional critic generally has a wide knowledge of art, and frequently has worked as an artist. The critic's knowledge and experience include an awareness of art's functions, styles, social and historical contexts, and a familiarity with particular artists and their work. With an extensive knowledge of art, one generally acquires the ability to relate to a wide range of creativity.

Written art criticism appears in periodicals, exhibition catalogs, and books; spoken criticism is heard in classrooms and in the statements of artists and art historians. Art critics generally inform people about the quality of exhibitions and events through written reviews. Such reviews may influence the sale of an artist's work. Criticism in the classroom is intended to help students develop understanding and aesthetic sensitivity. More important than passing personal judgment on a work is a teacher's or critic's ability to help others make their own evaluations.

As long as there have been art patrons and critics, the relationship between them and artists has been problematic. We are looking over the artist's shoulder in Pieter Bruegel's drawing THE PAINTER AND THE CONNOISSEUR. Or are we? Maybe we do not wish to be identified with the "connoisseur," who clutches his money pouch as he looks through his spectacles with what appears to be false fascination at Bruegel's work-in-progress. Of course, because Bruegel did the drawing, he gave us the story from the artist's point of view. The drawing has been done in such a way that, if we identify with anyone, it is Bruegel.

True connoisseurs, patrons, or critics do not have to feign understanding. Their astute sense of discrimination has been formed through study and experience. Such people play an important role in keeping the arts alive.

Ideally, each person who views a work of art will make his or her own evaluation of its quality, but preconceptions may cloud the process. Many of us read the artist's names and titles of works in museums before we allow ourselves to

35 Pieter Bruegel.
THE PAINTER AND THE CONNOISSEUR. c. 1568.
Pen and bistre. 10″ × 8⅜″.
Albertina Collection, Vienna.

36   People viewing MONA LISA through bullet-proof glass.

37   Leonardo da Vinci.
MONA LISA. c. 1503–1506.
Oil on wood. 30¼″ × 21″.
Louvre Museum, Paris.

respond. We have heard that Leonardo da Vinci's painting MONA LISA is a great work of art. If this is foremost in our minds when we see MONA LISA, our own direct experience of the painting becomes conditioned by acceptance of the idea that it is great art. Our judgment is likely to be further influenced by the fact that it is in the famous Louvre Museum in Paris, in a special case behind bulletproof glass, and largely obscured by crowds of people who flock to see it. The painting's fame prevents many people from making their own judgment.

The issue of evaluation is both complicated and enriched by the fact that today we often see reproductions rather than original artworks. Photomechanical reproductions make the world's art available to anyone who has access to books, magazines, posters, and postcards. Yet the size, color, texture, and material presence of the original art object is changed in even the best color reproductions. Three-dimensional works suffer the most by two-dimensional reproduction. They are generally presented from only one angle, thereby losing their multi-dimensional character.

Most of us have critical opinions on works of art, regardless of how familiar we are with art or art criticism. Although procedures exist for describing, analyzing, interpreting, and appraising art, there are no absolutely correct ways to evaluate works of art.

When we look at a work of art and find that we are pleased or displeased, we may seek to find out why. We derive added pleasure when we recognize the elements or qualities in a work that evoke our responses. The tendency to like what is familiar makes it necessary to develop knowledge and awareness in order to increase enjoyment. Art professionals and other educated viewers can contribute their experiences and add to the satisfaction we may get from a given work. In this sense, art criticism is a sharing of discoveries about art and life.

PART TWO

The Language of Visual Experience

. . . the creative act is not performed by the artist alone; the spectator brings the work in contact with the external world by deciphering and interpreting its inner qualifications and thus adds his contribution to the creative act.

Marcel Duchamp[1]

Marc Chagall.
I AND THE VILLAGE. 1911.
(See page 53.)

3

Visual Communication

The language of vision determines, perhaps even more subtly and thoroughly than verbal language, the structure of our consciousness.

S. I. Hayakawa[1]

The world we know through our senses has meaning for us apart from verbal language. When we speak of a "language of visual experience," we are referring to the elements and groupings of visual phenomena to which humans have typically similar responses. In art, it is the visual perception that is important, not the words used to describe that perception. However, words can help us analyze—and therefore better understand—the infinite ways in which artists work with the elements of visual form to communicate ideas and meanings.

REPRESENTATIONAL, ABSTRACT, AND NONREPRESENTATIONAL ART

Before we can investigate the various elements that comprise visual form, it is necessary to clarify the most basic terms used to identify what we respond to in art, and in all visual experience. When we understand these terms, we can become more consciously aware of our responses to visual form—regardless of whether it has subject matter or verbal interpretation.

Subject or *subject matter* refers to recognizable and nameable objects or themes to which the viewer responds. Understanding the full significance of a work of art, however, involves more than simply recognizing the objects portrayed.

The terms *representational*, *abstract*, and *nonrepresentational* describe the overall handling of visual form. *Representational* art (sometimes called *objective* or *figurative*) depicts the appearance of things. Objects in the everyday world are *re*presented—presented again. In chapter 2, for example, we discussed three representational works by Käthe Kollwitz (pages 28-29).

Abstract art emphasizes visual form and may or may not include subject or theme. The verb "to abstract" means to extract the essence of a thing or idea. An abstract artwork may depict actual objects, with the natural appearance of the subject changed or distorted in order to emphasize or reveal certain qualities or content; or an abstract image can be far removed from anything recognizable.

The application of the term abstract to either representational or nonrepresentational works can be confusing. In a basic sense, all art is an abstraction, because it is not possible for an artist to reproduce exactly what is seen. According to dictionary definitions, abstract can mean either (1) works that are totally nonrepresentational, without reference to natural objects; or (2) works that retain representational characteristics expressed in altered or generalized form. The second meaning is generally used throughout this book.

Varying degrees of abstraction are evident in Theo van Doesburg's series of drawings and paintings, and Picasso's series of lithographs. Both artists based their series on the form of a bull, although Van Doesburg's are titled "Cow." Let's look at a few examples from each sequence.

Van Doesburg began his series with a shaded side-view drawing. He suggested strong sunlight

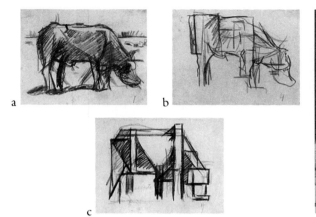

a   b

c

by the highlight on the animal's back and the shadow on the ground. A shadow and a horizon line also suggest the field in which the animal is standing. Van Doesburg paid attention to the horizontal and vertical structure of the animal, and to the relationship of this structure to similar lines in the landscape. In the second drawing, Van Doesburg began to abstract the image by simplifying the basic forms into rectangular shapes. By the third drawing, the light and shadow of the first drawing were transformed in an even more abstract image. At this point, the drawing is so abstract that the subject is no longer recognizable. The process of abstraction continues in the two paintings, until animal qualities have been completely replaced by a rhythmic composition of separate, colored rectangles. By contrast, Picasso emphasized curving lines rather than geometric shapes in a sequence that gradually reduces the complex image to a few lines. (See also the steps to abstraction in paintings by Piet Mondrian on pages 398–399).

Nonrepresentational art presents a visual form with no specific reference to anything outside itself. Such art is also called *nonobjective* and *nonfigurative*. Although Louise Nevelson's works (pages 32–33) have titles that indicate

d

e

38 Theo van Doesburg.
ABSTRACTION OF A COW, five stages.
a, b, and c. Studies for COMPOSITION (THE COW). n.d.
Pencil, 4⅝″ × 6¼″.
Collection, The Museum of Modern Art, New York. Purchase.
d. COMPOSITION (THE COW). 1916.
Gouache. 15⅝″ × 22¾″.
Collection, The Museum of Modern Art, New York. Purchase.
e. COMPOSITION (THE COW). 1916–1917.
Oil on canvas. 14¾″ × 25″.
Collection, The Museum of Modern Art, New York. Purchase.

39 Pablo Picasso.
THE BULL.
a. 3rd state, Dec. 18, 1945.
b. 7th state, Dec. 28, 1945.
c. 11th state, Jan. 17, 1946.
Lithographs.
National Gallery of Art, Washington, D.C.
Alisa Mellon Bruce Fund.

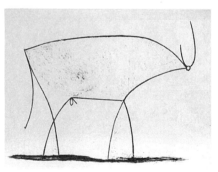

a   b   c

themes, the pieces are not meant to represent specific, nameable things—thus they are nonrepresentational.

Representational works may seem easier to relate to than nonrepresentational works; but it is important to realize that visual forms, like audible sounds, evoke responses in us whether or not they represent nameable subjects. In fact, literal subject matter can be a minor element in many of the arts—most notably in music. Given significant form (that is, good composition or design), a literal subject is unnecessary. Subject alone does not make art.

The Belgian painter René Magritte presents the viewer with a clear statement about the nature of representational art. The subject of the painting is clearly a pipe, but we see written in French on the painting, "*Ceci n'est pas une pipe*" ("This is not a pipe"). The viewer is made to wonder, "If this is not a pipe, then what is it?" A painting! Magritte's title, THE TREASON OF IMAGES, gives us a clue to his thinking.

Matisse once told of an incident that illustrated his views on the difference between art and nature. A woman who was visiting his studio pointed out, "But surely, the arm of this woman is much too long." Matisse replied, "Madame, you are mistaken. This is not a woman, this is a picture."[2]

FORM AND CONTENT

Form is what we see; content is what we interpret as the meaning of what we see. In art, *form* is the total effect of the combined visual elements – or various aspects of the work. *Content* is the message or meaning of the work of art—what the artist expresses or communicates to the viewer. Content determines form and is expressed through it; thus the two are inseparable. As form changes, content changes, and vice versa.

By developing a sense for the expressive potential of all form, we encourage within ourselves the ability to enjoy and create new relationships with the world around us. The first step toward becoming more visually sensitive is to increase awareness of what we see, and how we feel about what we see.

Form includes such elements as materials, color, shape, line, and design. Each form evokes or is capable of evoking some kind of response in us. In other words, *every* thing has form, and all form has some sort of content or spirit.

Subject matter can interfere with our perception of form. One way to learn to see form exclusive of subject is by looking at pictures upside down. Inversion of recognizable images frees the mind from the processes of identifying and

40 René Magritte.
LA TRAHISON DES IMAGES
(THE TREASON OF IMAGES).
c. 1928–1929.
Oil on canvas. 23⅝" × 37".
Los Angeles County Museum of Art.
Purchased with funds provided by
the Mr. and Mrs. William Preston
Harrison Collection.

Ceci n'est pas une pipe.

naming things. Familiar objects become unfamiliar. Learning to see form is made more challenging and rewarding if we search for pictures that are similar in form, but dissimilar as nameable objects. Such comparisons become visual metaphors.

The form of a work of art—and the meaning communicated by the artist through the form—is generated by the intention of the artist and the character of the materials used. The artist is the source or sender; the work is the medium carrying the message. We, as viewers, must receive and experience the work if the communication is to be complete.

Clearly, effort is required to produce a work of art. Less obvious is the fact that responding to a work of art also requires effort. Contemporary American composer John Cage brings this to our attention:

Most people mistakenly think that when they hear a piece of music, that they're not doing anything, but something is being done to them. Now this is not true, and we must arrange our music, we must arrange our Art, we must arrange everything, I believe, so that people realize that they themselves are doing it, and not that something is being done to them.[3]

We guide our actions by reading the content of the form of people, things, and events that make up our environment. We have an amazing ability to remember certain visual forms. We interpret content based on our previous experiences with these forms. A stranger who looks like someone we know may cause feelings of like or dislike, depending on how we feel about the acquaintance. When we see faces and figures of people whom we have seen before, they are familiar.

41 VISUAL METAPHOR.

We see and respond to the character of the form when we perceive any object, person, or place. Artists manipulate form in order to express specific content. Subject matter is not the same as content: the same subject can be changed in form to express radically different content. For example, the valentine ♥ heart, which is used to represent the human heart, is a symbol of love. If someone were to give you a huge, beautifully made red-velvet valentine, so large it had to be pulled on a cart, you would probably be overwhelmed by this gesture of love. The content would be LOVE! But if you were to receive a faded mimeographed outline of a heart on a sheet of cheap paper, you might read the content as: love—sort of—a very impersonal kind. Or, if you were to receive a shriveled, greenish-brown, slightly moldy image of the heart symbol, the content might be UGH, HATE!

One way to understand how art communicates human experience is to examine works that have the same subject, but which vary in form and content. THE KISS by Auguste Rodin and THE KISS by Constantin Brancusi show how two sculptors interpret an embrace. In Rodin's work, the life-size human figures represent ideals of masculine and feminine form. Rodin captured the sensual delight of the highly charged moment when lovers embrace. Our emotions are engaged as we overlook the hardness of the marble out of which the illusion was carved. The implied natural softness of flesh is accentuated by the rough texture of the unfinished marble on which the figures sit.

In contrast to Rodin's sensuous rendering, Brancusi chose to use the solid quality of the block of stone to express lasting love. Through minimal cutting of the block he symbolized, rather than illustrated, the concept of two becoming one. Brancusi chose geometric abstraction rather than naturalism to express love.

43 Constantin Brancusi.
THE KISS. c. 1912.
Limestone. 23″ × 13″ × 10″.
Philadelphia Museum of Art, The Louise and Walter Arensberg Collection.

42 François Auguste René Rodin.
THE KISS. 1886.
Marble. Height 5′11¼″.
Musée Rodin, Paris (S1002).
Photograph: Bruno Jarret.

44   Pablo Picasso.
A MOTHER HOLDING A CHILD AND FOUR STUDIES OF
HER RIGHT HAND. 1904.
Conté crayon. 13½″ × 10½″.
Fogg Art Museum, Harvard University.
Bequest of Meta and Paul J. Sachs.

Artists from very different times and cultures have depicted the universal relationship between mother and child. Contrasting images of the same subject are all valid expressions of the ideals, intentions, and experiences of individual artists as well as expressions of the cultures from which they came.

Pablo Picasso made his conté crayon drawing A MOTHER HOLDING A CHILD as a study for a painting of a circus family. Picasso drew the right hand of the mother several times in order to capture a gesture of tenderness as she holds her baby. The relationship of love between the mother and child is suggested by the graceful lines of the child's upreaching arm and the mother's inclining head and fallen lock of hair.

The mood of elegant calm expressed in Picasso's drawing contrasts sharply with the brutal anguish of a mother holding her dead child in a detail of his painting GUERNICA (see a reproduction of the full painting on page 411). In this image Picasso abstracted and distorted anatomy in order to portray anguish, thus increasing the emotional impact of his protest imagery.

Contemporary artist Elizabeth Catlett's carved MOTHER AND CHILD is an expression of an artist who is also a mother. The gesture of the mother figure suggests anguish, perhaps over the struggles all mothers know each child will face. Both figures have been abstracted to their essence in a composition of curves, bold lines, and solid shapes. The smoothly polished cedar is inviting to the touch.

Italian Renaissance painter Andrea Mantegna's highly realistic image of the Madonna must have been a surprise to the people of his time. There are no halos on the fully lifelike painting of mother and child, and no red robe or blue mantle to identify Mary. If it were not for the title, MADONNA AND CHILD, viewers might not realize that this tender scene is meant to be Christ and Mary. Mantegna's Madonna is a

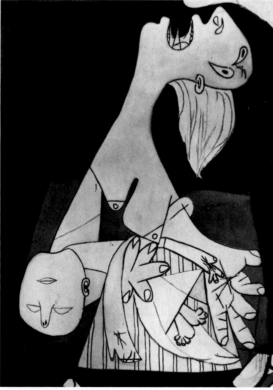

45   Pablo Picasso.
Detail of GUERNICA, 1937.
(See page 411).

humble, accessible woman, and Christ is a sleeping infant. The visual clues to their identity are subtle. The shroud-like swaddling cloth in which the infant is wrapped is a symbol of death, and the closed eyes of the Christ child are interpreted as a reference to the crucifixion.

Different interpretations of the mother and child theme show how various forms convey quite different content, even when the subject remains relatively similar. All artworks are the product of their time, the materials and techniques used to make them, and the individual experiences and concerns of the artists who created them.

Form conveys content even without narrative subject matter. But when nameable subjects are present, content often includes meaning based on traditional interpretations of certain subjects. *Iconography* is the symbolic meaning of subjects and signs and the conventions governing their use. Not all artworks contain iconography; but in those that do, it may be the symbolism, rather than the obvious subject, that carries the deepest level of meaning.

47 Andrea Mantegna.
MADONNA AND CHILD. c. 1475–1495.
Tempera on canvas. 16⁹/₁₆″ × 12⅝″.
Staatliche Museum, West Berlin.

46 Elizabeth Catlett.
MOTHER AND CHILD #2. 1971.
Walnut. 38″.
Collection of Alan Swift. Photograph courtesy of Samella Lewis.

48 Albrecht Dürer.
THE KNIGHT, DEATH AND THE DEVIL. 1513.
Engraving. 9¾″ × 7⅜″.
The Brooklyn Museum, Gift of Mrs. Horace O. Havemeyer.

Today, the term iconography usually refers to a religious or cultural area of iconographic study such as Christian or Egyptian iconography. The identification and specific meanings of significant subjects, motifs, forms, colors, and positions are the central concern of iconographic interpretation. Examples of iconography from different times and places reveal the wealth of meaning communicated by some works of art.

The primary subject in Albrecht Dürer's THE KNIGHT, DEATH AND THE DEVIL is a man in armor on horseback; behind him are a corpse-like figure and a horned monster. Meanings of the objects in the detailed scene would have been obvious to Christians of Dürer's time, because they were familiar with Christian iconography. The man in armor, for instance, represents the Christian knight who follows the right path in spite of the persistence of death and the devil. The knight, symbolizing the good Christian, must ride through the darkness of the "valley of the shadow of death" in order to reach the City of God, seen in the background. An hour-glass in the hand of death symbolizes mortality, or the brevity of human life. Serpents in death's hair are ancient symbols of death, and are also Christian symbols of the devil. The dog, a symbol of faithfulness in both religion and marriage, symbolizes the faith the knight must have if he is to reach his goal. A dragon-like lizard is an emblem of evil, and is seen here going in an opposing direction. The dead tree stump may refer to the original sin of Adam, and redemption through Christ. Dürer organized all these separate references in a way that leaves no doubt that the Christian knight is going to reach his goal. The idealized form and dominant central position of the knight and his horse convey a sense of power and assurance.

One of the world's finest works of relief sculpture, known as DESCENT OF THE GANGES, was carved in a huge granite outcropping in the town of Māmallapuram in southern India. Included in the large composition are over a hundred figures of humans, deities, flying pairs of angels, life-size elephants, and a variety of other animals, all converging at the River Ganges in an elaborate depiction of intertwining Hindu legends. As in

49 DESCENT OF THE GANGES.
Māmallapuram, India. 7th century.
Granite. Height approximately 30'.
Photograph: Jerome Feldman, Hawaii Loa College.

Dürer's engraving, the composition is filled with symbolic subject matter.

The carving is believed to represent the descent of the sacred Ganges from heaven to earth, to make the earth fertile. The cobra-like figures of the King and Queen of the Nagas are serpent deities that portray the River Ganges. Though these serpent figures dominate the center of the relief, other legends are incorporated into the composition with little or no concern for narrative or chronological sequence. Among the best known of these depictions is "Arjuna's Penance," a characteristically complex and involved Hindu myth. Arjuna appears in the upper left, standing on one foot in the posture of an ascetic. As the result of his penance, he receives redemption and special powers from Shiva.

In front of the largest elephant is a wonderful depiction of a cat and mice. According to an old folktale, a cat pretending to be an ascetic stood beside the Ganges with upraised paws and gazed at the sun. The cat convinced the mice that she was holy, and thus worthy of worship. As the mice closed their eyes in reverence, the cat snatched them for dinner.

The whole sculpture relates to the annual miracle of the return of the life-giving waters of the Ganges River. Appropriately, the many figures appear to be emerging from the stone.

In chapter 4, we will continue to explore visual language. We will see how a knowledge of art terminology can help us to analyze, and therefore better understand, the expressive potential of the elements of visual form.

56   Vincent van Gogh.
THE FOUNTAIN IN THE HOSPITAL GARDEN. 1889.
Pen and ink. 18⅞″ × 17¹¹/₁₆″.
National Museum Vincent van Gogh, Amsterdam.

57   David Hockney.
THE ARTIST'S MOTHER, BRADFORD. 1972.
Pen and Ink. 17″ × 14″.
© *David Hockney 1972.*

Drawn lines can also create light and dark patterns and the sensation of surface textures. In THE FOUNTAIN IN THE HOSPITAL GARDEN, Vincent van Gogh used a Japanese bamboo pen and ink for his vigorous lines. He varied the darkness of lines by using both full-strength and diluted ink. Rhythmic line groups suggest quality of light as well as rich variation in surfaces.

Perception of lines is not limited to two-dimensional art and objects. Lines are visible all around us in the form of tree branches, corners of buildings, human figures—in the edges of anything three-dimensional.

A *contour line* describes the edge of a three-dimensional object in space. It indicates the last visible portion of a surface that bends away from the viewer. Such a bend is, of course, not really a line, but only appears as an edge that may be drawn as a line. David Hockney employed contour lines to define the perceived edges of the figure and chair in his drawing THE ARTIST'S MOTHER. Notice the differences in line quality in the drawings by Hockney and van Gogh.

When we talk about lines we are usually referring to visible ones; but there are also invisible or implied lines. *Implied lines* can be felt to connect points of emphasis within a work, often giving overall structure to the design. In I AND THE VILLAGE, Marc Chagall used dotted and other implied lines as essential elements of the composition. Our eyes connect the incomplete sections of the circles and fill in the breaks between the dotted lines. Chagall used lines to integrate visually the charming scene, which treats Russian Jewish life and folklore in a highly imaginative manner.

SHAPE

Shape is a two-dimensional area or space defined by visible boundaries. Shapes become visible when a line encloses an area or when an apparent change in value (lightness or darkness), color, or texture sets an area apart from its surroundings.

We can approach the infinite variety of shapes through two general categories, organic and geometric—although there is no clear-cut division between the two. The most common shapes in nature are organic—soft, relaxed, curvilinear, and irregular. The most common shapes people make, at least in Western cultures, are geometric—hard, rigid, regular, and often rectangular. Geometric shapes are the shapes of geometry, such as triangles, circles, and rectangles.

Chagall's I AND THE VILLAGE is a subtle blend of organic and geometric shapes. The major shapes implied in the composition are triangles and circles, as shown in the diagram. Yet Chagall softened the geometric severity so that there is a natural flow between the various sections of the painting. Chagall simplified and abstracted the forms of the natural subjects he portrayed in order to strengthen their visual impact.

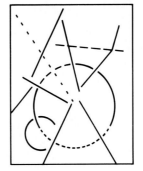

58 Marc Chagall.
I AND THE VILLAGE. 1911.
Oil on canvas. 75⅝″ × 59⅝″.
Collection, The Museum of Modern Art, New York, Mrs. Simon Guggenheim Fund.

Thus far, discussion of shape in I AND THE VILLAGE has focused on subject shapes. This is only half of what must be considered, however, because any shape appearing on a *picture plane*—that is, the flat picture surface—simultaneously creates a second shape out of the background area. Subject, active, or dominant shapes are called *positive shapes*; neutral or passive background areas are *negative shapes*. The artist must consider both positive and negative shapes simul-

taneously and as equally important to the total effectiveness of an image. Positive shapes are called *figure* shapes, whether or not they portray human figures or objects. Negative shapes are called *ground* shapes, and are part of the background. Figure shapes create ground shapes. Interactions between figure and ground shapes are discussed as *figure-ground relationships*. Figure/ground is the fundamental law of perception which allows us to sort out and interpret what we see. Because we are conditioned to see only objects, and not the spaces between and around them, it takes a shift in awareness to see the shapes of spaces.

59 Kenojuak.
THE RETURN OF THE SUN. 1961.
Relief print. 24″ × 36″.
West Baffin Eskimo Co-operative Limited, Cape Dorset, Northwest Territories, Canada.

60 M. C. Escher.
SKY AND WATER I. 1938.
Woodcut. 17⅛″ × 17¼″.
*Vorpal Galleries: San Francisco,
New York, and Laguna Beach.*

In THE RETURN OF THE SUN by Eskimo artist Kenojuak, the white negative shapes are not
recognizable as subject matter, yet they contribute to the vitality of the work as a whole. Inspired by the rich mythological tradition of her
people, Kenojuak filled her print with shapes that
symbolize the interacting forces of nature. The
dark, positive shapes are derived from shadows
seen against the snowy white environment. Although both are important, figure and ground
in Kenojuak's work retain their clear distinction.

In contrast, M. C. Escher's woodcut SKY
AND WATER I depends on the interchangeabil-
ity of figure and ground. As our awareness shifts,
the fish and bird shapes trade places or pop back
and forth, a phenomenon appropriately called
figure-ground reversal. It is not necessary for figure
and ground to be as highly elaborate or structured
as they are in Escher's work—an amazing variety
of images can evoke the reversal phenomenon.

61 FIGURE-GROUND REVERSAL.

MASS

A two-dimensional area is referred to as a shape; a three-dimensional area is a *mass*—the physical bulk of a solid body of material. Mass is often a major element in sculpture; in painting, mass is simulated or implied. Like other visual elements, mass is an aspect of total form, not a separate entity. Whether it is actual (as in sculpture) or implied (as on a two-dimensional surface), mass is inseparable from space, because three-dimensional objects always relate to the space they occupy.

Volume is a three-dimensional enclosed quantity which may be either a solid or a void. This word is sometimes used interchangeably with both mass and space.

The following contrasting pieces of sculpture demonstrate the expressive possibilities of actual mass in three-dimensional works. Massiveness was one of the dominant characteristics of ancient Egyptian architecture and sculpture. Egyptians sought this quality and perfected it because it fit their desire to make their works last forever. QENNEFER, STEWARD OF THE PALACE was carved from hard black granite and retains the cubic, block-like appearance of the quarried stone. None of the limbs project out into the surrounding space. The figure is shown in a sitting position, knees drawn up, arms folded, the neck reinforced by a ceremonial headdress. The body is abstracted and implied with minimal suggestion. This piece is a prime example of *closed form*: it exists in space, but does not openly interact with it. It is a solid, massive sculpture, and a strong symbol of permanence. A common function of Egyptian portrait sculpture such as this was to act as a symbolic container for the soul of an important person, to insure eternal life.

62   QENNEFER, STEWARD OF THE PALACE.
c. 1450 B.C.
Black granite. Height 2'9''.
British Museum, London.

In contrast to the massive Egyptian portrait, contemporary sculptor Alberto Giacometti's MAN POINTING evokes feelings of a fleeting presence rather than permanence. The tall, thin figure appears eroded by time—barely existing. Giacometti used little solid material to construct the figure, so we are more aware of space than mass. The *open form* of the figure reaches out and clearly interacts with the surrounding space, which seems to overwhelm it, suggesting the impermanent nature of human existence.

Giacometti's art reveals his obsession with mortality, which began at age twenty following the death of an older companion. Later, the fleeting essence of human life became a dominant concern in his work. For Giacometti, both life and the making of art were continuous evolutions. He never felt that he succeeded in capturing the changing nature of what he saw, and therefore considered all of his works unfinished.

63   Alberto Giacometti.
MAN POINTING. 1947.
Bronze. 70½'' high,
at base 12'' × 13¼''.
Collection, The Museum of Modern Art, New York.
Gift of Mrs. John D. Rockefeller III.

64   Henry Moore.
RECUMBENT FIGURE. 1938.
Green hornton stone. Length 54″.
The Tate Gallery, London.

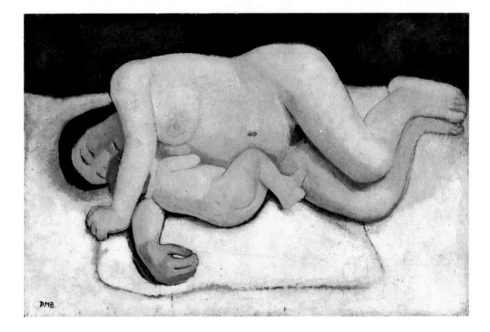

65   Paula Modersohn-Becker.
MOTHER AND CHILD. 1907.
Oil on canvas. 18 cm. × 24 cm.
Private collection, Bremen, Germany.

British artist Henry Moore's RECUMBENT FIGURE is massive in a way quite different from Egyptian solidity, and seems to have nothing in common with Giacometti's work. Moore's abstract figure relates to the wind-worn stone and bone forms he collected in his youth. Moore made his figure compact in its mass, and at the same time opened up holes in the figure that allow space to flow through as well as around the mass. In this way, he created a dynamic, interactive relationship between mass and space.

Compare the sculptural quality implied in the painting MOTHER AND CHILD by German artist Paula Modersohn-Becker with the actual three-dimensional form of Henry Moore's RECUMBENT FIGURE. Modersohn-Becker's figures look solid because she applied paint in gradual shifts from light to dark, giving the appearance of light from above falling on curving surfaces. The texture of the thick paint further emphasizes the solid quality of the figures.

A drawing by Picasso titled HEAD OF A YOUNG MAN shows a use of lines that seem to wrap around and define a head in space, implying a solid mass. The drawing gives the appearance of mass because the lines both define the surface directions and build up areas of light and shade. Picasso's control over the direction and grouping of his lines convince us that we are seeing a fully rounded head. At the same time, the vigor of Picasso's lines reminds us that the image is a drawing on a flat surface.

66 Pablo Picasso.
HEAD OF A YOUNG MAN. 1923.
Conté crayon. 24½" × 18⅝".
The Brooklyn Museum, New York.
Carrll H. DeSilver Fund.

67 Eero Saarinen.
TWA TERMINAL. Kennedy Airport, New York.
1956–1962.
a. Exterior.
 Photograph: Ezra Stoller © ESTO.
b. Interior.
 Photograph: Duane Preble.

SPACE

Space is the indefinable, great, general recepta-cle of all things–the void. It is continuous and infinite and ever present. It cannot exist by it-self because it is in and around everything. The visual arts are sometimes referred to as *spatial* arts, because in most of these arts, forms are or-ganized in space. Music is a *temporal* art, because musical elements are organized primarily in time. Film, television, dance, and other theater arts organize form in both time and space.

The concept of space is important not only in art, but in our daily lives. For example, we each have a sense of personal space–that area surrounding our bodies, which others may not enter unless invited. The extent of this invisible boundary varies from person to person and from culture to culture. Our experience of space in everyday life is determined by our position in re-lation to other people, objects, surfaces, and voids at various distances from the viewer. The eyes are the starting point; each move of our eyes and head brings a corresponding shift in our orientation to all directions. In architecture, we experience space by moving through the struc-tures; in sculpture, we usually perceive it by moving around the work.

The space of a picture's surface is defined by its edges and the two dimensions of the picture plane. Yet within these limited boundaries, a seemingly infinite number of spatial qualities can be implied. The major difference between the uses of space in two-dimensional and three-dimensional art forms is this: in two-dimen-sional works, we see space all at once; in three-dimensional objects and spaces, we must move around to get the full experience.

In Eero Saarinen's TWA TERMINAL, mass en-closes the interior space in such a way that peo-ple moving through the terminal are involved in dramatically shaped space. Four huge shells of reinforced concrete make up the basic struc-ture of this sculptural building. Two of the shells stretch out like the wings of a bird, making the exterior of the building a symbol of flight. Space moves around and through the structure, uniting the interior and exterior in a continuous flow of undulating rhythms. Saarinen intended his architectural space to lift the spirits as well as accommodate utilitarian functions.

On the edge of the Japanese city of Kyoto is a small garden that is part of Ryōan-ji Temple. In this famous garden, there are no plants; vegetation is all around, but separated from the garden by a wall. RYŌAN-JI GARDEN is a flat, rectangular area of raked gravel punctuated by five groups of rocks. It is not possible to see all the rocks at once from any one viewing position. The garden is mostly space – a void – which illustrates the Zen Buddhist concept of incompleteness or potentiality. It is a place for quiet meditation; its quality of "no-thing-ness" promotes inner reflection, and is designed to foster spiritual enlightenment. The apparent emptiness of the garden is intended to induce an egoless state in which the outer world of form and the inner world of formless intuition are experienced as one.

We would experience the space very differently if we were able to walk around Ryōan-ji Garden, rather than view it from the single vantage point of a photograph. The perception of actual three-dimensional space involves a sequence of impressions accumulated over time, while pictorial space on a two-dimensional surface is perceived all at once. A single photograph, taken from one position, can only suggest the experience of actual three-dimensional space. English artist David Hockney's multiple photographic image reveals an understanding of the way we see actual three-dimensional space.

68 RYŌAN-JI GARDEN. Kyoto, Japan. c. 1490.
Photograph: Prithwish Neogy.

69 David Hockney.
SITTING IN THE ZEN GARDEN AT THE RYŌAN-JI TEMPLE, KYOTO, JAPAN, FEBRUARY 19, 1983.
Photographic collage. 50" × 38½"
© *David Hockney, 1983.*

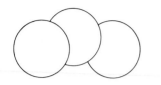

a. Overlap.

b. Overlap and diminishing size.

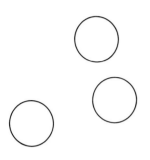

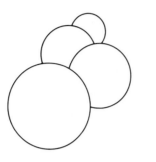

c. Vertical placement.

d. Overlap, placement, and diminishing size.

70 CLUES TO SPATIAL DEPTH.

71 Mu Qi (Mu Ch'i)
SIX PERSIMMONS. c. 1269.
Ink on paper. 17⁵⁄₁₆″ × 14¼″.
Ryoko-in, Daitoku-ji, Kyoto, Japan.

The traditional surfaces for drawings, prints, photographs, and paintings are flat or two-dimensional. Artists working on a picture plane are dealing with actual space in two directions or dimensions: across the surface up and down (height), and across the surface side to side (width). Yet almost any mark on a picture plane begins to give the illusion of the third dimension–depth. Clues to spatial depth learned in infancy or early childhood are the basis for ways to indicate space on a picture plane. The accompanying diagrams show the most basic of these.

The first diagram shows the spatial effect of *overlap*. When shapes overlap, we immediately assume from experience that one is in front of the other. This is the most basic way to achieve the effect of depth on a flat surface. In the second diagram, the effect of overlap is strengthened by *diminishing size*, which gives a sense of greater intervening distance between the shapes. Our perception of distance depends on the observation that distant objects appear smaller than near objects. A third method of achieving the illusion of depth is with *vertical placement*. Objects placed low on the picture plane appear to be closer to the viewer. This is how we see most things in actual space.

For centuries, Asian painters have handled the illusion of depth on the flat picture plane with careful attention to the relationship between the flat reality of the picture surface and the subtle implied depth they wish to create. Mu Qi's (Mu Ch'i's) SIX PERSIMMONS has only a slight suggestion of depth in the overlap of two of the persimmons. By placing the smallest persimmon lowest on the picture plane, Mu Qi further minimized the illusion of depth.

The persimmons appear against a pale background that works both as flat surface and infinite space. The painted shapes of the fruit punctuate the open space of the ground or picture surface and remind us of the well-placed rocks in the garden at Ryōan-ji. Imagine what would happen to this painting if some of the space at the top were cut off. Space is far more than just what is left over after the important forms have been placed; it is an integral part of total visual design.

72 A POND IN A GARDEN. Fragment of a wall from a
tomb in Thebes, Egypt. c. 1400 B.C.
Paint on dry plaster.
British Museum, London.

Paintings from ancient Egypt show little or
no depth. Early Egyptian painters made their images clear by portraying objects from their most
easily identifiable angles and by avoiding the visual confusion caused by overlap and the appearance of diminishing size. A POND IN A GARDEN
demonstrates how they did this. The pond,
viewed from overhead, is shown as a rectangle,
while the trees, fish, and birds are all pictured
in profile (or side view). The Egyptians felt no
need for a single point of view or vantage point.

73 Shaykh Zadeh.
INCIDENT IN A MOSQUE.
Persia. c. 1527.
Opaque watercolor on paper.
28.9 cm. × 17.8 cm.
Private collection.

The Persian miniature painting INCIDENT IN A MOSQUE by Shaykh Zadeh manages to show all the important figures, their positions in space in relation to each other, and their positions in relation to the interior of the mosque. Would a photograph of such a scene reveal as much? Certainly not. Within the flat, decorative surface, each figure and architectural form is presented from the angle that shows it best, and all are stacked up across the surface as if seen from a high vantage point. The result is an intricate organization of flat planes fitted together in shallow, implied space.

Islamic painters have typically shown human activity going on both inside and outside architectural spaces in order to clarify important aspects of the story. Here we see people looking through a window, and others looking over a wall, as well as people inside the mosque. The floor, with its tile pattern and richly decorated carpets, is seen as if from above. There is no diminishing size in the figures or in the steps to the raised chair to indicate distance from the viewer. Depth is shown by overlap and vertical placement, with those figures farthest from us placed highest in the composition. The painting has its own spatial logic consistent with the Persian style. Persian perspective emphasizes narrative clarity and richness of surface design.

Medieval pictorial space was intended to be symbolic and decorative, rather than logical or "real." In Angelo Puccinelli's painting TOBIT BLESSING HIS SON, is it possible to tell whether the angel is behind or in front of the son? It does not matter, of course, since angels do not usually appear in logical, earthly space.

In general usage, the word perspective refers to point of view. In the visual arts, *perspective* can refer to any means of representing the appearance of three-dimensional objects in space on a two-dimensional surface. It is correct to speak of the perspective of Persian miniatures, Japanese prints, Chinese Sung dynasty paintings, or Egyptian paintings—although none of these styles uses a system that is in any way similar to the linear perspective system we use, which was developed during the Italian Renaissance. It is a difference in intention rather than skill that results in various methods for depicting depth.

74 Angelo Puccinelli.
TOBIT BLESSING HIS SON.
c. 1350–1399.
Tempera on wood. 14⅞" × 17⅛".
Philbrook Art Center, Tulsa, Oklahoma.
Samuel H. Kress Collection.

77 a. Raphael Sanzio.
THE SCHOOL OF ATHENS. 1509.
Fresco. Approx. 18' × 26'.
Stanza della Segnatura, Vatican, Rome.

b. Detail showing foreshortening.

c. Perspective lines.

78 FORESHORTENING.

a. Foreshortened rod.

b. Unforeshortened rod.

In THE SCHOOL OF ATHENS, architecture in the Renaissance style provides a grand setting for the figures. Raphael achieved a balance between interest in the group of figures and the pull into implied deep space created by linear perspective. The size of each figure is drawn to scale according to its position in space relative to the viewer; thus the entire group seems natural. Lines superimposed over the painting reveal the basic one-point perspective system used by Raphael. The cube in the foreground is not parallel to the walls of the building and is in two-point perspective.

An artist can use perspective for symbolic emphasis. We infer that Plato and Aristotle are the most important figures in this painting, because they are placed at the center of the series of arches and are framed by the one farthest away. Perhaps more important is the fact that they are placed on either side of the vanishing point in the zone of greatest implied depth. At the point at which the viewer is pulled farthest back in space, the two figures come forward, creating a dynamic tension between push and pull in implied deep space. If the two main figures were removed, our eyes would be drawn right through the painting. The resulting "hole" would be so distracting that it would be difficult to see anything else in the painting.

One of the most difficult challenges for an artist is the problem of showing an elongated form with the long axis extending toward the viewer. An object in such a position is said to be *foreshortened*. Foreshortening is particularly evident in Raphael's rendering of Aristotle's right arm and right foot. Less extreme foreshortening is seen in the book in Aristotle's left hand.

A nonlinear means for giving an illusion of depth is *atmospheric* or *aerial perspective*. Here the artist creates the illusion of depth by changing color, value, and detail in accordance with the desired degree of distance between the viewer and distant objects. As the distance between an observer and large objects such as buildings and mountains increases, the increasing quantity of air, including moisture and dust, causes the objects to change in appearance. As objects recede,

79   Claude Lorrain.
THE HERDSMAN. c. 1635.
Oil on canvas. 47¾″ × 63⅛″.
National Gallery of Art, Washington, D.C.
Samuel H. Kress Collection.

they appear less distinct and bluer in color; color intensity is lessened and light/dark contrast is reduced.

The Renaissance idea of a painting as a window onto nature is readily apparent in THE HERDSMAN, which was painted by Claude Gellée of Lorraine, known as Claude, or one of his followers. Atmospheric perspective is effectively employed in the painting to heighten the illusion of deep space, yet our interest is held in the foreground by the figure of the herdsman and his flock. The vantage point is low. From this position, we feel invited to walk right into the painted landscape, as though its suggested space were an extension of our own space. However, the sun and its light come toward us from the distance, balancing the visual pull into implied deep space.

Artists of the Orient have used atmospheric perspective differently than their European counterparts. The soft, rolling shapes of mountains stack up in rhythmic layers of suggested space in this Chinese painting in the style of Mi Fei. The Sung dynasty master Mi Fei developed a technique of daubing ink on the silk surface to build up forms without outlines. Atmosphere is implied by the way the mist seems to progressively dissolve the lighter, distant hill shapes.

THE HERDSMAN, on the previous page, draws the viewer's eye into and through the suggested deep space. In contrast, the Mi Fei-style Chinese painting leads the eye up and down in shallow space close to the picture plane. Mi Fei, painting in the Chinese tradition, worked with the two-dimensional reality of the picture plane; Claude, following the Renaissance tradition, sought to deny the picture plane in order to achieve an illusion of three-dimensional space.

80 Paul Cézanne.
THE TURN IN THE ROAD.
1879–1882.
Oil on canvas. 23⅞″ × 28⅞″.
Museum of Fine Arts, Boston,
Bequest of Robert Treat Paine, II.

81 Attributed to Mi Fei.
MISTY LANDSCAPE: ROUNDED MOUNTAIN PEAKS
AND TREES. c. 1090.
Hanging scroll, ink on silk. 59¹/₁₆″ × 31″.
Courtesy of the Freer Gallery of Art, Smithsonian Institution,
Washington, D.C. (08.171).

MISTY LANDSCAPE was painted from memory. The implied high vantage point of the viewer is not an actual observation point, but a device that offers a detached view of distant hills in a relatively flat pattern. Traditional Chinese landscape paintings are poetic symbols of experience with landforms, rather than realistic representations. See page 275 for a discussion of the philosophical concepts behind "space" in Chinese painting.

Paul Cézanne constructed another kind of pictorial space in THE TURN IN THE ROAD. Because our vantage point is high above the ground plane, we are not led into this painting as we were in Claude's landscape. Cézanne intentionally tipped up the road plane, making it a major shape in the composition. In a departure from the idea of a window view from one vantage point, he adjusted all the planes in order to strengthen the overall dynamics of the composition. The space implied in THE TURN IN THE ROAD is relatively shallow. Although Cézanne did not use linear or atmospheric perspective, the suggestion of depth within the painting is a major element. Cézanne's goal was to reconcile in his own way the three dimensions of nature with the two dimensions of the picture plane. After four hundred years of the painting-as-a-window tradition, Cézanne's approach led Western artists to rethink pictorial space.

Linear perspective is simply one device an artist may or may not choose to use. Many leading artists of the twentieth century have chosen to avoid illusions of depth in their work. Paul Klee rarely employed perspective; but when he did, he used it imaginatively. In UNCOMPOSED OBJECTS IN SPACE, he created a dreamlike mood in which objects seem to be moving into, or emerging from, the dark space framed by the tallest rectangle.

82   Paul Klee.
UNCOMPOSED OBJECTS IN SPACE. 1929.
Watercolor. 12⅝″ × 9⅞″.
Private collection.

83   Paul Klee.
FIRE AT EVENING. 1929.
Oil on cardboard. 13⅜″ × 13¼″.
Collection, The Museum of Modern Art, New York.
Mr. and Mrs. Joachim Jean Aberbach Fund.

In the same year, Klee painted FIRE AT EVE-NING, in which he avoided any illusion of three-dimensional space. The painting is one of a series made after a trip to Egypt, where his imagination was stimulated by patterns of agriculture, and the glow of fires used for cooking, warmth, and light.

Although there is no perspective in this composition of horizontal and vertical rectangles, push and pull in space is suggested by contrast between warm and cool, light and dark colors. Rhythmic bands of muted colors capture the magic of twilight, and set off the advancing red-orange "fire." At the top, a glowing pink above an intense blue suggests the last fading light of day along the horizon. Klee achieved a feeling of landscape while maintaining the flatness of the picture plane.

Painters such as Paul Klee have reaffirmed the two-dimensional reality of the picture surface and used it to create spatial configurations, multiple views, and even a sense of time and motion relevant to the changing insights and concerns of our age (see pages 382-395).

TIME AND MOTION

Time is a nonspatial continuum in which events occur in succession. We live in a time/space environment; time is different from space, yet inseparable from it. Although time itself is invisible, it can be made perceptible in art, becoming an important element in some works.

In many Asian cultures, the experience of time is cyclic. The Wheel of the Law in Buddhism originated in ancient Hindu symbolism and stands for the view of time seen in the cycle of the seasons; in the cycle of birth, death, and rebirth; and in longer cycles of celestial creation,

84   WHEELS OF THE SUN CHARIOT.
Konarak, India. c. 1240.
Photograph: Prithwish Neogy.

preservation, dissolution, and *re*creation. This view of time is one of the symbolic references expressed in WHEELS OF THE SUN CHARIOT of Surya Deul Temple at Konarak, India.

In Western culture, we think of time as linear—continually moving forward. Sassetta implied the passage of linear time in his painted narration of THE MEETING OF SAINT ANTHONY AND SAINT PAUL. The painting depicts key moments during Saint Anthony's progression through time and space, including the start of his journey at the city barely visible behind the trees. He first comes into view as he approaches the wilderness; we next see him as he encounters the centaur; finally, he emerges into the clearing in the foreground, where he meets Saint Paul. The road upon which he travels implies continuous movement in time.

The comic strip is a contemporary narrative art form that relies on implied sequential time. In comics, the stories are read from left to right and each panel frames a segment of the action through time. Continuity in the dialogue and consistency in the identifying features of the figures make the illusion of passing time understandable.

The various interpretations of time found in different cultures suggest that the concept of time may be a human invention. In any case, the desire to stop time, or at least to record events in time, goes back to early history. This urge was part of the inspiration for the development of photography. Initially, only static, inanimate objects could be recorded, because the photosensitive material required a long exposure. By 1839, improvements in the process made it possible to photograph people standing or sitting very still; and by the late 1850s, images of slowly moving people and things could be photographed. (See the discussion of photography on pages 150–153.)

85 Sassetta and assistant.
THE MEETING OF SAINT ANTHONY AND SAINT PAUL. c. 1440.
Tempera on wood. 18¾ " × 13⅝".
National Gallery of Art, Washington, D.C.
Samuel H. Kress Collection.

LIGHT

Everything we see is made visible by the radiant energy we call *light*. Sunlight—natural light—perceived as white, actually contains all the colors of light that make up the visible part of the electromagnetic spectrum (see diagram on page 84). Light can be directed, reflected, refracted (bent), diffracted, or diffused. Various types of artificial light include incandescent, fluorescent, neon, and laser. The source, color, intensity, and direction of light determine the way things appear. As light changes, the things that are illuminated by it also appear to change.

A simple shift in the direction of light dramatically changes the way we perceive the sculpture of ABRAHAM LINCOLN by Daniel Chester French. When the monumental figure was first installed in the Lincoln Memorial in Washington, D.C., the sculptor was disturbed by the lighting. The entire character of the Lincoln figure was altered by the light which came from a low angle through the open doorway of the building. The problem was corrected by placing spotlights in the ceiling above the statue that were stronger than the natural light coming

93 Daniel Chester French.
Full-size copy of ABRAHAM LINCOLN
demonstrating lighting problem. 1922.
a. Original daylight.
b. With the addition of artificial light.

through the doorway. Light had altered the appearance of the form, and therefore had changed French's intended content.

Light coming from a source directly in front of or behind objects seems to flatten three-dimensional form and emphasize shape. Light from above or from the side, slightly in front, most clearly reveals three-dimensional objects in space as we are accustomed to seeing them.

In art terminology, the word *value* refers to the relative lightness and darkness of surfaces. The amount of light reflected from a surface determines its value. Values range from white through grays to black, and may be seen as a property of color or independent of color. Subtle relationships between light and dark areas determine how things look. Gradual shifts from lighter to darker tones can give the illusion of a curving surface, while an abrupt value change usually indicates an abrupt change in surface direction.

Diagram 94 shows that we perceive relationships, rather than isolated forms. The gray bar is of uniform value, yet appears quite different when the value of its background is changed.

The drawing of light falling on a sphere illustrates how a value gradation, or gradual shifting from light to dark, suggests a curved surface. The use of gradations of light and shade in which forms are determined by the meeting of lighter and darker areas, rather than by sharp outlines, is called *chiaroscuro*. This technique, developed in the Renaissance, makes it possible to create the illusion that objects depicted on a flat surface are three-dimensional. Chiaroscuro, originally an Italian word, is now used in English to describe the interaction of light and shade in two-dimensional art. The derivation of the word gives its meaning: *chiaro* means light or clear, and *oscuro* means dark or obscure.

Pierre-Paul Prud'hon created the illusion of roundness in STUDY OF A FEMALE NUDE by using black and white chalk on a middle-value blue-gray paper. Because the paper is a value halfway between white and black, it acts as a connective value between the highlights and shadows. If you follow the form of the figure, you will see how it appears first as a light area against a dark background (note the right shoulder),

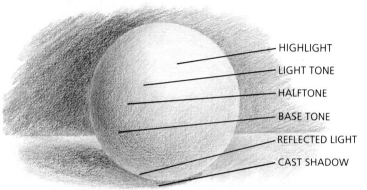

then as a dark area against a lighter background (as in the under-part of the breast on the same side). The background remains the same, appearing first dark, then light. Most objects become visible in this way. Sometimes, as in the area between the shoulder and the breast on this figure, the edge of an object will disappear when its value at that point becomes the same as the value behind it, and the two surfaces merge. Usually we do not "see" this, however, because our minds fill in the invisible line of the continuous edge. We know the form is continuous, so we perceive it as continuous.

In the "real" world, we always see values along with other color properties and textures. Works of art in which color is an important element obviously suffer when reproduced only in black and white. Most drawings and many prints are intentionally created in black and white, and early photography was possible only in black and white or brown and white. Today, despite the availability of high-quality color film and processing, many serious photographers choose to limit their work to black and white because the graphic clarity of black and white works better with the visual statements they wish to make. Black-and-white photographs are abstractions from the natural world of color. By eliminating the layer of information given by color, photographers can avoid the problem of presenting too much information.

94 DARK/LIGHT RELATIONSHIPS.
Value scale compared to uniform middle gray.

HIGHLIGHT
LIGHT TONE
HALFTONE
BASE TONE
REFLECTED LIGHT
CAST SHADOW

95 VALUE STUDY.
Illusion of light falling on the curving surface of a sphere.

96 Pierre-Paul Prud'hon.
STUDY OF A FEMALE NUDE. C. 1814.
Charcoal and black-and-white chalks on blue paper.
11″ × 8¾″.
Philadelphia Museum of Art. The Henry P. McIlhenny Collection in memory of Frances P. McIlhenny.

97   Francisco de Zurbarán.
SAINT SERAPION. 1628.
Oil on canvas. 47⁹/₁₆″ × 41″.
Wadsworth Atheneum, Hartford, Connecticut.
The Ella Gallup Sumner and Mary Catlin Sumner Collection.

Value alone can clearly express various moods and feelings. When gradations of value are eliminated, images take on a more forceful appearance. If no gray values are present, black and white areas adjoin one another directly. The resulting strong contrast between light and dark gives impact to the work that may be essential to its content.

Strong value contrast emphasizes the dramatic impact of Francisco de Zurbarán's SAINT SERAPION. In simple compositional terms, the major shape is a light rectangle against a dark background.

Minimal value contrast is a major aspect of Kasimir Malevich's WHITE ON WHITE. The simplicity of this unique painting is enhanced by the closely keyed value relationship of one white square placed on top of another. Malevich's painting calls attention to the visual quality of minimal value contrast, yet a subtle warm/cool color shift also plays a major role in the work. A very different example of minimal value contrast is INJURED BY GREEN by Richard Anuszkiewicz (see page 91). Both paintings have minimal value contrast; yet Malevich minimized color contrast, while Anuszkiewicz maximized it.

A two-dimensional image with minimal value contrast that uses light or high values exclusively is said to be *high key*; if it only employs dark or low values the work is *low key*. The painting WHITE ON WHITE is high key. By controlling value ranges, the artist creates particular moods within the work that are uniquely different from the more common mood created by an equal balance of light and dark values. The terms high key and low key can also be used to refer to the combined effect achieved by limiting the values of wall and floor covering, furniture, and room illumination in interior design. Hospitals tend to be high key; bars tend to be low key.

98 Kasimir Malevich.
SUPREMATIST COMPOSITION: WHITE ON WHITE.
1918 (?).
Oil on canvas. 31¼″ × 31¼″.
Collection, The Museum of Modern Art, New York.

99 Stephen Antonakos.
WALK ON NEON. 1968.
Neon, glass, aluminum, timing programmers.
120″ × 108″ × 144″.
Photograph: © *1968 Stephen Antonakos.*

Color, direction, quantity, and intensity of light have a major effect on our moods, our mental ability, and our general well-being. California architect Vincent Palmer has experimented with the effect that changes in the color and intensity of interior light have on people, and has found that he can modify the behavior of his guests by changing the light around them. Light quality affects people's emotions and physical comfort, thus changing the volume and intensity of their conversation and even the length of their visit.

Light has been an important element in art since prehistoric times. Early cave paintings were painted and viewed by flickering torchlight. The sun's changing rays illuminate the stained glass walls of Gothic cathedrals, filling their interiors with colored light. In the twentieth century, we have a variety of ways to produce and control light.

Light must be carefully considered in photography, cinematography, television, stage design, architecture, and interior design. As light technology and awareness of the impact and use of light have increased, lighting designers have become more important. Light technicians, engineers, and artists have combined their skills, using the unique qualities of light and light mixture to produce exciting visual forms.

Some artists even use artificial light as their medium. Since the 1960s, neon light has been the favorite sculpture material of Stephen Antonakos. In WALK ON NEON, tubes of colored light flash on and off in pre-set sequences. The work modifies space in a cycle of timed illumination.

Thomas Wilfred was one of the first to realize the potential of colored electric light as a legitimate medium for artists. His experiments in 1905 led to the development of the Clavilux Lumia, an organ-like instrument that played projected moving light instead of music. Wilfred is noted for separating kinetic light compositions from dependence on music or sound. When he played his first public recitals on the instrument in the early 1920s, audiences were thrilled by his unique and beautiful presentations. A single color that covered a large screen would gather itself into a shape, then break into moving patterns of various colors, then merge again. His original compositions, such as LUMIA SUITE OP. 158, have been recorded and are now projected on a smaller scale by automated light-projecting machines. Wilfred worked out a system for reflecting light from moving mirrors onto a translucent screen. A continuously changing image of colored light appears from the front of the screen.

Light used in combination with other media has become of increasing interest to contemporary artists. The art of lighting has become important in performances of all kinds. Since the mid-1960s, light shows, influenced by Wilfred's early work, have been presented with rock and other forms of contemporary popular music.

100 Thomas Wilfred.
LUMIA SUITE OP. 158. 1963.
a. Third movement: elliptical
b. First movement: horizontal
Composition of light in form, color, and motion.
Commissioned by the Museum of Modern Art, New York.
Mrs. Simon Guggenheim Fund.

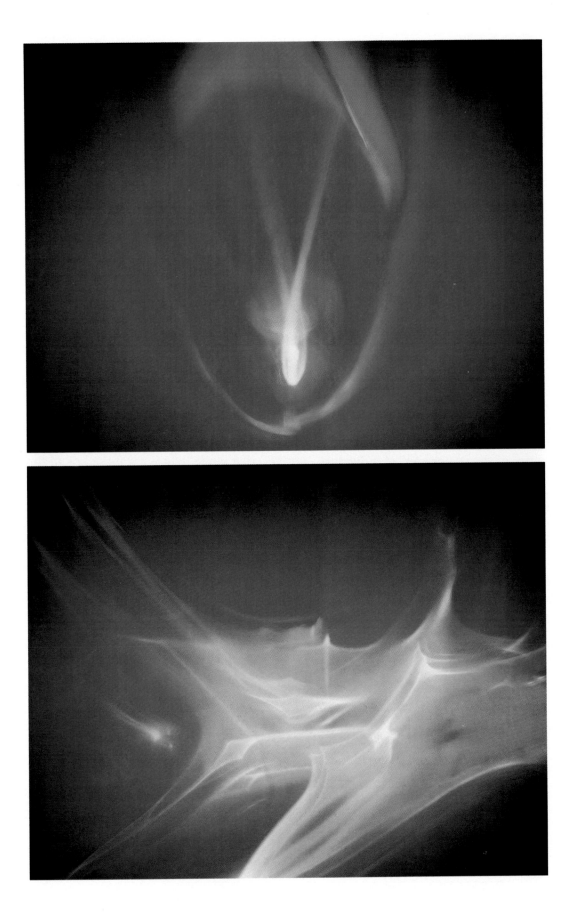

COLOR

Color affects us directly by modifying our thoughts, moods, actions, and even our health. Although the impact of color is substantial, we are often unaware of its effect. Psychologists, as well as designers of schools, offices, hospitals, and prisons, have acknowledged that colors can affect work habits and mental conditions for better or for worse. People surrounded by expanses of solid orange or red for a long period of time often experience nervousness and increased pulse and blood pressure. In contrast, some blues have been shown to have a calming effect, with blood pressure, pulse, and activity rates dropping to below normal levels.

Most of us have favorite colors, and many prefer different colors for different things. Such color preferences are one way we express our personal differences. When given a choice, most of us choose to wear and live with those colors we find particularly appealing. Leading designers of everything from clothing and cars to housewares are well aware of the importance of individual color preferences, and spend considerable time and expense to determine color choices for their products.

Most cultures use color symbolically, according to established conventions. Leonardo da Vinci was influenced by earlier traditions when he wrote, "We shall set down for white the representative of light, without which no color can be seen; yellow for earth; green for water; blue for air; red for fire; and black for total darkness."[5]

Some painters of the past found color so dominating that they avoided pure, unmixed colors to enable viewers to see the essence of the subject without being distracted. In China and Japan, traditional painters have often limited themselves to black ink on a white surface. Prior to the twentieth century, pure bright colors were seldom used in Western art. The French impressionist painters and their followers led the way to the free use of color we enjoy today (see pages 358–361).

What we call "color" is the effect on our eyes of light waves of differing wavelengths or frequencies. When combined, these light waves make white light. Individual colors are components of light.

The phenomenon of color is a paradox: it exists only in light, but light itself seems colorless to the human eye. All objects that appear to have color are merely reflectors or transmitters of the color that must be present in the light that illuminates them. In 1666, Sir Isaac Newton discovered that white light is composed of all the colors of the spectrum. He found that when the white light of the sun passes through a glass prism, it is separated into the bands of color that make up the *visible spectrum*. Each color has a different wavelength and travels through the glass of the prism at a different speed. Red, which has the longest wavelength, travels more rapidly through the glass than blue, which has a shorter wavelength. Rainbows result when sunlight is

101 ELECTROMAGNETIC SPECTRUM.

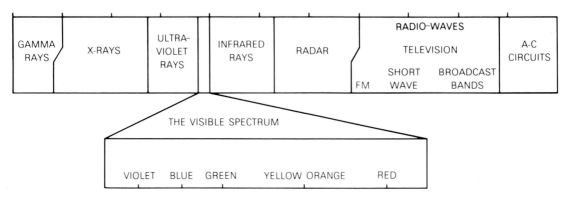

refracted and dispersed by the spherical form of raindrops, producing a combined effect like the glass prism. In both cases, the sequence of spectral colors is red, orange, yellow, green, blue, indigo, and violet.

Pigments and Light

Our common experience with color is provided by light reflected from pigmented surfaces. Therefore the emphasis in the following discussion is on pigment color rather than color coming from light alone.

When light illuminates an object, some of the light is absorbed by the surface of the object and some is reflected. The color that appears to our eyes as the apparent color of the object (called *object color* or *local color*) is determined by the wavelengths of light being reflected. Thus a red surface in white light appears red because it reflects mostly red light and absorbs the rest of the spectrum. A green surface absorbs most of the spectrum except green, which it reflects; and so on with all the hues of the spectrum.

If all the wavelengths of light are absorbed by an opaque object, the object appears black; if all the wavelengths are reflected, the object appears white. A black space is a space without light. Completely transparent objects appear to be the color of the light they transmit. Black and white are not true colors. White, black, and their combination, gray, are *achromatic*, or *neutral*—without the property of hue.

Color varies in three basic ways: hue, value, and intensity:

☐ *Hue* is the particular wavelength of spectrum color to which we give a name (see the prism diagram). Colors of the spectrum are called hues. Spectrum-intensity red is spoken of as the hue red and distinguished from the hue orange, its neighbor on the spectrum, and so forth.

☐ *Value* is the relative lightness or darkness of a color (see the value scale, page 86). Black and white pigments can be important ingredients in changing color values. Black added to a hue produces *shades* of that hue. For example, when black is added to orange, the result is a brown; and when black is mixed with red, the result is maroon. White added to a hue produces a *tint*. Lavender is a tint of violet; pink is a tint of red.

Hues in their purest form are also at their usual value. For example, the value of pure yellow is much lighter than the value of pure violet. Pure yellow is the lightest of hues and violet is the darkest. Red and green are middle-value hues.

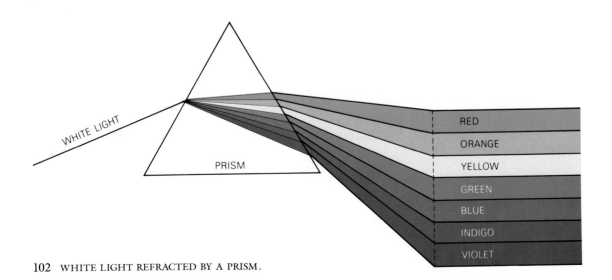

102 WHITE LIGHT REFRACTED BY A PRISM.

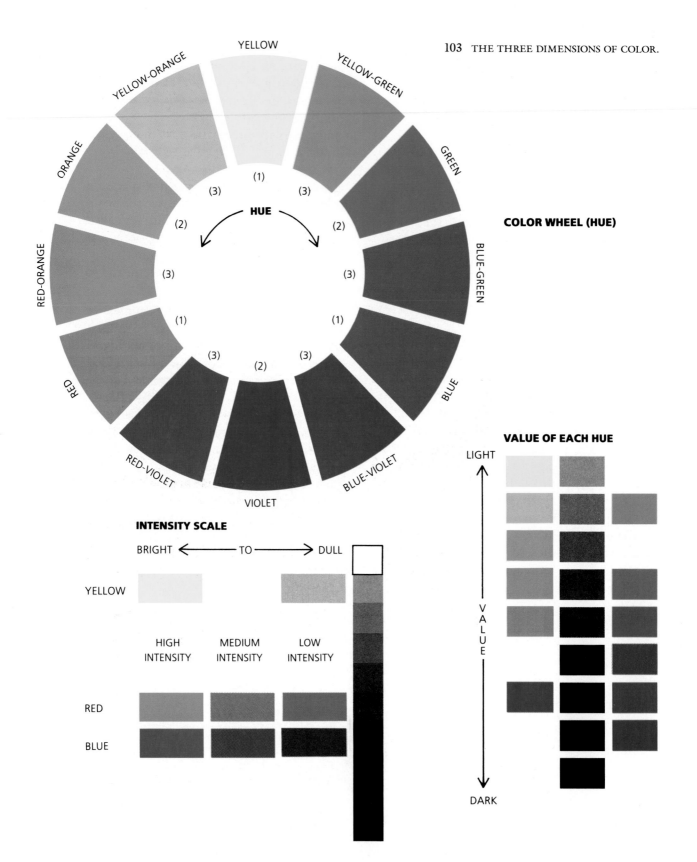

103   THE THREE DIMENSIONS OF COLOR.

COLOR WHEEL (HUE)

INTENSITY SCALE

VALUE OF EACH HUE

☐ *Intensity*, also called *saturation* and *chroma*, is the purity of a hue, or color. A pure hue is the most intense form of a given color; it is the hue at its highest saturation, in its brightest form. With pigment, if white, black, gray, or another hue is added to a pure hue, intensity diminishes and the color is dulled or modified.

When the pigments of different hues are mixed together, the mixture appears duller and darker because pigments absorb more and more light as their absorptive qualities combine. For this reason, pigment mixture is called *subtractive color mixture*. Mixing red, blue, and yellow will produce a dark gray, almost black, depending on the proportions and the type of pigment used.

Most people are familiar with the three pigment primaries: red, yellow, and blue. Printers use *magenta* (red), *yellow*, and *cyan* (blue), because magenta and cyan provide the specific purplish red and greenish blue that work best for printing. There are also three light primaries: red, green, and blue or blue-violet. When the three light primaries are combined, the result is white light. Such a mixture is called *additive color mixture*. Combinations of the light primaries produce lighter colors. Red and green light when mixed make yellow light, and so forth. Color television employs additive color mixture. A working knowledge of the character and mixing properties of light colors is essential for color photographers, film and video artists, and stage light designers.

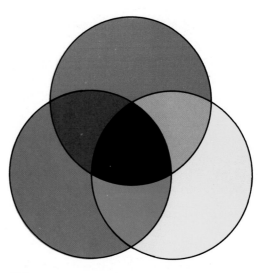

104 PIGMENT PRIMARIES: SUBTRACTIVE COLOR MIXTURE.

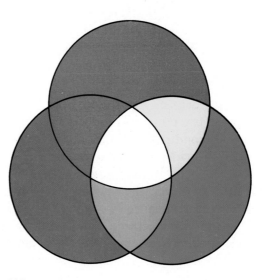

105 LIGHT PRIMARIES: ADDITIVE COLOR MIXTURE.

The Color Wheel

Several major pigment color systems are in use today, each with its own basic hues. The *color wheel* presented here is one contemporary version of the circle concept first developed in the seventeenth century by Newton. After Newton discovered the spectrum, he found that both ends could be combined into the hue red-violet, making the color wheel possible. Numerous color systems have followed since that time. The

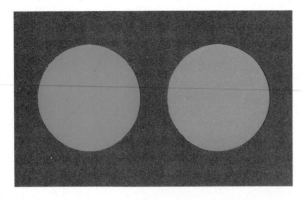

106 WARM/COOL COLORS.

color system presented here is based on twelve pure hues, and can be divided into the following groups:

☐ *Primaries*: red, yellow, and blue. These are the pigment hues that cannot be produced by an intermixing of other hues. They are also referred to as primary colors (see 1 on the color wheel on page 86).

☐ *Secondaries*: orange, green, and violet. The mixture of two primaries produces a secondary hue. Secondaries are positioned between the two primaries of which they are composed (see 2 on the color wheel). When we mix them ourselves, the secondaries do not have the pure brilliance of oranges, greens, and violets manufactured from pigments specifically chosen to produce those pure hues.

☐ *Intermediates*: red-orange, yellow-orange, yellow-green, blue-green, blue-violet, and red-violet. Their names indicate their components. Intermediates are located between the primaries and the secondaries of which they are composed (see 3 on the color wheel).

The blue-green side of the wheel is *cool* in psychological temperature, and the red-orange side is *warm*. Yellow-green and red-violet are the poles dividing the color wheel into warm and cool hues. The difference between warm and cool colors is chiefly due to psychological association. Relative warm and cool differences can be seen in any group of hues. Color affects our feelings about size and distance as well as temperature. Cool colors appear to contract and recede and warm colors appear to expand and advance (see diagram).

Malevich's WHITE ON WHITE (see page 81) is based on a subtle warm/cool difference. The diagonally placed square is painted a cool blue-white, which sets it apart from the warm yellow-white background.

Color sensations more vibrant than those achieved with actual pigment mixture can be obtained when dots of pure color are placed together so that they blend in the mind, creating the appearance of other hues. This is called *optical color mixture*. For example, rich greens appear when many tiny dots or strokes of yellow-green and blue-green are placed close together.

Painter Georges Seurat developed this concept in the 1880s as a result of his studies of impressionist paintings and then-recent scientific discoveries of light and color. He wanted his paintings to capture the brilliance and purity of light. His method, divisionism—popularly called *pointillism*—is similar to modern four-color printing in which tiny dots of printers' primaries—magenta (a red), yellow, and cyan (turquoise blue)—are printed together in various amounts with black on white paper to achieve the effect of full color. Seurat, however, used no black. Compare the detail of Seurat's SUNDAY AFTERNOON ON THE ISLAND OF LA GRANDE JATTE with the color separations and the enlarged detail of the reproduction of Botticelli's BIRTH OF VENUS. (See the complete paintings on pages 362 and 324.) The eye perceives subtle blends as it optically mixes tiny dots of intense color in both Seurat's painting and in four-color printing.

a. Yellow.

b. Magenta.

c. Yellow and magenta.

d. Cyan.

e. Yellow, magenta, and cyan.

f. Black.

g. Yellow, magenta, cyan, and black.

h. Color printing detail of Botticelli's BIRTH OF VENUS showing mechanical dot pattern of offset photolithography. *(See complete painting on page 324.)*

108 OPTICAL COLOR MIXTURE.
Detail of Seurat's SUNDAY AFTERNOON ON THE ISLAND OF GRAND JATTE showing divisionist technique. *(See complete painting on page 362.)*

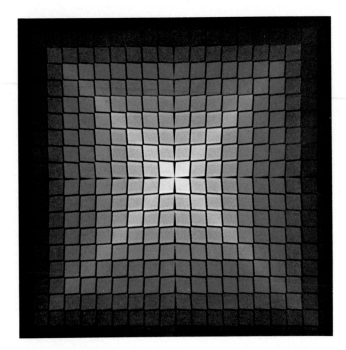

109 Victor Vasarely.
UNTITLED. 1967.
Screenprint. 23½″ × 23¼″.
Honolulu Academy of Arts.

Printed color reproductions and projected color slides can be quite different in color from the original artwork. Images from projected slides are often more brilliant because they are made with projected light, and because they are seen in a darkened room.

Color groupings that provide certain kinds of color harmonies are called *color schemes*. The most common of these are monochromatic, analogous, complementary, and polychromatic:

☐ *Monochromatic*: variations in value and intensity of a single hue. In this color scheme, a pure hue is used alone with black and/or white, or mixed with black and/or white. Victor Vasarely's screenprint is a monochromatic work that employs a pure blue and its tints and shades.

☐ *Analogous*: hues adjacent to one another on the color wheel, each containing the same hue—for example, yellow-green, green, and blue-green, which all contain the hue green. Ben Cunningham's CORNER PAINTING uses analogous color. Tints and shades of each analogous hue may be used to add variations to this color scheme.

110 Ben Cunningham.
CORNER PAINTING. 1948–1950.
Oil on canvas. 25½″ × 36½″ × 25½″ × 21½″.
Collection of Mrs. Ben Cunningham.

Cunningham went beyond the usual rectangular format in CORNER PAINTING. His manipulation of color relationships in precise perspective planes gives a fascinating illusion of depth. Cunningham mastered in one painting the spatial effects of color as transparent film, as hollow volume, and as impenetrable surface. One can look at, through, and into Cunningham's paintings.

☐ *Complementary*: two hues directly opposite one another on the color wheel. When mixed together in almost equal amounts, complementary hues form neutral grays; but when placed side by side as pure hues, they contrast strongly, and intensify each other. Because they can be identical in value, the complementary hues red-orange and blue-green tend to "vibrate" more when placed next to each other than do other complements. The complements yellow and violet provide the strongest value contrast possible with pure hues. The complement of a primary is the opposite secondary, which can be obtained by mixing the other two primaries. For example, the complement of yellow is violet. The interaction of the complementary hues red and green is the dominant feature of the painting INJURED BY GREEN by Richard Anuszkiewicz.

☐ *Polychromatic*: the use of many hues and their variations. When painters choose their palettes, they visualize color combinations in terms of their familiarity with certain available pigment colors. Most artists work intuitively with color harmonies which are more complex and sophisticated than the basic schemes described here.

The appearance of a given color in an object is always relative to adjacent colors and light conditions. A hue can appear to change as colors around it change. In INJURED BY GREEN, Richard Anuszkiewicz painted a uniform pattern of dots in two sizes. Behind these, the red-orange background appears to change, but is the same hue throughout.

Intensity builds from the outer edges of the painting toward the center, where we are "injured"—or temporarily color-blinded—by a

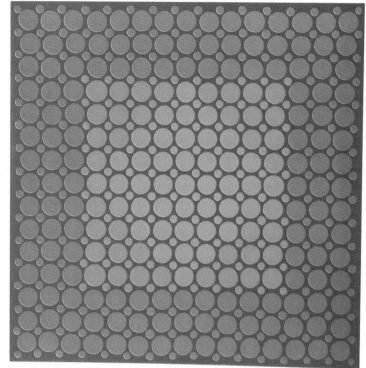

111 Richard Anuszkiewicz.
INJURED BY GREEN. 1963.
Acrylic on board. 36″ × 36″.
Collection of Janet S. Fleisher, Philadelphia.

diamond-shaped area containing yellow-green dots of the same value as the red background. The diamond is surrounded by a square of blue-green dots. These two hues are on either side of green on the color wheel—and green is the complement of red. The yellow-green and blue-green form the split complements of red. Anuszkiewicz used split complements of matching value to give this central area its pulsing energy. He said,

My work is of an experimental nature and has centered on an investigation into the effects of complementary colors full of intensity when juxtaposed and the optical changes that occur as a result.[6]

The eye sees an *afterimage* when prolonged exposure to a visual form causes excitation and subsequent fatigue of the retina. Color afterimages are caused by partial color blindness temporarily induced in the normal eye by desensitizing some of its color receptors. For example, staring at a red spot for thirty seconds under a bright

112 Jasper Johns.
Detail of FLAGS. 1965.
Oil on canvas with raised canvas.
Full painting 72″ × 48″.
Private collection.
© *Jasper Johns/VAGA New York, 1988.*

white light will tire the red receptors in that segment of the retina on which the red spot is focused and make them less sensitive to red light, or partially red-blind. When the red spot is removed, the eye sees a blue-green spot on the white surface, because the tired red receptors react weakly to the red light reflected by that area of the surface. The blue and green receptors, meanwhile, respond strongly to the reflected blue and green light, producing an apparent blue-green dot that is not actually present on the surface. On a neutral surface, therefore, the hue of an afterimage will always be the complement of the hue of the original image or stimulus.

Try this more complex example of the afterimage phenomenon. Stare for about thirty seconds at the white dot in the center of the flag in the detail of Jasper Johns's painting FLAGS, and then look at a white area of paper of the same size or larger.

Any color is modified by its association with surrounding colors and by such factors as intensity, angle, and warm or cool properties of light. As light decreases, individual colors become less distinct. In bright light, colors reflect one another, causing changes in the appearance of local color. In his painting THE BREAKFAST ROOM, Pierre Bonnard emphasized these shifts in local color and added many personal poetic color relationships of his own invention.

Color is central to Bonnard's art. Here he began with a somewhat ordinary scene and heightened its effect on us by concentrating on the magical qualities of light and color on a sunny day. The rich, seductive color portrays Bonnard's feelings about the mood of that day.

Bonnard's color is the result of a personal search. During the 1890s, he worked with subdued color. About 1900, he began to use brighter colors in what he described as a personal version of impressionism. As his color sense matured, his paintings became filled with rich harmonies of warm and cool colors, subtly played off against each other.

113 Pierre Bonnard.
THE BREAKFAST ROOM. c. 1930–1931.
Oil on canvas. 62⅞″ × 44⅞″.
Collection, The Museum of Modern Art, New York.
Anonymous gift.

TEXTURE

Texture refers to the tactile qualities of surfaces or to the visual representation of such qualities. What would life be like without the sense of touch? Young children explore their surroundings by touching everything within reach, and learn to equate the feel with the look of surfaces. As adults we know how most things feel, yet we still enjoy the pleasures that touching gives. We delight in running our hands over the fur of a pet, or the smooth surface of highly polished wood. We note the rough texture of bark or the smooth texture of glass, and we enjoy textural contrasts in such things as clothes and furnishings.

All surfaces have textures which may be experienced by touching, or through suggestion by sight alone. Textures may be categorized as actual or simulated. *Actual* textures are those we can feel by touch, such as polished marble, wood, sand, or lumps of thick paint. *Simulated* (or implied) textures are those that have been created to look like something they are not. Some painters simulate textures that look like real smooth paint. Textures invented by human imagination can be actual or purely visual (simulated). The texture of combed concrete is rough to the touch, while the invented texture of the painted background in Gustav Klimt's THE KISS is purely visual, and would have little or no textural feeling if we touched it.

Meret Oppenheim's notorious fur-covered teacup is about tactile experience. She presented an intentionally contradictory object designed to evoke strong responses ranging from revulsion to amusement. The actual texture of fur is pleasant, as is the smooth texture of a teacup, but the combination makes the tongue "crawl." Social and psychological implications are abundant and intended.

Sculptors and architects work with the actual textures of their materials, and the relationships between them. They can also create other textures in the finishing of surfaces. Compare the eroding surfaces of Alberto Giacometti's figure on page 57 with the youthful, skin-like textures of the figures in Rodin's THE KISS on page 42, which in itself has strong textural contrast. Each artist used texture to heighten emotional impact.

114   Meret Oppenheim.
OBJECT. 1936.
Fur covered cup, saucer, and spoon.
Cup, diameter 4⅜"; saucer,
diameter 9⅜"; spoon, length 8";
overall height 2⅞".
*Collection, The Museum of Modern Art,
New York. Purchase.*

115 Gustav Klimt.
THE KISS. 1908.
Oil on canvas. 71″ × 71″.
Osterreichische Galerie, Vienna.

116 Vincent van Gogh.
Detail of STARRY NIGHT. 1889. *(See page 367.)*

117 Jan van Eyck.
Detail of GIOVANNI ARNOLFINI AND HIS BRIDE.
1434. *(See page 320.)*

A painting may have a rich tactile surface as well as implied or simulated texture. Actual texture on a two-dimensional surface is seen in the detail of van Gogh's STARRY NIGHT (see the entire painting on page 367). With brush strokes of thick paint, called *impasto*, van Gogh invented textural rhythms which convey his emotional intensity. An earlier Dutch painter, Jan van Eyck, used tiny brush strokes to show, in minute detail, the incredible richness of ordinary materials. In GIOVANNI ARNOLFINI AND HIS BRIDE, van Eyck simulated a variety of textures. In this section of the painting we see the textures of the mirror and its carved wood frame, amber beads, and a whisk broom (see the entire painting on page 320).

Repetitive, ordered surface designs are called *patterns*. A pattern may or may not also have textural qualities, depending on its scale. When precisely structured textures are enlarged, they can appear as patterns, and some small patterns can be seen as textures. In Klimt's painting THE KISS (on page 95), the simulated textures of skin and hair are set off by the elegant invented texture of the gold background, by the decorative patterns of the garments, and by the floral area on which the figures kneel.

The preceding discussion of the elements of visual form has included the dominant aspects of what we see. The process of structuring these elements into works of art is called "design." When we know something about the expressive potential of the visual elements and how they can be effectively organized using the principles of design, we can better understand why we respond the way we do to a work of art.

5

Principles of Design

Organized perception is what art is all about.
Roy Lichtenstein[1]

In the context of art, *design* is both the process of organizing the elements of visual form and the product of that process. We perceive design as well as create design. In both cases, design grows from the basic human need to find and make meaningful order.

We are continually affecting and being affected by our own designs and the designs of others. Whenever we make plans, we are designing. We design when we do such things as select clothing or arrange furnishings in a room. The selection and ordering of elements in daily life is similar to the design process in art; in both, the design process is at its best when it is a lively, open dialogue between the intention and intuition of the designer and the characteristics of the materials used.

Artists make many design choices regarding size, materials, and ways in which visual elements may be used and organized. Such decisions are guided by the artist's expressive goal and sense of design. *Principles of design* are concepts that guide the process of developing significant form. They refer to the quality of relationships within a work of art and between a work and its surroundings. These principles are not rules, but important considerations during the selection process as one seeks to make form "work" visually. Each of us has some sense of what looks right or wrong, yet we may find it difficult to know why we feel the way we do, or what to do about problems in our own artwork. People who have worked with and studied design generally know why certain configurations work best or

feel right, and can explain their decisions when improvements are needed. They find that design principles become an intuitive part of their developed sensitivity.

The following discussion will introduce terms for some of the fundamental principles of design. The principles illustrated here can be applied to all works of art as well as to design problems of a simpler nature, such as laying out the title page of a term paper or arranging announcements on a bulletin board. The guiding principles discussed here are *scale and proportion*, *unity and variety*, *repetition and rhythm*, *balance*, *directional forces*, *emphasis and subordination*, and *contrast*. There are as many approaches to design terminology as there are to terms for visual elements. No matter what terms we use to describe these relationships, the inner dynamics of visual form remain one of the most central and intriguing issues in art.

The word *composition* is often used interchangeably with *design*—the broader term—when speaking of two-dimensional arts such as painting and photography. Although there have been many "rules for composition," none guarantee successful results. If excellence could be achieved by following rules, great artists would be commonplace. To become an effective artist, one needs to develop one's own sense of design through trained perception and visual experience. Good design is a matter of awakened intuition, feeling, and awareness, rather than formulas. For this reason, design cannot be taught

121 Michelangelo Buonarroti.
PIETA. St. Peter's Basilica, Rome. 1501.
Marble. Height 6'8½".

122 Master of the Beautiful Madonna.
PIETA. c. 1415.
Polychromed stone.
St. Mary's Church, Gdansk, Poland.

Changes in proportion can make major differences in how we experience a given subject. This is apparent in the following two *pietàs* (*pietà* is Italian for "pity," and refers to a depiction of Mary holding and mourning over the body of Jesus).

Creating a composition in which an infant appears on its mother's lap is much easier than showing a fully grown man in such a position. In his most famous PIETA, the young Michelangelo solved the problem by dramatically altering normal human proportions. Michelangelo greatly enlarged Mary's body in relation to that of Jesus and concealed her immensity beneath folds of drapery. Her seated figure spreads out to accommodate the almost horizontal curve of Christ's limp body. Imagine what the figure of Mary would look like if it were standing. Michelangelo made Mary's body into that of a giant. If she were a human being rather than a work of art, she would be about nine feet tall! Her hands are about twice normal size. Michelangelo used abundant naturalistic details of drapery and anatomy, which cause us to overlook the unique proportions of Mary's figure; yet the distortion is essential to the way we experience the content of the work.

Compare Michelangelo's work with an earlier PIETA done by an unknown sculptor. In the earlier work, the proportions are true to life, yet at first they seem unnatural. Christ's body appears to hang uncomfortably, unsupported in space. The sense of discomfort caused by the more normal proportions in this version emphasizes the suffering appropriate to the subject. Such emphasis on suffering is quite different from the emphasis on serenity in Michelangelo's design.

125   Pieter de Hooch.
INTERIOR OF A DUTCH HOUSE. 1658.
Oil on canvas. 29″ × 35″.
Reproduced by courtesy of the Trustees, The National Gallery, London.

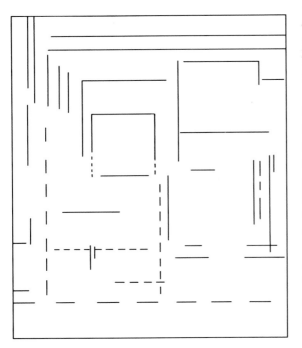

REPETITION AND RHYTHM

The recurrence of a design element provides continuity, flow, and dramatic emphasis. Repetition may be exact or varied, and it may establish a regular beat. Visual rhythm, like audible rhythm, operates when there is ordered repetition. Rhythm may simply be repetitive, providing variations on a basic theme, or indicating a progressive development.

In Pieter de Hooch's INTERIOR OF A DUTCH HOUSE, a definite rhythmic structure is established by the rectangular pattern of floor tiles and windows played off against the larger rectangles of the map, painting, fireplace, and table. The overall rectangular theme repeats the horizontal and vertical directions that begin with the edges of the picture plane.

In art, the word pattern generally refers to repeated forms or decorative designs such as those found in textiles, tiles, and wallpaper. De Hooch built his picture by organizing patterns within patterns—from the smaller patterns of floor tiles, window panes, and rafters, to the large pattern of the entire two-dimensional composition.

In Raphael's MADONNA OF THE CHAIR, the curved shapes echo the circular format of the painting. But the repetition of curving elements—convex and concave, large and small—does not establish a rhythmic pattern. Instead, the repeated curves provide flow and continuity. The vertical axis of the chair post stabilizes the entire composition.

A progressive visual rhythm is set up across the picture plane in José Clemente Orozco's ZAPATISTAS. The line of related figures is a sequence of alternating light and dark diagonal shapes grouped in a rhythmic pattern that expresses the aggressive force of oppressed humans in revolt. The marchers and the repeated, yet varied shapes of the sombreros establish a strong visual beat.

Duchamp's NUDE DESCENDING A STAIRCASE is an example of rhythmic progression. The design indicates movement and change in a dynamic sequence of interacting lines and shapes (see page 394).

126 Raphael Sanzio.
MADONNA OF THE CHAIR.
c. 1514.
Oil on wood. Diameter 2′4″.
Pitti Gallery, Florence.

127 José Clemente Orozco.
ZAPATISTAS. 1931.
Oil on canvas. 45″ × 55″.
Collection, The Museum of Modern Art, New York.
Anonymous gift.

128   Hans Holbein.
ANNE OF CLEVES. 1539.
Oil on wood panel.
Louvre Museum, Paris.

BALANCE

The attraction and tension between opposing forces is one of the basic conditions of life. Equally basic is the dynamic process of balancing these dualities—of seeking equilibrium. *Balance* is the achievement of equilibrium among the various parts of a composition. Lack of balance is contrary to our sense of order and need for stability. Our sense of visual balance stems from our feeling for physical balance. For sculptors and architects, balance is more than a visual problem; it is a structural necessity, because the weight of materials must be supported.

The two general types of balance are symmetrical and asymmetrical. *Symmetrical balance,* sometimes called *axial balance,* is the more obvious of the two. It is achieved by the equal distribution of identical or very similar parts on either side of a central axis. Symmetrical balance is easier to achieve than asymmetrical balance. It creates the feelings of stability, formality, and dignity found in Hans Holbein's ANNE OF CLEVES. Symmetrical compositions always run the risk of being static, obvious, and boring—though that is certainly not the case with Holbein's painting, in which slight variations in the basic symmetry add life and interest to the formal pose. When used appropriately, symmetrical balance can be powerful.

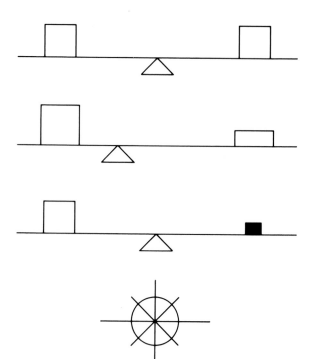

129   TYPES OF BALANCE.

A variation of symmetrical balance is *radial balance*, in which opposing forces rotate around, radiate from, or converge on an actual or implied central point. Vincent Topazio's award-winning illustration for a magazine article shows radial balance. Circular movement is suggested by the combined shapes of running children and shadows. The inclusion of more shadows than children gives the image a sense of mystery appropriate to the article for which the illustration was created.

In *asymmetrical balance*, sometimes called *informal balance*, a felt or implied center of gravity brings opposing or dissimilar elements into equilibrium. It is more difficult to achieve, but it is more flexible, subtle, and dynamic than radial or symmetrical balance. Dramatic asymmetry captures the viewer's attention in EXCALIBUR, Beverly Pepper's large outdoor sculpture. Actual physical balance of weight adds to the visual force of soaring diagonals.

131 Vincent Topazio.
ATLANTA–THE EVIDENCE OF THINGS NOT SEEN.
Reproduced by Special Permission of Playboy Magazine.
Copyright © 1981 by Playboy.

130 Beverly Pepper.
EXCALIBUR. San Diego Federal Building. 1976.
Painted steel. 35′ × 45′ × 45′.
Photograph: Philipp Scholz Ritterman.

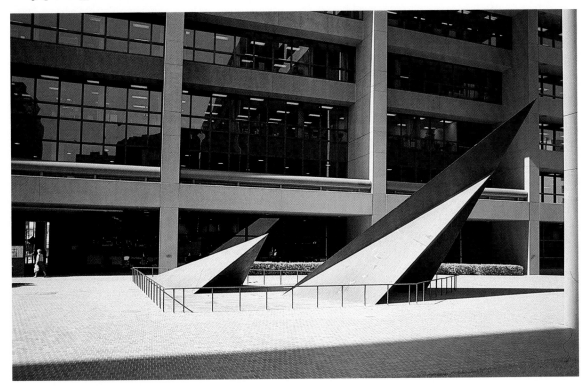

132 Francisco Goya.
BULLFIGHT. 1810–1815.
Etching. 12¼″ × 8⅛″.
Fine Arts Gallery of San Diego.

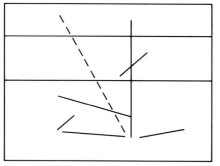

133 Henri Cartier-Bresson.
HYERES, FRANCE. 1930.
Photograph.

DIRECTIONAL FORCES

Implied or actual lines produce *directional lines* or *forces*, which determine the basic structure of a work. *Implied lines* are those we feel, rather than see. They may be suggested by the imagined connection between similar or related adjacent forms, or by the implied continuation from the ends of actual lines. An implied line may also be the unseen *axis* line that indicates the dominant direction of a single form. As we look at a work of art, our eyes tend to follow both implied and actual directional lines. Artists use such lines to help guide the viewer's eye movement and bind the art work into a single entity.

Vertical and horizontal lines repeat the human experience of standing and lying down. A horizontal line has a feeling of rest and inaction and provides a ground plane for a vertical. The mood of a vertical line is one of poise. This is true whether we are looking at an actual standing figure, a sculpture of a standing figure, or actual or implied vertical lines or forms, as in the facade of a building. Both horizontal and vertical lines are relatively motionless or static. Horizontal and vertical lines or directional forces, when placed together, can provide a sense of composure.

In contrast, diagonal lines are lines of action. They often seem to want to fall to horizontal or rise to vertical. Beverly Pepper's sculpture on page 107 creates tension because the diagonal edge lines and planes challenge our sense of balance.

Francisco Goya's etching BULLFIGHT is an example of dramatic asymmetrical balance. Most of the subject is concentrated in the left two-thirds of the rectangle. We are drawn to the *point of emphasis* by the intersecting horizontal lines behind the lower hand of the man on the pole. This linear movement holds the design together in spite of the tension and movement implied by the diagonal force lines of the bull and the man. Through design, Goya emphasized the feeling of suspense and potential danger.

In Henri Cartier-Bresson's photograph HYERES, FRANCE, the bicycle rider would lead our eyes out of the left side of the picture, if it were not for his relationship to the rest of the design. Cartier-Bresson skillfully balanced stationary and moving elements of his subject to create a dynamic tension that gives life and interest to the photograph. Selection is a major part of the creative process in all the arts, and it is crucial in photography. Cartier-Bresson spoke of the "decisive moment," when the photographer captures the significance of an event through the "precise organization of forms" (see page 156).

EMPHASIS AND SUBORDINATION

By emphasizing certain features in a work and subordinating others, an artist can establish a center of interest that focuses the viewer's attention. This strengthens the communication of the intended content. If the content is expressed by monotonous repetition, as in Andy Warhol's painting of soup cans (see page 434), emphasis will not be an active principle in the design because all elements will be given relatively equal weight. Goya's BULLFIGHT, however, emphasizes the large shapes of the bull, the bullfighter, and the line of the pole. The greatest emphasis is at the point of intersection of the pole with the bull's horns; the horizontal lines of the stadium are essential to the structure of the print, but are subordinate in terms of their attention gathering qualities. In Cartier-Bresson's photograph, the bicycle rider and the lines of the railing and curb are areas of emphasis, while the lines and shapes of stairs and cut stones are subordinate.

CONTRAST

Contrast can provide visual interest, emphasize a point, and express content. *Contrast* is the interaction of elements that express the dualities seen in opposites such as large and small, light and dark, simple and complex. In line, contrast may be between thick and thin areas of a single brush stroke. With shapes, contrast may be between regular geometric and irregular organic shapes, or between hard (sharp) and soft (blurred) edges.

Color contrasts are seen in a variety of ways, including contrast between hues, complements, values (light and dark), intensity (bright and dull), and temperature (warm and cool). All these types of color contrast are found in Ad Reinhardt's NUMBER 30. Reinhardt limited his design to geometric shapes as a way to focus attention on both shape and color interaction. The point of greatest emphasis is the red circle in the lower left; there are several points of secondary emphasis.

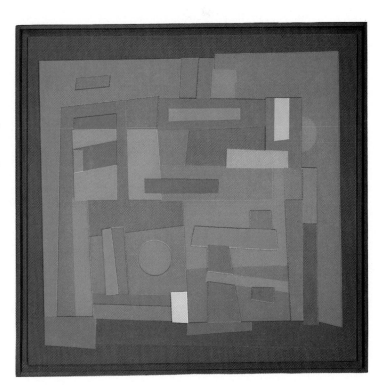

134 Ad Reinhardt.
NUMBER 30. 1938.
Oil on canvas. 40½″ × 42½″.
Whitney Museum of American Art.
Promised gift of Mrs. Ad Reinhardt (P.31.77).

DESIGN SUMMARY

As noted earlier, we perceive visual elements and principles of design all at once; yet, when we analyze design, we can speak or write about only one aspect at a time. In some works, only a few elements or principles are present or important.

Artists seek to achieve quality in their work by evaluating their own efforts. In his finished paintings, Matisse showed the results of a long search, not the search itself. Thus many of his paintings look easy—as if they were done with little effort.

The effort involved in his patient quest for the right design can be seen in the six working states of LARGE RECLINING NUDE shown here. Matisse attached pieces of colored paper to the surface of the painting to determine how the possible changes would look before he began repainting. In each state, he selected and strengthened those aspects of the image that contributed most to the overall composition. Finally, when he felt that everything worked together, he stopped.

In the earliest versions, Matisse had problems with awkward spacing and disjointed proportions. He gradually resolved these, and added the rhythmic background grid pattern, which contrasts with the sweeping, sensuous shapes of the figure. In the final painting, the bold distortions of the figure add up to an elegant abstraction of the subject.

135   Henri Matisse.
LARGE RECLINING NUDE (formerly called "The Pink Nude"). September 15, 1935. Oil on canvas. 26″ × 36½″. *The Baltimore Museum of Art: The Cone Collection, formed by Dr. Claribel and Miss Etta Cone of Baltimore, Maryland.*

136 Henri Matisse.
Photographs of six states of LARGE RECLINING NUDE
(formerly called "The Pink Nude").
The Baltimore Museum of Art. The Cone Collection.

a. State 1, May 3, 1935.

b. State 6, May 23, 1935.

c. State 9, May 29, 1935.

d. State 11, June 20, 1935.

e. State 13, September 4, 1935.

f. State 23, September 15, 1935.

137 Edvard Munch.
KISS BY THE WINDOW. 1892.
Oil on canvas. 72.3 cm. × 90.7 cm.
National Gallery, Oslo.

138 Edvard Munch.
THE KISS. 1895.
Drypoint and aquatint.
343 mm. × 278 mm.
Albertina Collection, Vienna.

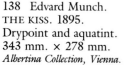

Artists can combine elements and principles of design in a number of ways. The following analysis of three works with the same subject done by one artist demonstrates how variations in media, format, balance, and the use of visual elements can effectively change the feeling and impact of a given subject.

In the 1890s, Edvard Munch, a young Norwegian painter, developed a new and intensely expressive way of depicting human passions and tragedies (see also page 371). These three works, all of which show a couple embracing, were completed over a period of six years.

In the painting KISS BY THE WINDOW, a couple stands to the side of the window, their figures joined. They appear to be hiding behind the curtain. Munch's way of showing a couple's feeling of oneness is already present in the greatly simplified composite shape of the embracing figures. The tree balances the couple, and creates an interesting asymmetrical tension. The nearly monochromatic blue-green tends to cool an otherwise passionate subject. Simple curves play off against straight edges, contrasting the figures and curtain with the lines of the window. Intersections of lines cause our eyes to move throughout the painting.

139   Edvard Munch.
THE KISS. 1897–1898.
Woodcut. 465 mm. × 467 mm.
Albertina Collection, Vienna.

The second work is a drypoint print in which the couple is nearly centered in front of the window. (Drypoint is discussed on page 142.) Munch boldly emphasized the outlines of the figures and again made them into one relatively simple shape. By removing the line that would normally indicate the division between the faces, he emphasized their unity. Drawn lines create a texture on the figures that adds to the rhythmic movement and energy of their outlines. The shapes of the dark curtains frame the embracing couple and add dramatic emphasis by providing strong value contrast with the light of the window. This contrast suggests the difference between public and private realms and contributes to a feeling of passion which is not present in the other two images. Subtle shifts between light and dark areas within the figures give a suggestion of solid mass to the bodies.

For the painting, Munch chose a dominantly horizontal format, which offsets the many vertical directional lines and active diagonal curves within the frame. The drypoint's format is vertical, which gives the image a more active quality in spite of its almost symmetrical composition. In the third work, a woodcut, the nearly square format produces a relatively quiet balance of directional forces. Here shapes have become flattened and even more simplified than the shapes in the painting. The entire image is very abstract. Wood texture, printed from an uncut second block, provides a vertical rhythmic sequence, which offers a counterpoint to the gently curving lines and single shape of the embracing couple. By removing the indications of light and shadow and eliminating suggestions of spatial depth, location, and all unnecessary details of anatomy, Munch created maximum dramatic effect with a minimum of means. He simplified his concept to its essence. He did not achieve this result all at once; it evolved from one work to the next in a series that included several versions not shown here. Of Munch's many versions of THE KISS, the woodcut is the best known, perhaps because it so effectively symbolizes an idea and a feeling.

It is not necessary to know anything about the artist to analyze a work of art in terms of visual elements and principles of design. Such knowledge, however, stirs interest and adds another dimension to our understanding and enjoyment. Munch employed subjects chosen for their emotional significance in order to depict internal rather than external life. Munch stated,

There should be no more paintings . . . of people reading and women knitting. In the future they should be of people who breathe, who feel emotions, who suffer and love. [3]

His best-known works relate to death, loneliness, sexuality, and love. Munch's view of love is often seen as a basic struggle between the sexes. The early loss of his mother and sister—the two women closest to him—undoubtedly contributed to his obsession with male-female love. His adult life included at least one long, unhappy love affair. One cannot help but wonder if the works reproduced here spring in part from Munch's need for love, and his unfulfilled desire for a lasting, loving relationship with a woman.

Munch often repeated a work two, three, or more times, usually starting with a painting and moving on to prints. In the process, he strengthened and clarified his composition, and added impact to the message of his imagery. In all three of the images on pages 112 and 113, Munch demonstrated his sensitivity to the format he chose and to the unique character of each medium. By following the evolution of an artist's idea, as we have done with Munch, we have examined the interdependence of meaning and design.

To be successful, the design process must involve making sensitive, effective decisions about all aspects of the form being created. The artist evaluates each decision as it is implemented, and makes changes as needed, as Matisse did in PINK NUDE. The goal is to remain true to what is best in terms of all the relationships within the evolving form—to make the most of a particular set of circumstances. What is right in one context may be totally wrong in another.

The elements and principles of visual design affect us continually—whether we are engaged in activities of daily living or looking at works of art, whether we understand design or even notice it. The design of the objects and spaces we live with makes a big difference in how we feel. Learning to read visual form leads to a conscious awareness of the visual qualities in our surroundings, and their effect on us. We respond to the visual character of people's homes, and of various indoor and outdoor environments. The effect of designed or undesigned spaces, light, colors, shapes, textures, and sizes can give us pleasure or cause discomfort. An awareness of visual form and its effect on us helps us discriminate between what contributes to our lives and what does not, and leads to self-renewing decisions related to all that we perceive.

PART THREE

The Visual Arts

Each art exists because the ideas special to it cannot be transmitted otherwise. . . .

Vernon Blake[1]

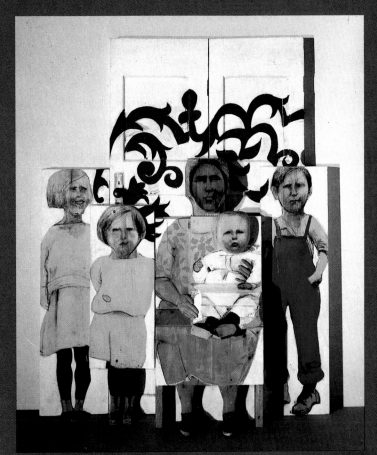

Marisol.
THE FAMILY. 1962.
(See page 187.)

The visual arts were invented and continue to evolve as ways to meet human needs. Throughout the history of art, the development of new materials and techniques have been stimulated by, and in turn have supported, the emergence of new ways of seeing and thinking. Subsequent stylistic changes often depend on the most recently developed media.

Whether the art form is graphic design or architecture, drawing or photography, basic visual elements and principles of design remain the same. The results, however, are often very different, because each material has its own form-making possibilities and limitations. As the artist shapes the material, the material, in turn, contributes its unique qualities to the work.

A particular material, along with its accompanying technique, is called a *medium*. (The plural of medium is *media*, or less frequently, *mediums*.) Artists select media that best suit the ideas and feelings they wish to present. In each case, the artist must have a developed sensitivity to the character of the material used. An artwork that combines different media is referred to as *mixed media*.

Certain media that have long been favorites include clay, fiber, stone, wood, and oil paint. More recently developed media such as photography, cinematography, and video, and materials such as polyester resin and electric light, enable us to communicate insights and concerns in ways not previously possible.

The Western tradition has divided the visual arts into two categories: fine art and applied art. *Fine arts*, such as painting and sculpture, are intended primarily for contemplation or visual enjoyment. *Applied arts*, such as furniture design and advertising art, are intended to serve utilitarian as well as visual functions.

The terms fine art and applied art were coined before the Industrial Revolution, when artists or artisans were the sole suppliers of utilitarian objects for everyday use. The arts of painting, sculpture, and architecture were considered to be of a "higher" order, since they were not functional in the practical sense, and were involved primarily with aesthetics and the intellect. The inclusion of architecture in the traditional list of fine arts is problematic. Buildings worthy of being called architecture are more than ordinary construction; yet most successful architecture is utilitarian as well as aesthetically and intellectually stimulating. Nor does a clear line separate the fine and applied arts in the craft area. Craftsmen, no longer charged with the responsibility of providing all of our household goods, are now free to use so-called craft media to create visual forms whose only purpose is to delight the eye or stimulate the mind. How do we classify Gerhardt Knodel's woven installation on page 204, or Toshiko Takaezu's ceramic forms on page 196? Are they fine or applied art? They are made from materials traditionally associated with applied art, but they are certainly fine art in intention and result.

The split between art and industrial production grew wider from the beginning of the Industrial Revolution in England in the mid-eighteenth century until the early twentieth century. Then, in the 1920s, the split began to heal. The Bauhaus, a German school of art and design, brought artists together with industrial technology and created fields such as industrial design. Since then, technological advances have led to an increase in the number of jobs for artists and designers in many areas of industry and communications. Artists can now use new imaging technology to enhance or diminish human awareness. As always, the ultimate criteria for success are the quality of the artist's creativity, imagination, and ability to follow through on the personal expressive idea or the design problem to be solved for others.

Part Three surveys the traditional visual arts, and also looks at newer media such as video and computer graphics. Chapter 6 looks at two-dimensional media; Chapter 7 at three-dimensional media; and Chapter 8 explores the design professions.

6

Two-dimensional Media

DRAWING

Drawing is the most immediate and accessible way to communicate through imagery. Children draw long before they learn to write, and some continue to draw into adulthood. Developing drawing skills may be easier than learning to write, because drawing is less abstract than writing. The most important factors are interest, and an understanding that seeing and drawing are learned processes.

Those who are intrigued by the rich complexity of the visual world can develop their awareness by drawing. Many artists keep a sketchbook handy to serve as a visual diary—a place to keep track of whatever catches their eye or imagination. From it, ideas may develop and reach maturity as complete works in drawing or other media.

In his book *The Zen of Seeing*, Frederick Franck describes drawing as an awareness tool:

I have learned that what I have not drawn, I have never really seen, and that when I start drawing an ordinary thing I realize how extraordinary it is, sheer miracle: the branching of a tree, the structure of a dandelion's seed puff.[1]

Betty Edwards and other effective drawing teachers help people learn how to draw by helping them learn new ways to see. Student drawings from her book *Drawing on the Right Side of The Brain*[2] show the typical change in seeing ability achieved in just a few weeks by using her approach.

140 Frederick Franck.
Pencil drawing from his book *The Zen of Seeing*.

141 a. Gerardo Campos, September 2, 1973.
b. Gerardo Campos, November 10, 1973.
From Betty Edwards, *Drawing on the Right Side of the Brain*.

142   Vincent van Gogh.
CARPENTER. c. 1880.
Black crayon.
22″ × 15⅕″.
Rijksmuseum Kroller-Muller,
Otterlo, Netherlands.

143   Alberto Giacometti.
SELF-PORTRAIT. 1959.
Ballpoint pen on paper napkin.
7¼ ″ × 5″.
Private collection.

Drawing from direct observation is neither more nor less important than drawing from imagination or memory. Great drawings—and, more important, great understandings—can come from any approach. However, the process of drawing from observation is a unique way to strengthen one's awareness of the visible world as well as one's ability to depict imagery from either memory or imagination.

Vincent van Gogh learned a great deal about seeing and image making by drawing. He was just beginning his short career as an artist when he made this drawing of a carpenter. Although clumsy in proportion, the drawing reveals Van Gogh's careful observation. The drawing on page 52, made nine years later, shows that Van Gogh had learned a great deal about seeing and drawing in the intervening years.

Drawing is a good way to note what you see. Alberto Giacometti drew his face as he saw it reflected in a mirror, using the materials at hand—a ball point pen and a napkin. The idea of exhibiting or selling this SELF-PORTRAIT was undoubtedly far from his mind. His primary impulse was to satisfy his compulsion to respond to what he saw.

Good drawing may appear deceptively simple. It can take years of patient work to be able to draw easily and effectively. According to one account, a person viewing a portrait drawn by Matisse with great economy of line asked the artist with some disgust, "How long did it take you to do this?" "Forty years," replied Matisse.

In the most fundamental sense, to draw means to pull, push, or drag a marking tool across a surface to leave a line or mark. Artists working in most of the visual arts practice drawing as a basic means of recording and develop-

144 Henri Matisse.
PORTRAIT. c. 1916.
Crayon.
Location unknown.

ing ideas. Drawing and painting are closely related, even overlapping, disciplines. One could say that some paintings are simply drawings made with paint. However, painting is rarely used as a preliminary step in the process of creating works in other disciplines. Objects as diverse as postage stamps, transportation systems, and paintings usually begin with drawings.

A drawing can function in one or all of the following ways:

☐ as a personal notation or record of something seen, remembered, or imagined

☐ as a study for something else, such as a sculpture, a film, or a painting

☐ as an end in itself—a finished work of art

145 Claes Oldenburg.
LATE SUBMISSION TO THE CHICAGO TRIBUNE ARCHITECTURAL
COMPETITION OF 1922: CLOTHESPIN (VERSION TWO). 1967.
Pencil, crayon, watercolor. 22″ × 23¼″.
*Des Moines Art Center. Gift of Gardner Cowles by exchange and
partial gift of Charles Cowles, New York (1972).*

The potential of drawing as a means for developing and presenting ideas originating in the imagination is apparent in Claes Oldenburg's drawing for a monumental building in the shape of a clothespin. All three of the common uses of drawing are demonstrated here. Oldenburg documented something imagined, did a study for a work in another medium, and created a self-sufficient work of art all at once. Oldenburg first visualized the clothespin's size, then defined it on paper. Tiny figures and casual use of linear perspective help to give awesome scale to the enormous, somewhat humanized clothespin. Although the proposed building will probably never be constructed, it could be. One result of Oldenburg's imaginative drawings of monuments found final form in the huge CLOTHESPIN sculpture in Philadelphia shown on page 98.

A simple drawing, called a *study*, can function as the embryo of a large or complex work. Picasso did many studies in preparation for the painting GUERNICA, a large work measuring more than 11 feet high by 25 feet long. Forty-five of the studies are preserved, nearly all dated.

The first drawing for GUERNICA shows what can be identified in later stages as a woman with a lamp, apparently an important symbol to Picasso. The woman leans out of a house in the upper right. On the left, a bull appears with a bird on its back. Both the bull and the woman with the lamp are major elements in the final painting. Although the first drawing was probably completed in a few seconds, its quick gestural lines contain the essence of the complex painting.

Picasso recognized the importance of documenting the creative process from initial idea to final painting:

It would be very interesting to preserve photographically, not the stages, but the metamorphoses of a picture. Possibly one might then discover the path followed by the brain in materializing a dream. But there is one very odd thing to notice, that basically a picture doesn't change, that the first "vision" remains almost intact, in spite of appearances.[3]

146   Pablo Picasso.
First composition study for GUERNICA. May 1, 1937.
Pencil on blue paper. 8¼″ × 10⅝″.
Prado Museum, Madrid.

147   Pablo Picasso.
Composition study for GUERNICA. May 9, 1937.
Pencil on white paper. 9½″ × 17⅞″.
Prado Museum, Madrid.

148   Pablo Picasso.
GUERNICA. 1937.
Oil on canvas. 11′5½″ × 25′ 5¼″.
Prado Museum, Madrid.

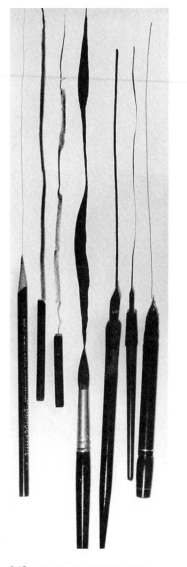

149 DRAWING TOOLS AND
THEIR CHARACTERISTIC LINES.

150 Alphonse Legros.
HEAD OF A MAN. 1892.
Silverpoint. 8¾″ × 7″.
*The Metropolitan Museum of Art,
New York. Gift of the artist, 1892
(92.13.18).*

Another type of preparatory drawing is the cartoon. The original meaning of *cartoon*, still used by art professionals, is a full-sized drawing made as a guide for a large work in another medium, particularly a fresco painting, mosaic, or tapestry. In common usage, the word cartoon refers to a narrative drawing that emphasizes humorous or satirical content. Cartoons and comics are among the most widely enjoyed drawings. Many young people find drawing cartoons so rewarding that it leads them to develop their drawing skills in other ways.

We tend to think of drawing as a medium without color because, historically, most drawings were done in black or brown on white paper. Today, rich, even vibrant color is possible with colored pencils, felt-tipped pens, and various types of chalks and oil pastels.

Each drawing tool and each type of paper has its own characteristics. The interaction between these materials and the will of the artist determines the nature of the drawing that results. Notice the different qualities of marks made by various common drawing tools.

Dry Media

151 TYPES OF HATCHING.

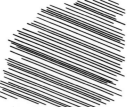

a. Hatching.

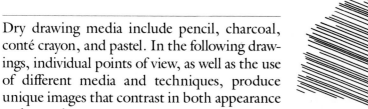

b. Cross-hatching.

c. Contour hatching.

Dry drawing media include pencil, charcoal, conté crayon, and pastel. In the following drawings, individual points of view, as well as the use of different media and techniques, produce unique images that contrast in both appearance and mood.

Prior to the invention of graphite pencils in the seventeenth century, most drawings were done with charcoal, brush and ink, or *silverpoint*. A stylus of silver or other similar metal used on a specially prepared ground produces a delicate silver-gray line that soon darkens with oxidation. No variation in width of line, or value gradation of individual lines is possible with this medium. Tones, or values, are built up with parallel lines called *hatching*, or with *cross-hatching* of various types. In his portrait study, HEAD OF A MAN, Alphonse Legros used hatching to create a sculptural, three-dimensional appearance. Legros chose to use silverpoint, even though he lived at a time when many other drawing materials were available.

A variety of pencils can be used for drawing. In addition to a wide range of soft to hard graphite pencils, high-quality colored pencils are available in a great many colors. Line quality is determined by the degree of hardness of the pencil, and the texture of the surface to which it is applied. Paper with some *tooth* or surface grain will receive pencil marks more readily than paper that is smooth. Pencil lines may vary in width or length, may be made by using the side of the pencil point in broad strokes, and can be repeated as hatching. A considerable range of values can be produced by varying the pressure on a medium-soft drawing pencil.

An amazing variety of marks made with drawing pencils fills Jennifer Bartlett's drawing IN THE GARDEN #119. Richly developed light and dark shapes, patterns, and textures play off against each other in lively improvisation. The drawing contains highly abstract references to the garden and pool that are the subject of a series of Bartlett's drawings and paintings.

152 Jennifer Bartlett.
IN THE GARDEN #119. 1980.
Pencil on paper. 26″ × 19¾″.
Private collection. Photograph courtesy of Paula Cooper Gallery, New York.

153 William Abbott
Cheever.
RAM'S HEAD.
Charcoal on paper.
19¹³⁄₁₆″ × 23¹³⁄₁₆″.
*Addison Gallery of American
Art, Phillips Academy,
Andover, Massachusetts.*

Charcoal is probably the oldest drawing medium. The drawing charcoal used today is little different from the charcoal used by prehistoric people to draw on cave walls. The various hard and soft grades of charcoal used for drawing provide a flexible medium for both beginning and advanced draftsmen. Because the charcoal particles do not bind to the surface of the paper, charcoal is easy to smudge, blur, or erase. This quality is both an advantage and a drawback. It enables one to make changes readily, but also causes finished works to smear and be easily damaged. A completed charcoal drawing may be "fixed" with a thin varnish called *fixative*, which is sprayed over it to help bind the charcoal to the paper.

William Cheever's RAM'S HEAD shows the rich value range and varied strokes possible with charcoal. Sharp outlines give definition to the horns, making them look hard; soft, feathery strokes create the illusion of fur. Charcoal is an ideal medium for creating velvety blacks such as those in the nose and shadow areas. There is vitality throughout as the illusion of a ram's head is played off against the reality of charcoal on paper.

Natural chalks of red, white, and black have been used for drawing since ancient times. Fabricated chalks and pastels, produced since the nineteenth century, have characteristics similar to natural chalk. They have a freshness and purity of color because they are comprised mostly of pigment, with very little binding material. They give the artist the ability to work without the changes of color that occur in some paints as they dry. Artists often begin pastel drawings with an outline drawing in charcoal that serves as a guide. Soft pastels do not allow for fussy details, so they force the user to work in other ways. Blending with fingers or a paper stump made for the purpose produces a soft blur, and can be used to slightly mix colors. Pastels yield the most exciting results when not overworked.

French artist Edgar Degas shifted from oil painting to pastels in his later years, and occasionally combined the two. He enjoyed the vibrant strokes of color and subtle blends possible with pastel. His carefully constructed compositions look like fleeting glimpses of everyday life. In BREAKFAST AFTER THE BATH, bold contours give a sense of movement to the whole design.

Conté crayon is a semi-hard chalk with enough oil in the binder to cause it to adhere to smooth paper. It can produce varied lines or broad strokes that are relatively resistant to smudging. Wax-based crayons such as those used by children are seldom used by serious artists—they lack flexibility, and many are not fade resistant. It is difficult to obtain bright color mixtures with wax crayons, because the strokes do not blend or fuse easily.

Georges Seurat used conté crayon to build up the illusion of three-dimensional form through value gradations (chiaroscuro) in the drawing of his mother sewing. Seurat actually drew a multitude of lines, yet in the final drawing the lines are obscured by the total effect of light and dark finely textured areas. He selected conté crayon on rough paper as a means to concentrate on the interplay of light and shadow.

154 Georges Seurat.
THE ARTIST'S MOTHER (WOMAN SEWING). c. 1883.
Conté crayon on paper. 12¼″ × 9½″.
The Metropolitan Museum of Art, New York. Purchase.
Joseph Pulitzer Bequest, 1955 (55.21.1).

155 Edgar Degas.
BREAKFAST AFTER THE BATH
(YOUNG WOMAN DRYING HERSELF). c. 1894.
Pastel on paper. 98.7 cm × 58.7 cm.
Presented by the Gilman Foundation, New York to the
Tel Aviv Museum and the Tel Aviv University.

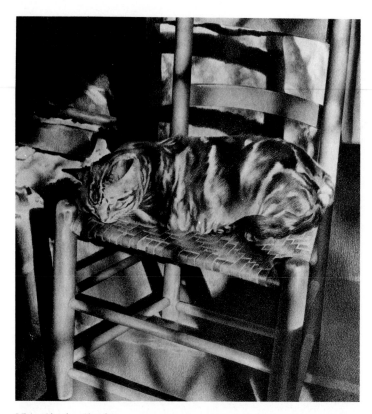

156   Charles Sheeler.
FELINE FELICITY. 1934.
Crayon. 14⅛″ × 13¼″.
Fogg Art Museum, Harvard University. Louise E. Bettens Fund.

157   Charles White.
PREACHER. 1952.
Ink on cardboard. 21⅜″ × 29⅜″.
*Collection of Whitney Museum of American Art, New York.
Purchase.*

Charles Sheeler also used conté crayon, but differently from Seurat. FELINE FELICITY is a detailed image in which crisp edges and light and shade work together in an intricate pattern. Sheeler was a leading photographer as well as a painter and draftsman. In all media, his work has a strong sense of structured order.

Liquid Media

Pen and ink and brush and ink are liquid or wet drawing media. Some brush drawings are made with *washes* of ink thinned with water. Such ink drawings are similar to watercolor paintings. Felt- and fiber-tipped pens are widely used recent additions to traditional pen and ink media.

Charles White used cross-hatched ink lines in PREACHER to build up the figure's mass and gesture in a forceful manner. Through the use of contour hatching, White gave the figure sculptural solidity. The strongly foreshortened right hand and forearm add to the drawing's dramatic impact.

Nineteenth-century Japanese artist Hokusai was a skilled and prolific draftsman—he is said to have created about thirteen thousand prints and drawings during his lifetime. He experienced the feelings of self-doubt known to many, yet prevailed against them with courage and humor. His statement about the development of his artistic ability should encourage any young person to persevere:

I have been in love with painting ever since I became conscious of it at the age of six. I drew some pictures which I thought fairly good when I was fifty, but really nothing I did before the age of seventy was of any value at all. At seventy-three I have at last caught every aspect of nature—birds, fish, animals, insects, trees, grasses, all. When I am eighty I shall have developed still further and will really master the secrets of art at ninety. When I reach one hundred my art will be truly sublime, and my final goal will be attained around the age of one hundred and ten, when every line and dot I draw will be imbued with life.

*(signed) Hokusai
The art-crazy old man*[4]

158 Hokusai.
TUNING THE SAMISEN. c. 1820–1825.
Brush drawing. 9¾″ × 8¼″.
Courtesy of Freer Gallery of Art, Smithsonian Institution,
Washington, D.C. (04.241).

In TUNING THE SAMISEN, the expressive elegance of Hokusai's lines was made possible by the responsiveness of his brush. In the Orient, writing and drawing are done with the same or similar brushes, often using the same strokes. Oriental brushes are ideal for making calligraphic lines because they hold a substantial amount of ink and can produce both thick and thin lines. Hokusai played the uniformly thin lines detailing head, hands, and instrument against the bold, spontaneous rhythms indicating the folds of the kimono. He captured a moment of concentration with humor and insight.

Rembrandt van Rijn also used brush, ink, and ink wash to create a wash drawing of his wife, Saskia. The result, SASKIA ASLEEP, is at once bold and subtle, representational and abstract, finished and unfinished. As a total image, it is complete. Rembrandt's spontaneous line technique bears comparison to the Oriental brush painting tradition seen in the works of Hokusai.

159 Rembrandt van Rijn.
SASKIA ASLEEP. c. 1642.
Brush and wash. 9½″ × 8″.
British Museum, London.

PAINTING

To many people, the word art means painting. The long history of painting, the strong appeal of color, and paint media's great image-making possibilities probably account for its prominence.

At least seventeen thousand years ago, early humans painted on cave walls with colors found in nature: black from charred wood and bones, red and yellow from clays, and white from chalk deposits. Today, many types of ready-made paints are available, each with its own distinctive properties.

Paints consist of three components: pigment, binder (or medium), and vehicle. The *pigment* provides color; the *binder* is the substance that holds the pigment particles together without dissolving them, and attaches the pigment to the ground; and the *vehicle* is the dispersing agent for spreading the pigment. With oil paints, turpentine is the vehicle and linseed oil is the binder. With traditional tempera, water is the vehicle and egg yolk is the binder.

Pigments are powdered coloring agents which have long been derived from plant, animal, or mineral sources. In the nineteenth and twentieth centuries, major advances in the chemical industry have made it possible to extend the range of colors and improve the durability of both natural and synthetic pigments. Most of the same pigments are used in the various paint media as well as in dry drawing media such as colored pencils and pastels. The character and slight color of each binder affects the hue, value, and intensity of common pigments in different ways. Thus the same pigments look slightly different in each of the various paint types.

Because art terminology is notoriously ambiguous, it is helpful to note the overlapping meanings of the term medium. As mentioned earlier, the word medium, in the broad context of the whole field of visual arts, means a material and its accompanying technique. In the context of painting, medium can also refer to the binder, or mixture of binder and vehicle, added to paint to facilitate its application without diluting color intensity.

Paints are usually applied to a flat *support*, such as stretched canvas for oils, or paper for watercolors. The surface of the support is generally prepared by sizing or priming, or both, to achieve a *ground*—the prepared surface to which paint is applied. Because supports are often too absorbent to permit controlled application of paint, a *size* or penetrating sealer is often applied to lessen absorbency and fill in the pores of the material. Size is particularly needed on paper and canvas to protect them from disintegration caused by the drying action of linseed oil in oil paint. To complete the preparation of a surface for painting, an opaque *prime* coat or *ground*, usually white, is often applied after or instead of sizing. For watercolors, sizing and priming are unnecessary; a paper surface provides both the support and the ground.

Watercolor

Watercolor paintings are made by applying pigments suspended in a solution of water and gum arabic to white paper. Rag papers are the preferred support because of their superior absorbency and unchanging whiteness. Blocks of paint available in metal or plastic boxes are modern versions of the dried blocks of watercolor that have been in use for thousands of years. Both blocks and watercolor packaged in tubes use gum arabic as the binder and water as the vehicle.

Paint is laid on in thin transparent washes. The transparency of watercolor paint allows light to pass through the layers of color and be reflected back up from the white paper. Highlights are obtained by leaving white areas unpainted. Opaque (nontransparent) watercolor—

160 Joseph Mallor William Turner.
THE BURNING OF THE HOUSES OF PARLIAMENT.
1843.
Watercolor from a sketchbook. 9¼″ × 12¾″.
British Museum, London.

called *gouache*—is sometimes added for detail. In the hands of a skilled painter, watercolors are well suited to spontaneous application. In spite of the simple materials involved, however, it is a difficult medium to handle and does not allow for easy changes or corrections. Overworking a watercolor painting results in the loss of the medium's characteristic freshness.

The fluid spontaneity possible with watercolor makes it a favorite medium for landscape painters, who use it to catch quick impressions out of doors, rather than in the studio. Transparent washes of color are masterfully combined in William Turner's watercolor sketches, as in THE BURNING OF THE HOUSES OF PARLIAMENT. This immensely prolific English painter was fascinated by the moods created by atmospheric qualities of light and color.

161 John Marin.
MAINE ISLANDS. 1922.
Watercolor. 16¾″ × 20″.
The Phillips Collection, Washington, D.C.

John Marin used both transparent and opaque areas in his watercolor paintings. Marin developed his own fusion of representational and abstract elements. In MAINE ISLANDS, he combined suggestions of a panoramic view with diagonal lines that fragment the picture plane, giving viewers the feeling of seeing through transparent planes into deep space. The look of transparency is consistent with the major characteristic of the watercolor medium.

Carolyn Brady's elaborately developed photorealist watercolors stress the interplay of patterns found in familiar surroundings. WHITE TULIP is so filled with visual information that our eyes do not remain long on any one part of the composition. Exuberant color and decorative surface reflections are held together in an

unusual, carefully composed design. Brady must have worked on the painting for many hours, yet her mastery of the medium enabled her to retain a fresh, spontaneous quality.

Traditional Chinese watercolor technique employs ink as well as color. The artist and the viewer are expected to know the basic precepts of Chinese painting and the attitudes that animate them (see pages 272–276). Paintings may be developed with opaque, individually significant brush strokes, as well as with washes of ink or color. Ink diluted with water can be applied in thin washes to achieve a wide range of values. Dao Ji probably painted A MAN IN A HOUSE BENEATH A CLIFF with a single brush. The vigorous strokes indicate a mountain cliff filled with the *qi* (*ch'i*) or energy force, that Dao Ji must have felt, both within himself and in nature. Areas of light color provide a balance to the dynamic power of the brush-drawn lines.

Gouache is opaque watercolor—that is, watercolor to which opaque (nontransparent) white pigment in the form of precipitated chalk has been added. With gouache, a painter can create effects similar to those obtainable with oil paint, and with less trouble and expense. However, gouache is not as permanent or as flexible as oil, and colors dry much lighter in value than they appear when wet. Because gouache dries quickly, brush strokes cannot be blended as easily as with oil. The thickness of the gouache and the artist's individual brush strokes are evident in Paul Wonner's painterly landscape titled L.A. Many leading artists have enjoyed the simplicity and versatility of gouache, often using it to make quick studies for paintings done in other media. Its ease of correction makes gouache a good medium for children and other beginners.

163 Dao Ji (Tao Chi or Shih T'ao).
A MAN IN A HOUSE BENEATH A CLIFF. c. 1800.
Ink and light color on paper. 9½″ × 11″.
C. C. Wang Family Collection, New York.

164 Paul Wonner.
L. A. 1965.
Gouache on paper. 11¼″ × 17½″.
Collection of Karl Ichida, Honolulu.
Photograph: Tibor Franyo, Honolulu.

162 Carolyn Brady.
WHITE TULIP. 1980.
Watercolor on paper. 31½″ × 44″.
Private collection. Photograph courtesy of
Nancy Hoffman Gallery, New York.

165   Andrew Wyeth.
THAT GENTLEMAN. 1960.
Egg tempera on board. 23¼″ × 47¾″.
Dallas Museum of Art. Dallas Art Association Purchase.

Tempera

Tempera was used by the ancient Egyptians, Greeks, and Romans; it was highly developed during the Middle Ages, when it was the primary medium for small paintings made on wood panels (see the Byzantine Madonna on page 311). Since ancient times, the principal tempera medium has been egg tempera, in which egg yolk, or occasionally egg white, is the binder. (The binding qualities of egg yolk are well known to anyone who has washed breakfast dishes.) Today the word *tempera* is sometimes used to include water soluble paints with binders of glue, casein, egg, or egg and oil emulsion.

All tempera paints are water-thinned. Egg tempera has a luminous, slightly *matte* (nonshiny) surface when dry. The luminous quality is the result of painting on a ground of very white gesso. *Gesso* is a preparation of chalk or plaster of Paris and glue which is applied to a support as a ground for tempera, oil, and metalpoint drawings.

Egg tempera is good for working in precise detail and will not darken with age. Its main disadvantages are color changes during drying and the difficulty in blending and reworking due to rapid drying. Traditional tempera painting requires complete preliminary drawing and pale underpainting due to its translucency and the difficulty in making changes. Overpainting is made by applying layers of translucent paint in small, careful strokes. Because tempera does not have much flexibility, movement of the support may cause the gesso and pigment to crack. A rigid support such as a wood panel is preferred.

American artist Andrew Wyeth is one of the few contemporary painters to work in egg tempera. In THAT GENTLEMAN, Wyeth interwove rich detail and subtle color to evoke a quiet mood of inner reflection. The many fine brushstrokes used in egg tempera technique capture the variety of carefully observed textures. Many of Wyeth's paintings, including this one, have a disquieting, isolated feeling. His realism often suggests nostalgia for a simpler life.

Oil

Oil paint has been a favorite painting medium for five hundred years. Pigments mixed with various vegetable oils, such as linseed, walnut, and poppyseed, were used in the Middle Ages for decorative purposes; but it was not until the fifteenth century that Flemish painters fully developed the use of paint made with linseed oil for representational paintings. In this early period, artists applied oils to wood panels covered with smooth layers of gesso, as in the older tradition of tempera painting.

Oil has many advantages not found in other traditional media. Because of the flexibility of dried oil film, it was possible to replace wood panels with canvas, which could be unstretched and rolled for transporting. In comparison to tempera, oil paint can provide both increased opacity, which gives it better covering power, and greater transparency. The slow drying time of oil, first considered a major drawback, soon proved to be a crucial advantage because it allowed strokes of color to be blended and repeated changes to be made during the painting process. In contrast to tempera, gouache, and acrylics, oil colors change very little when drying; oil medium, however, darkens and yellows with age.

Jan and Hubert van Eyck did not invent oil painting, but they were the first great masters of the medium. The brothers often worked together. According to the inscription, the Ghent Altarpiece was begun by Hubert and completed by Jan. It is not known which of the brothers painted THE KNIGHTS OF CHRIST, one of sixteen panels of the huge altarpiece. Within the context of their religious subject, the Van Eyck brothers demonstrated their enthusiasm for the delights of the visible world. Atmospheric perspective contributes to the feeling of infinite

166 Hubert and Jan van Eyck.
THE KNIGHTS OF CHRIST. From the Ghent Altarpiece.
Cathedral of St. Bavo, Ghent, Belgium.
Completed in 1432.
Oil on panel. Panel 54″ × 18¾″.

167   Attributed to a follower of Rembrandt van Rijn.
HEAD OF SAINT MATTHEW. c. 1661.
Oil on wood. 9⅞" × 7¾".
National Gallery of Art, Washington, D.C. Widener Collection (1942).

space. The development of oil painting went hand in hand with the Renaissance concern for naturalism.

The painter began THE KNIGHTS OF CHRIST panel with a brush drawing in tempera. He then proceeded with thin layers of oil paint, moving from light to dark and from opaque to transparent. The luminous quality of the surface is the result of successive oil glazes.

A *glaze* is a very thin, transparent film of color applied over a previously painted surface. To produce glazes, oil colors selected for their transparency are diluted with glazing medium—usually a mixture of oil, thinner, and varnish. Glazes give glowing depth to painted surfaces because they allow light to pass through and to be reflected from lower paint layers.

Artists generally begin traditional representational paintings with monochromatic underpaintings called *grisaille*, to establish the design and the modeling of light and dark areas. The image is then painted in full color, and glazes may or may not be applied as a finish.

Oil can be applied thickly or thinly, wet into wet or wet onto dry. When applied thickly, it is called *impasto*. In HEAD OF SAINT MATTHEW, attributed to a follower of Rembrandt, the impasto of light and dark paint defines both a solid-looking head and an exciting display of painterly brushwork.

The wide range of approaches possible with oil paint is apparent when we compare the Van Eycks' rich detail and subtly glazed colors with the impasto used in HEAD OF SAINT MATTHEW and Hans Hoffmann's THE GOLDEN WALL.

In both his art and his teaching, Hofmann emphasized the translation of personal states of being into nonrepresentational form. In THE GOLDEN WALL, he worked with the dynamics of advancing and receding color, movement and countermovement. Static, hard-edge rectangles assert their presence in a field of vigorous, irregular shapes. The painting creates its own self-contained environment.

168 Hans Hofmann.
THE GOLDEN WALL. 1961.
Oil on canvas. 60″ × 72¼″.
Mr. and Mrs. G. Logan Prize Fund
(1962.775). © 1988, The Art Institute
of Chicago. All rights reserved.

169   Frank Stella.
HIRAQLA 1. 1968.
Polymer and fluorescent polymer paint on canvas.
10' × 20'.
Private collection.

170   Audrey Flack.
WHEEL OF FORTUNE. 1977–1978.
Oil over acrylic on canvas. 8' × 8'.
Collection of Louis, Susan, and Ari Meisel.
Photograph courtesy of Louis K. Meisel Gallery, New York.

Acrylic

Synthetic painting media are now in wide use. The most popular are loosely called *acrylics*. Pigments are suspended in acrylic polymer medium, which provides a fast-drying, flexible film. Acrylics are relatively permanent and may be applied to a wider variety of surfaces than can older painting media. Most acrylics are water-thinned and water-resistant when dry. Because acrylic resin medium is highly transparent and nonyellowing, colors can maintain a high degree of intensity. Unlike oil paint, acrylics are not likely to darken or yellow with age. Their rapid drying time, however, restricts blending and reworking possibilities.

When dry, acrylic paint is inert and will not damage cloth fibers over a long period of time the way oil paint does. Thus acrylics can be applied directly to unprimed canvas. This quality has resulted in a variety of staining techniques in which the paint, thinned with water, acts more as a dye than as a coating on top of the canvas. Helen Frankenthaler used this technique in INTERIOR LANDSCAPE (see page 428).

Interwoven bands of both muted and intense day-glo acrylic polymer colors pull together in a tight spatial sandwich in HIRAQLA 1 by Frank Stella. Acrylic paints lend themselves to uniform application and to the use of tape to obtain shapes with precise edges—a style called *hard edge*.

In recent years, many painters have used airbrushes to apply their paint. An *airbrush* is a refined, small-scale paint sprayer, capable of projecting a fine, controlled mist of paint. It creates a smooth, even surface, well suited to the impersonal imagery found in many paintings of the 1960s and 1970s (see Don Eddy's painting PRIVATE PARKING X on page 450).

Audrey Flack used both oil and acrylic in her huge airbrush painting WHEEL OF FORTUNE. Working from a dressing-table still life, Flack achieved a photographic sense of realism. She paints from a combination of photographs, and adds to the photographic imagery as she works. Objects seen from different angles, combined in illogical ways, give her finished paintings surprising twists and turns. Her surfaces are jammed with material opulence, of both personal and universal significance. WHEEL OF FORTUNE even includes an early photograph of the artist. The physical delights, pictured with such fresh enthusiasm by the early Flemish painters, have here turned to provoke and overwhelm the viewer. Old, modern, and personal symbols of time, chance, vanity, and death remind us of the search for meaning in life.

Encaustic

In the ancient medium of *encaustic*, pigments are suspended in hot beeswax. Encaustic paintings have lustrous surfaces that bring out the full richness of colors. It is difficult to keep the wax binder at the right temperature for proper handling, however, and encaustic is not a popular medium with today's painters. One of the few contemporary artists who works in encaustic is Jasper Johns (see his TARGET WITH FOUR FACES on page 431).

Early Christian Egyptians known as Copts developed encaustic painting to a high art in the second century Coptic sarcophagus portraits such as MUMMY PORTRAIT OF A MAN were painted on wood, and retain their brilliant color after almost two thousand years. In these portraits, lifelike vigor and individuality remain strong.

171 MUMMY PORTRAIT OF A MAN. 160–170 A.D.
From Fayum, Egypt.
Encaustic on wood. 14″ × 18″.
Albright-Knox Art Gallery, Buffalo, New York.
Charles Clifton Fund (1938).

Intaglio

Intaglio printing is the reverse of relief, because the areas below the surface hold the ink. *Intaglio* comes from the Italian *itagliare*, meaning "to cut into." The image to be printed is either cut into a metal surface by engraving or drypoint tools, or is etched by acid. To make a print, the printmaker first coats the plate with viscous printer's ink, then wipes it clean, leaving ink only in the cuts. The pressure of a printing press transfers the ink to slightly damp paper. Intaglio printing was traditionally done from polished copper plates, but now zinc, steel, or aluminum is often used for economic reasons.

In *engravings*, lines are cut into the polished surface of the plate with a *burin* or engraving tool. This process takes strength and control. Lines are made by pushing the burin through the metal to carve a small groove, removing a narrow strip of metal in the process. A clean line is desired, so any rough edges of the groove must be smoothed down with a scraper. Engraved lines cannot appear as freely drawn as etched lines due to the differences in the two processes. The precise, smooth curves and parallel lines that are typical of engravings can be seen in the engraved portraits that appear on the paper currency we carry with us every day.

The complex richness of engraved lines may also be seen in Albrecht Dürer's magnificent engraving THE KNIGHT, DEATH AND THE DEVIL, which is reproduced here close to its actual size. Thousands of fine lines define in detail the shape, mass, space, value, and texture of the objects depicted. The precision of Dürer's lines seems appropriate to the subject—an image of the noble Christian knight moving with resolute commitment, unswayed by the forces of chaos, evil, and death which surround him (see discussion of the print's iconography on page 46).

Drypoint is similar to line engraving. Using a pencil-like thin, pointed tool that has a steel or diamond tip, the artist digs lines into the relatively soft copper or zinc in a way that leaves a burr, or rough edge, similar to the row of earth left by a plow. The burr catches the ink and leaves a slightly blurred line characteristic of drypoint prints. Because the burr is fragile, and deteriorates rapidly as prints are pulled, drypoint editions are by necessity small. Skillful draftsmanship is required, because drypoint lines are difficult to execute and almost impossible to correct. The soft, somewhat sketchy line quality in Berthe Morisot's gentle depiction of LITTLE GIRL WITH CAT is typical of drypoint prints.

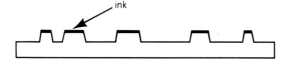

175 RELIEF BLOCK.

176 ENGRAVED PLATE.

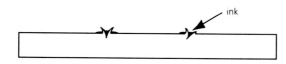

177 DRYPOINT PLATE.

178 Berthe Morisot.
LITTLE GIRL WITH CAT. 1889.
Drypoint. 6″ × 5″.
National Gallery of Art, Washington, D.C. Rosewald Collection.

179 a. Albrecht Dürer.
THE KNIGHT, DEATH AND THE DEVIL. 1513.
Engraving. 9¾″ × 7⅜″.
The Brooklyn Museum. Gift of Mrs. Horace O. Havemeyer.

179 b. Albrecht Dürer.
Detail of THE KNIGHT, DEATH AND THE DEVIL.
See page 143.

180 Rembrandt van Rijn.
a. Detail of CHRIST PREACHING.

b. CHRIST PREACHING. c. 1652. Etching. 6¹/₁₆″ × 8⅛″.
*The Metropolitan Museum of Art, New York. Bequest of Mrs. H. O. Havemeyer,
1929. The H. O. Havermeyer Collection (29.107.18).*

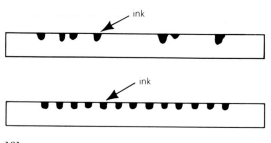

181 ETCHED PLATE AND AQUATINT PLATE.

182 Mary Cassatt.
WOMAN BATHING. 1891.
Drypoint and aquatint. 14⅛″ × 10⅛″.
Museum of Fine Arts, Boston. Hayden Fund.

An *etching* is made by drawing lines through
a protective coating made of a mixture of beeswax, asphalt, and resin, which covers a copper
or zinc plate. The plate, with its back and sides
protected with varnish, is then placed in acid.
Where the drawing has exposed the metal, acid
"bites" into the plate, making a groove that varies in depth according to the strength of the acid
and the length of time the plate is in the acid
bath.

To see the difference in line quality between
an etching and an engraving, compare the detail of Rembrandt's etching CHRIST PREACH-
ING with the detail of Dürer's engraving
KNIGHT, DEATH AND DEVIL. Etched lines are
generally more relaxed or irregular than engraved
lines. In his depiction of Christ preaching, Rembrandt worked in a wide range of values, using
drypoint as well as etched lines. Skillful use of
light and shadow draws attention to the figure
of Christ, and gives clarity and interest to the
whole image.

Aquatint is an etching process used to obtain various uniform values in black-and-white or color prints. The artist first sifts a protective layer of powdered resin onto the plate, then heats the plate to melt the particles so that they will attach to the surface. Areas to remain either white, or a value different from the aquatint area being worked on, are *stopped out*—that is, protected from the acid with varnish. When the plate is placed in acid, the exposed areas between the resin particles are eaten away to produce a rough surface capable of holding ink. Values thus produced can vary from light to dark, depending on how long the plate is in the acid. As with etched line, the longer the plate is in the acid, the deeper the bite; and the deeper the bite, the more ink will be held on the surface. Because aquatint is not suited to making thin lines, it is usually combined with a linear print process such as engraving, drypoint, or line etching.

American artist Mary Cassatt's prints and paintings were influenced by the strong flat shapes and elegant lines of the Japanese prints she saw in an exhibition in Paris in 1890. WOMAN BATHING is one of a series of highly original color prints she produced the following year. Aquatint provides flat light and dark areas of subtle color, and drypoint lines give definition and linear movement to the composition.

Lithography

Lithography is planographic (surface) printing based on the mutual antipathy of oil and water. The process lends itself well to a direct manner of working, because the artist draws an image on the surface of the stone or plate without any biting or cutting of lines. Its directness makes lithography faster and more flexible than other methods, and difficult to distinguish from drawing.

The artist draws the image on smooth, fine-grained Bavarian limestone (or on a metal surface developed to duplicate the character of such stone) using special litho-crayons, pencils, or a greasy ink called *tusche*. After the image is complete, it is chemically treated to "fix" it on the

183 Honoré Daumier.
RUE TRANSNONAIN. 1834.
Lithograph. 11¼″ × 17⅜″.
The Cleveland Museum of Art. Gift of Ralph King.
(CMA 24.809).

184 LITHO STONE OR PLATE.

upper layer of the stone. Then the surface is dampened with water and inked. The ink is repelled by the moisture in the blank areas, but adheres to the greasy area of the image. As in other print processes, when the surface is covered with paper and run through a press, the image is transferred to the paper.

Although lithography was a relatively new medium in the early 1800s, it had a major impact on society because of its comparative ease and speed of execution. It provided the illustrations for newspapers, posters, and handbills. Honoré Daumier, one of the first great lithographers, made his living drawing satirical and documentary lithographs for French newspapers. His personal style was well suited to the direct quality of the lithographic process.

In RUE TRANSNONAIN, Daumier carefully reconstructed an event that occurred during a period of civil unrest in Paris in 1834. The militia claimed that a shot was fired from a building on Transnonain Street. Soldiers responded by entering the apartment and killing all the oc-

185 Henri de Toulouse-Lautrec.
JANE AVRIL. c. 1893.
Photograph.

186 Henri de Toulouse-Lautrec.
JANE AVRIL. c. 1893.
Oil study on cardboard.
38″ × 27″.
Private collection.

cupants. Daumier's lithograph of the event was published the following day. The lithograph clearly reflects the artist's feelings, but it also conveys information in the way photographs and television do today. Rembrandt's influence is evident in the composition of strong light and dark areas that increase the dramatic impact of Daumier's image.

The freedom and directness possible in the drawing phase of lithography made the technique well suited to the spontaneous, witty approach of Henri de Toulouse-Lautrec. In the space of about ten years, this prolific artist created over three hundred lithographs. Many of them were brush-drawn posters advertising people and products ranging from nightclub entertainers to bicycles. His posters of cabaret singer and dancer Jane Avril made her a star, and simultaneously gave Parisians of the 1890s a firsthand look at "modern art" by a leading artist. Toulouse-Lautrec's innovations in color lithography created a widely copied style in poster design which has had a major influence on graphic design in the twentieth century. His images set a new standard for instant appeal, quick comprehension, and memorable impact, each of which is an important function of posters.

The popular lithographic poster shown here appears to have begun with an awkward photograph and come to life in a dynamic and colorful oil sketch. The sketch was then incorporated as the key element in a strong lithograph drawn with brush and liquid tusche on the litho stone. Compare the angles of feet and legs in the photograph with the sketch and print. Toulouse-Lautrec used diagonal lines and curves to give a sense of motion missing in the photograph. In the print, he placed the figure in a nightclub setting, offset by the silhouetted shape of a bass player. Strong black shapes and fluid brush lines retain much of the lively vigor and dramatic pattern of the sketch, and also reflect Toulouse-Lautrec's admiration for Japanese prints. He used descriptive line to enclose flat shapes of color, which become dominant elements in the design.

187 Henri de Toulouse-Lautrec.
JANE AVRIL. JARDIN DE PARIS. c. 1893.
Lithograph printed in color. 48⅝″ × 35⅛″.
Collection, The Museum of Modern Art, New York.
Gift of A. Conger Goodyear.

188   Mayumi Oda.
GODDESS COMING TO YOU;
CAN YOU COME TO HER? 1976.
Screenprint. 33″ × 24″.
Collection of the artist.

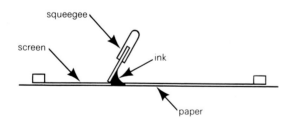

189   SCREEN PRINTING.

Screenprinting (Serigraphy)

Screenprinting, the most recently perfected print-making process, is a refinement of the ancient technique of stencil printing. Early in this century, stencil technique was improved by adhering the stencil to a silk fabric screen stretched across a frame (synthetic fabric is used today). The screen is placed on paper or any other flat surface and a rubber-edged tool called a squeegee pushes the paint or ink through the open pores of the fabric to print the design. Because silk was the traditional material used for the screen, the process has also been known as *silkscreen* or *serigraphy*.

Screenprinting is well suited to the production of images with numerous flat color areas. Each separate color change requires a different screen, but registering and printing are relatively simple. Pure colors, fluid lines, and ample curving shapes fill Mayumi Oda's colorful multilayered screenprints. GODDESS COMING TO YOU; CAN YOU COME TO HER? is representative of the lyrical exuberance of her work. Her dual Japanese and American cultural background is evident in her integration of Japanese traditional art, mythology, and Zen Buddhism with modern concepts of form.

The latest development in screenprinting is the photographic stencil or *photo screen*, achieved by attaching light-sensitive gelatin to the screen fabric. A developing solution and exposure to light make the gelatin insoluble in water. The gelatin is first exposed to light through a positive image on film. Soluble, unexposed areas are then washed away, leaving open areas in the fabric that allow ink to pass through to the print surface. Photo screens are often used for printing items such as posters and T-shirts. Photographic elements in Robert Rauschenberg's mixed-media painting TRACER are screen printed on the large canvas (see page 186).

Combined Print Techniques

190 Duck Jun Kwak.
REAGAN AND KWAK. 1981.
Photo screenprint. 53.5 cm × 36.8 cm.
Collection of the artist, Kyoto, Japan.

Korean artist Duck Jun Kwak employed photo screenprinting to provide mass media impact and political content in his print REAGAN AND KWAK. The technique relates the image to the form and content of news reporting. Kwak combined a photograph of himself with one of the newly elected President Reagan on the cover of *Time* magazine.

The 1960s ushered in a virtual explosion of innovations in printmaking. Many artists have been pushing the limits of traditional printmaking in a variety of ways, including developing equipment and techniques for making very large prints, and combining several different print techniques in a single work. Because artistic motivation is more important than technique, many artists combine different media or techniques to achieve the results they desire. Misch Kohn's LABYRINTH is an example of such combined print techniques. In it, Kohn employed engraving, aquatint, woodcut, and embossment. *Embossed* areas are created by pressing a raised, uninked design into the paper with a printing press, which leaves a low-relief impression on the paper.

191 Misch Kohn.
LABYRINTH. 1978.
Engraving/aquatint/color woodcut/embossment.
17½″ × 21¾″.
Honolulu Academy of Arts. Gift of Mr. Kei-Pak Lo.

PHOTOGRAPHIC AND ELECTRONIC ARTS

Photography

Much of our present understanding of the world, the universe, and people beyond our family and friends comes from images made with still, motion picture, and television cameras. The camera arts have made a great wealth of information and poetic vision available to us. As we get caught up in the compelling realism of photography, film, and television, we tend to overlook the fact that these media are relatively recent extensions of a long pictorial tradition which grew out of the desire to create a lifelike illusion of reality. Each new technique in the history of art relies heavily on its predecessors. Photography has been influenced by painting (and in turn has influenced painting); cinematography relies on still photography; and television has been influenced by painting, photography, and cinematography.

With the mass-media circulation of photographic images, we lost our innocence and simultaneously increased our concern for others and for the future of our planet. Poverty, famine, nuclear weapons, the human rights movement, environmental protection, the beauty and unity of Earth all have entered our consciousness through the medium of photography and its children, film and television.

Photography has been slow to gain full acceptance as an art, perhaps because the same term is used to refer to everything from a purely mechanical reproductive process to fine art.

Photography can be considered a form of printmaking. As a technique, it involves the science of capturing optical images on light-sensitive or photosensitive surfaces. As an art, the process reveals the quality of seeing of the individual who makes the photograph. Making a significant photograph involves far more than merely "taking" what is in front of the camera. Before releasing the shutter, a serious photographer makes many choices: subject, light, angle, focus, distance, and composition, as well as type of camera, lens, and film. The best photographers have learned to visualize their photographs before releasing the shutter.

Ten different photographers working with the same subject will make ten different photographs, with each photographer conveying those aspects of the subject he or she feels is significant. Individual styles would not be evident in photographs if photography were not a means of personal expression and communication. Although ads for some cameras would have us

192 R. P. Athanase Kircher.
CAMERA OBSCURA. 1646.
*International Museum of Photography
at George Eastman House, Rochester, New York.*

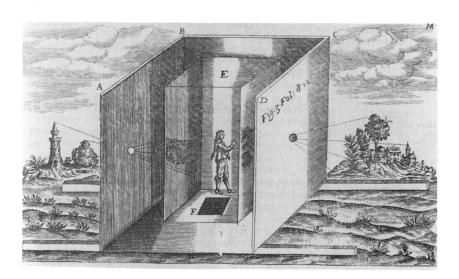

believe a particular brand will almost automatically produce "great pictures," it is the photographer, not the equipment, that makes the difference between an ordinary snapshot and a work of art. In the following statement, photographer Ansel Adams speaks of the need to give considerable time and effort to the making of a photograph if the result is to be worthwhile:

I have often thought that if photography were difficult in the true sense of the term—meaning that the creation of a simple photograph would entail as much time and effort as the production of a good watercolor or etching—there would be a vast improvement in total output. The sheer ease with which we can produce a superficial image often leads to creative disaster. We must remember that a photograph can hold just as much as we put into it, and no one has ever approached the full possibilities of the medium.[6]

Edwin Land, who developed the Polaroid camera, also puts emphasis on the process when he describes the way even automatic, "instant" cameras can help us learn to see:

At its best, photography can be an extra sense, or a reservoir for the senses. Even when you don't press the trigger, the exercise of focusing through a camera can make you better remember thereafter a person or a moment. When we had flowers in this office recently to use as test objects, it was a great experience to take pictures of them. I learned to know each rose. I now know more about roses and leaves, and that enriched my life. Photography can teach people to look, to feel, to remember in a way that they didn't know they could.[7]

Photograph literally means "light-writing," but a more accurate description would be "light-drawing." The basic concept of the camera preceded actual photography by more than three hundred years. A *camera obscura*, or darkened room, was one of several optical sighting devices developed in the sixteenth century as aids for drawing and painting. It was too large and cumbersome to be useful until it evolved into a portable dark box, with a lens and an angled mirror which righted the inverted image so that it could be traced with a pen or pencil.

193   TABLE MODEL CAMERA OBSCURA.
International Museum of Photography at George Eastman House, Rochester, New York.

The development of the camera was motivated by the desire of Renaissance artists to make accurate depictions of nature. Because visual perception results from a combination of optical and mental phenomena, this idea can never be fully realized with a mechanical device; yet the desire for "accurate" pictures was the impetus behind the eventual invention of photography as we know it.

The first vague photographic image was made around 1826 by Joseph Nicephore Niepce. He recorded and fixed on a sheet of pewter an image made by exposing the sensitized metal to light for eight hours! During the next decade, the painter Louis Jacques Mandé Daguerre further perfected Niepce's process, and produced the first satisfactory photographs. Images produced by Daguerre's process became known as *daguerreotypes.*

194   Louis Jacques Mandé Daguerre.
LE BOULEVARD DU TEMPLE. 1839.
Daguerreotype.
Bayerisches National Museum, Munich.

At first, because the necessary exposure times were too long, photography could only be used to catch images of stationary objects. In Daguerre's photograph of Paris in 1839 (the year his process was made public), the streets appear deserted because moving figures made no lasting light impressions on the plate. However, one man, having his shoes shined, stayed still long enough to become part of the image. He is visible in the lower left, the first person to appear in a photograph. It was a significant moment in history. Now images of actual things, including people, could be made without the skillful hand of a traditional artist. Although some painters at the time felt the new medium constituted unfair competition and spelled the end of art, the invention of photography actually marked the beginning of a period when art would be more accessible to all.

Before the development of the camera, it was usually only royalty, aristocrats, and wealthy merchants who could afford to have their portraits made by artists. By the mid-nineteenth century, people were coming in great numbers to portrait studios to sit unblinking for several minutes in bright sunlight to have their likenesses made. It even became popular to have one's portrait printed on visiting cards to give to friends. From the beginning, portrait photography was heavily influenced by the traditions of portrait painting. In turn, the increasing availability of photographs and cameras in the late nineteenth century contributed to the decline of representational, particularly naturalistic, painting.

It wasn't long before the art of portrait photography was raised to a very high level by English artist Julia Margaret Cameron. In 1864, she became an ardent amateur photographer and began to create some of the most moving portraits ever made with a camera. Cameron pioneered the uses of the close-up and carefully controlled lighting to enhance views of her subjects, who were often her family and famous friends. In the portrait of British actress ELLEN TERRY AT THE AGE OF SIXTEEN, the dominant light comes from behind the subject, leaving the face in shadow and giving the portrait an introspective mood. The design of shapes within the circular format gives memorable structure to the image.

Many nineteenth-century photographers looked for ways to duplicate what painters had already done, and therefore failed to find their medium's unique identity. Painters, meanwhile, partially freed by photography from their ancient role as recorders and narrators of people, places, and events, looked for other avenues of discovery.

One of photography's special strengths is its ability to serve the human desire to halt time. Since prehistoric times, artists have tried to capture the appearance of people and animals in motion. It took about forty years after Daguerre made the first photograph of a human being for photographic technology to be able to stop figures in motion. Eadweard Muybridge pioneered stop-action photography. He accomplished the world's first serious studies of people and animals in motion, and provided the groundwork for the development of motion pictures.

195 Julia Margaret Cameron.
ELLEN TERRY AT THE AGE OF
SIXTEEN. 1863.
Carbon print. Diameter 240 mm.
The Metropolitan Museum of Art,
The Alfred Stieglitz Collection, 1949 (49.55.323).

196 Eadweard Muybridge.
GALLOPING HORSE. 1879.
Photograph.
International Museum of Photography
at George Eastman House, Rochester, New York.

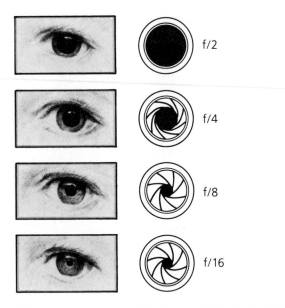

197   PUPIL OF HUMAN EYE AND APERTURE OF CAMERA.

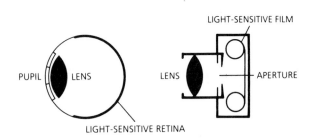

198   HUMAN EYE AND CAMERA.

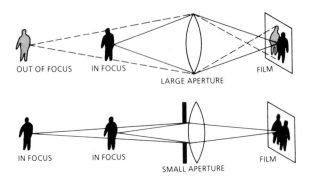

199   CHANGES IN DEPTH OF FIELD WITH
APERTURE ADJUSTMENTS.

The basic camera can be compared to a simplified mechanical replica of the human eye. The major differences are that the eye brings a continual flow of changing images that are interpreted by the brain, whereas the still camera depends on light-sensitive film to record an image, and can only pick up a single image at a time. Pairs of eyes see in stereoscopic vision, in contrast to the monoscopic vision of the camera. Motion picture and television cameras come closer to the human visual experience because they usually record sequences that involve motion, rather than fixed images.

The adjustable aperture in the lens of a sophisticated camera is similar to the changing pupil of the human eye. By changing the aperture, a photographer adjusts the amount of light entering the camera and simultaneously determines the depth of the area in sharp focus—called the *depth of field*—in the photograph. A large aperture gives a relatively shallow depth of field. By closing down the size of the opening, the photographer increases the area in focus, as shown in the diagram. The smaller the aperture, the greater the depth of field. To understand how this works, hold up your thumb about a foot in front of your eyes and focus your eyes on it. Notice how objects behind it are out of focus. Now curl the fingers of your other hand to make a very small tunnel and hold it up to your eye. The light reflected off your thumb will pass through the tunnel to your eye. As you look at your thumb through the small opening or aperture, you will notice that both your thumb and what is just behind it come into sharper focus.

Although the technology of modern cameras is highly sophisticated and complex, the basic unit is still simply a lightproof box with an opening or *aperture* set behind a *lens* designed to focus or order the light rays passing through it. It also has a *shutter* to control the length of time the light is allowed to strike the light-sensitive film or plate held within the body of the camera.

The various types of amateur and professional *film* are essentially transparent plastic strips or single sheets, coated with a layer of light-sensitive emulsion. Exposed and developed print film is called a *negative*, because the light and dark areas of the original subjects are reversed. Color positive film, such as slide film, produces a positive image capable of being projected or printed.

In a darkroom, the photographer or technician prints a negative by placing it in an *enlarger*, which projects and enlarges the negative image onto light-sensitive paper. The paper, when developed through chemical action, darkens in those areas where it has been exposed to light. After being chemically *fixed* to prevent further change, a positive image is produced.

In manufactured cameras of all types, the quality of the lens is most important. Lenses are designed to gather and concentrate a maximum amount of available light in order to transmit a sharply focused image quickly. The most versatile cameras allow for interchangeable lenses capable of various angles of view. Diagram 200 shows the approximate angles of view in *normal, telephoto,* and *wide-angle lenses.* A *zoom lens* permits the focal length of the lens to be adjusted to various distances from close to far.

Photography is not always as objective as many would believe. It can stretch the truth, and even mislead. In this capacity, it is sometimes used to editorialize for one point of view or another. The accompanying photographs were taken on the same street, from the same position, using different lenses. A telephoto lens compresses distance, thereby making the street look crowded with bumper-to-bumper traffic, while a wide-angle lens makes the street look spacious and relatively uncrowded.

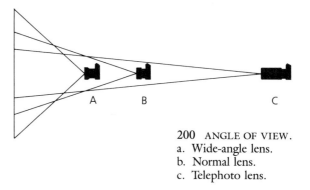

200 ANGLE OF VIEW.
a. Wide-angle lens.
b. Normal lens.
c. Telephoto lens.

201 PHOTOGRAPHS OF A STREET
a. With a 200 mm. telephoto lens.
b. With a 24 mm. wide-angle lens.

202 Dennis Oda.
REBOUND. 1987.
Photograph.
Courtesy of the artist, Honolulu.

Today it is common for cameras to have shutter speeds up to 1/1000 of a second. High shutter speeds and corrresponding film and film processing are crucial for sports photographers and others who seek to stop action in their photographs. Dennis Oda's REBOUND arrests the ball in mid air, and, with the help of a telephoto lens, brings the viewer into the action at a moment of great intensity. The unusual overhead vantage point gives a unique view of the action.

Henri Cartier-Bresson created another type of stop-action photograph in BEHIND THE GARE ST. LAZARE, PARIS. Although the actual image was caught in an instant, Cartier-Bresson made many important choices that led him to the point when he could quickly release the shutter at just the right time. He chose the moment when all significant forms within the selected area went together to make a memorable photograph. A fraction of a second later the man's foot would have hit the pavement, and the picture would have been nothing special. Many of the silhouetted shapes are balanced by their reflections. Most amazing of all is the way the shape of the running man is echoed by the dancer on the poster in the background as well as by his own reflection. Cartier-Bresson called such split-second designing the "decisive moment."[8]

To me, photography is the simultaneous recognition, in a fraction of a second, of the significance of an event as well as of a precise organization of forms which give that event its proper expression.[9]

203 Henri Cartier-Bresson.
BEHIND THE GARE ST. LAZARE,
PARIS. 1932.
Photograph.

204 Margaret Bourke-White.
AT THE TIME OF THE LOUISVILLE FLOOD. 1937.
Photograph.
LIFE Magazine © *1954, Time, Inc.*

In the 1930s, the concept of the photographic essay was introduced by Margaret Bourke-White, whose approach was soon adopted by other photographers. A *photo essay* is a collection of photographs on a single subject, arranged to tell a story or convey a mood in a way not possible with a single photograph. Photo essays, now an important part of journalism, have become major sources of information.

A number of photographers led the way toward a renewed concern with social reform. Margaret Bourke-White's photograph AT THE TIME OF THE LOUISVILLE FLOOD confronts us with the brutal difference between the glamorous life of advertising promises and the actual reality that many face every day.

The wide range of Bourke-White's creativity is demonstrated by the diversity of her imagery—from the social commentary of her photo journalism to emphasis on the monumental effects of human enterprise. Bourke-White was an early master of aerial photography. In her photograph CONTOUR PLOWING (see next page), the large curving shape that dominates the design is made up of rhythmically vibrating furrow lines. The plow provides a sense of scale.

205 Margaret Bourke-White.
CONTOUR PLOWING. 1954.
Photograph.
LIFE Magazine, © 1954, Time, Inc.

206 Ernst Haas.
CORNER OF 38TH STREET. 1952.
Dye transfer print (photograph).
© *Ernst Haas.*

By necessity, photography began as a black-and-white (and sometimes brown-and-white) process. For the first hundred and fifty years, black and white was preferred by most serious photographers. Even when fairly accurate color became available, many photographers felt that color tended to dilute the abstract, one-step-removed-from-nature power of the black-and-white image. Color was considered a layer of unnecessary information.

The development of color photography took a step forward in 1907 with the invention of "autochrome" positive color transparencies. In 1932, Eastman Kodak Company began making color film based on the divisionist color theories of Seurat (see page 362). Major developments in the versatility and accuracy of color film, in the relative permanence of original color prints, and in the processing of color reproductions have led to a recent burst of creative activity in color photography. The best color photographers work with color as an integral and very important aspect of total form.

For those who accept its potential and its limitations, color expands expressive possibilities by employing the most emotionally evocative element of visual form. In CORNER OF 38TH STREET, Ernst Haas celebrates the color and mystery of a reflected city scene caught in dramatic light.

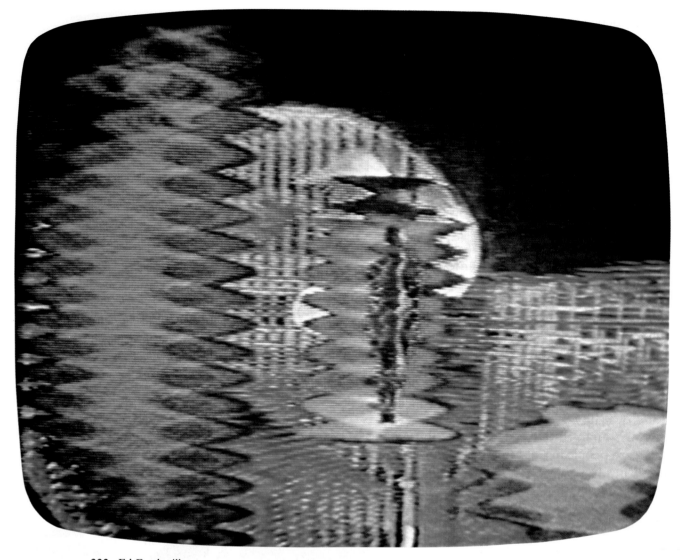

222 Ed Emshwiller.
SCAPE-MATES. 1973.
Computer-generated video. 30 minutes.
The Television Laboratory, WNET, New York.

Ed Emshwiller began as a painter, switched to filmmaking in the 1960s, and then to video in 1972. Although he had achieved national recognition as an avant-garde filmmaker, he saw more possibilities and freedom in video. Emshwiller feels video has some of the immediacy of painting, and greater image-making flexibility than film. Video's flexibility is demonstrated in SCAPE-MATES, a thirty-minute kaleidoscopic fantasy that blends two dancers with an ever-changing computer-generated environment. Emshwiller orchestrated his visions with the help of skilled video engineers. His choreography began with black-and-white artwork, from which he designed basic shapes and movements electronically with a computer. The dancers were then color-keyed into the environment. He added final background and color with a synthesizer.

The development of video art in the mid-1960s coincided with the growing desire of many leading artists to move away from the emphasis on art as precious finished objects, to art as creative processes.

As we have seen, people working in each new medium usually begin by copying the style and content of the medium's closest predecessor. The phenomenon is exaggerated by the practical and profit-making applications of new media. Television, like printmaking, has gone from serving a recording or transmission function for other art forms, to becoming a medium of conscious creativity. Video art can produce a broad spectrum of images–from free forms related to non-representational painting, to the photographic realism of cinematography and the rhythm and movement of the performing arts. Video brings liveness, immediacy, flexibility, and extraordinary manipulations of form and color to the vocabulary of the visual arts.

Computer-generated Imagery

The spatial gymnastics of rotating letters or logos often seen in television program openers and commercials are not produced by film or television techniques, but by computers (see page 214). Like TV screens, computer screens are cathode ray tubes (CRTs). Computer graphic capabilities range from producing finished artworks to helping to solve problems and generate ideas for works that are ultimately made in another medium.

Within art specializations, filmmakers, videographers, photographers, painters, sculptors, designers, and architects are among those who have enjoyed the computer's graphic capabilities.

The computer's capacity to store images-in-progress enables the user to save an unfinished image in order to follow other avenues of exploration that might contribute to solving a problem in the original image. Computer marking tools include a wide variety of electronic "drawing" and "painting" instruments. The effect is similar to having a collection of pens and brushes of different widths capable of producing various line qualities. Some computers and programs even allow the user to smear or blend one color into another.

Lillian Schwartz has been a pioneer in the establishment of the computer as an artistic tool. After studying drawing, painting, printmaking, and sculpture, she became increasingly interested in merging art and technology. She began draw-

223 Lillian Schwartz.
From the TELEVISION ANNOUNCEMENT FOR THE REOPENING OF THE MUSEUM OF MODERN ART. 1984.
Computer-generated video.
© *Courtesy of The Museum of Modern Art, New York.*

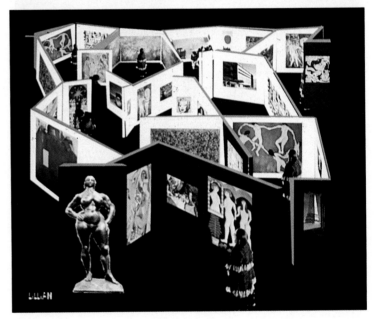

224 Lillian Schwartz.
TWO PROFILES = ONE A1–22. 1987.
Computer generated. 32″ × 48″.
© *1987 Lilyan Productions, Inc.*

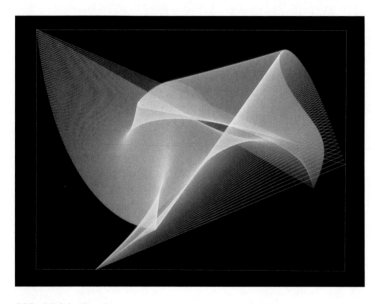

225 Melvin Prueitt.
GOLD WING. 1981.
Computer.
Courtesy of the artist.

ing with a light pen in 1968, and has since used computers to make graphics, film, and video, as well as images that resemble watercolors and oil paintings. As a consultant for AT&T Bell Laboratories, Schwartz collaborated with engineers and physicists in the development of computer-generated color images and effective techniques for the use of computers in film and animation. In 1984, she created the first computer-generated graphics commissioned by the Museum of Modern Art, to announce the reopening of the expanded museum. We show two frames of her award-winning thirty-second television spot on page 175.

In her more recent work, Schwartz has combined her research in visual perception and creativity with her use of computers. She has analyzed the color and structure of works by Picasso and others as part of her ongoing investigations of the creative process. Throughout history, artists have produced works "after" other artists, but Schwartz is going about it in a whole new way.

Nuclear physicist Melvin L. Prueitt has been building intricate free-form images from his numerical programs for more than two decades. In GOLD WING, Prueitt took advantage of the computer's ability to draw three-dimensional illusions in full color using the mathematics of linear perspective. Prueitt was not trained as an artist; his work suggests the opportunities for aesthetically sensitive people who are skilled computer programmers.

The invention of the computer and its application as a tool for image making will have an influence on other art forms similar in impact to the changes in the nature of painting brought about by the invention of photography. Modern tools, however, are simply facilitators. No matter how complex and sophisticated they are, tools, by themselves, do not necessarily make art or turn their users into artists.

7

Three-dimensional Media

The arts introduced in this chapter involve both three-dimensional objects and performances. In most cases, movement is necessary to complete the piece—movement of the viewer around a sculpture, of the work in space, or of the performer. Clearly, the difference between viewing an original work of three-dimensional art and its photographic reproduction is even greater than with paintings, prints, and drawings.

SCULPTURE

Sculpture is both a visual and a tactile art form. The earliest art objects known are hand-size prehistoric sculptural pieces that were apparently intended to be held (see the PALEOLITHIC FIGURE on page 258). Although the touch of many hands can eventually wear away a work of sculpture, the tactile dimension is an important consideration for the sculptor.

A sculpture that projects from a background surface is in *relief*. In *low-relief* (or *bas-relief*) sculpture, the projection from the surrounding surface is slight and no part of the modeled form is undercut. As a result, shadows are minimal. In *high-relief* sculpture, more than half of the natural circumference of the modeled form projects from the surrounding surface, and figures are often substantially undercut. Sculpture meant to be seen from all sides is called *in-the-round* or *freestanding*. Because forms in high relief may be almost detached from the background, they

226
APOLLO. c. 415 B.C.
Greek silver coin. Diameter 1⅛″.

begin to look freestanding. When we view freestanding sculpture, we receive impressions from each side as we move around the piece. The total experience of the work is the sum of its surfaces and profiles.

A piece of sculpture may be small enough to hold in the hand and admire at close range. Most coins, for example, are works of low-relief sculpture. A high point in the art of coin design was reached on the island of Sicily during the classical period of ancient Greece. The APOLLO coin, shown here more than twice its actual size, has a strong presence in spite of being in low relief and very small.

236   Fausta Squatriti.
SILENCE IS GOLDEN. 1986.
Iron and brass. 100 cm. × 80 cm. × 220 cm.
Collection of the artist.

By the late 1920s, cutting and welding metals had developed into an important sculptural technique, which has since become widely used. The invention of oxyacetylene welding in 1895 provided the necessary tool, but it took three decades for sculptors to realize its potential. David Smith (see page 427), an early practitioner of metal construction, used such industrial materials as I-beams, pipes, and rolled metal plates for raw materials, and adopted industrial methods of fabrication.

Metal fabrication provides Italian sculptor and designer Fausta Squatriti with the precision she is looking for in her work. Her sculpture is the outgrowth of a carefully defined and controlled aesthetic theory based on the transformation of simple geometric forms. Squatriti structures mass and space so that emptiness and fullness play off against each other. In many of her works, a given mass is cut into equal parts and rearranged so that an equal amount of void counterbalances the solid. Nothing is removed, only displaced. She says, "The empty is attractive. . . . I conceive infinity as a void. . . . I try to outflank space, to suggest it by subtraction."[2] "I demonstrate that the empty is worth as much as the full, or three times as much."[3]

Since the 1970s, Deborah Butterfield has been making horses from found materials such as sticks and mud, and scrap metal. She spends much of her time on a ranch in Montana, where she trains and rides horses and makes sculpture. Painted, crumpled, rusted metal certainly seems an unlikely choice of media for making sculpture of an animal, yet Butterfield's ADAN and other abstract horses have a surprising naturalness and presence. The artist intends her sculpture to *feel* like horses rather than look like them. The old car bodies which make up the substance of her welded and wired metal horses add a note of irony; the horseless carriage becomes a horse.

Alexander Calder, along with David Smith, was among those who gave renewed life to the blacksmith's ancient craft. The traditional emphasis on mass is replaced in Calder's work by an emphasis on shape, space, and movement. Calder was also among the first to explore the possibilities of *kinetic sculpture*—sculpture that moves. By 1932, he was designing wire and sheet-metal constructions, such as BIG RED, which are moved by natural air currents. Marcel Duchamp christened them *mobiles*, a word he had coined for his own work in 1914 (see page 402).

The finished surface of a piece of sculpture is an important element in its design. Sculptors may choose between highly refined finishes that obscure their tool marks and finishes that reveal some of the process. Elizabeth Catlett gave her wood MOTHER AND CHILD on page 45 a smooth, polished finish, which brought out the grain of the wood. Michelangelo's unfinished AWAKENING SLAVE (page 182) and Barlach's MAN DRAWING HIS SWORD (page 183) reveal tool marks, which add textural energy to the works and invite vicarious participation in the carving process. Louise Nevelson finished each of her wood and metal constructions with a unifying coat of paint (pages 32–33). Some artists design their sculptures to be weathered or oxidized over time, thus allowing for natural change; others cover their pieces with colorful paint. Alexander Calder used bright red to add to the playfulness of BIG RED. To protect and maintain surface qualities created by the artist, it is necessary to care for sculpture, particularly outdoor pieces, as one would care for the surface of a fine piece of furniture, an expensive automobile, or a house.

237 Deborah Butterfield.
UNTITLED (ADAN). 1986.
Steel. 77″ × 104″ × 25″.
Photograph: Yura Adams.
Courtesy Edward Thorp Gallery, New York.

238 Alexander Calder.
BIG RED. 1959.
Painted sheet metal and steel wire. Height 74″.
Collection of Whitney Museum of American Art.
New York. Purchase with funds from the Friends of the
Whitney Museum of American Art (61.46).

239 Andy Warhol.
CLOUDS. 1966.
Helium-filled mylar. Each 48″ × 42½″.
Photograph courtesy of Leo Castelli Gallery, New York.

Andy Warhol took advantage of the distinctive reflective surface of mylar in his whimsical dance of floating pillows called CLOUDS. The environmentally inclusive work consisted of helium-inflated containers made of thin sheets of metalized plastic. In the gallery, the pillows drifted and bumped against the ceiling and each other, activating the entire space and creating a silent, continually changing interplay in which viewers participated.

Artists such as Robert Smithson (see page 438) and Herbert Bayer (page 461) have worked with the environment on a large scale. Each of their earth sculptures (*earthworks*) uses materials from its area and is conceived in terms of the character of the site. Earthworks, environmental and interior installations, and assemblages (discussed in chapter 16) are just some of the ways in which contemporary sculpture has gone beyond traditional forms and media.

MIXED MEDIA

It is easiest to discuss materials and techniques when works involve only one medium. Today's artists, however, frequently use a variety of media in a single work. Rather than present a long, awkward list of materials, artists often identify such combinations as *mixed media*. The different media may be all two-dimensional, all three-dimensional, or a mixture of the two. Although painters and printmakers frequently use more than one medium to achieve the results they want, the term mixed media is usually applied to works comprised of very different media.

Among the most common mixed-media works are *collages*, in which various materials are attached to flat surfaces. Collage gives the artist a means for incorporating reality, rather than

240 Robert Rauschenberg.
TRACER. 1964.
Mixed media. 84″ × 60″.
Private collection.
Photograph courtesy of Leo Castelli Gallery, New York.

imitating it, in a work. Collage also relates to a particular way of experiencing objects and relationships in time and space.

Mixed-media works by their very nature break through habitual media-related preconceptions. American artist Robert Rauschenberg has been a pioneer of mixed media. In TRACER, he combined painting with modified parts of art reproductions and documentary photographs, incorporated with the help of the new technique of photographic screenprinting. References to art history, the Vietnam War, national symbolism, and street life interact.

Mixed media is a wide-open category. It embraces the work of many artists who have gone beyond identification with a particular medium. For example, we can describe Rauschenberg as a painter and printmaker who sometimes makes mixed-media "combine paintings," which include sculpture (see page 430). Marisol, on the other hand, is a sculptor who incorporates drawing and painting in her work.

The humble folks in Marisol's sculpture THE FAMILY are seen as if sitting for a family photograph. Typical of Marisol's work is the combination of actual common objects such as shoes and doors with careful carpentry, carving, casting, drawing, and painting. A wry sense of humor often characterizes her work.

In the late 1960s, Betye Saar began building mixed-media assemblages in boxes. She has since concentrated on combining objects, materials, and pictorial elements in poetic presentations loaded with personal and social content. Her FRIENDS AND LOVERS capitalizes on the symbolism of carefully selected photographs and other memorabilia to create a mysterious energy and evoke the power of memory by association.

241   Marisol.
THE FAMILY. 1962.
Painted wood and other materials in three sections. 6'10⅝'' × 65½''.
Collection, The Museum of Modern Art, New York. Advisory Committee Fund.

242   Betye Saar.
FRIENDS AND LOVERS. 1974.
Mixed media assemblage. 13¼'' × 11¼'' × 1''.
Photograph: F. J. Thomas. Courtesy of the artist.

PERFORMING ARTS AND PERFORMANCE ART

All the arts can be said to be an extension of the expressive qualities of the human body. In dance and drama, however, the body becomes the primary medium for visual expression. Because performing is a basic ingredient in film and television, the development of these media created a bridge between the visual arts and the traditional performing arts.

In *mime* or *pantomime*, an ancient form of silent drama, the artist mimics real situations or persons and portrays imaginary events by means of exaggerated gestures and full-body movements. The traditional boundaries of mime have been greatly extended by Mummenschanz, an international performing company created by André Bossard, Floriana Frassetto, and Bernie Schürch. Their name comes from two German words—*mummen*, meaning game or play, and *schanz*, meaning choice—and evokes the essence of their purely visual, abstract mime. The players went from facial masks in their early work to what they call "whole body masks," in which flexible space-age materials become giant soft sculptures, activated from within. Enormous stagehands and a creature resembling a cross between an octopus and a flower suggest the variety of their inventive forms.

The acts are usually brief, humorous comments on the human condition. The only sounds are the swishes and shuffles of the body masks, and laughs, coughs, and comments from the audience. Without sound or facial clues, the basic visual elements of line, shape, light, color, and motion become the vehicles for content. Mummenschanz magic encourages viewers to reactivate their own imaginations. According to Bossard, people have fun because of "the power of the audience to see things in the shapes that we make, to project its fantasy on the environment we create. . . . They participate in creating our show, unlike most of the entertainments they see, where they are dragged passively from one visual thrill to another."[4]

Dance is another performing art based on the poetry of the human body in motion. The sculptural qualities of the body offer variations

243 Mummenschanz.
THE NEW SHOW. 1987.
a. Show opener, "stage hands."
b. Octopus.
Photograph: Christian Altorper. © Mummenschanz, Ltd. 1982.

in shape, line, and mass, which extend into space by means of movement. Cultures around the world find foundations for their art in dance; states of mind and dramatic or narrative content can be eloquently expressed through body movement.

The Alvin Ailey American Dance Theater, formed in 1958, was originally dedicated to preserving the black tradition in American dance. Starting in the 1970s, the company's founder and director has taken a more universal approach to subject matter and choreography. The company receives international acclaim for high-energy performances of striking beauty and strength. Projected light adds color and intensity to the moods created by the dancers.

Performance art is a visual arts term for works that draw on aspects of painting, sculpture, film, mime, drama, and dance, yet are none of these. Performance (as it is often called today) began in about 1910 with the Italian futurists (see pages 392–393), who staged outrageous acts designed to destroy all things solid and serious connected with "Art" and "Culture." The idea flourished in Zurich as poets, writers, and artists who called themselves dadaists (see page 402) turned to performance as a way to shake the public out of complacency.

In the 1920s, the highly influential Bauhaus school in Germany was a major center for further development of performance art. Oskar Schlemmer, painter, sculptor, teacher, designer, and pioneer of modern dance choreography, provided the direction and inspiration. His 1926 PLAY WITH BUILDING BLOCKS was characteristic of his many inventive performances. The mannequin-like figures he created in his paintings were brought to life on stage. Geometrically organized movements, and props such as blocks, gave the overall design a pure simplicity of form that expressed the Bauhaus concern for an international, nonreferential aesthetic capable of synthesizing art and technology.

The surrealists (see page 407) were among those who helped keep the idea of performance alive as a valid expressive medium for visual arts. Since the 1960s, performance art has picked up momentum again. Artists began to collaborate, each adding his or her specialty to inventive mixtures of music, dance, and theater with sculptural overtones. Performance art became important in the 1970s and 1980s (see pages 446–447).

244 Elizabeth Roxas and Rodney Nugent in Alvin Ailey's THE LARK ASCENDING.
Photograph: © Jack Vartoogian, New York.
Courtesy Alvin Ailey American Dance Theater.

245 Oskar Schlemmer.
BAUHAUS DANCES, PLAY WITH BUILDING BLOCKS.
Performed at the Bauhaus Stage, Dessau by
Werner Siedhoff, Fischer and Albert Mentzel in 1926.

CRAFT MEDIA

All art begins with craft. If a work is not well made, there is little chance that it will be experienced as art; but craftsmanship alone does not make art.

Today's crafts grew out of ancient traditions, yet they now play either traditional or totally new roles. Until the Industrial Revolution, artisans made all articles for the sustenance of daily life. Now, of course, the vast majority of everyday objects are produced by mechanical methods. Before mechanization, shoppers were able to influence the design of objects made for convenience and pleasure by explaining their personal preferences to craftsworkers before the items were produced. Although technological development has severed the direct contact between consumer and craftsman, mechanization has also made it possible for craftspeople to make handcrafted objects without the limitations caused by earlier demands for quantity, economy, and practicality. In fact, industrialization made it possible for some craft-artists to produce purely expressive "fine" rather than "applied" or functional art. Today we treasure the work of the artist-craftsmen whose products radiate the kind of inner vitality found in the best handmade articles of pre-industrial times.

Since the beginning of civilization, crafts were—and in some cultures still are—an integral part of everyday life. Historically, few saw the crafts as separate or "minor" arts, as they are sometimes called today. As much artistic thought probably went into a painting on a Greek vase as into a wall painting. When machines took over weaving cloth, making dishes, and stamping out metal utensils, the close relationship between the maker and the individual object was lost.

We can derive lasting satisfaction from using our own hands to make utilitarian objects, and we feel a related pleasure when we use something handmade. Well-designed handcrafted works made for visual and utilitarian purposes offer a personal touch not found in machine-produced objects. Of course, there is good and bad design in both handmade and factory-made articles.

Craftsworkers tend to divide themselves into three groups. The first are those without academic training, including folk artists (see pages 16–20) and amateurs, most of whom make things for pleasure rather than for income. The second group of craftsmen make a living doing marketable work. The third group, whom we will call craft-artists, aims to produce objects of artistic merit, regardless of sales value. Artists from the third group tend to lead the way in inventive design and innovative use of materials. In part because of them, there has been an increased mixing of media and techniques in nearly all areas of artistic expression during the last several decades.

Some craftsmen produce only one-of-a-kind works, while others engage in limited production of multiple originals, often working with assistants who reproduce or help work on the designs. It is important to realize that even production handcrafting is very different from factory mass production.

Ceramics and weaving have been the most widely practiced of the crafts. The recent revival of interest in handwork, however, has resurrected a wide variety of other craft art, including jewelry making, enameling, and glassblowing. Previously accepted limits of traditional materials, techniques, and purposes have been set aside as artists and craftspeople explore new ideas and means of expression. As we have seen, the tendency to categorize and separate objects identified as "craft" from those considered "art" has been heavily challenged and in many cases discarded. Yet it is useful to realize that the word "art" is still applied to works in which form and content are primary, and "craft" to works in which material and function are dominant. The "fine art" explorations of the craft movement have brought about a merger of these traditionally separate concerns. Although there is no name for the new phenomenon, it is a continuing pleasure to see works of art in which form and content, medium and function, become one.

Organizations and exhibitions continue to carry the word "craft," even though a large portion of the works involved could also be classified as sculpture. Today, a high percentage of artworks made of traditional craft media have no function other than to evoke pleasure or a sense of beauty, or to provoke thought. In other words, some works still called "craft" carry a depth of content traditionally associated only with the fine arts.

Clay

Ceramics is the art and science of making objects from clay. The earth provides a variety of clays that can be mixed with one another and refined to obtain desired characteristics. Clay has long been a valuable raw material. It offers ample flexibility as well as relative permanence due to its capacity to harden when exposed to heat.

A person who works with clay is called either a *potter* or a *ceramist*. Potters and ceramists create functional pots or purely sculptural forms using hand-building methods such as slab, coil, or pinching, or by *throwing* clay—that is, shaping it on a wheel that may be driven by motor, hand, or foot. A potter can create form from a shapeless lump of clay as if by magic. Wheel throwing may look effortless, but it takes time and practice to perfect.

The term ceramics includes a wide range of objects made of fired clay, including tableware, vases, bricks, sculpture, and many kinds of tiles. Most of the basic ceramic materials were discovered, and processes developed, thousands of years ago. Ceramics, one of the oldest crafts, reached peaks of achievement in ancient China and Egypt. Originally, pots were made by pinching or building up with coils. Since the invention of the potter's wheel in Mesopotamia about six thousand years ago, potters have been able to produce circular and cylindrical forms with greater speed and uniformity.

The ceramic process is relatively simple. When a piece of pottery is thoroughly dry, it is *fired* in a *kiln*, a kind of oven. Heat transforms it chemically into a hard, stonelike substance. The pot-

246 JERRY MEEK THROWING A POT.

ter may add *glazes* or other decoration for color and textural variation. The silica in the glaze vitrifies during firing, fusing with the clay body to form a glassy, nonporous surface. Glaze can be transparent or opaque, glossy or dull, depending on its chemical composition.

Until the twentieth century, new processes evolved very slowly. In recent years, new formulations and even synthetic clays have become available. The biggest changes have come in more accurate methods of firing and improved techniques and equipment.

250 Isamu Noguchi.
BIG BOY. 1952.
Karatsu ware. 7⅞" × 6⅞".
Collection, The Museum of Modern Art,
New York. A. Conger Goodyear Fund.

To create his expressive sculpture BIG BOY, Isamu Noguchi pinched clay to form the hands, legs, and feet, and rolled out a slab of clay for the child's garment. He pressed the slab into the other pieces of clay to form a single unit. Noguchi used modeling, cutting, and assembling to achieve the final, playful result.

Robert Arneson considers all art self-portraiture, and underscores his assertion by making whimsical images of himself. He made CALIFORNIA ARTIST in reply to an attack on his work by a New York critic, who said that, due to California's spiritual and cultural impoverishment, Arneson's work could have no serious depth or meaning. Arneson responded by creating a ceramic self-portrait with gaping holes in place of eyes, revealing an empty head. The inside of the head is even glazed Catalina blue. The figure is a portrait of the artist as a combination cyclist and aging California hippie—complete with the appropriate clichés on and around the base. Those who think that clay is only for making bricks and dinnerware were acknowledged by Arneson, who put his name on the bricks, as any other brickmaker would. Arneson stated his point of view when he said,

I like art that has humor, with irony and playfulness. I want to make "high" art that is outrageous, while revealing the human condition which is not always high.[5]

In the mid-1950s, Peter Voulkos brought craft traditions together with art expectations, and thus extended the horizons for both art and craft. With a group of his students, he led the California sculpture movement that broke through barriers of preconception about the limits of clay as a medium. Voulkos's radical, almost anarchistic spirit opened the way for a revitalization that has transformed ceramic art, and touched off new directions in various media. His monumental GALLAS ROCK brings the emotional energy of abstract expressionist painting (see page 421) into three-dimensional form.

252 Peter Voulkos.
GALLAS ROCK. 1960.
Clay. Height, approx. 6'.
University of California at Los Angeles.

251 Robert Arneson.
CALIFORNIA ARTIST. 1982.
Glazed ceramic. 78″ × 28″ × 21″.
San Francisco Museum of Modern Art.

Peter Voulkos and Toshiko Takaezu have both been influenced by the earthiness and spontaneity of some traditional Japanese ceramics as well as by expressionist painting, yet their work has taken very different directions. Voulkos's pieces are rough and aggressively dynamic, while Takaezu's offer subtle, restrained strength. Takaezu's sculptural forms become the foundation for rich paintings of glaze and oxide. She comments on her love of the clay medium:

When working with clay I take pleasure from the process as well as from the finished piece. Every once in a while I am in tune with the clay, and I hear music, and it's like poetry. Those are the moments that make pottery truly beautiful for me.[6]

For many years, Marilyn Levine has been making mind-teasing clay reconstructions of well-worn leather objects. The selection of subjects such as SPOT'S SUITCASE, and her amazing technical ability, have defied accepted notions about the limits and appropriate uses of clay. By crafting clay to look like leather, Levine has violated the long-accepted craft principle of "truth to materials." Yet her work has truth of another kind—truth to the subject's appearance and to the way objects, particularly those that are worn, tell of the lives of their owners and even seem to take on lives of their own.

253 Toshiko Takaezu.
CERAMIC FORMS. 1986. Stoneware.
Photograph: Macario, Kaneohe, Hawaii.

254 Marilyn Levine.
SPOT'S SUITCASE. 1981.
Ceramic and metal buckles.
8½″ × 29″ × 18″.
Photograph courtesy of the artist.

Glass

Glass is an exotic and enticing art medium. Chemically, glass is closely related to ceramic glaze. As a form-creating medium, however, it offers a wide range of possibilities that are unique to glass. Hot or molten glass is a sensitive, amorphous material that can be shaped by blowing, casting, or pressing into molds. As it cools, glass solidifies from its molten state without crystalizing. After it is blown or cast, glass may be cut, etched, fused, laminated, layered, leaded, painted, polished, sandblasted, or slumped (softened for a controlled sag). The fluid nature of glass produces qualities of mass flowing into line and translucent volumes of airy thinness.

Glass has been used for at least four thousand years as a material for practical containers of all shapes and sizes. In recent centuries, it has also been used in architecture as clear and stained glass windows and mirrors, and in decorative inlays in a variety of objects, including jewelry. Elaborate, colored blown glass pieces have been made in Venice since the Renaissance. Because our primary contact with glass is with utilitarian objects such as food and beverage containers and windows, we often overlook the fact that glass can also be an excellent sculptural material. Although it can be said that the character of any material determines the character of the expression, this is particularly true of glass. Molten glass requires considerable speed and skill in handling. The glassblower combines the centering skills of a potter, the agility and stamina of an athlete, and the grace of a dancer to bring qualities of breath and movement into crystalline form.

Line, shape, light, and sensuous color unite to tease the senses in Harvey Littleton's YELLOW CROWN II. Littleton has been the leading figure in the American studio glass movement which began in the 1960s. Before he began to experiment with glass, Littleton was a successful professional ceramist. His first glass pieces were functional vases, but he soon began to

255   Harvey K. Littleton.
YELLOW CROWN II. 1984.
Glass. Approximately 23″ × 28″ × 23″.
Private collection. Photograph: Brian Westveer.
Courtesy of Maurine Littleton Gallery, Washington, D.C.

make forms that had no function other than to delight the eye. Although he spent about two years mastering the techniques of glass, his search was for significant expressive form. He feels that technique is the easy part, something that anyone can learn, but the art is in how technique is used. Glass is so seductive and intriguing that some lesser artists never get beyond the beauty of the material itself.

Albert Paley began his metalworking career making jewelry, and gradually shifted to larger pieces such as the GATE commissioned for the entrance of the Renwick Gallery museum shop. He enjoys handling a material that physically resists him. Few modern artists possess the exacting technical skill required to forge red-hot iron. Whether Paley is working on small pieces or large ones, he employs a variety of metals, woven together in harmonious interplay. A lively relationship between lines and spaces creates the high energy of his ornamental gates. The curves have the sensual fluidity of pliable heated metal, while the center verticals recall the strong rigidity of iron and steel. Bundles of straight lines unify and solidify the composition. The twelve-hundred-pound gates took Paley and his assistant seven months to complete.

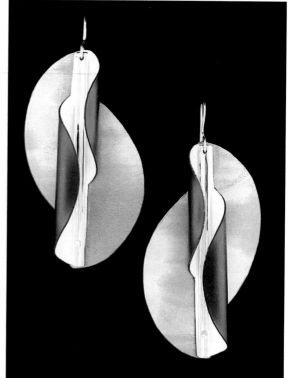

258 Mark Pierce.
EARRINGS. 1982.
Polished brass and luminar.
2¼″ × 1⅜″ × ½″.

Mark Pierce has found ways to create exciting jewelry forms by merging his experience as a painter with his work as a jewelry designer. He is among the many craft-artists who have been exploring uses of new materials and techniques. Through research, Pierce developed a polymer-aluminum process for creating unique, eye-catching jewelry.

259 Albert Paley.
GATE. 1974.
Steel, brass, copper, hand-wrought and forged.
90¾″ × 72″.
National Museum of American Art, Smithsonian Institution, Washington, D.C.
Commissioned for the Renwick Gallery (1975.117.1).

Wood

Life and growth characteristics of individual trees remain visible in the grain of wood long after trees are cut, giving wood a vitality not found in other materials. Its abundance, versatility, and warm tactile qualities have made it a favored material for human use. The living spirit of wood is given second life in crafted forms.

Many contemporary designers have been inspired by art from nonindustrial cultures. Traditional peoples have demonstrated extraordinary imagination and sensitivity toward materials in their design of articles for daily use, survival, and spiritual fulfillment. Generations of traditional artisans have refined the design of such objects in order to improve their practical and expressive functions (see the COCONUT GRATER on page 289).

The natural colors, textural patterns, and grain of various woods are fully explored by Bob Stocksdale in his bowl forms. Shape, size, and wall thickness are largely determined by Stocksdale's sensitivity to the characteristic of each block. As Stocksdale shapes each bowl, he shows off the color variations, knots, and growth rings that make each piece of wood unique.

Most furniture purchased for today's homes is produced by industrial mass-production methods. However, those with the skill to make their own, or enough money to buy custom pieces, can enjoy the special experience of living with handcrafted furniture.

Sam Maloof makes unique pieces of furniture and also repeats some designs he finds particularly satisfying. The designs Maloof creates express his love of wood and of the hand processes he uses to shape wood into furniture. He employs assistants who help him duplicate his best designs, but he limits quantity. Because he enjoys knowing that each piece is cut, assembled,

261 Bob Stocksdale.
TURNED WOOD BOWLS. 1982.
Clockwise from top right: ebony, 10¾″ diameter; ash, 8½″ diameter; blackwood, 11¼″ diameter; macadamia, 4½″ diameter; ironwood, 6½″ diameter.
Photograph: Nora Scarlett.

260 Sam Maloof.
ROCKING CHAIR. 1986.
Fiddleback maple.
Photograph courtesy of the artist.

262 Stephen Whittlesey.
"LAKE QUEEN" (VANITY/DESK WITH SEAT). 1985.
Recycled wood. Vanity/desk 5′ × 5′ × 22″.
Collection of Delta Burke, Los Angeles.
Photograph courtesy of Umbrello Gallery, Los Angeles, and the artist.

and finished according to his own high standards, Maloof has turned down offers from manufacturers who want to mass-produce his designs. He prefers to retain quality control and the special characteristics that are inevitably lost when even the best designs are factory-produced rather than handmade. Many pieces of furniture are pleasing to look at, and many comfortable to use, but relatively few fulfill both functions as successfully as those by Maloof.

Stephen Whittlesey's attitude toward making wood furniture is very different from Maloof's. He assembles each piece the way a painter composes a canvas, or a sculptor constructs an assemblage, rather than with the sensibility of a conventional furniture maker. His education in painting and sculpture and his work as both a painter and carpenter have led him to work with wood in a new way.

When Whittlesey first began to make furniture out of found pieces of wood, he allowed the shapes of the wood to influence the result to a great extent. Subsequently, he made a conscious decision to change the way he worked. He began to impose his own sense of design more completely on his constructions, while continuing to retain and incorporate the shapes, scars, and old paint of salvaged wood into his unique furniture. Always on the lookout for wood he can use, Whittlesey is particularly attracted to fragments that bear the marks of their former lives.

Fiber

Fiber art includes weaving and a host of other processes—such as stitching, knitting, crocheting, and knotting—that use natural and synthetic fiber in both traditional and innovative ways. The field has undergone a major rebirth and redefinition heralded by a name change from "weaving" to "fiber art." Modern on- and off-loom constructions share with other art forms the heritage of art history along with involvement in current trends.

All weaving is based on the interlacing of lengthwise fibers, *warp*, and the cross fibers, *weft* (also called *woof*). Weavers create patterns by changing the numbers and placements of interwoven threads.

Alice Parrott's weaving MESA VERDE uses warm, intense colors to create an abstract image of the ancient protected community built high in the overhanging cliff of a Colorado mesa. Such modern wall hangings extend traditional tapestry and rug-making concepts.

Weavers can choose from a variety of looms and techniques. A large tapestry loom, capable of weaving hundreds of colors into intricate forms, may require several days of preparation before work begins. In contrast, a small weaving on a simple hand loom may be finished in a few hours.

263 Alice Parrott.
MESA VERDE. 1976.
Wool and linen, tapestry and soumac techniques. 48″ × 62″.
Collection of Paul M. Cook, Atherton, California.

264 Gerhardt Knodel.
GRAND EXCHANGE. 1981.
Handwoven fabric, nylon cords,
metal framework. Ceiling height 52'.
Cincinnati Bell of Ohio, atrium.
Photograph: Balthazar Korab.

there to relax. The suspended fabric planes suggest stairs, parts of a landscape, or spatial constructions. Knodel applied his sensitivity to light, color, planes in space, and surface textures in the creation of a kind of open cloth architecture. Inspiration for this work came in part from his observation of the magical effects of theater curtains. Other sources of inspiration for Knodel's work include fiber arts he has seen in such places as Indonesia, India, and Afghanistan.

Recent innovations in off-loom fiber work have taken the fiber arts beyond their traditional roles as functional or simply decorative crafts. Marcia Donahue has used leather as a medium for fiber sculpture. In NEST, she twisted and pulled leather to make it resemble wood; she also cut it into strips and wove it to give it the appearance of plant fiber. She plaited and formed the vegetable-tanned cowhide while it was wet. NEST has a remarkable presence. The face suggests a nature spirit or wood nymph emerging, or perhaps revealing itself just for a moment.

Fiber forms have warmed us, provided cushioned floor coverings, and offered interior color, texture, and sound control. Pioneering fiber artist Gerhardt Knodel has added to these traditional functions by exploring other environmental possibilities of fiber. Knodel's large hanging work GRAND EXCHANGE, designed for the Cincinnati Bell atrium, has transformed a rather stark and awkward space into a place that is inviting and calming to the employees who go

265 Marcia Donahue.
NEST. 1979.
Leather.
27" × 13¾" × 6".
Collection of the artist.

266   Magdalena Abakanowicz.
BACKS. 1976–1982.
80 pieces, burlap and glue: 24″ × 19⅝″ × 21⅝″;
27¼″ × 22″ × 26″; 28¼″ × 23¼″ × 27¼″.
Photograph: Dirk Bakker.
Courtesy of Marlborough Gallery, New York.

Polish artist Magdalena Abakanowicz uses fiber in highly inventive ways. Since the 1960s, she has been at the leading edge of nontraditional uses of fiber. Both art and life have been a struggle for Abakanowicz. She was nine years old when the horrors of World War II in Poland became part of her life. Later, she faced the need to support herself in a poor country; battled an educational system in which new approaches were not allowed; was forced to work in small spaces; and finally, struggled against prevailing traditional ideas about acceptable and unacceptable uses of fiber. The form and content of much of her work suggests the difficulties she has faced.

Her powerful series called BACKS has an unforgettable quality—at once personal and universal. The earthy textures and color of the formed burlap seem to tell of humankind's capacity to endure dire hardships and challenges. The artist speaks of her motives:

I like the surface of threads that I make, every square inch differs from the others, as in the creations of nature.

I want the viewer to penetrate the inside of my forms.

For I want him to have the most intimate contact with them, the same contact one can have with clothes, animal skins, or grass.[8]

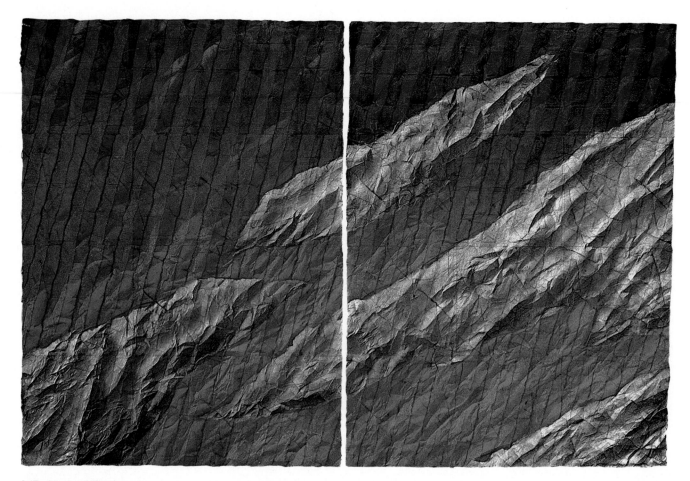

267 Nance O'Banion.
MIRAGE SERIES: TOO. 1984.
Handmade abaca paper, paint on bamboo. 4′ × 6′.
Photograph: Elaine Keenan.
Courtesy of the Allrich Gallery, San Francisco.

In recent years, there has been a revival of the ancient craft of making paper by hand. Inventive artworks have greatly expanded our understanding of paper's potential as an expressive medium. Some artists accustomed to drawing, painting, and making prints on manufactured paper have joined fiber artists in exploring unconventional possibilities of handmade paper.

Nance O'Banion worked in printed textiles prior to her involvement in papermaking. She often combines her handmade paper with other types of fiber. In the diptych (two-part composition) MIRAGE SERIES: TOO, O'Banion created an intriguing interplay of textures, patterns, shapes and colors. Cloud-like forms appear in relief, accentuated by subtly painted shadows. Their light, majestic shapes are set off by the contrasting warm/cool colors of the rhythmically striped background. MIRAGE SERIES: TOO has been exhibited in the direction seen on the *Artforms* cover, and as shown here. It is an effective, memorable image either way.

The fibers we are closest to in everyday life are in the form of clothes. Recently, some fiber artists began working with the concept of wearable art (see page 218). Artists involved in "art to wear" want their imagination to have free reign, and not be held back by requirements of mass production or practicality.

Art to wear, along with other avenues of investigation and innovation in craft media, demonstrate the craft-artist's important role in bringing art to life. Craft media are used today in both traditional and new ways, and increasingly overlap and combine with the practices and sensibilities of drawing, painting, sculpture, and printmaking.

8

Design Disciplines

Every manufactured object we buy or use has been designed by someone. As consumers, we are aware that some objects are well designed, and some are not. If the form and function of an object do not complement each other, the object is poorly designed. Good design solves problems; bad design creates problems.

Design shapes as well as transmits material culture. A professional designer's role is to enhance living by applying a developed sense of aesthetics and utility to the creation of a wide variety of images, objects, and spaces intended to meet human needs. From small objects to large buildings, and from personal to public spaces, design is a necessity, not a cosmetic addition.

In the Western world, twentieth-century design has been heavily influenced by the Bauhaus school founded by Walter Gropius in Weimar, Germany, in 1919. The Bauhaus merged the Weimar schools of fine and applied arts into a single, interdisciplinary institution, and brought together many leading artists, architects, theatrical innovators, and designers. Working as an inspired team, they combined the study of fine arts such as drawing and painting with crafts such as weaving and furniture making, and developed an aesthetic based on visual structure and sound craftsmanship. The Bauhaus stressed functionalism and good design in everyday life, and aimed to solve the problems of visual design created by industrialization. Through the 1920s, the school and its outstanding faculty attracted students from all over the world. In 1933, however, Hitler closed the school because he considered Bauhaus art and ideas degenerate.

After the Bauhaus closed, some of the faculty moved to the United States. László Moholy-Nagy opened the Institute of Design in Chicago to carry on the Bauhaus goals. The teaching of design in the United States continues to reflect the influence of the Bauhaus philosophy, with its emphasis on formal visual structure over personal expression, functional simplicity, and honest use of materials. The impact of the all-embracing design concepts of the Bauhaus is very much with us today, evident in disciplines as diverse as architecture, industrial design, textile design, typography, and painting.

The Bauhaus was not only a design movement, it was a social movement as well. Central to its vision was the belief that people must command machines and use them for creative purposes in order to control human destiny. The underlying mission was to improve society through improved design, to bring humanistic and artistic sensitivity to the industrial world.

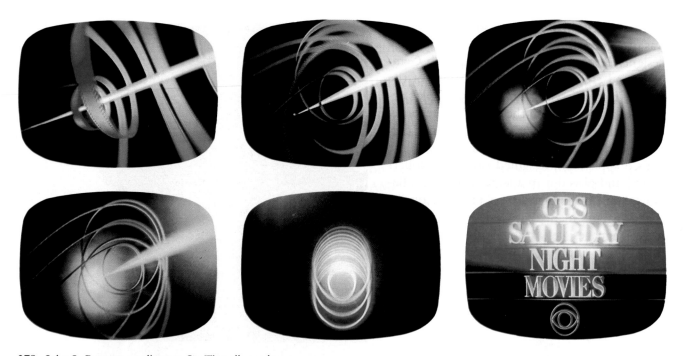

279   John LePrevost, art director; Jay Tietzell, producer.
CBS MOVIE OPENER. 1983.
Computer-generated animation.

In 1952, when William Golden was creative director for advertising for the Columbia Broadcasting System, he designed the eye symbol, which for several decades has served as the CBS trademark. One variation of the symbol is a five-second computer-animated sequence used to announce the "CBS Saturday Night Movies."

ILLUSTRATION

An *illustration* is a picture or decoration, usually used in conjunction with a text, created to enhance the appearance of written material or to clarify its meaning. Illustration, along with writing, evolved from early pictographs. With the development of printing, the art of hand-painted illumination such as that found in the Book of Kells (see page 314) declined. Modern illustration has evolved along with the modernization of printing processes. As noted on page 145, Daumier was among those who used lithography for illustration in the nineteenth century. More recent photomechanical reproduction processes have enabled illustrators to employ a wide variety of drawing, painting, and photographic techniques. Computers have further extended the capabilities of illustrators.

Since illustrations are often drawings, paintings, or photographs, the distinction between illustrations and works displayed in galleries and museums has to do with the purpose the work is intended to serve, rather than the medium out of which the work is made.

Illustrators create images to be printed in books, magazines, reports, record covers, greeting cards, advertisements, and the like. Although a great deal of illustration is now done with photography, some areas—notably children's books, fashion illustration, and greeting cards—continue to rely heavily on drawn or painted images.

American illustrator Norman Rockwell is best known for the many *Saturday Evening Post* covers he created between 1916 and 1963. He specialized in warm, humorous, often sentimental scenes of everyday small-town life, drawn with a wealth of meaningful detail. His TRIPLE SELF-PORTRAIT is intriguing on several levels. The face looking back at us from the mirror looks anxious and somewhat comical, with a drooping pipe, and blank reflections for eyes; the Rockwell on the easel appears handsome and jaunty, without glasses, and with his pipe more firmly clenched. Perhaps the real Norman Rockwell is the third figure, with his back to us. Self-portraits by Dürer, Rembrandt, Picasso, and Van Gogh are tacked to the right corner of his easel. He may be suggesting that "painters" can show themselves as they look, feel, or imagine they are; while "illustrators" are self-effacing types who rarely depict themselves—and, when they do, aren't sure where they fit in the art world.

In the mid-1950s, there was a fairly clear distinction between the fine arts of drawing and painting and the commercial art of illustration. Since then, however, the two areas have moved closer together. Challenges to the dominance of abstract and nonrepresentational painting, starting about 1960, led to a return to representational styles; the pop art of the 1960s celebrated commercial art; and the photorealist artists of the 1970s employed an approach to imagery used by illustrators in the 1950s. In the 1960s, 1970s, and 1980s, some magazine editors encouraged personal expression, which led a number of illustrators to move in the direction of more abstract, symbolic, or poetic depictions, bringing their work closer to that of gallery artists.

280 Norman Rockwell.
TRIPLE SELF-PORTRAIT. Cover for *Saturday Evening Post*. February 13, 1960.
Oil on canvas.
© *1960 Curtis Publishing Company.*

Brad Holland is an illustrator who belongs to this new breed. His images are specific, but not literal, and he is more concerned with meeting his own criteria than those of anyone else. Holland began his career by working very briefly in a tattoo parlor, then worked for a year as a book illustrator at Hallmark in Kansas. He proceeded to New York, where his struggle to make a living was hampered by his insistence that he be allowed to work in his own way. He succeeded, however, and his distinctive style has had an influence on many other illustrators, some of whom appear to copy his approach. Many of Holland's illustrations have an eerie, demonic quality, which may have made him a logical choice to do the KHOMEINI cover for *Time*'s "Man of the Year" issue in 1980.

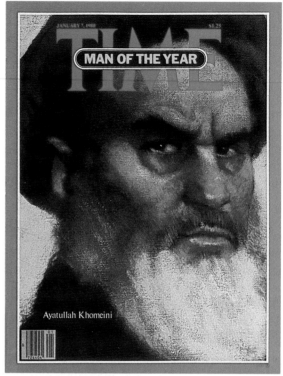

281   Brad Holland.
KHOMEINI. January 7, 1980. *Time.* 1980.
© *1980 Time Inc. All rights reserved. Reprinted by permission from Time.*

Editors generally seek an illustrator after they have selected a story or article that they want illustrated. To Holland's surprise and delight, a few editors have reversed this, giving writers story assignments intended to accompany his existing drawings. That was how Holland intended his work to be used, though it is not customary in the field of illustration.

Leo and Diane Dillon have chosen to work together as a "combined artist." They pass their work back and forth, critique one another, and take over one another's work. In their illustrations for books, magazines, and record covers, they use a variety of techniques, including woodcut, stencil, and airbrush, choosing the media that will produce the desired result. They conceived the illustration for the book GIFT OF THE BLACK FOLK to convey both strong feelings and information.

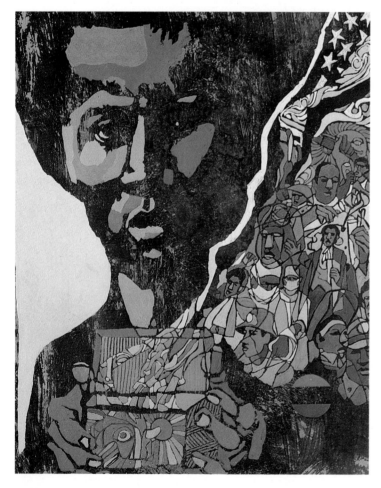

282   Leo and Diane Dillon.
Illustration for *Gift of the Black Folk* by W. E. B. Dubois. 1960.
Mixed media with casein and felt-tip markers. 10″ × 12½″.
Collection of Society of Illustrators, Museum of American Illustration, New York.

Maurice Sendak's name has become synonymous with children's book illustration. He has illustrated many books by other authors, but he is best known for those he wrote himself. His style varies from quite simple line drawings, with little or no background, to elaborate crosshatched and textured drawings in which every inch of the composition is filled.

Sendak's surreal, make-believe creatures delight adults as well as children. His READING IS FUN poster uses animals from his book *Where The Wild Things Are*. Sendak rejected the notion that illustrations for children's books must be benign—devoid of anything frightening. His playfully menacing creatures provide children with a healthy way to confront some of their fears of the unknown. Sendak's work has had a strong influence on other illustrators.

Surprisingly, given his fame as an illustrator, Sendak believes that illustrations should be secondary to the text. His view is in contrast to that of Brad Holland, who prefers to see his work,

if not more important than the text, at least to precede it in concept. When illustration is at its best, however, pictures and text seem inseparable. This is particularly true with favorite children's books, and is perhaps what illustration is really all about—not only to enhance a text, but to become part of it.

CLOTHING DESIGN

No potential art form could be physically closer to us than clothing. For this reason, fashion design has been called "art for the near environment." We express ourselves by the manner in which we dress; clothing is visual communication.

Clothing designers begin with an awareness of the lines, proportions, and movements of the human body, the ways fabric drapes and molds itself, and the look they are trying to achieve. Ideas usually begin with visualization and drawings. Line, shape, color, and texture are major considerations.

Apparel design applies to mass-produced clothing of all types as well as to unique custom garments that may cost thousands of dollars. Each season, new fashions of famous designers are brought to public attention through newspapers, magazines, and television. Although their designs often seem extreme and far removed from the everyday world, fashion designers have a great deal of influence on popular taste and style selection.

The United States was the first country to mass-produce good-looking clothes, enabling people of modest means to buy, rather than make their own clothes. Here and abroad the public, encouraged by the garment industry, has developed an enormous appetite for new ideas and new styles in clothing.

READING IS FUN!
INTERNATIONAL YEAR OF THE CHILD 1979

283 Maurice Sendak.
READING IS FUN. Poster.
© 1979 by Reading Is Fundamental, Inc. Reprinted with permission.

284 Issey Miyake.
Clothing design.
Photograph: Eiichiro Sakata/Time, Inc.

285 Sandra Rubel
COAT. 1983.
Silk, painted, pieced, beaded.
Photograph: © Kathy A. McGinty, 1983.

Japanese designer Issey Miyake is a man of great openness and imagination, who creates colorful, inventive clothes. Miyake uses beautiful fabrics that he and his associates design. He first drapes the fabric over his own body to give him the feel of the cloth. He then lets the way the cloth falls suggest the design. Only after he decides how he wants to use the fabric does he drape a model and then make drawings for the garment. He recognizes that clothes are not only seen from the outside, but felt from within. Miyake's garments free the body, in contrast to Western clothes, which tend to constrict the body with their clearly defined shapes. His designs invite wearers to interpret his garments in their own ways. Miyake's clothes can be seen as both ancient and futuristic, Japanese and Western. They do not go out of style, because they are beyond fashion as it has been known.

Sandra Rubel combined a mastery of color and fiber art with a knowledge of clothing construction in her one-of-a-kind handcrafted COAT. Deep pleats penetrate the elaborate yoke to create an exciting design for the back of the garment. The pleats fall gracefully and move with the body when the coat is worn. Piping and beads add delicate finishing touches that are well integrated with the overall design.

Rubel's coat was included in the exhibition "Art to Wear: New Handmade Clothing" at the American Craft Museum II in New York in 1983. The concept of wearable art brings art out of museums and galleries.

TEXTILE DESIGN

As media categories, fiber arts and textile design overlap. *Textile design* generally refers to designs to be mass-produced by either weaving or printing.

Anni Albers has been a weaver who designed for machine production, and also continued to make one-of-a-kind experimental weavings. She studied at the Bauhaus, where she developed an aesthetic sensitivity suited to commercial production. When the Bauhaus was closed, she and her husband, the painter Josef Albers, came to the United States. The Albers were proponents of rectilinear design, which has been a major part of twentieth-century modernism.

Jack Lenor Larsen has become one of America's best-known weavers and textile designers. An enthusiastic traveler, he finds inspiration in the fabrics he studies and collects in various parts of the world. Larsen says he weaves his experiences into his fabrics. He uses techniques, color, and materials from many cultures, and synthesizes them into designs and collections that are uniquely his own. He is a major innovator as well as a sound traditional craftsman.

The majority of Larsen's designs are now woven on power looms, but he continues to weave most of the first samples by hand. Some of his large commissions are woven in places such as India and Africa, where the traditional techniques Larsen employs originated. This practice has helped to revitalize ancient crafts and has proved to be of benefit to local economies.

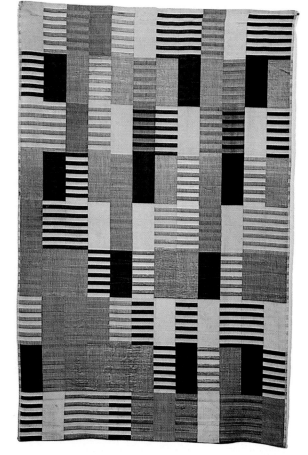

286 Anni Albers.
UNTITLED WALLHANGING. 1926.
Silk, triple weave. 72″ × 48″.
*Courtesy of the Harvard University Art Museums
(Busch-Reisinger Museum). Museum purchase.*

287 Jack Lenor Larsen.
LABYRINTH. 1981.
Upholstery fabric, Jacquard "repp," worsted wool and cotton, worsted wool face.
Project Director: Mark Pollock, Larsen Design Studio.

288 MARIMEKKO FABRIC DESIGNS.
1963.
Cotton.

In the early 1950s, Armi Ratia started the Marimekko company in Finland. Designer Maija Isola joined her, and together they caused a revolution in the textile printing industry. Marimekko broke away from conventional floral motifs and monotonous ornamentation. The firm became known for its bold designs using large areas of color. As fabric design moved into the expressive domain enjoyed by painters and graphic designers, people often stretched Marimekko fabrics on frames and hung them on the wall like paintings.

INTERIOR DESIGN

Interior living spaces are designed consciously and unconsciously by those who inhabit them. Professional and amateur designers need to have both an awareness of the expressive character of architectural spaces and the ability to visualize how the surfaces and objects placed within the spaces can be selected so they contribute to the total effect.

Enjoyable interiors are determined by the values and lifestyles of the occupants. For this reason, some of the best interior design is done by individuals for themselves. Important aspects of the process include developing ideas about the intended purpose of the space and desired mood; relating interior and exterior when applicable; organizing rooms, and objects within rooms, to suit specific needs; selecting and arranging furniture for comfort and ease of circulation; and coordinating materials, colors, and textures.

Interior designers Robert Bray and Michael Schaible are primarily concerned with spatial qualities. Bray's studio apartment was designed to be a starting point to which other elements could be added at a later date. After he began living in the apartment, however, Bray decided that he did not want to add anything—that he preferred the beauty of the walls to the beauty of paintings. The uncluttered simplicity gives a spacious feeling to the small room, and makes the apartment a tranquil refuge from the intensity of Manhattan. A variety of floor levels divides the room, providing visual interest without making the space appear smaller. The highest level is flush with the window sills, creating a flow between interior and exterior space.

Interior design frequently may include interior architecture. When they work with clients, Bray and Schaible feel that getting spaces down to basic, functional essentials is the first and most important step, even when clients already own beautiful furnishings and art objects. Such an approach enables those with limited funds to add furniture and art objects slowly.

289 Bray-Schaible Design, Inc.
BRAY RESIDENCE.
Photograph: Jaime Ardiles-Arce.

290 Sam and Alfreda Maloof.
MALOOF RESIDENCE.
Photograph: © Jonathan Pollack, 1984.

Sam and Alfreda Maloof have created a home that supports and expresses their way of life. Their home and workshop are located in California on seven acres of rural land. Sam designed and built the house—from the supporting structure to the elegant details. Even the door latches and hinges are beautifully handcrafted. The house is filled with Sam's furniture (see his rocking chair on page 201) and with ancient and contemporary art collected by the Maloofs. Persian rugs and an outstanding collection of Native American rugs, pots, and baskets complement the natural wood of the house. In the large kitchen-dining area, walls of concrete block painted orange and magenta contrast with the walls of rough-hewn redwood. The house is an ongoing work of love that has engaged the Maloofs for more than thirty years.

291 William Tapley.
APARTMENT INTERIOR.
Photograph: Robert Perron.

Fancy, expensive architecture and costly furniture are not prerequisites for exciting interior design. Paint alone can do wonders when selected and applied with skill and imagination. Masking tape can be used for a clean separation between colors. William Tapley designed "super graphics" to enliven an otherwise ordinary apartment. Stripes and triangles in muted and contrasting hues integrate with, and at times offer counterpoint to, the architecture.

ARCHITECTURE

The oldest of the design professions is architecture, the art and science of designing and constructing buildings for practical, aesthetic, and symbolic purposes. Architecture affects our lives directly and continually because it provides environments for human life. Since it grows out of human needs and aspirations, architecture offers one of the clearest records of the cultural values of past and present civilizations. Within the last two hundred generations—five thousand years—people in various parts of the world have developed impressive techniques for the construction of ceremonial, commercial, institutional, and domestic buildings that go beyond mere shelter to celebrate and enhance life. Today, architects continue to play a central role in the creation of living spaces and cultural symbols.

The organization of space, defined by horizontal, vertical, and diagonal planes, and curving surfaces, forms the essence of architecture. Time is also important, because it is through a succession of experiences that a building is understood. The interplay of light and shadow inside and outside a building is another crucial factor. Unity and interest are enhanced by the sensitive selection and combination of surface qualities, including textures and colors.

The world's architectural structures have been designed in relation to the limitations of available materials and the structural systems devised to utilize them. Structures can be analyzed according to how they deal with downward forces created by gravity. Architecture is designed to withstand the forces of compression or pushing (→ ←), tension or pulling (← →), bending or curving (↶ ↷), or a combination of these in different parts of the structure. The diagrams illustrate ancient as well as modern structural systems and the relationships between them.

Prior to the twentieth century, two dominant structural types were in common use: post-and-beam (or post-and-lintel) and arch systems, including vaulting. In the late nineteenth and twentieth centuries, the technologies of steel and steel-reinforced concrete led to the development

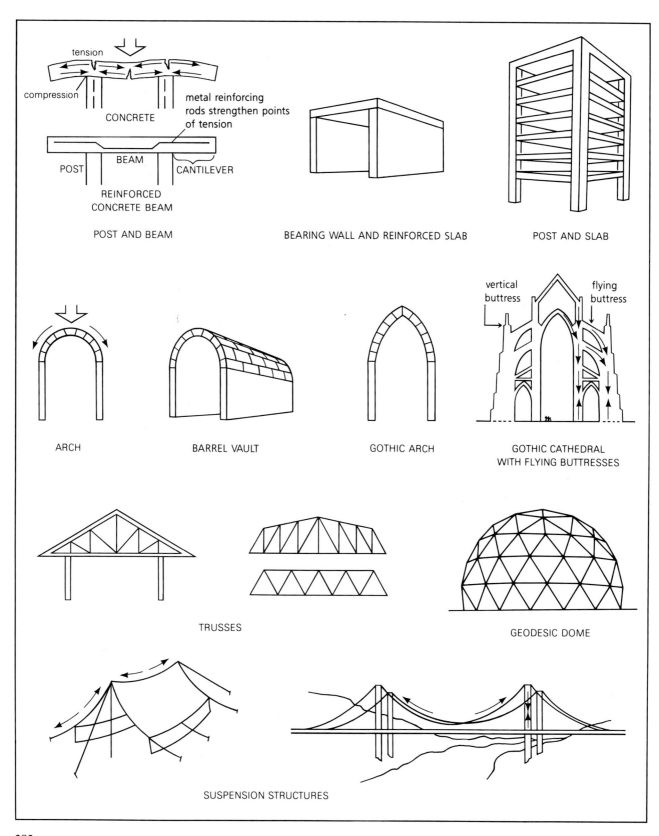

292 BASIC STRUCTURAL SYSTEMS.

293 Beverly Hoversland.
ARCHITECTURAL DRAWINGS.

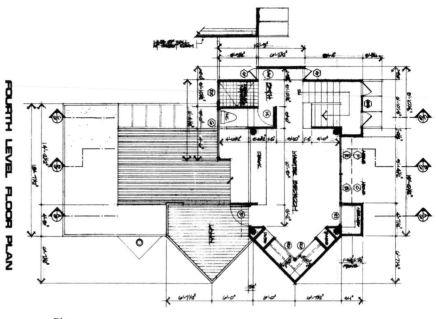

FOURTH LEVEL FLOOR PLAN

a. Plan.

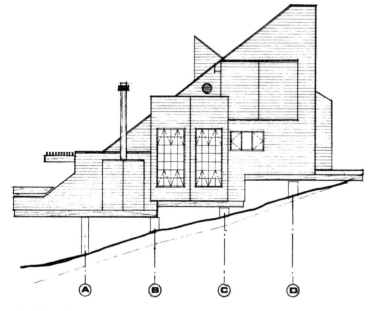

b. Elevation.

of highrise structures and other forms not previously possible. The late twentieth century has seen many new variations on basic structural types: domes, shells, folded plates, hanging roofs, and free-form castings.

To develop and present their ideas, architects make drawings and scale models. Architectural drawings include (a) *plans*, in which the structure is laid out in terms of linear patterns of spaces as seen from above; (b) *elevations*, in which individual exterior walls are drawn to scale as if seen straight on, thus indicating the exact proportions of such elements as wall heights and window placement; (c) *sections*, in which slices or cross sections are drawn showing details along an imaginary vertical plane passing through the proposed structure; and (d) *perspective renderings*, which give pictorial rather than diagrammatic views of finished buildings as they will appear on the site. Perspective renderings indicate such features as land contours, landscaping, and adjacent streets and buildings, if any.

Today's architecture has three essential components, which can be compared to elements of the human body: a supporting *skeleton* or frame; an outer *skin*; and vital *equipment*, similar to the body's vital organs and systems. The equipment includes plumbing; electrical wiring; appliances for light; hot water; and air-conditioning for cooling, heating, and circulating air as needed. Early brick and stone wall structures had no such equipment, and the skeleton and skin were one. We are again seeing the union of skeleton and skin in contemporary architecture built with folded plate, shell, and *pneumatic* or air-inflated structures.

Each major historic style has been based on the invention of a new method of construction arrived at through experimentation undertaken to meet the needs of a new way of life. In earlier times, it was necessary to design structural systems for the available materials—primarily wood, stone, or brick. Today's technology makes it possible to invent new building materials to suit the type of structure desired. Major twentieth-century innovations in the materials and techniques of construction have given builders the opportunity to enclose space with increasing ease and speed, and with a minimum of material.

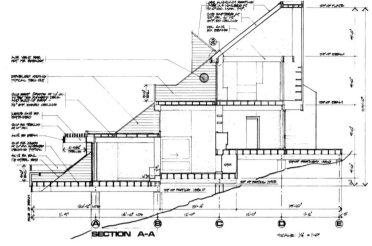

c Section.

d. Perspective rendering.

298 ST. SAVIN-SUR-GARTEMPE. Poitou, France.
c. 1095–1115.
Choir-and-nave.

it possible to further develop the vault construction of western Asia. Great vaults and domes such as the Pantheon (see page 306) covered large, open floor areas. Roman builders also developed the *groin vault*, which is formed by the intersection between two vaults. Vaults made of separate blocks pressing one on another exert both downward and outward pressure. To prevent collapse, supporting walls must be thick or reinforced from the outside. Barrel vaults were only rarely used outside the Roman Empire.

During the early Middle Ages, the Roman art of vaulting died out with the loss of technical knowledge for engineering such structures. In the eleventh and twelfth centuries, the architects of northern Europe, seeking to replace the fire-prone wooden roofs of churches with something less flammable and more dignified, returned to building barrel vaults based on the Roman concept. Until then, medieval builders had used

arches only for bridges and arcades along the side walls of church interiors and courtyards. The style that resulted from the adoption of Roman construction for medieval buildings is known as Romanesque. Romanesque architecture is massive, dark, and heavily enclosed, with emphasis on basic geometric forms. Because the walls support the roof, windows in churches such as ST. SAVIN-SUR-GARTEMPE had to be small and thus admit little light into the interior.

The first great structural breakthrough after the semicircular arch was the pointed arch. This seems a small change, but its effect on the whole structure of buildings was spectacular. Given the same starting point and width, the *pointed arch* is higher and therefore capable of embracing more space. Height, space, and light are the key features of Gothic church architecture.

Gothic cathedrals, built in Europe from the twelfth to the sixteenth centuries, are among the most inventive and awe-inspiring architectural achievements of all time. Their enthusiastic spirit of ascendance symbolizes an era of renewed faith, economic prosperity, and freedom of inquiry. In contrast to the heavy, dark interiors of their Romanesque predecessors, Gothic interiors are open, full of light, and seem almost weightless as they soar to great heights.

No single element in Gothic architecture was new. The innovation of Gothic architects was to combine and integrate such elements as pointed arches, ribbed groin vaults, and major external buttressing, which transformed the massive load-bearing walls of Romanesque into the slender supports and large windows of the Gothic style.

Vaults based on the pointed arch can vary in width yet retain the same height and thus provide greater flexibility than barrel vaults. The curved edge at the junction of two intersecting vaults is called the *groin*. Stone ribs placed along the groins act as arches and thrust the weight of the vault out as well as down. Although a pointed arch is steeper and therefore sends its weight more directly downward, a substantial sideways thrust must still be held in check. Gothic architects accomplished this by building elaborate buttresses on the outside of the building. In the most developed High Gothic cathedrals, the outward force of the arched vault is carried to large vertical buttresses by stone half-arches called *flying buttresses*. By placing part of the structural skeleton on the outside, Gothic builders were able to make their cathedrals higher and lighter in appearance. The added external support of the buttresses relieved cathedral walls of much of their structural function; they could then be opened up to include enormous, non-load-bearing stained glass windows. From the floor of the sanctuary to the highest part of the interior above the main altar, the windows increase in size, causing the upper part of the interior to appear dissolved in light.

Diagonal and transverse ribs of the groin vaults cross between opposite arcades, and carry the major weight of the vaults downward to supporting columns. The columns, called compound piers, look like bundles of slender ribs. The rib vault concept in combination with the pointed arch and the flying buttress produced the stone framework of Gothic architecture. Linear forms emphasize verticality and give the cathedral its active sense of vitality and upward thrust. Spiritual qualities of light, soaring interior space, and the resonance of music and spoken words express the devotion and spiritual aspirations of the people who built these monuments to the Age of Faith.

No basic structural variation was added to Western architectural vocabulary after the Gothic arch and vault until the inventions of steel and reinforced-concrete construction in the late nineteenth century. From the Renaissance to the nineteenth century, architects designed complex and at times innovative structures in which combinations of borrowed or eclectic elements play an important role. Forms and ornamentation from the Greek and Roman periods were brought back again and again.

By the mid-nineteenth century, the world was being transformed by science, industry, and the quest for speed. New inventions of the industrial age led to a revolution in architecture. First cast iron, then steel, then steel-reinforced concrete, electricity, and the invention of the high-speed elevator gave architects a set of materials and technologies that changed the design of buildings.

299 NOTRE DAME DE CHARTRES. Chartres, France.
c. 1200–1400.
Interior. Nave, approx. height 122′, width 53′, length 130′.

300 Joseph Paxton.
CRYSTAL PALACE. London. 1851 (destroyed by fire in 1936).
Interior. Cast-iron and glass.
(Engraving by R. P. Cluff.)
British Architectural Library, RIBA London.

With the advent of mechanized mass-production, iron became an important building material. It was found to be stronger and more fire resistant than wood, and could be more easily shaped than stone. Factories, bridges, and railway stations were among the new types of buildings for which iron was used.

The CRYSTAL PALACE, designed by Joseph Paxton, was a spectacular demonstration of what iron could do. It was designed and built for the Great Exhibition of the Works of Industry of All Nations, held in London in 1851. There is no eclecticism in this building. Paxton used the new methods of the industrial age—prefabricated cast iron, glass, and wooden sections. His successful innovation was a new application of the concept that "form follows function," expressed earlier by Renaissance architect Leon Battista Alberti, and later made famous by Louis Sullivan.

In the CRYSTAL PALACE, the light, decorative quality of the glass and cast-iron units was created not by applied ornamentation, but by the structure itself. Most significant was the use of relatively lightweight preformed *modules*–standard-size structural units repeated throughout the building. They provided enough flexibility for the entire structure to be assembled on the site, right over existing trees, and later disassembled and moved across town. Unfortunately, the building burned in 1936.

New building techniques and materials, as well as new functional needs, demanded a fresh approach to structure and form. The architects who met this challenge during the last one hundred years were articulate thinkers who developed a philosophy of architecture closely linked in their minds to social reform. The movement began to take shape in commercial architecture, became symbolized by the early skyscraper, and found one of its first opportunities in Chicago, where the big fire of 1871 had cleared the way for a new start.

In Henry Hobson Richardson's huge MARSHALL FIELD WHOLESALE STORE, the heavy, Romanesque character of its masonry exterior was pierced by superimposed window arcades reminiscent of Roman aqueducts. The thick walls carried their own weight, as did their ancient predecessors; but within the building, an iron skeleton supported the seven floors of the structure, which occupied an entire city block. The logical simplicity and strength of this building, with its opened vertical window bays, linked the beauty of ancient stone structures of the past with the uniquely modern architecture that was to follow.

The next major breakthrough in large-scale construction methods came between 1890 and 1910 with the development of structural steel, and steel as the reinforcing material in reinforced concrete. The extensive use of cast-iron skeletons in the mid-nineteenth century had prepared the way for *steel-cage construction* in the 1890s.

Leading the Chicago school was architect Louis Sullivan. He is regarded as the first great modern architect, because he rejected eclectic practices (borrowing of earlier styles) and made an all-out effort to meet the needs of the present by using building methods and materials made available by new technology. Sullivan had a major influence on the early development of what became the twentieth century's dominant architectural form: the skyscraper.

Sullivan's first "tall" building, the WAINWRIGHT BUILDING in St. Louis, Missouri, was made possible by the earlier invention of the elevator and the development of steel used for the structural skeleton. The building breaks with nineteenth-century tradition in a bold way. Its exterior design reflects the internal steel frame and emphasizes the height of the structure by underplaying horizontal elements in the central window area. Sullivan demonstrated his sensitivity and adherence to the harmony of traditional architecture by dividing the building's facade into three distinct zones, reminiscent of the base, shaft, and capital of the Greek column. These areas also reveal the various functions of the building, with shops at the base and offices in the central section. The heavily ornamented band cornice at the top acts as a capital, stopping the vertical thrust of the piers between the office windows. All of Sullivan's buildings bear his distinctive terra cotta ornamentation.

The interdependence of form and function is found in nature and well-designed human forms. Sullivan's observation that "form ever follows function"[2] eventually helped architects to break with the reliance on past styles and rethink architecture from the inside out, according to its purpose.

In this spirit, a new architecture arose in Europe between 1910 and 1930. It rejected decorative ornamentation, as well as traditional stone and wood construction, and broke away from the traditional idea of a building as a mass. The principles of cubist painting and especially the "pure" geometric planes of Mondrian's paintings (see page 399) greatly influenced what came to be called the *international style*.

301 Henry Hobson Richardson.
MARSHALL FIELD WHOLESALE STORE. Chicago. 1885–1887 (demolished in 1930).
Photograph: Barnes and Crosby (ICHi-19131), Chicago Historical Society.

302 Louis Sullivan.
WAINWRIGHT BUILDING. St. Louis. 1890–1891.

gained national recognition for his pastel drawings of highly stylized architectural fantasies. Now some of his fantasies are realities, and Graves is known as both a superstar and the *enfant terrible* of postmodernism. With colorful, idiosyncratic designs that evoke history, rather than imitate it, Graves has infused architecture with new life and interest. He seeks to replace modern-industrial with postmodern-heroic.

Reinforced concrete and steel have provided the raw materials for a variety of new structural forms. The giant roofs of Kenzo Tange's indoor stadiums, built in Tokyo for the 1964 Olympics, are hung from steel cables, using a suspension system of the type employed previously for bridge construction. Tange's two OLYMPIC STADIUMS are beautifully interrelated structures. The buildings reveal a unique harmony between spatial, structural, and functional requirements.

In the main building, which houses the swimming pools, Tange and structural engineer Yoshikatsu Tsuboi designed an interior space with seating for fifteen thousand. The vast open area under the roof was made possible by suspending the roof from cables strung from huge concrete abutments at either end of the building, rather than supporting the roof with interior columns. In spite of the structure's large size, the proportions of the smaller units to each other and to the entire building provide a sense of human scale. This is noticeable in the diving platforms, seats, and air conditioning vent pipes on the end wall, which are part of the unified, sculptural design.

The aerial view shows how the sweeping curves of the buildings unite the two structures and energize the spaces between and around them. The proportions of the many curves, both inside and out, give the complex a sense of graceful motion and balance. Balance in architecture

309   Kenzo Tange.
OLYMPIC STADIUMS.
Tokyo, Japan. 1964.

a. Exterior, natatorium.

b. Interior, natatorium.

c. Aerial view.

involves bringing actual opposing physical forces into equilibrium as well as working with a sense of visual stability.

Inventor, architect, and structural engineer R. Buckminster Fuller sought to bring about a new era when humanity would work together to preserve and enhance life on Earth. He pointed out that carefully guided technology can provide maximum benefit with minimum cost. Fuller put this concept to work when he developed the principles of the geodesic dome, inspired by polyhedrons found in nature. His goal was not to imitate nature, but to recognize and employ her principles. The strength of the geodesic dome makes it possible to enclose more space with less material than with any other structural system.

One of Fuller's domes can be erected from lightweight, inexpensive standardized parts in a very short time. Usually a skeleton is constructed of small, modular, linear elements joined together to form single planes; these, in turn, join together to form the surface of a dome, such as the U.S. PAVILION, EXPO-67. The resulting structure can be covered with a variety of materials to make the enclosed space weatherproof. In contrast to the relatively heavy supports used in traditional vaults and domes, the weight in Fuller's dome is carried by the entire structure, producing a high strength-to-weight ratio. Fuller's geodesic domes provide practical shelter and embody his goal of doing more with less. Geodesic domes have served a wide variety of functions, including housing, research facilities, and greenhouses.

Buckminster Fuller was one of the most forward-thinking men of our time. His ideas for better living and his numerous inventions suggest ways to solve immediate problems. Significantly, the physical projection of his thoughts reached far ahead into the future, yet were in harmony with structures in nature and in the human past.

The Kalapalo Indians of Brazil have traditionally built dome-like houses reminiscent of Fuller's domes. Over a period of months, saplings are curved and then fastened in an arc to giant posts. A single structure may house several families, each with its own space for hammocks and a cooking fire.

310 R. Buckminster Fuller.
U.S. PAVILION, EXPO-67. Montreal. 1967.
Photograph: © 1967 Dennis Stock/Magnum Photo, Inc., New York.

311 KALAPALO INDIANS HOUSE.
Aifa, central Brazil. 1967.
Photograph: Stan Wayman. Life Magazine © 1967, Time, Inc.

312   Frank Lloyd Wright.
KAUFMANN HOUSE. Bear Run, Pennsylvania. 1936.
Photograph: Thomas A. Heinz.

By necessity, the creators of indigenous architecture follow a principle of building in harmony with nature that relates to the concerns of both Fuller and his older contemporary, Frank Lloyd Wright. When Louis Sullivan was designing the Wainwright Building, Wright was his chief draftsman. Wright, who went on to become the most influential American architect of the twentieth century, was the first to use open planning in houses. In a break with the tradition of closed, box-like houses and rooms, Wright eliminated walls between rooms, enlarged windows, and discovered that the best way to open a box-like room was to place windows in corners. By so doing, he created flowing spaces that opened to the outdoors, welcomed natural light, and related houses to their sites and climates.

Major influences on today's domestic architecture came through Wright from Japan, where he lived from 1916 to 1922. He saw the asymmetrical balance, large extended eaves, and open plan of traditional Japanese houses as dynamic and more sensitive to nature than the often static, closed-box symmetry of Western homes.

When a beam or slab is extended a substantial distance beyond a supporting column or wall, the overhanging portion is called a *cantilever*. Before the use of steel and reinforced concrete, cantilevers were not used in any significant way, because available materials could not extend far enough to make it a viable concept. Early demonstrations of the possibilities of this structural idea include the extensive overhanging roof of Frank Lloyd Wright's ROBIE HOUSE on page 387, and the extended slab in Le Corbusier's drawing of 1914–1915 on page 232. One of the boldest and most elegant uses of the principle occurs in Wright's KAUFMANN HOUSE (also known as Falling Water) at Bear Run, Pennsylvania. Horizontal masses cantilevered from supporting piers echo the huge rock outcroppings and almost seem to float above the waterfall. The intrusion of building on such a unique and beautiful location seems justified by the harmony Wright achieved between the natural site and his equally inspiring architecture.

One of the first considerations an architect gives to any building is the relationship it will have to the site and its climate. Remmert W. Huygens's HOME IN WAYLAND, MASSACHUSETTS and Peter Jefferson's COTTAGE IN THE BAHAMAS were built to relate well to their climates and locations. The house in Massachusetts is comfortably enclosed against harsh winters. The house in the Bahamas is open in form and reaches out to allow the moderate weather to enter. In both, mass and space work together and with the surroundings to provide settings for enjoyable living.

The sharp increase in energy costs in recent years has motivated some architects to reexamine their design concepts. They began designing with nature, rather than striving to conquer it. After building up a mass of costly technology designed to shield us from climatic changes, they realized that energy-saving architecture can be designed to offer comfortable year-around temperatures by taking advantage of renewable energy sources. The need to find ways to conserve energy has led to a rediscovery of the logic of earlier indigenous structures.

313   Remmert W. Huygens.
HOME IN WAYLAND, MASSACHUSETTS.
Photograph: Phokion Karas.

314   Peter Jefferson.
COTTAGE IN THE BAHAMAS.
Photograph: Ezra Stoller © Esto.

315 INDIGENOUS ARCHITECTURE,
designed for various climates.

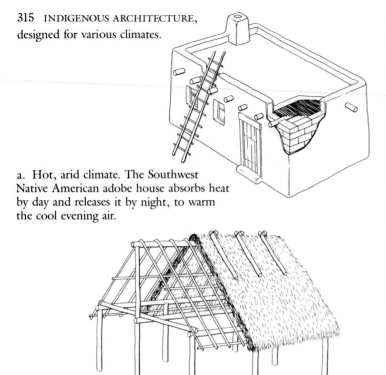

a. Hot, arid climate. The Southwest
Native American adobe house absorbs heat
by day and releases it by night, to warm
the cool evening air.

b. Hot, humid climate. The Seminole Indian
house in Florida permits air circulation and
lowers the humidity.

c. Cool climate. The Eskimo igloo's heat-saving
entrance and snow-block walls rely on the
insulating principle of trapped air.

For early societies, the sun was the only reliable source of heat. It was a matter of comfort and even survival to understand how to build in good relation to the sun and the daily and yearly warming and cooling cycles. The traditional adobe brick of the Southwest insulates against the extreme temperature changes of the desert. Thick adobe walls are the key to success for both ancient pueblo and some contemporary solar structures designed for the Southwest. New forms of regional architecture designed for spe-

cific climates and related to the dwellings of past societies are gradually being developed.

Houses based on the concept of using solar radiation from walls were first built in the late 1930s, but they collected too much heat by day and lost too much heat at night. This heat-storage problem is solved in David Wright's houses in which the masses of the buildings store solar heat and retain it for long periods with the help of full external insulation.

In 1979, David Wright designed a home called SUN CAVE, which was constructed near Santa Fe, New Mexico, by builder Karen Terry. It is an earth-sheltered house inspired by Southwest pueblo-style architecture, and based on the concept of a direct-gain *passive* (nonmechanical) solar heating system.

The entire house is a solar collector and heat-storage system. On sunny days, heat from the sun passes through south-facing double-glass windows and is absorbed by red-brick flooring and 12-inch-thick adobe walls. The floor is the primary heat-storage area. After absorbing heat during the day, both floor and walls radiate the collected heat during the night and during overcast periods of daylight. Air circulates naturally to counterbalance day and night and seasonal warming and cooling cycles. The building enclosure is capable of storing enough heat to keep the home comfortable for several sunless days. Cooling is provided by good cross ventilation. SUN CAVE comfortably handles temperature changes from below 0° F to 85° F with changes of as much as fifty degrees in a single twenty-four hour period. The success of this house is largely due to the simplicity of its design.

In the mid-nineteenth century, as people harnessed water power to run saw mills, production of precut, standardized lumber caused a revolution in home building. Lumber, plywood, wallboard, and window frames are now manufactured in standard sizes, and architects design with such sizes in mind. Cabinets, once handcrafted on the site, are now usually factory produced. Even an architect-designed, custom-built house such as SUN CAVE may contain many standardized components. Cost-cutting standardization is a major aspect in the transition of architecture from handcraft to industrial produc-

316 David Wright.
SUN CAVE. Santa Fe, New Mexico. 1979.

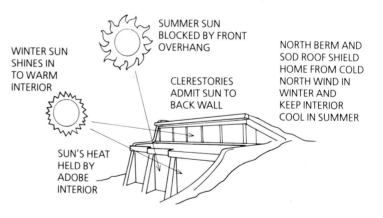

WINTER SUN
SHINES IN
TO WARM
INTERIOR

SUMMER SUN
BLOCKED BY FRONT
OVERHANG

CLERESTORIES
ADMIT SUN TO
BACK WALL

NORTH BERM AND
SOD ROOF SHIELD
HOME FROM COLD
NORTH WIND IN
WINTER AND
KEEP INTERIOR
COOL IN SUMMER

SUN'S HEAT
HELD BY
ADOBE
INTERIOR

tion. Prefabrication offers the best hope for meeting the urgent international need for low-cost, quality housing.

Our immediate environment has measurable effects on us. Therefore what we understand about architectural possibilities will make a difference in how we live. It is the goal of architects to design buildings that serve practical functions, and also offer inspiration and delight. Buildings enhance human life when they provide durable shelter, facilitate their intended function, complement their site, suit the climate, and stay within the limits of economic feasibility. The client who pays for the building and defines its function is as important to the outcome as the architect. The responsibility for good and bad building design belongs to both clients and architects; the level of understanding and communication between the two is crucial. Ultimately, the meaning and purpose of architecture is contained in the way it meets human physical, emotional, and spiritual needs.

322   Elliott Erwitt.
FREEWAY. 1968.
Photograph.

Cars beget highways and highways discourage alternate means of transportation in a vicious cycle. Suburban developments are annexed to cities seemingly overnight, creating rings of residential commuter towns for miles around city centers. Daly City is just one of thousands of places in which frantic growth has caused open space to be devoured by urban sprawl, with little thought to creating a life-enhancing environment.

Some environmental designers have suggested that we do not need concentrated urban forms: they no longer offer protection, they are not necessary for commerce, and they are hardly needed at all for communication. Others point out that dense urban complexes save agricultural, recreational, and wilderness land. Some suggest that the design of urban areas should take an even denser form than present zoning laws permit.

In 1922, Le Corbusier envisioned that constructing highrise apartment towers on urban land would open space for continuous park areas and make it possible to separate pedestrian space from automobile space. In his plan for a CITY OF THREE MILLION, housing was split between widely spaced tall towers at subway stops, and lowrise garden apartments. Industry was banished to the outskirts, and business was to be

323   Le Corbusier.
DRAWING FOR A CITY OF THREE MILLION. 1922.

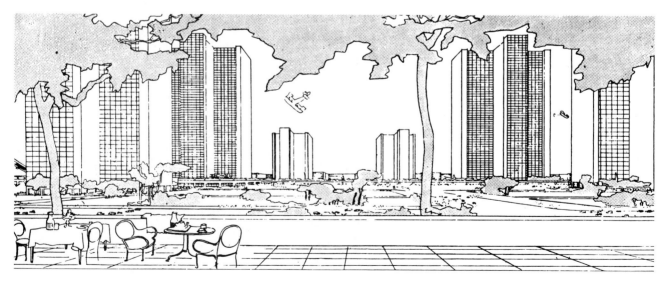

concentrated in towers at the center. Unfortunately, Le Corbusier's ideas led to the vast, dehumanized housing projects that have become places of crime and social decay. Individuals and families in these areas are caught in barren wastelands, cut off from those elements of cities that give identity and safety to traditional dwellings and neighborhoods.

The growth pattern that results from placing one house on one lot consumes enormous amounts of land. If the single-family house in suburbia is affordable, its location too often offers housing, but not jobs. Many suburban developments have not been planned to meet all the major needs of their residents. They are bedroom communities, which simply provide places to sleep and cause huge transportation, air pollution, and energy-consumption problems because residents are forced to commute daily to jobs in the city.

The planned town or community concept is one approach to minimizing consumption of land and retaining open green space. The idea involves concentrating people in specific communities capable of meeting all their basic daily needs, including stores, schools, services, and job opportunities. The best planned communities usually include apartments, townhouses, and cluster houses, with shared open space and extensive recreational facilities.

Columbia, Maryland, is one of many planned cities built since 1960 which initially have not been able to provide enough jobs. A percentage of Columbia residents commute to jobs in Baltimore or Washington, D.C. However, Columbia is gradually attracting corporations interested in moving away from high land costs in older cities, and relocating in or near the new community where land is cheaper and a labor force is nearby.

324 HYGIENIC APARTMENTS IN THE MAN-MADE DESERT.
Photograph: Orlando Cababan.

325 Downtown COLUMBIA, Maryland.
Photograph courtesy of the Rouse Company.

326   Moshe Safdie and David Barott. Boulva Associated Architects.
HABITAT '67. Montreal. 1967.

327   NORTH PUEBLO. Taos, New Mexico.
Photograph: Laura Gilpin.

Architect Moshe Safdie has designed new forms of stacked modular living units as an alternative to urban sprawl and highrise apartments crowded together. He is motivated by the idea that relatively low-cost housing can be designed to minimize land consumption, yet provide privacy and a sense of individual living units. This concept is related to traditional multi-unit structures in the Southwest that are energy efficient, climate-related, high-density communities surrounded by open space

Safdie's HABITAT '67, built for the World Exposition in Montreal in 1967, was his first demonstration of these concepts. He minimized costs by prefabricating apartment units in a factory and stacking them on the site. Although the components were standardized, they could be placed in a variety of configurations, thus keeping the total structure from becoming monotonous. The roof of one unit becomes the garden for another. Walkways and covered parking areas are included. The design allows for a dense concentration of people, yet provides many of the advantages of single, unattached dwellings. Much of Safdie's design philosophy is summarized in his phrase, "For everyone a garden."

The visionary drawings of Paolo Soleri portray total cities as single, self-contained structures. The Italian-born architect worked with and was highly influenced by Frank Lloyd Wright. In 1958, Soleri began to design multileveled buildings that he conceived as complete cities. His idea is to concentrate carefully planned, integrated cities in order to eliminate urban sprawl and its inevitable destruction of countryside. Soleri's ideas have had a wide influence on more conservative architects, planners, and urban designers who see promise in his consideration of inhabitants' work and social activities and his desire to disturb the natural environment as little as possible.

Soleri's ideas, such as the megastructure BABELDIGA, help to stimulate our thinking about alternatives to uncontrolled horizontal and vertical growth. Soleri uses the term *arcology* to describe his concept, which combines the ideals of architecture and ecology. His designs for vast self-sufficient communities are unique responses to problems of overpopulation and urban decay. To provide a sense of the scale of his thinking, Soleri included an outline of the Empire State Building on the right side of his drawing. A smaller version of his interconnected megastructure concept is slowly being built in the desert of Arizona by Soleri and his colleagues.

Changing the overall design of existing cities is economically impossible and in most cases undesirable. Yet relatively small changes within cities are going on all the time, with some sensitive blending of old and new. Often there has been no blend, and occasionally incredible confrontations occur between the old and the new. The sizes of many new buildings cause them to dwarf older, smaller structures.

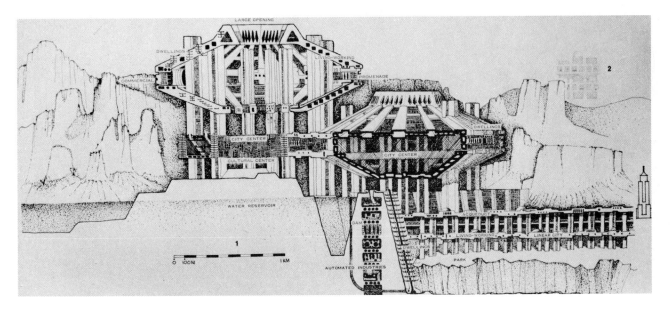

328 Paolo Soleri.
Drawing for BABELDIGA with Empire State Building.
1965.

329   Henry Hobson Richardson.
TRINITY CHURCH. 1877.
I. M. Pei and Partners.
JOHN HANCOCK TOWER. 1974.
Copley Square, Boston.
Photograph: © *Steve Rosenthal.*

The JOHN HANCOCK TOWER on Copley Square in Boston has been widely publicized because of safety problems resulting from falling glass window panels. Aside from that issue, many people find it offensive because of its dominating size and incompatibility with the styles of nearby older buildings. Others enjoy its monumental scale and the dramatic contrast of its sheer crystalline form with Henry Richardson's nineteenth-century TRINITY CHURCH. The upper part of the Hancock building reflects the sky and seems to dissolve into it, while the lower portion reflects the church.

The commercial development in BATTERY PARK CITY is a large complex built on a long-vacant section of landfill just west of the World Trade Center in Manhattan. The development was first conceived in 1966, but a series of changing plans and financing problems held up the project for over ten years. In 1979, the New York State Urban Development Corporation took over the project. Under its subsidiary, Battery Park City Authority, an unusual combination of city management and private investment was formed. As a first step, a master plan and urban design guidelines for the area were prepared by Cooper-Eckstut Associates. The plan, based on studies and comparative analysis, defined street patterns, building masses, public and private space, waterfront treatment, and connections and relationships to the adjoining section of lower Manhattan. Later, architect Cesar Pelli found the guidelines both helpful and time saving. Both the planner and architect made a conscious effort to relate the new complex to the older, nearby buildings, rather than to the tall box skyscrapers built in the 1950s, 1960s, and 1970s. The planners' guidelines specified that the buildings be stepped back at the third, ninth, and twenty-fourth floors to relate them both physically and symbolically to old, lower Manhattan building heights and profiles.

The postmodern BATTERY PARK commercial complex is built on fourteen of the ninety-two acres of the city within a city. It includes four tall office buildings and two lower domed, octagonal buildings, joined by a three acre tree-shaded plaza with a terrace that steps down to the Hudson River. The buildings have different

330 Cooper-Eckstut Associates and Cesar Pelli.
BATTERY PARK CITY. 1979–1987.
a. Aerial view.
Photograph: Philip Greenberg,
courtesy of Battery Park City Authority.
b. Detail of commercial complex. 1987.
Photograph: Duane Preble.

331 BACKYARD SLUM.
San Antonio River bank,
San Antonio, Texas.
c. 1935.

332 RIVER WALK,
SAN ANTONIO
RIVER PARK.
San Antonio, Texas.
c. 1969.
Photograph: Zintgraff, Inc.

tops and heights, but are unified by indentical granite and glass facades. The spectacular complex, with its mile-long waterfront walkway, is a landmark addition to New York City. It is also an unusual achievement of state and city management combined with private investment in a mutually beneficial partnership.

Lake and ocean shorelines, rivers, and streams are important natural resources communities can preserve and enjoy. Towns and cities all over the world have grown up beside waterways. The present city of San Antonio, Texas, began as a small settlement on the bank of the San Antonio River. As was customary at the time, the river functioned both as an upstream water source and downstream waste-disposal system. After a major flood in 1921, there was serious talk of enclosing the small river with concrete and making a street above it. Fortunately, a flood-prevention plan was begun instead, and by 1938 the full aesthetic potential of the river was recognized. Citizens and government officials worked with landscape architect Robert H. H. Hugman to transform what had become a backyard slum into a frontyard garden and riverfront linear park. Arched bridges augment the natural beauty of the river, and walkways, restaurants, and boating facilities line its banks. The river park area has become a major income-producing attraction for residents and tourists alike.

Generations ago, many towns were built around an open area known as the village square or common. Most of our cities have sizeable parks, established long ago by citizens and planners who recognized the need for open green space within a metropolitan area. As cities continue to increase in size and population, the need for park space grows; yet land in cities becomes ever more expensive. The concept of small or "vest-pocket" parks has evolved to meet this need in a practical way. Such parks can be sprinkled liberally throughout the city. When an old building is torn down, a tiny park can be built on a single lot that is too small to allow for substantial new construction. In business districts, such parks provide refuge for workers and tired shoppers (see GREENACRE PARK, page 23). In residential areas, they provide recreational and play areas easily accessible to nearby residents.

The city of Davis, California, has placed linear parks within the community. They pass under streets and thus provide people with easy, safe access to shopping, recreational areas, and schools along pleasant pathways.

Urban renewal once meant the wholesale demolition of neighborhoods. But in recent years, economic factors as well as social concerns have led away from this idea. The concept of *historic preservation* includes the restoration and reuse of old buildings to preserve the character of existing neighborhoods. Buildings may serve the same purposes for which they were originally designed; many times, however, the intended functions are no longer viable, so such structures are converted to meet current needs. Many fine old buildings have already been destroyed simply because people in positions to take action were unable to visualize each building's potential.

333 M. Paul Friedberg and Associates.
LEFFERTS PLACE PARK.
Brooklyn, New York. 1963.
Photograph courtesy M. Paul Friedberg and Partners.

334 LINEAR PARK WITH BIKEWAY.
Davis, California. 1977.
Photograph: Alison Portello.

335   ICE HOUSE I. San Francisco, California. Built 1914, restored 1969 and 1986.
a. Interior.
b. Exterior.

Some old buildings have been converted to restaurants and shops, others are used for apartments and offices. The old icehouses in San Francisco, which in the nineteenth century provided storage for natural ice brought in from Alaska by ship, have been converted for office use. The Harper & Row office in ICEHOUSE 1 was designed to expose the dramatic inner structure of the building, and to provide modern, practical working space. Nearby new buildings were designed to harmonize with the icehouses and other early buildings in the neighborhood. The preservation and restoration of significant old buildings help give continuity and a sense of identity to cities.

Environmental designers help establish and work within *zoning laws* that determine land use and population density through open-space requirements; and by such restrictions as height limits on buildings and *set-back* laws, which establish the distance a building must be from property lines. Visual contact with natural and manufactured features can be preserved or created through *view corridors* and *view planes*. A band of continuous parks, farmland, or wilderness areas called a *greenbelt* may be designated or developed at the edge of a city as a boundary or planned stopping point to keep the city to its optimum size, and to prevent haphazard urban growth from spreading into rural and nearby communities areas.

Environmental design specialists often work with community groups during the process of making design decisions. Citizens who live in areas under consideration for development or change are increasingly asking to become involved in what is called *participatory planning*. Their ideas and feelings are often very important to the success of the final projects or plans in both environmental planning and design. Even the best design professionals cannot, and should not, solve environmental problems alone. Success or failure of their efforts is often determined as much by economic, political and social forces, as by the quality of environmental design plans.

PART FOUR

Art of the Past

To me there is no past or future in art. If a work of art cannot live always in the present it must not be considered at all. The art of the Greeks, of the Egyptians, of the great painters who lived in other times, is not an art of the past; perhaps it is more alive today than it ever was. Art does not evolve by itself, the ideas of people change and with them their mode of expression.

Pablo Picasso[1]

MAYAN MAN AND WOMAN.
(See page 284.)

353 EARTHENWARE ARMY OF THE FIRST EMPEROR
OF QIN. Xian, China. c. 210 B.C.
Terra cotta. Life size.
a. Detail of cavalryman and saddle horse.
*Photograph: Cultural Relics Bureau, Beijing, and
Metropolitan Museum of Art, New York.*
b. Excavation view.
Photograph: Overseas Archaeological Exhibition Corporation, Beijing.

have a style-less realism. Traces of color that remain on the surface indicate that the figures were
realistically painted in full detail. The heads, including hairstyles and facial features, as well as
clothing, were carefully individualized. The desire for realism came from the function of the
figures. This vast retinue was made to substitute
for living soldiers and animals, who, in earlier
times, would have been buried alive with the
ruler when he died.

Recent excavations of Han dynasty tombs have
revealed more aesthetically rewarding figures, including the magnificent second-century FLYING
HORSE found at Wu-Wei in Kansu. The sculptor gave a feeling of weightlessness to the horse
by delicately balancing it on one hoof atop a

354 FLYING HORSE. Wu-Wei. Han dynasty, 2nd century. Bronze. 13½″ × 17¾″.

flying swallow. The elegant horse is typically Chinese in its dynamic, curvaceous form and powerful vitality.

Through most of Chinese history, animals have been the preferred subject for sculptors. Aside from tomb figures, the early Chinese were reluctant to represent the human body in art. When a period of major sculpture based on the human figure did develop in China, it came with

355 SEATED GUAN YIN (KUAN YIN).
Song (Sung) dynasty, c. 12th century.
Wood covered with gesso. Height 55½".
Museum of Fine Arts, Boston. Harvey Edward Wetzel Fund.

the introduction of Buddhism. Chinese artists adopted the idealized, sacred images of India with only minor changes. Some of the finest figures are those which express Buddhist compassion. They are known as Avalokitesvara in India, Guan Yin (Kuan Yin) in China, and Kwannon in Japan. The gentle smile and relaxed posture of the GUAN YIN symbolize kindness, patience, and wisdom.

Chinese painting and sculpture reveal an attitude of reverence for nature. Traditionally, the aim of Chinese painting has been to manifest the spirit residing in every form. The painter was advised to meditate before wielding a brush, in order to achieve a balance between the impression received through the eyes and the perception of the mind. Through the art of painting, individuals nourished spiritual harmony within themselves and revealed the creative power of divine energy to others.

About the eleventh century, a gradual shift occurred in the function and meaning of painting in China. The new ideas that brought about change came from a group of artists of the Northern Sung period, who were among the intellectual elite of China. Artistic expression of their ideals is known as *literati painting.* The concepts came, in part, from calligraphy, which has long been greatly valued in China, and is still considered a higher art than painting. Literati painters drew inspiration from poet, statesman, and master calligrapher Wang Hsi-chih.

A key idea held that the artist's true character and personal emotions could be expressed through the abstract forms of calligraphic characters, and even through individual brush strokes. Literati painters sought to elevate painting to the levels that calligraphy and poetry had attained, by introducing calligraphic techniques for expressive purposes. These gentlemen painters also held that there does not need to be a connection between the expressive and the representational content of a work of art. Many of the early literati painters were both political leaders and accomplished calligraphers. They were critical of those who painted for commercial rather than aesthetic reasons.

Mi Fei was one of the first literati painters to paint landscapes, but few, if any, of his paintings have survived (see page 70).

For centuries, traditional Chinese painters have spent years copying the works of earlier artists in order to assimilate fully the rich tradition they inherited. It was common to base a composition on the work of an earlier painter, but the artist was also expected to add an individual interpretation to the traditional theme.

The brushwork used for both written characters and painted subjects was highly developed, and the artists often included poems within the paintings. Painting and writing complement each other in both form and content; whether written or painted, each brushstroke was considered important in the total design. Artists used many different kinds of brushstrokes, and identified them by descriptive names such as "raveled rope," "raindrops," "ax cuts," "nailhead," and "wrinkles on a devil's face."

After prolonged contemplation of nature, the artist produced the painting from memory. Paintings were executed with ink and light color on silk or paper, using watercolor technique.

The Song (Sung) dynasty court painter Fan Kuan was regarded by his contemporaries as the greatest landscape painter of the period. In his large hanging scroll TRAVELERS AMONG MOUNTAINS AND STREAMS (see next page), the intricate brushwork captures the spirit of trees and rocks. "Raindrop" and other types of brushstrokes emphasize the texture of the vertical face of the cliff. Men and donkeys in minute scale travel a horizontal path dwarfed by high cliffs rising sharply behind them. The artist painted the waterfall using a wash technique, with the white of the water suggested by the off-white color of the unpainted silk. The vertical emphasis of the composition is set off by the almost-horizontal shape of the light area behind the rocks in the lower foreground. Rising mists are suggested at the base of the cliffs that divide the composition into lower one-third and upper two-thirds.

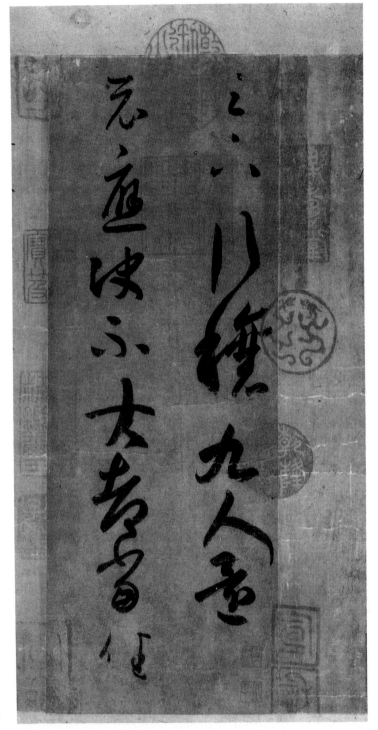

356 Hsing-jang t'ieh. Detail of early T'ang tracing copy of a letter written by Wang Hsi-chih. 4th century. Letter mounted as a handscroll, ink on *ying-huang* paper. 24.4 cm × 8.9 cm. *The Art Museum, Princeton University. Anonymous loan (L.1970.175).*

357 Fan Kuan (Fan K'uan).
TRAVELERS AMONG MOUNTAINS AND STREAMS.
Early 11th century.
Hanging scroll, ink on silk. Height 81¼".
National Palace Museum, Taipei, Taiwan.

When a vertical line intersects a horizontal line, the opposing forces generate a visual attraction that acts as a strong center of interest. Fan Kuan took advantage of this phenomenon by extending the implied vertical line of the upper falls to bring attention to the travelers.

Figures give human significance to the painting and, by their small scale, indicate the vastness of nature. Effectiveness of the monumental landscape is achieved by grouping the fine details into a balanced design of light and dark areas.

The painting embodies philosophical ideas of Daoism and Neo-Confucianism, which see nature as both emptiness and substance, interacting passive and active forces (*yin* and *yang*) which regulate the universe. When humans have humility, they are in harmony with these universal forces.

Though mountains in many Chinese paintings may appear to us to be fantastic inventions, in both central and southern China steep, mist-shrouded peaks such as Huangshan Mountain have inspired Chinese painters for centuries. In the seventeenth century, Li Li-Weng wrote, "First we see the hills in the painting, then we see the painting in the hills." This statement reminds us that, although art depends on our perception of nature, we often perceive nature with heightened awareness inspired by art.

Northern Song (Sung) literati painters helped prepare the way for another school of painting, which flourished in Buddhist monasteries. Chan (as Zen Buddhism is called in China) painters in the thirteenth century developed a bold style that used abbreviated, abstract references. Compared to the detailed representation in Fan Kuan's TRAVELERS AMONG MOUNTAINS AND STREAMS, the priest Yu-Jian's painting of MOUNTAIN VILLAGE IN A MIST shows a simplified, gestural impression of a landscape. In this painting, the relationship of human beings to nature is again expressed with figures and barely suggested roof lines in an atmosphere of mist-obscured mountains. The white, unpainted surface is as visually strong as the brushwork. Fan Kuan's painting is descriptive and formal, while Yu-Jian's is suggestive and informal.

雨
花
雲
脖
欲
長
沙
隱
隱
殘
虹
帶
晚
霞
最
好
市
橋
官
柳
外
酒
旗
摇
曳
弄
思
家
山
市
晴
嵐

358 Yu-Jian (Yü-Chien). MOUNTAIN VILLAGE IN A MIST.
13th century.
Ink on paper.
Idemitsu Museum of Arts, Tokyo.

Before the twentieth century, no European or American artist would have left such large areas unpainted. Traditional Chinese painters, however, see space as a ground of possibilities, as positive rather than negative. Forms are suspended, as in Yu-Jian's painting. They emerge and vanish in ambiguous ways. Here the paper refers to sky, clouds, or mist, implying that what cannot be seen at this moment will appear at another moment and then disappear again. Chinese philosophy emphasizes the changing, interactive nature of thing-ness and no-thing-ness.

The same area of silk or paper that can stand for sky or clouds can also be a surface to write upon, as in the left side of MOUNTAIN VILLAGE IN A MIST. Brush marks that indicate the landscape are expected to evoke a remembered experience rather than present what the eyes see. The accompanying writing is a poem that also stimulates the memory image. The poem and the painting are parallel expressions. Such a spontaneous painting was to have great influence on later Japanese Zen painters of the "splash-ink school."

The practice of adding inscriptions to paintings beyond dates and signatures reached maturity with the literati painters of the thirteenth and fourteenth centuries, and has continued in Chinese painting.

359 HUANGSHAN MOUNTAIN AFTER A RAIN. c. 1980.
Photograph.

Dragons are another major motif in Chinese art. In Christian art, the dragon is usually a symbol of evil forces; but for the Chinese it is a symbol of vitality associated with the sun, water, storms, and the power of Heaven, or the Spirit. In spite of its ferocious appearance, the dragon has long been regarded as a beneficial power.

Chen Rong (Ch'en Jung), China's best-known painter of dragons, had an unusual technique. According to contemporary accounts, Chen Rong began by blocking in areas of tonal contrast with a cloth dipped in ink. He then used a brush to paint dragons, clouds, water, and rocks. He added texture to the surface by snapping the end of his brush to splatter ink over the painting. Forms emerge and disappear in swirls of ink that represent clouds, water, or mist, evoking the mysterious world of dragons. The dragons in the NINE DRAGONS scroll show a marvelous blend of ferocious energy, cunning, and playful—even friendly—beneficence.

JAPAN

Nature worship, a major practice in ancient Japan, became known as Shinto, the indigenous or native religion. Forests and huge stones were considered holy places where gods dwelled. The Shinto shrines at Ise are on one such site. The present MAIN SHRINE AT ISE has been completely and exactly rebuilt every twenty years since the seventh century. Builders take wood for the shrine from the forest with gratitude and ceremonial care. As a tree is cut into boards, the boards are numbered so that the wood that was one in the tree is reunited in the building. No nails are used; the wood is fitted and pegged. Surfaces are left unpainted in keeping with the Shinto concept of purity. The shrines at Ise combine simplicity with subtlety. Refined craftsmanship, sculptural proportions, and spatial harmonies express the ancient religious and aesthetic values of Shinto.

In a wave of cultural borrowing more than a thousand years ago, the Japanese imported elements that are major factors in Japanese society today. Included are Buddhism, the Chinese

360 Chen Rong (Ch'en Jung).
Detail of NINE DRAGONS. Mid-13th century.
Handscroll, ink on paper. Height 46.3 cm.
Museum of Fine Arts, Boston. Francis Gardner Curtis Fund.

361 MAIN SHRINE. Ise, Japan. c. 685, rebuilt every twenty years.

362 Unkei.
Detail of MUCHAKU. c. 1208.
Wood. Height 75″.
Kofuku-ji Temple, Nara, Japan.

writing system, and the art and architecture of Tang dynasty (seventh to tenth centuries) China.

Buddhism came to Japan by way of Korea in the sixth century. The subsequent conversion to Buddhism stimulated an outpouring of art. One of the greatest Buddhist artists of Japan was the sculptor Unkei. His portrait-like sculpture of MUCHAKU, a legendary Indian priest, was made of blocks of wood that were joined, carved, and painted to produce a feeling of life-like realism. The sculpture by Unkei is one of the relatively few naturalistic figures known in Asia in which the force of individual personality is used to portray spiritual values. MUCHA-KU's face expresses the sublime tranquility sought in Buddhism.

Zen Buddhism, which spread to Japan in the fourteenth century, provided a philosophical basis within which aesthetic activities were given meaning beyond their physical form. A Zen in-fluence on Japanese aesthetics has continued in poetry, calligraphy, painting, flower arranging, and tea ceremony. The Zen Buddhist priest Ses-shū is considered the foremost Japanese master of ink painting. In 1467, he made a trip to China where he studied the works of Southern Song (Sung) masters, and saw the countryside that in-

spired them. Chinese Zen paintings such as Mu Qi's SIX PERSIMMONS (page 62) and Yu-Jian's MOUNTAIN VILLAGE IN A MIST were greatly admired, and many were brought to monasteries in Japan.

Sesshū adapted the Chinese style and set the standard in ink painting for later Japanese artists. He painted in two styles. The first was formal and complex, while the second was a simplified, somewhat explosive style, which came to be called *haboku*, meaning "flung ink." HABOKU LANDSCAPE is abstract in its simplification of forms and freedom of brushwork. Mountains and trees are suggested with single, soft brush strokes. The sharp lines in the center foreground indicating a fisherman, and the vertical line above the rooftops in the distance representing the staff of a wine shop, are in contrast to the thin washes and darker accents of the suggested landscape.

In THE FIST THAT STRIKES THE MASTER, Zen monk Sengai illustrated the story of a Zen priest, Rinzai, who found enlightenment and struck his teacher. Rinzai's gesture was not in anger or frustration, but was an intuitive expression of new insight. Sengai's brush drawing was made in the spirit of this event.

Many Japanese artists used the format of horizontal handscrolls (thought to have originated in China) as a way of leading the viewer on a journey through landscape. Some scrolls measure as long as 50 feet, and all were meant to be seen, a small section at a time, by only two or three people. In Japan, the handscroll was also used for landscape and was found particularly advantageous for long narrative compositions that depict the passage of time. BURNING OF THE SANJO PALACE is from HEIJI MONOGATARI, a scroll that describes the Heiji insurrection of 1159. We can understand this vivid scene without knowing the incident it depicts.

363   Sesshū.
HABOKU LANDSCAPE. 15th century.
Hanging scroll, ink on paper. 28⅚" × 10½".
Cleveland Museum of Art. The Norweb Collection (CMA 55.43).

As the scroll is unrolled from right to left, the viewer is enticed into following a succession of events expertly designed to tell the story. The horror and excitement of the action are connected through effective visual transitions. The story builds from simple to complex events, reaching a dramatic climax in the scene of the burning palace. This is one of the most effective depictions of fire in the history of art. The color of the flames emphasizes the excitement of the historic struggle. Use of parallel diagonal lines and shapes to indicate the palace walls adds to the sense of motion and provides a clear geometric structure in the otherwise frantic activity of this portion of the scroll. Compare this depiction of fire with Turner's BURNING OF THE HOUSES OF PARLIAMENT (page 129). Today such epic drama would be presented through film or television.

Folding screens provide functional art in sparsely furnished Japanese interiors. Artists have been highly original in the ways they used the unique spatial properties of the screen format.

364 Sengai.
THE FIST THAT STRIKES
THE MASTER. c. 1800.
Ink on paper.
41.3 cm. × 27.8 cm.
*Idemitsu Museum of Arts,
Tokyo.*

365 BURNING OF THE SANJO PALACE, from HEIJI
MONOGATARI. 13th century.
Section of the handscroll, ink and color on paper.
Height 43.3 cm.
Museum of Fine Arts, Boston. Fenollosa-Weld Collection.

366　Anonymous. TAGASODE.
Painted screen.
Courtesy of the Freer Gallery of Art, Smithsonian Institution,
Washington, D.C. (07.127).

367　Tawaraya Sōtatsu.
WAVES AT MATSUSHIMA. Early 17th century.
Painted screen, paper. Each panel 59⅞″ × 141¼″.
Courtesy of the Freer Gallery of Art, Smithsonian Institution,
Washington, D.C. (06.231).

Often, natural subjects are portrayed life-size. The strong, environmentally affecting presence of a painted screen within the living space of a home is quite different from the window-onto-nature quality of a post-Renaissance European easel painting. The usefulness of a screen is portrayed on the screen known as TAGASODE.

Tawaraya Sōtatsu's large screen painting WAVES AT MATSUSHIMA consists of a pair of six-panel folding screens. (Only one is shown here.) The screens are designed so that together, or separately, they are complete compositions.

In keeping with well-established Japanese artistic practices, Sōtatsu created a composition charged with the churning action of waves, yet as solid and permanent in its design as the rocky crags around which the waters leap and churn. He translated his loving awareness of natural phenomena into a decorative, abstract design. Spatial ambiguity in the sky and water areas suggests an interaction that is to be felt, rather than read as a literal transcription of nature. Boldly simplified shapes and lines are balanced by highly refined details and eye-catching surprises. Rhythmic patterns fill much of the surface. A flat, horizontal gold shape in the upper left, accentuated with a black line, signifies a cloud and also reaffirms the picture plane. The strongly asymmetrical design, emphasis on repeated patterns, and relatively flat spatial quality are all typical of much Japanese painting from the sixteenth to the nineteenth centuries.

By the mid-seventeenth century, the art of woodcut printing had developed to meet the demand for pictures by the newly prosperous merchant class. Japanese artists took the Chinese woodcut technique and turned it into a popular art form. For the next two hundred years, hundreds of thousands of these prints were produced. The prints are called *Ukiyo-e*, which means "floating world." They depict scenes of daily life, particularly as it was lived in the entertainment centers of the time.

Kitagawa Utamaro's woodcut of a woman looking at herself in a mirror transforms an ordinary subject into a memorable image based on bold, curving outlines and flat shapes. The center of interest is the reflected face of the woman,

368 Kitagawa Utamaro.
REFLECTED BEAUTY, from the series
SEVEN WOMEN SEEN IN A MIRROR. c. 1790.
Color woodblock print. 14¼″ × 9½″.
Honolulu Academy of Arts. Gift of James A. Michener.

369 KATSURA DETACHED PALACE. Kyoto, Japan.
17th century.
a. Gardens and Teahouse.
Photograph courtesy of Kenzo Yamamoto.
b. Aerial view.
Photograph courtesy of Obayashi-Gumi Construction Company.

set off by the strong curve representing the mirror's edge. Consistent with much of Japanese art, no shadows are indicated. The figure is thrust in from the right and cut off by the edge of the picture, rather than presented completely within the frame as in traditional European painting.

Japanese architects have also demonstrated sensitive orchestration of clearly defined forms. KATSURA PALACE, a seventeenth-century Japanese imperial villa, was built in Kyoto beside the Katsura River, the waters of which were diverted into the garden to form ponds. Land, water, rocks, and plants were integrated in a design that blends handcrafted and natural elements. The walls of the palace support no weight. They are sliding screens, which allow flexibility between interior and exterior spaces.

KATSURA is very humble when compared to VERSAILLES, another seventeenth-century imperial villa (see page 340). Unlike VERSAILLES, the KATSURA PALACE complex was planned with no grand entrances either to the grounds or to the buildings. Rather, one approaches the palace along garden paths. As one proceeds along the paths, unexpected views open up. Earth contours, stones, and waterways are combined to symbolize—on a small scale—mountains, rivers, fields, inlets, and beaches. The tea house, which imitates the traditional Japanese farm house, is constructed of common, natural materials. It provides the appropriate setting for the tea ceremony, which embodies the attitudes of simplicity, naturalness, and humility that permeate the entire palace grounds.

Domestic architecture has long been an important part of Japanese art. Modest houses, palaces, and Buddhist temples have traditionally employed many of the structural and aesthetic principles of Shinto shrines. In the past, Japanese homes were related to the land, and were usually set in or built around a garden. The gardens provided intimacy with natural beauty even in crowded city environments.

Traditional Japanese houses are built of wood using post-and-beam construction. The result is essentially a roof on posts, which frees walls to be sliding screens rather than supports. The Japanese use of unpainted wood and the concept of spatial flow between indoors and outdoors have had major influences on twentieth-century architects in the West. In fact, traditional Japanese sensitivity to designs that relate well to nature has produced a variety of art forms with broad international appeal.

370   INTERIOR OF A TRADITIONAL JAPANESE HOUSE. *Photograph: Francis Haar.*

371   MAYAN MAN AND WOMAN. Mexico. c. 700.
Buff clay with traces of color. 10½″ × 5¾″ × 3⅜″.
Honolulu Academy of Arts. Purchase.

NATIVE AMERICA

At the end of the last glacial age, while the cultures of India and China were emerging from the Neolithic stage, parallel developments were taking place in Central and South America. The major societies of this region were the Mayan, the Aztec, and the Inca.

The Mayans, who lived in what are now parts of Mexico, Guatemala, and Honduras, developed a written language, an elaborate calendar, advanced mathematics, and large temple complexes of stone. Mayans also made fine ceramic vessels and sculpture. Figures such as MAYAN MAN AND WOMAN stress body volume, natural gestures, and costume detail.

The hundreds of stone temples at Tikal suggest that Mayan priests had great power. TEMPLE 1 was built during the classical Mayan period, A.D. 300–900. It and others like it rise over a great plaza in a Guatemalan rain forest. The 200-foot-high pyramid has a temple at the top which consists of three rooms. Another Mayan temple pyramid contained a burial cham-

372   TEMPLE 1. Tikal, Guatemala. c. 300–900.
Photograph: Hans Namuth.

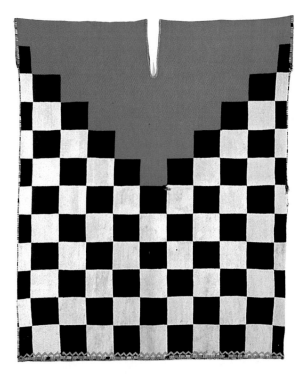

373 INCA SHIRT. Peru. c. 1438–1532.
Tapestry weave in alpaca wool. 34″ × 31″.

374 INCA STONE WALLS.
Photograph: © *Mario Fantin 1973.*

ber deep inside, similar to those found in Egyptian pyramids. Walls and roofs of Mayan stone temples were richly carved and painted.

In the Andes of South America, Inca culture flourished for several centuries prior to the Spanish conquest in 1532. The Incas made outstanding fabrics and metal objects. Although we have contemporary reports of their beauty, few remain; most Inca goldwork was taken by the Spanish and melted for reuse. Inca weaving is typified by rich color and geometric patterns such as those found in this sleeveless shirt.

The Incas are perhaps best known as supreme masters of shaping and fitting stone. Their masonry is characterized by mortarless joints and the "soft" rounded faces of granite blocks. It is believed that each stone was somehow placed in a sling and swung against the adjoining stones until the surfaces were ground to a precise fit. MACHU PICCHU, "the lost city of the Incas," was built on a ridge in the eastern Andes, in what is now Peru, at an elevation of 8,000 feet. The city, which escaped Spanish detection, was planned and constructed in such a way that it seems to be part of the mountain.

375 MACHU PICCHU. Peru. Early 16th century.
Photograph: Ewing Krainen.

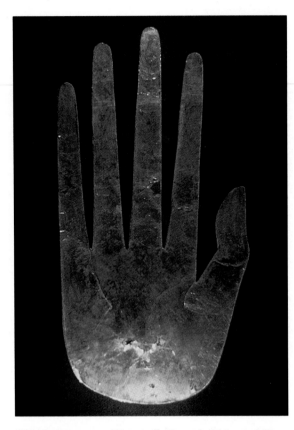

376   MICA HAND. Hopewell Mound, Ohio. c. 150.
Ohio Historical Society, Columbus, Ohio.

The native art of North America has received less attention than that of the urban cultures of Central and South America. At one time there were great numbers of North American tribes, each with its own unique culture and style of art. Only a handful of these societies survive today.

The MICA HAND found in a Hopewell burial mound has a striking, abstract quality. The Hopewell culture flourished from the second century B.C. to the sixth century A.D. Large burial mounds, most of which were built in what is now Ohio, contained rich offerings placed in elaborate log tombs. Hopewell artists included wood and stone carvers, potters, coppersmiths, and specialists who worked in shell and mica.

Pueblo Indian tribes of the Southwest have been among the few native American groups to succeed in keeping their cultures alive. Most Pueblo tribes recognize the spirits of invisible life forces. These spirits, known as Kachinas, are impersonated by masked and costumed male members of the tribes who visit the villages in

a variety of forms including birds, animals, clowns, and demons. During ceremonies they dance, give kachina dolls to delighted children, provide humor, and occasionally give public scoldings. The carved and painted dolls are made by Hopi and Zuni fathers and uncles as a means of teaching children their sacred traditions.

Much of what we know of Native American art is in the form of vessels (see the modern Acoma pottery on page 193). Before their cultures and most of their people were destroyed, native Americans of the Pacific Coast region produced some of the world's finest baskets. Pomo artists in northern California made baskets of such incredible tightness that they could hold

377   Marshall Lomakema.
HOPI KACHINA. 1971. Painted wood.
Courtesy of Museum of the American Indian, Heye Foundation, New York.

378   POMO FEATHER BASKET.
California. c. 1945.
3¼″ × 13½″.
Courtesy of the Southwest Museum, Los Angeles.

379   POMO STORAGE BASKET.
California. 19th century.
Coiled basketry. 13½″ × 21″.
*Courtesy of Museum of the American Indian,
Heye Foundation, New York.*

water. There was great variety in size, shape, and decoration—from large containers up to four feet in diameter to tiny gift baskets less than a quarter of an inch across. Pomos wove strong geometric designs into many of their baskets, and used ornaments such as feathers and shells to embellish others. Women were responsible for the highest artistic achievements in Pomo culture—the brightly colored feathered baskets. These treasured objects were made as gifts designed solely to delight the eye.

Northwest Coast tribes had highly imaginative arts related to their mythology. Tlingit and other Northwest Coast tribes are known for elegant and sophisticated abstractions of animal subjects. Their painted relief carvings are reminiscent of the abstract animal forms found on ancient Chinese bronzes (see page 269). On house walls, boxes, and blankets, major features of a totemic animal form are laid out in two-dimensional schematic patterns. The rounded shapes of totemic animals are presented in integrated symmetrical designs.

The TLINGIT COMMUNITY HOUSE is characteristic of the art and architecture of the region. Tlingit totem poles are shorter and thinner than those of other Northwest tribes, and combine original design elements with those borrowed from neighboring tribes.

380   TLINGIT COMMUNITY HOUSE.
Ketchikan, Alaska.
Photograph: Steve McCutcheon.

381   CANOE PROW FIGURE.
Maravo Lagoon, New Georgia,
Solomon Islands. Collected 1929.
Wood with mother-of-pearl.
Height 6½″.
Basel Museum, Basel, Switzerland.

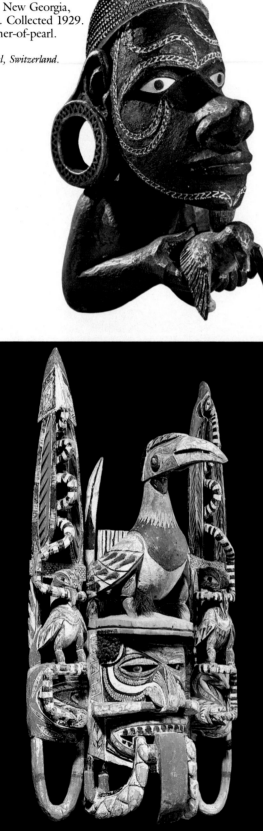

OCEANIA

Oceania is the collective name for thousands of Pacific islands. The term usually excludes the islands of Japan, Taiwan, the Philippines, and Indonesia, whose cultures are closely related to mainland Asia. The islands of Oceania are divided ethnologically and geographically into groups comprising Melanesia, Micronesia, and Polynesia. It is difficult and misleading to generalize about Oceanic art, because the cultures, physical environments, and raw materials vary greatly over an enormous area.

Oceanic peoples developed very little pottery due to a shortage of clay, and metal was unknown until it was introduced by traders in the eighteenth century. They used stone, bone, or shell for tools, and wood, bark, and small plants for houses, canoes, mats, and cloth. Feathers, bone, and shells were employed for utensils and sculpture, as well as for personal adornment.

In the Solomon Islands and New Ireland, part of Melanesia, wood-carvings and masks are designed to serve ritual purposes. In the art of many nonliterate societies, birds appear with human figures to act as guides or messengers between the physical world of the living and the spiritual world of deceased ancestors. The bird in the CANOE PROW FIGURE from the Solomon Islands seems to guide voyagers by acting as a protective spirit, watching out for shoals and reefs. The carving is only 6½ inches high, but it looks much larger because of the boldness of its form. Exaggerated nose and jaw help give the head its forward thrust. The wood is blackened and inlaid with mother-of-pearl, which provides white shapes for the eyes and forms the rhythmically curving linear ZZZ bands that unify the design. Like the Chinese bronze vessel on page 269, it expresses faith in the symbolic, protective power of art.

In New Ireland, masks are made for funerary rites that commemorate tribal ancestors, both real and mythical. Each of the colorfully painted

382   MASK. New Ireland. c. 1920.
Painted wood, vegetable fiber, shell. 94 cm. × 53 cm.
UCLA Museum of Cultural History, Los Angeles.

masks represents a specific ancestor. In this mask, the elaborately carved openwork panels are painted in strong patterns that establish large and small rhythms accentuating—and at times opposing—the dynamic forms of the carving. Snail-shell eyes give the mask an intense expression. As in the Solomon Islands CANOE PROW FIGURE, a bird is featured.

In contrast to the art of Melanesia, the works made in Micronesia and much of Polynesia are streamlined and highly finished. The Kapingamarangi COCONUT GRATER shows a fine integration of form and function. One sits on the "saddle" of the animal-like form, and grates coconuts using the serrated blade at its head. The angle and placement of the blade are important to the efficient removal of meat from nut halves. The STANDING FIGURE from Nukuoro Island has the same distinctive spare quality. Although both Kapingamarangi and Nukuoro are in the southern part of Micronesia, they are culturally Polynesian.

Polynesia covers a large, triangular section of the Pacific from New Zealand to Hawaii to Easter Island. It is not surprising that the widely separated Polynesian islands and island groups developed greatly varied arts. These include both delicate and boldly patterned bark cloth, feather-work, shell-work, wood-carvings, and huge rock-carvings. The rich color and stunning designs of Hawaiian feather helmets and cloaks are among the world's most magnificent royal attire. Captain James Cook (the first European to "discover" the Hawaiian Islands) described Hawaiian featherworks as comparable to "the thickest and richest velvet which they resemble both as to the feel and the glossy appearance."[1] In this FEATHER CAPE, geometric figure and ground shapes are in pleasing relationship to one another as well as to the overall shape of the cape.

384 COCONUT GRATER.
Kapingamarangi, Caroline Islands. 1954.
Wood with shell blade attached
with sennet. Height 17″.
Private collection.

383 STANDING FIGURE.
Nukuoro Atoll, Caroline
Islands. Probably 19th century.
Wood. Height 15⁹/₁₆″.
Honolulu Academy of Arts. Exchange.

385 FEATHER CAPE. Hawaii. 18th century.
Network with feathers knotted into the mesh.
Height 4′1″.
British Museum, London.

AFRICA

The traditional arts of black Africa are extremely varied. Most tribal styles are highly abstract, but some groups have produced naturalistic works. The principal art forms are masks and figures, usually made for ceremonial use. Much traditional African art has been made of perishable material because there was no desire to preserve it beyond the occasion for which it was made.

Tribal groups and urban kingdoms of traditional Africa have shared a number of basic concepts, including *animism*, the belief that all objects, whether animate or inanimate, have a spirit or life force. Sculpture from these areas does not simply symbolize a spirit; it is believed actually to embody or contain it. Where such traditions still prevail, the carver of sacred objects must be purified before carving. Sculpting tools are also considered sacred because of their purpose.

The Bambara people of Mali are famous for their carved wooden antelope headdresses,

386   MALE AND FEMALE ANTELOPE FIGURES (CHIWARA). Mali Republic, Bambara Tribe. Probably 20th century. Wood, brass tacks, string, cowrie shells, iron, quills. Height of female 79.8 cm., height of male 97.8 cm. *Ada Turnbull Hertle Fund (1965.6-7)* © *1988 The Art Institute of Chicago. All rights reserved.*

which they attach to basketry caps and wear on top of their heads during agricultural ceremonies. When a new field is cleared, the most diligent male workers are selected to perform a dance of leaps in imitation of the mythical *chiwara*, who taught humans how to cultivate crops. The dance always includes both male and female chi-wara figures. The female is identified by her baby on her back, and the male by a stylized mane. Organically abstracted antelope bodies become energized, almost linear forms. Rhythmic curves are accented by a few straight lines in designs that emphasize an interplay of solid mass and penetrating space.

As the Gothic era was beginning in twelfth-century Europe, a highly sophisticated art was being produced for the royal court of Ife, the sacred Yoruba city in southwestern Nigeria. There, a naturalistic style of courtly portraiture developed that was unlike anything to be found in Europe at the time and was equally unique among the inventive abstract forms created by most African cultures. The MALE PORTRAIT HEAD shown here is a representational portrait of an individual. The work demonstrates great skill in the difficult craft of lost-wax bronze casting. Scarification lines emphasize facial contours. Rows of small holes originally held hair and

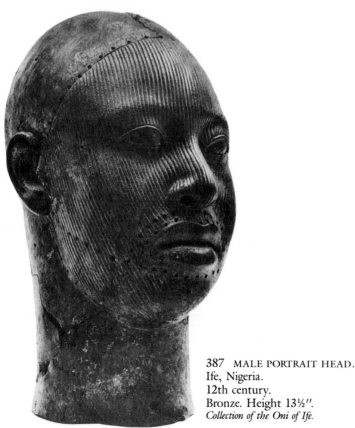

387   MALE PORTRAIT HEAD. Ife, Nigeria. 12th century. Bronze. Height 13½″. *Collection of the Oni of Ife.*

389 MASK. Benin district, Nigeria. 16th century. Ivory, iron inlays. Height 9⅜″. *The Metropolitan Museum of Art, New York.*

388 BENIN HEAD. Nigeria. 16th century. Bronze. Height 9¼″. *The Metropolitan Museum of Art, New York. The Michael C. Rockefeller Memorial Collection. Bequest of Nelson A. Rockefeller 1979 (1979. 206.86).*

beard, adding to the realism. Bronze artworks of comparable quality subsequently appeared elsewhere in Africa. It is believed that in the fourteenth century, a master sculptor from Ife brought bronze casting to the neighboring kingdom of Benin. The courtly style that developed in Benin was somewhat abstract in comparison to the naturalism of Ife portrait sculpture.

The ivory MASK from Benin was carved in the sixteenth century, but modern versions are still worn at the oba's (king's) waist during important ceremonies. The crown consists of a row of heads inspired by the "strange" dress and beard styles of Portuguese visitors. "Civilized" Europeans were amazed when they saw Benin sculptures, palaces, and city plans, because they could not imagine how people living in huts could create such refined art.

The bold, uninhibited style of Cameroon art looks far removed from the aristocratic, refined styles of nearby Ife and Benin, yet the Cameroon style is believed to have come from Nigeria. In sculpture and masks, the design elements tend to be divided into horizontal zones. The separate areas of the LARGE DANCE MASK are clearly defined by different patterns and textures.

390 LARGE DANCE MASK. Bamenda area, Cameroon, Africa. 19th century. Wood. Height 26½″. *Rietberg Museum, Zurich, von der Heydt Collection. Photograph: Wettstin and Kaaf.*

391 GOURDS. Northern Nigeria. 20th century.
UCLA Museum of Cultural History, Los Angeles.
Photographer: Richard Todd.

The art of Africa south of the Sahara was first known in Europe in the fifteenth century. It attracted little attention, however, until it was rediscovered around the turn of this century by a few European artists who were greatly impressed by its power, and brought it to the attention of their colleagues. Expressive and highly sophisticated abstract sculpture from Africa and Oceania quickly became a major influence on twentieth-century Western art (see page 383).

The art of pattern design is highly developed in many parts of Africa. In northern Nigeria, people embellish GOURDS with inventive incised patterns. The smooth surfaces lend themselves to carving and painting. Gourds are among the oldest plants cultivated in Africa, where they have been used for numerous purposes, including as storage and serving containers, musical instruments, and ritual objects.

Though greatly varied, the traditional arts of Native America, the Pacific Islands, and Africa have more in common with one another than with the arts of the long-established civilizations of Asia or the modern Western world. In all three geographic areas, abstraction is far more common than naturalism. Art from these areas was made primarily for specific utilitarian and ritual purposes.

Within the few remaining native communities of the Americas, the Pacific Islands, and Africa, many traditional arts are no longer being practiced. Even for those peoples who are still living in such societies, the arts have largely lost their crucial roles in maintaining meaningful survival and cultural continuity. Although artifacts of varying degrees of integrity are still produced in some of these areas, the introduction of modern schools, missions, and mass-produced material goods has rendered pointless and sterile the once-thriving artistic life of most traditional societies. Today, production of poor copies and tourist curios often dominates. Ironically, museums and private collections of the industrialized world preserve artistic evidence of ways of life made impossible by modern culture.

ISLAMIC ART

Islamic history began in 622 with Mohammed's flight, known as the Hegira, to what is now Medina on the Arabian peninsula. The new religion quickly spread into much of what had been the Eastern Roman and Byzantine empires, then went on to include North Africa, Spain, India, and areas of Southeast Asia.

Initially, the Muslims had little art of their own, and adopted the highly developed arts of the countries they overtook. The Islamic style of art that gradually evolved was derived primarily from the art of Eastern Christianity and the earlier art of Persia (now Iran), but also from the nomadic art of Central Asia.

Because orthodox Islam prohibits the representation of living creatures, an art based on geometric pattern and floral form developed. Intricate patterns cover entire surfaces of small utensils, manuscript pages, and walls. The most characteristic Islamic design is the arabesque, which is composed of angles and curves, crossed or interlaced. Like the animal style of the nomads (see page 312), Islamic design fills entire spaces, but with repeated patterns rather than the tangled ambiguity of the animal style. Even on buildings, Islamic artists use sacred writing instead of figurative painting and sculpture. Arabic writing developed into many elaborate and elegant calligraphic styles and was integrated into the arabesques. The decorative qualities of Arabic scripts combine well with nonverbal abstract design motifs.

As Muslim conquest spread, Islamic architects borrowed building techniques as well as surface designs from older styles. Their architecture consists of buildings directly related to the Muslim religion; even secular constructions have religious elements. A variety of arch forms have been used by Islamic builders, who found that horseshoe and pointed arches created larger and more open spaces than semicircular arches. Other notable features include onion domes, minarets from which worshipers are called to prayer, and open courtyards for preparing for worship. The MIHRAB, or prayer niche, in a mosque indicates the direction of Mecca, and usually contains a copy of the Koran.

Secular Islamic painting was greatly influenced by the Mongol invasion of the Middle East in the thirteenth century. A highly decorative style of painting emerged in which figures, landscape, and ornament combine in rich two-dimensional compositions (see page 64).

The geographic center of present-day Islamic culture coincides with the section of Iraq known in ancient times as Mesopotamia. We begin our discussion of the art of the ancient world with the early civilization which developed in this fertile plain.

392   MIHRAB. Iran. Early 16th century.
Tin-glazed earthenware tiles. Height 6'7".
Museum of Islamic Art, West Berlin.

393   SULTAN AHMET MOSQUE. Istanbul, Turkey.
1609–1616.
Photograph: Tom Klobe.

11

Ancient through Medieval

The cultures of ancient Mesopotamia and Egypt ran almost parallel in time, yet they were quite different from each other. Urban civilization began to develop earlier in the Tigris-Euphrates Valley than it did in the Nile Valley of Egypt. The Egyptians, who had the protection of a narrow river valley walled off by formidable deserts, enjoyed thousands of years of relatively unbroken self-rule; the Mesopotamians, however, were vulnerable to repeated invasion, and the area was ruled by a succession of different peoples. Because of these and other differences, each civilization developed its own distinctive art forms.

MESOPOTAMIA

The Greeks called the broad plain between the Tigris and Euphrates rivers Mesopotamia, "the land between the rivers." An early people who called the area Sumer, and subsequently became known as the Sumerians, developed the world's first writing.

In Sumeria, religion and government were one; authority rested in priests who claimed divine sanction. People worshiped a hierarchy of nature gods at huge *ziggurats*, which were at the center of each theocratic city-state. The ruins of many early Mesopotamian cities are still dominated by eroding ziggurats such the one at Ur. Massive ziggurats, each symbolizing the sacred mountain which links heaven and earth, were filled with sun-baked bricks and faced with fired

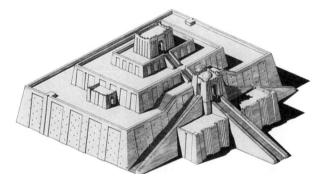

394 a. ZIGGURAT AT UR. Iraq. c. 2100 B.C.
b. Reconstruction drawing of the ZIGGURAT AT UR.
British Museum, London.

395   Reconstructed LYRE. From "The King's Grave"
tomb RT 789, Ur. c. 2650–2550 B.C.
Wood with gold, lapis lazuli, shell and silver.
The University Museum, University of
Pennsylvania, Philadelphia (T4-29).
a. Detail of soundbox.

b. Front panel.

bricks often glazed in different colors. Two or more successively smaller platforms stood on the solid base, probably with a shrine on the uppermost platform. On these heights, close to heaven, the city's god might dwell, and there the ruling priests had their sanctuaries.

We can imagine the splendor of Sumerian court life by studying the reconstruction of the elegant royal LYRE found in the king's tomb in the ancient city of Ur. The narrative panel on the front and the bull's head are original. The bearded bull's head is a symbol of royalty often seen in Mesopotamian art. In contrast, the bulls and other imaginative animals inlaid on the harp's soundbox are depicted in a simplified narrative style that seems somewhat comical to us. They take on human roles, as do the animals in the later, ancient Greek fables of Aesop. The upper panel, which shows a man embracing two bearded bulls, is a type of heraldic design developed by the Sumerians that was to influence the art of many later cultures. Both the top trio and the panel at the bottom, a goat attending a scorpion-man, are believed to be scenes from the great classic of Sumerian literature, the *Epic of Gilgamesh*.

About 2300 B.C., the scattered city-states that made up Sumeria had come under the authority of a single Akkadian king. The magnificent HEAD OF AN AKKADIAN RULER portrays such an absolute monarch. Clearly, this fully mature work evolved from a long tradition. The elaborate hairstyle and rhythmic patterning shows the influence of Sumerian stylization. The handsome face expresses calm inner strength. Superb blending of formal design qualities with carefully studied naturalism is a characteristic of both later Mesopotamian and Egyptian art.

396   HEAD OF AN AKKADIAN RULER. Niniveh. c. 2300–2200 B.C. Bronze. Height 12″. *Iraq Museum, Bagdad.*

EGYPT

Deserts on both sides of the Nile diminished outside influences and enabled Egypt to develop distinctive styles of architecture, painting, and sculpture that remained relatively unchanged for 2,500 years. It is astonishing to realize that ancient Egyptian culture lasted longer than the time from the birth of Christ to today. All of us alive today were born into an age of very rapid cultural and technological change. It is difficult for anyone conditioned by the concept of "new is better" to imagine such a stable society.

We are most familiar with Egyptian art that was made for the tombs of pharaohs, who were considered god-kings. Egyptian religious belief was distinguished by its emphasis on life after death. Preservation of the body and care for the dead were considered essential for extension of life beyond the grave. Upon death, bodies of royalty and nobility were embalmed and, together with accompanying artifacts, tools, and furniture, buried in huge pyramids or in hidden underground tombs. Architecture was the most important of the ancient arts, and, because of the extensive use of written language, the names of ancient Egyptian architects have been preserved. Among the finest and best-preserved examples of Egyptian architecture is the FUNERARY TEMPLE OF QUEEN HATSHEPSUT. The design and placement of ramps and colonnades echoes and complements the natural surroundings.

Egyptian sculpture is characterized by a preference for compact, solidly structured figures that embody some of the qualities of strength and geometric clarity found in Egyptian architecture. The final form of a piece of sculpture was determined to a great extent by the sculptor's tools and working methods, as well as by an underlying geometric plan that was first sketched on the surface of the block.

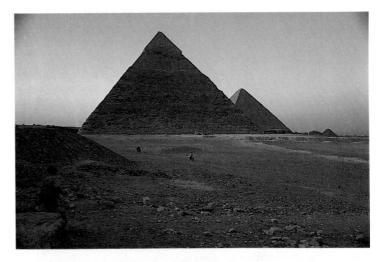

397   KING MYCERINUS AND QUEEN
KHAMERERNEBTY. 2599–2571 B.C.
Slate schist. Height 54½″.
Museum of Fine Arts, Boston.
Harvard Boston expedition.

398   GREAT PYRAMIDS OF GIZA. Egypt.
Khafre, c. 2600 B.C.; Khufu, 2650 B.C.

399   FUNERARY TEMPLE OF QUEEN HATSHEPSUT.
Deir el-Bahari. c. 1480 B.C.
Photograph: Jerome Feldman, Hawaii Loa College.

The sculptor of KING MYCERINUS AND QUEEN KHAMERERNEBTY paid considerable attention to human anatomy, yet stayed within the traditionally prescribed geometric scheme. The strength, clarity, and lasting stability expressed by the figures result from a particular kind of union between naturalism and geometric abstraction. With formal austerity, the couple stands in the frontal pose that had been established for such royal portraits. Even so, the figures express warmth and vitality; the queen touches Mycerinus in a sympathetic, loving way. Typical of monumental sculpture of the Old Kingdom are the formal pose with left foot forward, the false ceremonial beard, and figures that are still attached to the block of stone from which they were carved.

405 Ictinus and Callicrates.
PARTHENON. Acropolis, Athens.
448–432 B.C.
a. Copy of a model of the
Acropolis by G. P. Stevens
with artistic additions by
Sylvia Hahn.
*Courtesy of the Royal Ontario Museum,
Toronto.*

The city-state of Athens was the center of ancient Greek civilization when that culture was at its height. Above the city, on a large rock outcropping called the ACROPOLIS, the Athenians built one of the world's most admired structures. Today, even in its ruined state, the PARTHENON continues to express the high ideals of the people who created it.

This temple, one of several sacred buildings on the Acropolis, was designed and built as a gift to Athena Parthenos, goddess of wisdom, arts, industries, and prudent warfare, and protector of the Athenian navy. It expressed the gratitude of the Athenians for naval and commercial success.

When Ictinus and Callicrates designed the PARTHENON, they were following a well-established tradition in temple design based on the post-and-beam system of construction. In the PARTHENON, the Greek temple concept reached its highest form of development. It was located so that it could be seen against the sky, the mountains, or the sea from vantage points around the city, and was the focal point for processions and large outdoor religious festivals. Rites were performed on altars placed in front of the eastern entrance. The interior space was designed to house a 40-foot-high statue of Athena. The public was permitted to view the

magnificent figure through the eastern doorway, but the interior was used only by priests. The axis of the building was carefully calculated so that on Athena's birthday the rising sun coming through the huge east doorway would fully illuminate the gold-covered statue.

The proportions of the PARTHENON are based on harmonious ratios. The entire elevation of either end conforms to the Golden Section (see page 102). Below the triangular pediment, the proportions are based on a different ratio. The ratio of the height to the widths of the east and west ends is approximately 4 to 9. The ratio of the width to the length of the building is also 4 to 9. The diameter of the columns relates to the space between the columns at a ratio of 4 to 9, and so on.

None of the major lines of the building are perfectly straight. Experts believe that the subtle deviations from straight horizontal and vertical lines were designed to correct optical illusions. The columns have an almost imperceptible bulge (called *entasis*) above the center, which causes them to appear straighter than if they were actually straight-sided, and gives the entire structure a tangible grace. Even the steps and tops of doorways rise slightly in perfect curves. Corner columns, seen against the light, are somewhat larger in diameter to counteract the diminish-

b. THREE GODDESSES from the east pediment of the PARTHENON.
Marble. Over life-size.
British Museum, London.

ing effect of strong light in the background. The axis lines of the columns lean in a little at the top. If extended into space, these lines would converge 5,856 feet above the building. The unexpected variations are not consciously seen, but they are felt. They give the building its sense of perfection.

Although today we see Greek temples as white stone structures, analysis shows that some of the upper portions of exterior surfaces were brightly painted. In its original form, the PARTHENON exhibited the refined clarity, harmony, and vigor that comes from the heart of the Greek tradition.

Some of the finest of all Greek sculpture was carved for the upper areas of the PARTHENON. Much of it was removed by Lord Elgin in the early nineteenth century, and is now in the British Museum. Most of the remaining sculpture has been badly damaged by war, and the recent corrosive effects of air pollution (see also the discussion of preservation and restoration on pages 468–469).

The THREE GODDESSES from the right corner of the PARTHENON's east *pediment* (triangular end surface formed by the slopes of the roof), though now headless, are remarkable in their exaggerated naturalism. Deep creases and swirling folds reveal robust bodies beneath thin robes. By running fold lines of the drapery across the

c. View from the northwest.

limbs, the sculptor created the illusion of motion as well as mass.

Greek aesthetic principles provide the basis for the concept of classicism, which is referred to again and again in art history. *Classical* art emphasizes rational simplicity, order, and restrained emotion and is in contrast to the subjective, expressive, and emotional qualities found in late Greek art and in various subsequent periods.

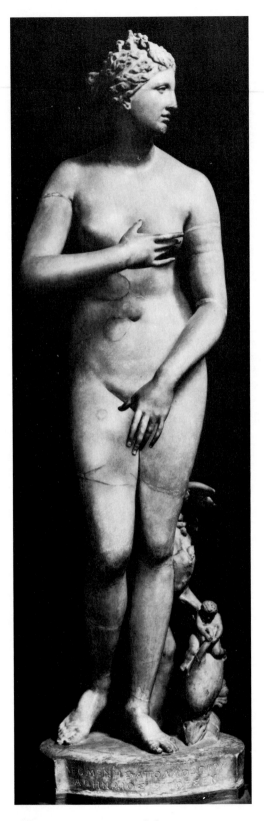

406   VENUS DE MEDICI. 3rd century B.C.
Marble. Height 5′.
Uffizi Gallery, Florence.

The classical Greek profile is one of the most obvious features of the Greek idealization of human figures. Aphrodite, the Greek goddess of love and beauty, was known as Venus by the Romans. VENUS DE MEDICI is a Roman copy of a fourth-century B.C. Greek original. The figure is more ideal than natural, because it was made to symbolize a goddess rather than to portray a real woman.

After the decline of the Greek city-states at the end of the fourth century B.C., the art of the Mediterranean changed. Though it continued to be strongly influenced by earlier Greek art, and was often executed by Greek artists, it was produced for, and according to, the preferences of non-Greek patrons. Mediterranean art during this era is called *Hellenistic*, meaning Greeklike. The transition from classical Greek to Hellenistic coincided with a loss of confidence in the material world, as well as a loss of security due to a realization that the gods had failed to sustain the glory of Greece. People turned to the subjective and imperfect aspects of life and humanity rather than the glorified idealizations of the classical period.

407   Agesander,
Athenodorus,
and Polydorus of Rhodes.
THE LAOCOÖN GROUP.
c. 150–30 B.C.
Marble. Height 95¼″.
Vatican Museum, Rome.

408 FEMALE PORTRAIT. c. 54–117.
Marble. Life-size.
Museo Profano Lateranese, Rome.

409 MALE PORTRAIT. c. 100.
Marble. Life-size.
Capitoline Museums, Rome.

In the Hellenistic period, Greek art became more dynamic and more naturalistic. Everyday activities, historical subjects, myths, and portraiture were more common than in the classical period.

THE LAOCOÖN GROUP is a late Hellenistic work. According to the myth, Laocoön was a priest who warned against bringing the Greek wooden horse into Troy during the Trojan War. Subsequently, he and his sons were attacked by serpents, an act interpreted by the Trojans as a sign of God's disapproval of Laocoön's prophecy. The event is presented with dramatic poses, tortured facial expressions, and strained muscles. Laocoön is shown in hierarchic proportion to his grown sons.

The rationalism, clarity, and restrained gestures that were typical of the sculpture of the classical period are here replaced by writhing movement, expressing emotional and physical anguish. When this sculpture was unearthed in Italy in 1506, it had an immediate influence on the young Michelangelo (see page 182) and many of his contemporaries.

ROME

By the second century B.C., Rome was the major power in the Western world. At its height, the Roman Empire included western Europe, North Africa, and the Near East, as well as the shores of the Mediterranean. The governance of a multitude of unique peoples and cultures was a prime example of the Roman genius for order and worldly action. Roman culture has affected our lives in many areas—our systems of law and government, our calendar, festivals, religions, and languages. We also inherited from the Romans the concept that art is worthy of historical study and critical appreciation.

The Romans were a practical, materialistic people, and their art reflects this. They made few changes in the general style of Greek art, which they admired, collected, and copied. But not all Roman art was imitative. Roman portraiture achieved a high degree of individuality rarely found in Greek sculpture. The naturalistic style probably grew out of the Roman custom of making wax death masks of ancestors for the family shrine or altar. Later, these images were recreated in marble to make them more durable. Roman sculptors observed and carefully recorded those physical details and imperfections that give character to each person's face.

The Romans' greatest artistic achievements were in civil engineering, town planning, and architecture. They created utilitarian and symbolic structures of impressive beauty and grandeur that were to have a major influence on subsequent Western architecture. As noted in chapter 8, the outstanding feature of Roman architecture was the semicircular arch, which the Romans utilized and refined in the construction of arcades, barrel vaults, and domes (see the diagrams on page 223 and the aqueduct at Nimes on page 227).

By developing the structural use of concrete combined with semicircular arch and vault construction, the Romans were able to enclose large indoor spaces. Although a type of concrete was commonly used in Roman construction, the quality of cement (the chemically active ingredient in concrete) declined during the Middle Ages and concrete was not widely used again until it was redeveloped in the nineteenth century.

In the PANTHEON, a major temple dedicated to all the gods, Roman builders created a domed interior space of immense scale. The building is essentially a cylinder, capped by a hemispherical dome, with a single entrance framed by a Greek porch or *portico*.

Romans developed the ability to build large domed and vaulted interiors to accommodate their preference for gathering inside. The interior is the primary focus of the PANTHEON, in contrast to the Greek Parthenon's exterior orientation. Romans conceived architecture as units of space shaped by enclosing walls, in contrast to Egyptians and Greeks, who designed primarily in terms of relationships between masses.

410   PANTHEON. Rome. 118–125.

411   Giovanni Paolo Panini.
INTERIOR OF THE PANTHEON. c. 1740.
Oil on canvas. 50½″ × 39″.
National Gallery of Art, Washington, D.C.
Samuel H. Kress Collection.

412 SACRED LANDSCAPE.
Wall painting from Pompeii.
c. 63–79. Fresco.
National Museum, Naples, Italy.

The Pantheon's circular walls, which support the huge dome, are stone and concrete masonry, 20 feet thick and faced with brick. The dome diminishes in thickness toward the crown, and is patterned on the interior surface with recessed squares called *coffers*, which both lighten and strengthen the structure. Originally covered with gold leaf, the coffered ceiling was designed to symbolize the dome of heaven. The dome was designed so that the distance from the summit to the floor is equal to the 144-foot diameter—making it a virtual globe of space. At the dome's crown, an opening called an *oculus* or eye, 33 feet in diameter, provides daylight and ventilation to the interior. Neither verbal description nor views of the exterior and interior can evoke the awe one feels upon entering the PANTHEON.

Roman wall paintings, such as the SACRED LANDSCAPE excavated at Pompeii, contain a wide range of subject matter, from complex architectural details to still lifes and landscapes. Here a wall was transformed into an illusionary window view. The idyllic landscape, painted as if seen from a high vantage point, includes people, animals, and architecture. Although the scene is imaginary, the artist made it look natural through the use of such devices as linear and atmospheric perspective. Some Roman painters were aware of linear perspective. In SACRED LANDSCAPE, however, the perspective lines are not systematically related to each other, nor is there a controlled use of the effect of diminishing size relative to distance. After the collapse of the Roman Empire, perspective was not applied, and the knowledge was forgotten until it was rediscovered and developed as a system during the Renaissance, one thousand years later.

THE MIDDLE AGES

Early Christian and Byzantine

By the time Emperor Constantine was converted to Christianity in the fourth century, Roman attitudes had changed considerably. The material grandeur of Rome was rapidly declining. As confidence in the material world fell, people turned inward to more spiritual values. Inevitably, this new orientation was reflected in the art of the time. Change is expressed in the colossal marble HEAD OF CONSTANTINE, once part of an immense figure located in the Basilica of Constantine in Rome. The style of this sculpture developed from conflicting attitudes. The superhuman head is an image of imperial majesty, yet the large eyes and immobile features express an inner spiritual life. The late Roman style of the facial features, particularly the eyes, was very different from the naturalism of earlier Roman portraits, and directly influenced later Byzantine images.

In 330, Constantine moved the capital of the Roman Empire from Rome to the city of Byzantium, which he renamed Constantinople (present-day Istanbul). Meanwhile, western Europe was increasingly dominated by "barbaric" invaders from the north and east, whose repeated attacks led to the final collapse of the western Roman Empire at the end of the fifth century.

The one-thousand-year period that followed the decline of the Roman Empire (in the fourth and fifth centuries) has been called the medieval period or Middle Ages because it came between the time of ancient Greek and Roman civilization and the rebirth, or renaissance, of Greco-Roman ideas in the fifteenth century. During the medieval period, Byzantine civilization flourished in Constantinople. There the heritage of Greece and Rome was preserved, and Christianity was brought to the various peoples of the Byzantine Empire, which included the area around the eastern Mediterranean. The Byzantine artistic heritage continues today in the

413   HEAD OF CONSTANTINE. c. 312.
Marble. Height 8'.
Museo dei Conservatori, Rome.

mosaics, paintings, and architecture of the Eastern Orthodox church.

In the first hundred years A.D., the early Christians had been against pictorial—particularly human—representations. Their position conformed to the Old Testament's second commandment, "Thou shall not make unto thee a graven image, nor any likeness of anything that is in heaven above, or that is in the earth beneath. . . ." To make representational images, or to worship such images, might cause confusion of the image with the personage or deity being worshiped. Such practice, called idolatry, makes a work of art into a fetish. Thus Christ was initially portrayed only with symbols such as the lamb, the fish, or the sacred monogram. The earliest figural representations of Christ portray him as a young shepherd.

The mosaic THE GOOD SHEPHERD SEPARATING THE SHEEP FROM THE GOATS is one of a series of mosaics which depict the life and teachings of Christ. In Saint Matthew's New Testament account, Christ in his glory, with the angels around him, will sit in judgement and separate the sheep (the faithful) from the goats (the unfaithful).

Christ, angels, and animals are depicted with heavy outline and stylized shading. A suggestion of space is created with overlap, yet the figures and animals appear to be confined to a narrow area between the surface and the background.

The many mosaics created in Ravenna, Italy in the fifth and sixth centuries show the transition from early Christian to Byzantine style. Naturalism and a sense of depth found in earlier Roman painting gradually gave way to abstraction and a flattening of pictorial space.

There was no sharp dividing line between early Christian art and the subsequent art of either the Eastern or the Western church. The art forms of the early Christian period were affected by an ongoing controversy between those who sought to follow the biblical prohibition against the worship of idols and those who wanted images to help tell the sacred stories.

The artworks connected with Constantine's reign (306–337) served to refuel the old opposition to idolatry. In 726, the Christian Byzantine emperor issued an edict prohibiting the use of representational images, and many representational works were destroyed. As a result, floral patterns and abstract symbols such as the cross were incorporated into Christian imagery during the next hundred years. Byzantine Christian abstractions stemmed from associations with Eastern religions, particularly Islam, which employed flat patterns and nonrepresentational designs.

414 THE GOOD SHEPHERD SEPARATING THE SHEEP
FROM THE GOATS.
Sant' Apollinare Nuovo,
Ravenna, Italy. c. 520. Mosaic.

415   CHRIST AS PANTOCRATOR.
Dome of the Church of the
Dormition, Daphni, Greece. c. 1080.
Mosaic.

Following the iconoclast period (726–843), when the making of icons, or graven images, was banned, the abstract style was integrated with more emotional, figurative imagery. Eastern influence continued in the hierarchical size and placement of subject matter in Byzantine church decoration, with Christ occupying the dome.

High in the center of the dome of the Church of the Dormition at Daphni, Greece, there is a Byzantine mosaic depicting CHRIST AS PANTOCRATOR, Lord of the Universe. This awesome religious work, created in the eleventh century, is one of the most powerful images of Christ.

The scale of the figure emphasizes its spiritual importance to worshipers. The early Christian HEAD OF CONSTANTINE and the Byzantine CHRIST AS PANTOCRATOR exhibit similar intensity and emphasis on the eyes. The artist who designed the Byzantine mosaic of Christ designed the features of the face to create a symbol of patriarchal authority.

A row of windows circles the base of the dome, bringing light to the church interior. The mosaic surfaces depend on the direction of light from the windows and from artificial sources such as candlelight. Each small *tessera* – piece of glass or ceramic tile – was placed on the adhesive surface and tilted to catch the light, producing a shimmering effect.

Beginning in the tenth and eleventh centuries, Byzantine artists created a distinct style that expressed Eastern Orthodox Christianity and also met the needs of a lavish court. The Byzantine style is still followed by artists working within the tradition of the Eastern Orthodox church. Clergy closely supervise the iconography and permit little room for individual interpretation. The effectiveness of an image depends on the artist's fidelity to established prototypes.

The abstract Byzantine style developed as a way to inspire the illiterate, while keeping the biblical commandment that forbids the making of graven images. The figures were painted in conformity with a precise formula. The intent was to symbolize, rather than represent. Small paintings, referred to as *icons* (from the Greek *eikon*, meaning image), are holy images from the Eastern Orthodox church which inspire devotion, but are not worshiped in themselves.

The making of portable icon paintings grew out of mosaic and fresco traditions. Artists of the Eastern Orthodox faith sought to portray the symbolic or mystical aspects of divine beings, rather than their physical qualities. The design of MADONNA AND CHILD ON A CURVED THRONE is based on circular shapes and linear patterns. Mary's head repeats the circular shape of her halo; circles of similar size enclose angels, echoing the larger circle of the throne. The lines and shapes used in the draped robes that cover the figures give scarcely a hint of the bodies beneath. Divine light is symbolized by the gold background that surrounds the throne in which the Virgin Mary sits. The large architectural throne symbolizes Mary's position as Queen of the City of Heaven. Christ appears as a wise little man, supported on the lap of a heavenly, supernatural mother. As a holy image, such a painting had to avoid naturalism and references to the real world; confusion with reality would constitute idol worship.

In order that they be worthy of dedication to God, icons are usually made of precious materials. Gold leaf was used here for the background and costly ground lapis lazuli for the Virgin's robe.

Convergence of Nomadic-Barbarian and Greco-Roman

When the Romans conquered the lands around the Mediterranean Sea between the first and third centuries B.C., they inherited and assimilated the knowledge and cultural traditions that had been developed by earlier civilizations. The Roman Empire came to include all the lands around the Mediterranean, and northward through what is now France and Britain.

As the Roman Empire declined from within during the third and fourth centuries A.D., it was simultaneously challenged from without by invading nomadic tribes. With the notable exception of the Celts, many of these nomadic peoples traveled across the Eurasian grasslands called the Steppes, which extend from the Danube River in Europe to the borders of China. The migrations occurred during a long period that began in the second millennium B.C. and lasted well into the Middle Ages. The Greeks called these uncivilized nomads (and other non-Greeks) "barbarians." What little we know about them is derived from artifacts and records of literate cultures of the Mediterranean, Near East, and China, to whom the nomads were a menace. The Great Wall of China and Hadrian's Wall in Britain were built to keep out such invaders.

416 Byzantine School.
MADONNA AND CHILD ON A CURVED THRONE.
13th century.
Tempera on wood. 32⅛″ × 19⅜″.
National Gallery of Art, Washington, D.C.
Andrew W. Mellon Collection.

A varied, but interrelated art, sometimes referred to as the *animal style*, was developed by various groups of Eurasian nomads. Because of their migrant way of life, their art consisted of small, easily portable objects such as items for personal adornment, pole-top ornaments, weapons, and horse trappings such as the bronze LURISTAN ORNAMENT from western Iran. The style is characterized by active, intertwining shapes, often depicting wild animals in combat, as seen in the SCYTHIAN ANIMAL ornament. The vigor of the art reflects the dynamic life of these mobile peoples. The art of the animal style rarely depicts humans; when it does, humans play subordinate roles to animals.

Nomadic metalwork often exhibits exceptional craftsmanship. Because of frequent migrations and the durability and value of the art objects, the style was diffused over large geographic areas. Among the best-known works of nomadic art are small gold and bronze ornaments produced by the Scythians, whose culture flourished between the eighth and fourth centuries B.C. Their abstracted animal forms appear to have

been adopted by groups in the British Isles, Scandinavia, and China. Similar animal forms appeared later in wood- and stone-carving and manuscript illumination, as well as in metal.

The gold and enamel PURSE COVER found in a grave at Sutton Hoo belonged to a seventh-century East Anglian king. Its motifs are distinctly varied, indicating that they are derived from several sources. The motif of a man standing between confronting animals appeared first in Sumerian art over three thousand years earlier (see page 295), and is seen again in the LURISTAN ORNAMENT.

A great deal of wood-carving was done in Scandinavia, where the animal style flourished longer than anywhere else in the West. Protective animal spirits, like those in both the early Chinese RITUAL VESSEL (see page 269) and the carving from Norway, were felt to have power and symbolic significance far beyond the decorative function we may associate with them. We know that Viking law required that figures such as the DRAGON'S HEAD be removed when a ship came into port so that the spirits of the land would not be frightened.

417 SCYTHIAN ANIMAL. 5th century B.C.
Bronze. Diameter 4″.
Hermitage Museum, Leningrad.

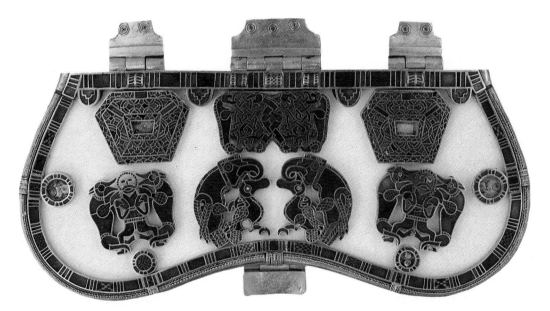

418 PURSE COVER.
From the Sutton Hoo Ship
Burial, Suffolk, England. Before 655.
Gold and enamel. Length 7½".
British Museum, London.

419 LURISTAN ORNAMENT. c. 900–700 B.C.
Bronze. Height 7¼".
Honolulu Academy of Arts. Bequest of Mr. and Mrs. J. Scott Pratt III.

420 DRAGON'S HEAD.
Found at Oseberg, Norway.
c. 820.
Wood.
© *University Museum of National
Antiquities, Oslo, Norway.*

422   Detail of CHRIST OF THE PENTECOST.
Saint Madeleine Cathedral, Vézelay, France. 1125–1150.
Stone. Height of the tympanum 35½″.

churches. Such figures were the first large sculpture since Roman times.

Deviation from standard human proportions enabled sculptors to provide appropriately symbolic form for figures such as CHRIST OF THE PENTECOST. The mystical energy and compassion of Christ is depicted in the relief carving above the doorway of Saint Madeleine Cathedral at Vézelay, France. As worshipers enter the sanctuary, the image above them symbolizes Christ at the time he asked the Apostles and all Christians to take his message to the world. Swirling folds of drapery are indicated with precise curves and spirals that relate to the linear energy of the

animal style and the CHI-RHO MONOGRAM. In abstract terms, the spiraling motion suggest Christ's cosmic power. The image of Christ is very large in scale to show his relative importance. The sculptor achieved a monumental quality by making the head smaller than normal, and by elongating the entire figure.

One of the major differences between the cultures of the East and the West is the restless energy of Europeans, which has resulted in frequent changes in attitude that can be seen in Western art. The Romanesque style had lasted barely a hundred years when the Gothic style began to replace it, in about 1145. The shift is seen most clearly in architecture, as the Romanesque round arch was superseded by the pointed Gothic arch, developed in the mid-twelfth century (discussed on page 228). Combined with the ribbed-groin vault and the flying buttress, the pointed arch allowed for greater interior height and larger window spaces. The basic structure of Gothic cathedrals was made of stones carved and assembled to form thin ribs and pillars; the result is a seemingly weightless "stone cage." Buttresses held in the sideways thrust of the vault, relieving the walls of some of their load-bearing function, and making possible curtain walls of stained glass that filled the interior with rich, luminous color. Inside, the faithful must have felt they had actually arrived at the visionary Heavenly City.

Cathedrals were expressions of a new age of faith that grew out of medieval Christian theology and mysticism. The upward-reaching forms symbolize the triumph of the spirit over the bonds of earthly life, evoking a sense of joyous spiritual elation.

Gothic cathedrals such as the one at Chartres were the center of community life. They were used as meeting places for people doing business, for lovers, for lectures, for concerts, and for morality plays—as well as for places of worship. The entire community cooperated in the building of NOTRE DAME DE CHARTRES (Our Lady of Chartres), although those who began its construction never saw it in its final form. The cathedral continued to grow and change in major ways for over three hundred years. Although the basic plan is symmetrical and logically organized, the architecture of CHARTRES has a rich, enigmatic complexity that is quite different from the easily grasped totality of the classical PARTHENON.

CHARTRES was partially destroyed by fire in 1194 and was rebuilt in the High Gothic style. It was one of the first cathedrals based on the full Gothic system, and helped set the standard for Gothic architecture in Europe. In its west facade, CHARTRES reveals the transition between the early and late phases of Gothic architecture. The massive lower walls and round arch portals were built in the mid-twelfth century. The north tower, on the left as one approaches the facade, was rebuilt with the intricate flamelike or flamboyant curves of the late Gothic style early in the sixteenth century, after the original tower collapsed in 1506.

Magnificent stained glass windows of this period are so well integrated with the architecture that one is inconceivable without the other. The scriptures are told in imagery that transforms the sanctuary with showers of color, changing hour by hour. At CHARTRES, the brilliant north rose window, known as the ROSE DE FRANCE, is dedicated to the Virgin Mary who sits in majesty, surrounded by doves, angels, and royal figures of the celestial hierarchy.

423   NOTRE DAME DE CHARTRES. Chartres, France. 1145–1513.
Cathedral length 427′; facade height 157′; south tower height 344′; north tower height 377′.

a. West front.
b. "ROSE DE FRANCE" WINDOW. c. 1233.

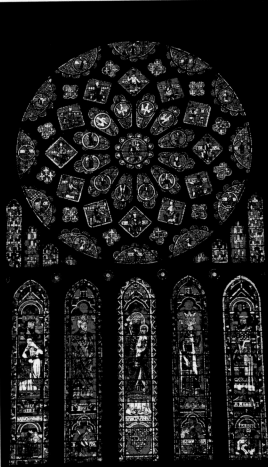

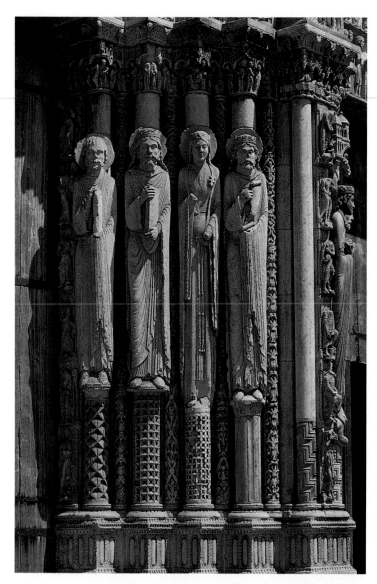

The statues of the OLD TESTAMENT PROPHET, KINGS, AND QUEEN to the right of the central doorway at the west entrance of CHARTRES are among the most impressive remaining examples of early Gothic sculpture. The kings and queen suggest Christ's royal heritage, and also honor French monarchs of the time. The prophet on the left depicts Christ's mission as an apostle of God. In contrast to active, emotional Romanesque sculpture, the figures are passive and serene. Their typically Gothic, elongated forms allow them to blend readily with the vertical emphasis of the architecture.

Although they are part of the total scheme, the figures stand out from the columns behind them. Their draped bodies, and especially their heads, reveal a then new interest in portraying human features. Such interest eventually led again to full portraiture and freestanding figures.

In spite of the great differences in form and content between Hindu (see page 264) and Christian architecture and sculpture, their basic purposes are similar. Both the cathedral and temple relate to an idea expressed by Abbot Suger, the man credited with starting the Gothic era. Art historian Erwin Panofsky has translated and paraphrased Suger's concept:

. . . *every perceptible thing, manmade or natural, becomes a symbol of that which is not perceptible, a stepping stone on the road to Heaven; the human mind, abandoning itself to the "harmony and radiance"* . . . *which is the criterion of terrestrial beauty, finds itself "guided upward" to the transcendent cause of this "harmony and radiance" which is God.*[1]

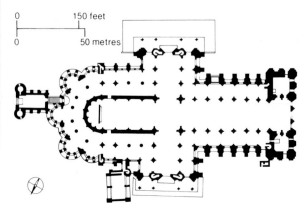

c. OLD TESTAMENT PROPHET, KINGS, AND QUEEN.
   c. 1145–1170. Door-jamb statues from West (or Royal) Portal.
d. View from the southeast.
e. Plan, based on Latin cross.

12

Renaissance and Baroque

THE RENAISSANCE AND MANNERISM

A major shift in attitude occurred in Europe as the spiritual mysticism of the Middle Ages was increasingly challenged by logical thought and the new philosophical, literary, and artistic movement called *humanism*, in which people and their capabilities are of major concern. Renaissance humanists did not discard theological concerns, but reaffirmed the human dimension, respected scientific exploration, and cultivated the classical literature of Greece and Rome. The beginnings of this transition became apparent in the late thirteenth century.

New directions in the course of human history are usually begun by a small group or single person of genius who seizes the opportunity that changing circumstances present. Such a person was the proto-Renaissance Italian painter and architect Giotto di Bondone, known as Giotto. By breaking with conservative Byzantine formulas and bringing a renewed sense of realism to painting, he, more than any other, determined the future of painting in Europe. In retrospect, we see him not only as a precursor of the Renaissance, but as the reinventor of naturalistic painting–which had not been seen in Europe since the fall of Rome a thousand years earlier, and which was to dominate Western art from the Renaissance until the beginning of the twentieth century.

Though Gothic sculptors of this period were developing greater naturalism, both Gothic and Byzantine painting featured relatively flat, symbolic styles designed to symbolize spiritual truth. By studying the way light defines form, Giotto

424 Giotto di Bondone.
LAMENTATION. Arena Chapel, Padua, Italy. c. 1305.
Fresco. 185 cm. × 200 cm.

was able to give a feeling of sculptural solidity to his figures. In LAMENTATION, Giotto depicted physical as well as spiritual reality; Giotto's people appear as individuals within a shallow, stage-like space. Their expressions depict personal feelings not often seen in medieval art.

The ancient Greeks were primarily concerned with idealized physical form. Roman artists emphasized physical accuracy. The Middle Ages focused attention on spiritual concerns rather than physical existence. As the Renaissance replaced the Middle Ages, it brought a renewed interest

425 Jan van Eyck.
GIOVANNI ARNOLFINI AND HIS BRIDE. 1434.
Tempera and oil on panel. 33″ × 22½″.
Reproduced by courtesy of the Trustees, The National Gallery, London.

in human potential within the earthly sphere; people expressed a desire to equal or surpass the glory of ancient Greece and Rome, and to imbue their achievements with the light of Christian understanding. It was the people of the time who named their period the *Renaissance* — rebirth — an apt description for the period of revived interest in the art and ideas of ancient Greece and Rome. It was a time of discovery — discovery of the world and of the seemingly limitless potential of individual human beings.

In both northern and southern Europe, art became more naturalistic, aided by a blending of artistic and scientific concerns. Artists began an intense study of anatomy, natural light, and applications of geometry for the logical construction of implied space through the use of linear perspective. The careful observation of nature initiated by Renaissance artists became essential to the growth of modern science.

Depictions of earthly reality began and developed in different ways in Italy and northern Europe. In the northern "Low Countries" of Belgium, the Netherlands, and Luxembourg, the leading artist was Jan van Eyck, known today as the "father of Flemish painting." He was one of the first to use linseed oil as a paint medium. The fine consistency and flexibility of the new medium made it possible to achieve a brilliance and transparency of color previously unattainable.

On the same type of small wooden panels previously used for tempera painting, Van Eyck painted in minute detail, achieving an illusion of depth, directional light, mass, rich implied textures, and the physical likenesses of particular people. Human figures and their interior setting took on a new, believable presence. In spite of Van Eyck's realistic detail, GIOVANNI ARNOLFINI AND HIS BRIDE has a Gothic quality in its traditional symbolism, formality, and the vertical emphasis of the figures.

At the time the portrait painting of the Arnolfini wedding was commissioned, the church did not always require the presence of the clergy for a valid marriage contract, thus it was easy to deny that a marriage had taken place. Van Eyck's painting is thought to be a testament to the oath of marriage between Giovanni Arnolfini and Giovanna Cenami. As witness to the event, Jan van Eyck placed his signature and the date, 1434, directly above the mirror.

Today the painting's Christian iconography, well understood in the fifteenth century, needs explanation. Many of the ordinary objects portrayed with great care have sacred significance. For example, the lone, lighted candle in the chandelier symbolizes the presence of Christ. The amber beads and the sunlight shining through them are symbols of purity. The dog indicates marital fidelity. The bride's hand is placed suggestively on her stomach because at that time it was stylish for a woman to appear to be pregnant as an indication of willingness to bear children. Green, the symbol of fertility, was often worn at weddings.

Almost one hundred years later, another Flemish painter, Joachim Patinir, continued to develop some of the techniques for landscape painting begun by the Van Eyck brothers (see page 133). In earlier Christian art, landscape had been merely background for religious scenes. Patinir's painting, REST ON THE FLIGHT INTO EGYPT, is in the religious tradition, but the

426   Joachim Patinir.
REST ON THE FLIGHT INTO EGYPT. 1515–1524.
Oil on wood. 6¾″ × 8⁵⁄₁₆″.
Koninklijk Museum, Antwerp, Belgium.

427 Masaccio.
THE HOLY TRINITY. Santa Maria Novella, Florence. 1425.
Fresco. 21'10½" × 10'5".

landscape appears more important than the flight of the Holy Family. What fascinated Patinir and the people for whom he painted was the way biblical stories could be brought to life through the new naturalistic painting.

Patinir emphasized the small scale of people in landscape in a way that is similar to the earlier Chinese tradition (see pages 274–275). But while Chinese painters maintained the symbolic, suggestive role of art, Patinir put emphasis on an illusion of actual landscape.

Atmospheric perspective, heightened by transparent glazes made possible by the oil medium, greatly enhances the sense of space. Patinir formulated and greatly refined a technique for representing receding distances. Warm, brownish colors and strong value contrast in the foreground gradually shift through greens to light blue-green cool colors in the distance. The implied deep space may express an awareness brought on by the new age of exploration. With such paintings, Patinir helped to establish a tradition of landscape painting that has continued into our time.

Another approach to the study and depiction of nature was taken by German artist Albrecht Dürer, a better known and longer lived contemporary of Patinir. Minute details in THE GREAT PIECE OF TURF (page 7) reveal careful observation, while THE KNIGHT, DEATH AND THE DEVIL (page 143) combines Christian symbolism with natural forms.

In southern Europe, about one hundred years after Giotto, Masaccio became the first major painter of the Italian Renaissance. He owed a great deal to the pioneering work of his countryman Giotto, to the naturalism already achieved in sculpture, and to the newly developed theory of scientific perspective. Linear perspective was known to the Romans in a limited way, but it did not become a consistent science until the architect Filippo Brunelleschi rediscovered and developed it in Florence early in the fifteenth century. It developed as a means to analyze and represent one person's unique view of the world from a particular position in space, at a particular moment in time.

THE HOLY TRINITY was the first Renaissance painting based on the systematic use of linear perspective. Perspective gave Masaccio the tool he needed to construct an illusion of figures in actual space. The single vanishing point is placed below the base of the cross, about five feet above ground, at the viewer's eye level. Masaccio's perspective measurements were so exact that one can actually compute the dimensions of the interior of the illusionary chapel, the interior volume of which is seen as a believable extension of the space occupied by the viewer. The architecture, with the barrel vault, adds greatly to the sense of space, and reveals Masaccio's knowledge of the new Renaissance architecture based on Roman prototypes. Even in its present deteriorated condition, Masaccio's fresco THE HOLY TRINITY has a monumentality not found in the realism of northern Renaissance painters such as Van Eyck and Patinir.

In Giotto's paintings, the body and drapery appear as one; Masaccio's figures are clothed nudes, with garments draped like real fabric. Two donors (those who paid for the painting) kneel on either side of an open chapel in which the Trinity appears as God the Father, Christ the Son (on the cross), and the Holy Spirit in the form of a white dove. Below, a skeleton is shown lying on a sarcophagus beneath the inscription, "I was what you are, and what I am you shall become." If we view the painting from bottom to top, we move from temporal reality to spiritual reality.

Fra Filippo Lippi added a worldly dimension to religious subject matter. He may have studied under Masaccio, whose influence is evident in his early paintings. Lippi later developed his own graceful, linear style, and became one of the finest colorists of his day. In Lippi's MADONNA AND CHILD, the long thin nose, small mouth, and tilt of the head reflect the lingering idealizations of the Byzantine tradition (see page 311); yet Lippi's Madonna is lifelike and quite expressive of the Renaissance interest in individuality. Attention to anatomical accuracy, light and shadow, and spatial depth are integrated to produce a naturalistic, yet poetic portrayal of the subject.

428 Fra Filippo Lippi.
MADONNA AND CHILD. c. 1440–1445.
Tempera on wood. 31⅜″ × 20⅛″.
National Gallery of Art, Washington, D.C.
Samuel H. Kress Collection (1939).

BAROQUE AND ROCOCO

The period known as the *baroque* includes the seventeenth and most of the eighteenth centuries in Europe. Although baroque generally refers to a period, the term is often used stylistically to describe the art that arose in Italy around 1600 and spread through much of Europe. The baroque period had far more varied styles than the Renaissance, yet its art is often characterized by exuberant energy, strong feeling, dramatic lighting, large scale, movement, and dynamic balance. (El Greco's emotional intensity, sense of movement, and strong use of light and shadow cause him to be classed by some historians as an early baroque painter.)

Many baroque painters used highlights and dark backgrounds to heighten illusions and focus attention. Baroque works often engage the viewer emotionally. Frequent use of curves and countercurves characterized painting, sculpture, and architecture alike. A new degree of naturalism in the depiction of light and space developed, and the art of landscape painting came to maturity. Simultaneous to this very broad baroque style were both a classical countermovement and a new level of realism best exemplified by the work of Dutch painters.

Italian painter Michelangelo Merisi da Caravaggio created the most vivid, naturalistic depictions of his time. He developed the use of light as a way to direct the attention of the viewer and unify and intensify the subject matter. Strong contrast between light and dark areas is characteristic of the work of Caravaggio and other baroque painters, such as Rembrandt and Zurbarán (see SAINT SERAPION, page 80). THE CONVERSION OF SAINT PAUL was an ideal subject for Caravaggio. Light creates a blinding flash, symbolizing the evangelist's conversion. "And suddenly there shined around him a light from heaven: and he fell to the earth" (Acts 9:3–4). The major figure is foreshortened and pushed into the foreground, presenting such a close view that we feel we are right there.

Although the subject matter is sacred, Caravaggio depicted ordinary people, dressed as they would have appeared on the street in his day. In keeping with the supernatural character of the event he portrayed, he evoked a feeling for the mystical dimension within the so-called ordinary world. He wanted his paintings to be accessible and self-explanatory, and for this purpose brought to the stories of the Bible the vivid emotional intensity of his own life. Some of the clergy for whom he painted rejected his style. His emotional realism was too strong for people accustomed to aristocratic images demonstrating little more than gestures of piety.

439   Michelangelo Merisi da Caravaggio.
THE CONVERSION OF SAINT PAUL. 1600–1601.
Oil on canvas. 100⁹⁄₁₆″ × 68¹⁵⁄₁₆″.
Santa Maria del Popolo, Rome.

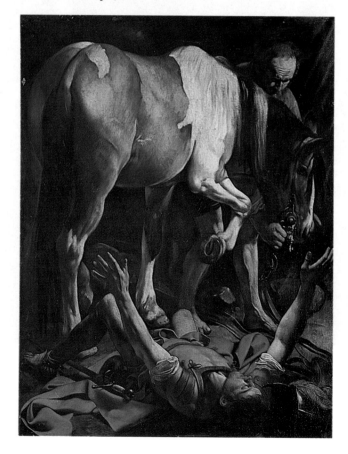

The spiritual intensity of baroque art is vividly apparent in THE ECSTASY OF SAINT TERESA, by Italian sculptor and architect Gian Lorenzo Bernini. The work features a life-sized marble figure of the saint, and represents one of her visions as she recorded it. In this vision, she saw an angel, who seemed to pierce her heart with a flaming arrow of gold, giving her great pain as well as pleasure and leaving her "all on fire with a great love of God."[3] Bernini makes the experience visionary, yet as vivid as possible, by portraying the moment of greatest feeling. Turbulent drapery heightens the expression of joy on Saint Teresa's face.

This was the time of the Counter-Reformation, a movement in the Roman Catholic church that sought to offset the effects of increasing secularism and the Protestant Reformation of the sixteenth century. The dramatic realism of baroque painting and sculpture was part of the Catholic effort to revitalize the church. In THE ECSTASY OF SAINT TERESA, Bernini symbolized spiritual ecstasy through expression of physical ecstasy.

Bernini designed not only the figures of Saint Teresa and the angel, but their altar setting and the entire CORNARO CHAPEL. Architecture, painting, and sculpture work together to enhance the drama of the central figures above the altar. Bernini intentionally crossed the lines usually drawn between architecture, painting, and sculpture, as well as those between illusion and reality. The chapel embodies much of the emotion felt in opera, a major musical art form of this period, which combined all the arts in elaborately staged musical narratives.

Above the saint and her heavenly messenger, sunlight shines through a hidden window, illuminating the work in such a way that it appears to dematerialize the figures. In box seats on either side of the altar, sculpted figures of the Cornaro family witness the event, and thus make a symbolic connection between sacred and secular experience.

440 Gian Lorenzo Bernini.
THE ECSTASY OF SAINT TERESA.
Detail of the altar, Cornaro Chapel,
Santa Maria della Vittoria, Rome. 1645–1652.
Marble. Life-size.

441 Gian Lorenzo Bernini (18th-century painting by an unknown artist).
CORNARO CHAPEL. 1645–1652.
Staatliches Museum, Schwerin, Germany.

444 Jan Vermeer
THE GIRL WITH THE RED HAT. c. 1660.
Oil on wood. 9⅛″ × 7⅛″.
National Gallery of Art, Washington, D.C.
Andrew W. Mellon Collection.

His intimate portrait THE GIRL WITH THE RED HAT has the quality of a chance encounter – a vivid moment. The painting is one of Vermeer's early works. It was painted on a small wooden panel similar in size to the frosted glass on which the image appeared in one type of camera obscura of the period. Vermeer evidently taught himself to see with photographic accuracy by copying images from the ground glass. In THE GIRL WITH THE RED HAT, the focus has a narrow range. Only part of the girl's collar and the left edge of her cheek are in sharp focus; everything in front of and behind that narrow band becomes increasingly blurred. The carved lion's head on the arm of the chair in the foreground looks like shimmering light, just as it would appear in an out-of-focus photograph.

For Vermeer, the camera obscura was an important tool. With it he was able to develop his perceptive powers, but he went beyond the imitation of surfaces. His sense of abstract design gave his compositions their great strength.

Vermeer's painting THE ARTIST IN HIS STUDIO may be an idealized self-portrait. Like his Spanish contemporary, Velázquez, Vermeer painted a behind-the-scenes view of an artist's world. The heavy curtain and other dark objects in the left foreground lead into the painting and give dynamic balance to the center of interest created by the black-and-white stripes on the artist's shirt. We look over the artist's shoulder at a painting in progress, then move left again to the figure of the woman who represents the Muse of History. She holds a book and trumpet, symbols of fame. The plaster cast and the book on the table symbolize the other arts.

Everything in the studio is illuminated by light coming through an unseen window on the left. Vermeer carefully noted the subtle ways light defined the precise character of each thing he observed. His exceptional awareness of qualities of light and reflected color give Vermeer's paintings extraordinary luminosity.

During the baroque period, French artists adopted Italian Renaissance ideas, but made them their own. By the end of the seventeenth century France had begun to take the lead in European art.

445 Jan Vermeer.
THE ARTIST IN HIS STUDIO. c. 1665.
Oil on canvas. 31⅜″ × 26″.
Kunsthistorisches Museum, Vienna.

We can glimpse a different view of seventeenth-century European life in the royal architecture and garden design of the French imperial villa of VERSAILLES built for King Louis XIV. The main palace with its gardens exemplifies seventeenth-century baroque architecture and landscape architecture. Throughout the palace and its gardens, cool classical restraint and symmetry balance the romance of baroque opulence and grand scale.

VERSAILLES expresses the absolute monarch's desire to surpass all others in the splendor of his palace. It is an example of royal extravagance, originally set in fifteen thousand acres of manicured gardens, twelve miles south of Paris. The vast formal gardens with their miles of clipped hedges proclaimed the king's desire to rule even over nature. It is revealing to compare the contrasting attitudes behind VERSAILLES and KATSURA, the Japanese imperial villa built during the same century (see page 282).

The heavy, theatrical qualities of baroque art gradually gave way to the light and airy *rococo* style in France early in the eighteenth century. Some of the movement, light, and gesture of the baroque remained, but the effect was quite different. The arts moved out of the marble halls of palaces such as Versailles into fashionable townhouses.

The pastel colors of the rococo style in France were particularly suited to the frivolous life of the court. Elegantly paneled interiors of palaces and wealthy homes were decorated with golden shells, garlands of flowers, and gay paintings. The word rococo comes from the French *rocaille*, which refers to the shells and rocks used for ornament in garden grottos. The curved shapes of the shells were copied in architectural ornament and furniture, and influenced the billowing shapes in paintings.

446 VERSAILLES. c. 1665.
Painting by Pierre Patel. Louvre Museum, Paris.

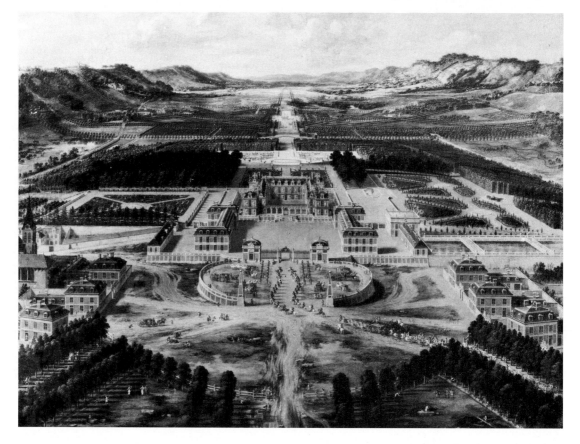

447 Antoine Watteau.
PILGRIMAGE TO THE ISLAND OF CYTHERA. 1717.
Oil on canvas. 50½″ × 76″.
Louvre Museum, Paris.

Antoine Watteau was the painter most responsible for setting the tone of early eighteenth century painting in France. Watteau designed
rococo interiors for the castles of nobility, but
his fame rests on his romantic painted visions of
life free from hardships, where musical parties
and festive picnics fill the days. His painting PIL-
GRIMAGE TO THE ISLAND OF CYTHERA por-
trays the legendary island where Venus rose from
the sea. Lovers depart after a day of romance on
the island of eternal youth and love. The robust
sensuality of the baroque is transformed by Watteau into a shimmering pastel world. Watteau's
graceful lines and feathered brushwork combine
with an overlay of transparent glazes inspired by
Venetian colorists such as Giorgione.

Jean-Honoré Fragonard's flamboyant temper-
ament was in contrast to the quiet melancholy
of Watteau. Fragonard drew inspiration from
many French, Italian, and Flemish sources, yet
he developed and retained his own identity. The
freedom of his brush technique and the vitality
of his landscapes are seen in THE BATHERS (see
next page). There is not a straight line in the entire composition—no hints of horizontal or vertical edges that might tie things down a bit.
Compositions during this period were playful
and richly decorative in keeping with the exuberant extravagances of the French court.

The rococo world of make-believe contrasts
with the straightforward look at the lives of ordinary people painted in the same period by
Fragonard's first teacher, Jean-Baptiste-Siméon
Chardin. Throughout his long life, Chardin

448 Jean-Honoré Fragonard.
THE BATHERS. c. 1765.
Oil on canvas. 25¼″ × 31¼″.
Louvre Museum, Paris.

449 Jean-Baptiste-Siméon Chardin.
GRACE BEFORE A MEAL. 1740.
Oil on canvas. 19¼″ × 15⅜″.
Louvre Museum, Paris.

painted still lifes and modest domestic interiors with careful attention to the spirit as well as the surface of each object he portrayed. His paintings, which reveal the beauty in ordinary objects and everyday life, were popular with members of the middle class. GRACE BEFORE A MEAL demonstrates Chardin's ability to paint textures and to present them within a well-structured composition. His sensitivity to composition is comparable only to Vermeer's similar treatment of figures in interiors (see page 339).

The Baroque era was soon to give way to the Age of Reason. By the middle of the eighteenth century, political and economic strains had developed in France; the fantasy and frivolity of rococo art no longer adequately expressed the prevailing experience or attitude. A more serious attitude led to the study and reinterpretation of the visual forms and symbolic content of classical Greek and Roman art.

PART FIVE

The Modern World

*In every new age there is a turning
point, a new way of seeing and
asserting the coherence of the world.*
Jacob Bronowski[1]

Wassily Kandinsky.
Detail of BLUE MOUNTAIN. 1908.
(See page 380).

13

The Late
Eighteenth
and Nineteenth
Centuries

Three revolutions—the Industrial Revolution, which began in Britain about 1760, the American Revolution in 1775, and the French Revolution in 1789—launched the period of great social and technological change we call the modern age. The Enlightenment, or Age of Reason, as the eighteenth century has been called, was characterized by a shift to a more rational and scientific approach to religious, political, social, and economic issues. Belief in self-determination and progress brought about an emphasis on secular concerns.

In art, a new self-consciousness and controversy about styles and stylishness led to increasing uncertainty about the place of art and artists in society. Earlier societies each had a dominant style that was simply the way things were done. Following the French Revolution, and the subsequent break with traditional art patronage in France, a variety of styles developed. Artists were freed from the artistic constraints imposed by their traditional patrons (royalty, aristocracy, wealthy merchants and bankers, and the church), but were left to struggle financially until a new system of patronage emerged. The support that developed has continued in the form of private collectors, museums, and commercial galleries.

NEOCLASSICISM

With the French Revolution in 1789, the luxurious life that centered on the French court ended abruptly, and French society and economy were disrupted and transformed. As social structure and values changed, tastes changed radically.

One of the men who led the way to revolution was the painter Jacques-Louis David. When he painted OATH OF THE HORATII, David intentionally used a rational and controlled neoclassical style. The term *neoclassical* refers to the emulation of the cultures of classical Greece and Rome. Much of the subject matter in neoclassical art was Roman, because Rome represented a republican, or nonmonarchial government.

David rejected what he saw as the frivolous immorality associated with the aristocratic rococo style. He believed that the arts should serve as political propaganda during the time of reform. The subject of OATH OF THE HORATII is a story of virtue and readiness to die for liberty, in which three brothers pledge to take the sword offered by their father to defend Rome. The painting acquired political meaning, and proved to be prophetic when Louis XVI was executed during the revolution.

David's neoclassicism emphasized a geometric structuring of the composition, creating rational clarity, in strong contrast to the vague softness

450 Jacques-Louis David.
OATH OF THE HORATII. 1784.
Oil on canvas.
10'10" × 14'.
Louvre Museum, Paris.

of the rococo. Strong directional light emphasizes the figures in the foreground and creates an image with the quality of classical relief sculpture. Even the folds in the garments are more like marble than soft cloth. The three arches set on columns give strength to the design and provide a historically appropriate setting for the Roman figures. The two center columns separate the three major parts of the subject. Vertical and horizontal lines parallel the edges of the picture plane to form a stable composition that resembles a stage set.

In architecture, the practice of borrowing and combining from diverse sources is called *eclecticism*. By the nineteenth century, historic styles had been carefully catalogued so that architects in Europe, the United States, and other parts of the world could borrow and adapt freely, depending on the tastes of architects and their clients. In church design, the Byzantine, Romanesque, and Gothic styles dominated. For public and commercial buildings, Renaissance, Greek,

and Roman designs were preferred, and often mixed. These preferences lasted well into the twentieth century, as the major old buildings in American cities attest.

American architecture achieved international stature for the first time with the work of American statesman and architect Thomas Jefferson. His design for his home, MONTICELLO, was initially derived from Palladio's sixteenth-century interpretation of Roman country-style houses (see page 331). During his years in Europe as Minister to France between 1784 and 1789, Jefferson was strongly influenced by French, Italian, and surviving examples of ancient Roman architecture. Thus, when he rebuilt his home between 1793 and 1806, he had the second story removed from the center of the building and replaced by a dome on an octagonal drum. He added a large Greco-Roman portico, making the entire design reminiscent of the PANTHEON (see page 306) by way of contemporary French neoclassical architecture. In comparison with the

451   Thomas Jefferson.
MONTICELLO. Charlottesville, Virginia. 1793–1806.
Photograph: J. T. Tkatch.
Courtesy of the Thomas Jefferson Memorial Foundation.

first Monticello, the second version has a monumental quality that reflects Jefferson's increasingly classical conception of architecture.

Jefferson also designed the University of Virginia, which was built shortly before his death. Both Monticello and the University of Virginia are examples of the Roman phase of neoclassical architecture (often called the Federal or Jeffersonian Style). Jefferson's aim was for an architecture capable of expressing the values of the new republic. His architecture has an originality in its fusion of classical Greek, Roman, Palladian Renaissance, Georgian English, and contemporary French forms that makes his work stand above other more imitative works. Jefferson's neoclassical synthesis set the style for much of American architecture until the Civil War. Neoclassical architecture can be found in practically every city in the United States, and continues to dominate Washington, D.C.

ROMANTICISM

The literary and artistic movement called *romanticism* emerged in Europe toward the end of the eighteenth century as a reaction against the rigid rules of neoclassicism. The incentives behind the movement were desires to assert the validity of subjective experience and to escape what the romanticists saw as the neoclassicists' fixation on classical forms and formulas at the expense of content and feeling. Although the basic aims of the romanticists varied widely, they shared a concern for the common person and an emphasis on the senses over reason and intellect. In contrast to neoclassicism, romanticism is not a clearly defined or easily recognizable, unified style. The literature of the time, including the historical novels of Sir Walter Scott and the poetry of Lord Byron and William Wordsworth, as well as music such as Wagner's operas, were sources of inspiration for romantic painters and sculptors. The romantic movement dominated European art from about 1825 to 1850.

Spanish artist Francisco Goya was an independent romantic painter and printmaker. A contemporary of David, he was aware of the French Revolution, and personally experienced some of the worst aspects of the ensuing Napoleonic era. Because his sympathies were with the revolution, and he had lost confidence in the king of Spain, Goya at first welcomed Napoleon's invading army. But he soon discovered that the occupying army was destroying rather than defending the ideals he had associated with the revolution. Madrid was occupied by Napoleon's troops in 1808. On May 2, a riot broke out against the French in the Puerto del Sol. Officers fired from a nearby hill and the cavalry was ordered to cut down the crowds. The following night, a firing squad was set up to shoot anyone who appeared in the streets. Goya vividly and bitterly depicted these brutalities in his powerful indictment of organized murder, THE THIRD OF MAY, 1808, painted in February 1814.

The painting is large, yet so well conceived in every detail that it delivers its meaning in a single, visual flash. A clearly structured pattern of light and dark areas organizes the scene and gives

452 Francisco Goya.
THE THIRD OF MAY, 1808. 1814.
Oil on canvas. 8'9" × 13'4".
Prado Museum, Madrid.

it impact. Value shifts define a wedge shape formed by the edge of the hill and the edge of the brightly lighted area on the ground, which helps to bring attention to the soldiers. From their dark shapes, we are led by the light and the lines of the rifle barrels to the man in white. The entire picture is focused on this man, who raises his arms in defiance as more people are forced into the light to be shot. The irregular shape of his shirt is illuminated by the hard, white cube of the soldier's lantern. Mechanical uniformity marks the faceless firing squad, in contrast with the ragged group that is the target.

Goya was appalled by atrocities committed during the French occupation. His sensitivity, magnified by the total deafness of his later years, made the visual experience of war all the more vivid. THE THIRD OF MAY, 1808 is not a heroic reconstruction of history; it is a universal statement of protest against war.

English painting in the early nineteenth century was dominated by an interest in landscape —brought on, in part, by the need to escape the growing effects of the Industrial Revolution. Romantic painters John Constable and William Turner became recognized masters and led the way to later developments in painting.

453   John Constable.
THE HAY WAIN. 1821.
Oil on canvas. 50½″ × 73″.
Reproduced courtesy of the Trustees. The National Gallery, London.

The son of a wealthy miller, Constable grew up in the country and developed a love of nature that was to stay with him all his life. Nature and paintings by earlier masters of European landscape became his sources of inspiration. Although his final detailed paintings were developed in the traditional way in his studio, they were preceded by numerous oil sketches completed outdoors. Constable was not the first to paint studies on location, but he was unique in the attention he gave to intangible qualities of light and weather. He decried what he saw as the decline of art caused by "the imitation of preceding styles, with little reference to nature."[1]

When Constable's painting THE HAY WAIN was exhibited in the annual Paris exhibition of 1824, French artists were amazed by the English painter's vision of landscape. Eugène Delacroix is said to have been so inspired by the way the sky was painted in THE HAY WAIN that he repainted the sky in one of his own major works in a similar manner. Constable broke away from conventional formulas of color and technique. His innovative use of broken strokes of varied color (rather than the traditional method of laying down continuous areas of a single color) and his use of flecks of white to suggest shimmering sunlight brought him ridicule from some critics and, two generations later, praise from French impressionists.

Turner's freely expressive approach to painting was in some ways more indicative of things to come than Constable's naturalism. While Constable gave attention to the wonder of so-called ordinary subjects and humble settings, Turner often chose to interpret dramatic forces in nature. Upon seeing one of Turner's early paintings, Constable said it was "the most complete work of genius I ever saw."[2]

Turner's interests in light and color, atmosphere, and direct, expressive brush strokes anticipated, yet were different from, the interest of the less romantic French impressionists. In SNOWSTORM: STEAMBOAT OFF A HARBOR'S MOUTH, the mast and sidewheel of a steamboat are barely visible in a swirling vortex of snow and wind. Turner based his painting on a unique experience. So that he could fully understand the wrath of a blizzard at sea, Turner had sailors lash him to the mast, where he remained for four hours. He wasn't sure he would survive, but vowed to paint the storm if he did. Turner's visionary land and seascapes symbolize human emotion and vulnerability in the face of nature's awesome power.

The work of romantic painter Thomas Cole helped to stimulate enthusiasm for the vast American wilderness. Cole, America's first popular landscape painter, is recognized as the founder of the Hudson River school. In THE OXBOW, Cole employed an approach to landscape that became widely used by other Hud-

454 Joseph Mallord William Turner.
SNOWSTORM: STEAMBOAT OFF
A HARBOR'S MOUTH. 1842.
Oil on canvas. 35½" × 47½".
The Tate Gallery, London.

455 Thomas Cole.
THE OXBOW. 1836.
Oil on canvas. 51½" × 76".
*Metropolitan Museum of Art,
New York. Gift of Mrs. Russell
Sage, 1908 (08.228).*

456   Eugène Delacroix.
THE DEATH OF SARDANAPALUS. 1827.
Oil on canvas. 12'1½'' × 16'2⅞''.
Louvre Museum, Paris.

son River school painters. A broad, panoramic view that included a variety of physical features, carefully rendered details, and a light-filled atmosphere became the basis for the practice of landscape painting for several generations. Cole began with elaborate on-site oil and pencil sketches, but made his large paintings in his studio.

Eugène Delacroix was the leading French Romantic painter. Both Goya and Delacroix used baroque lighting to heighten the emotional impact of their work. Delacroix's painting THE DEATH OF SARDANAPALUS exhibits the many qualities that distinguish romanticism from the neoclassicism of David and his followers. The turbulent sensuality is based on Byron's poem, in which the legendary Assyrian ruler watches from his deathbed after ordering that his palace and all its contents be destroyed. The romantic ideal stresses passionate involvement, color (equal in importance to drawing), and spontaneous movement, in contrast to the cool, detached formal qualities of neoclassicism. Delacroix's rich color and *painterly* execution (open form, sensual use of paint, with shapes defined by changes in color rather than line) was greatly admired by later painters, particularly the Dutch expressionist Vincent van Gogh.

Both neoclassical and romantic painters of the mid-nineteenth century were known to employ historical, literary, mythical, and exotic subjects. The French Academy of Fine Arts, *L'École des Beaux Arts*, gave official sanction to highly illustrative approaches to painting. See Couture's neoclassical ROMANS OF THE DECADENCE on page 352 and Delacroix's romantic DEATH OF SARDANAPALUS. *Academic art* is art that follows formulas laid down by an academy or school, and is often used to refer to types of painting and sculpture preferred by the nineteenth-century French Academy.

PHOTOGRAPHY

One of the nineteenth-century inventions that changed life forever was the camera perfected by the painter Daguerre (see page 152). Portrait painters initially saw photography as a threat to their livelihood, yet it largely freed all painters from the roles of narrator and illustrator. Except for color, the realistic portrayal of subject matter could be handled by the new medium; this gave painters the opportunity to explore dimensions of inner experience that had scarcely been considered previously. At the same time, photography offered new opportunities to fuse images of objective reality with personal visions.

Delacroix was one of the first to recognize the difference between camera vision and human vision. He understood the unique qualities of each. For him, the camera and the photographic process developed by Daguerre were of great benefit to art and artists: " . . . let a man of genius make use of the daguerreotype as it is to be used, and he will raise himself to a height that we do not know."[3]

Delacroix drew and painted from metal daguerreotypes and prints on paper. He set up a painter's composition with a model; then with the help of his friend and colleague, the photographer Eugène Durieu, he made a photograph. In this way, a photograph rather than a drawing became the basis for a painting. In an essay for students, Delacroix wrote,

A daguerreotype is a mirror of the object, certain details almost always overlooked in drawing from nature take on in it characteristic importance, and thus introduce the artist to complete knowledge of construction as light and shade are found in their true character.[4]

457 Eugène Durieu.
FIGURE STUDY. c. 1855.
Photograph.
Bibliotheque Nationale, Paris.

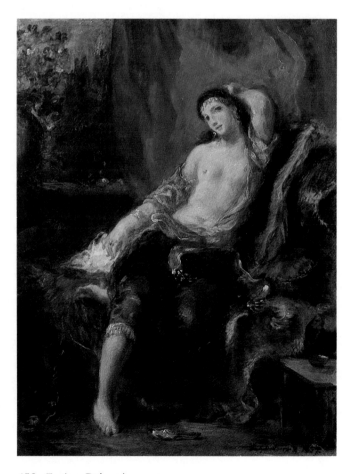

458 Eugène Delacroix.
ODALISQUE. 1857.
Oil on canvas. 35.5 cm × 30.5 cm.
Private collection.

In an effort to prove that photography could be art, many photographers worked in the academic manner. They used the medium so suited to staying in touch with the actual world to create photographs designed to look like paintings. With exceeding care, painter and photographer O. G. Rejlander combined over thirty negatives to achieve his technically ambitious and morally explicit photograph THE TWO WAYS OF LIFE.

Rejlander was devoted to the new medium of photography and went to great lengths to prove that it was possible to create photographs equal in importance to paintings. His opportunity came when he entered this print in the "Manchester Art Treasures Exhibition" of 1857. Queen Victoria, who was an amateur photographer, purchased the work.

459   O. G. Rejlander.
THE TWO WAYS OF LIFE. 1857.
Photograph. 16″ × 31″.
Royal Photographic Society Collection, Bath, England.

Rejlander was working within the same academic style as Thomas Couture. Couture's huge painting ROMANS OF THE DECADENCE is a romantic subject in a neoclassical setting typical of nineteenth-century French academic art. This painting represents the dying gasp of pictorial themes that had been worked and reworked since the Renaissance. It nominally criticized Roman decadence, but also presented an eroticism that was appealing in an age of repressed sexuality. Vast changes in art, however, were about to topple the dominance of the French Academy.

REALISM

The term *realism* is often used to describe a style in art and literature in which the aim is to depict ordinary existence without idealism. By midcentury, a growing number of artists pursued an interest in the visual appearance of everyday life. Realism was based on the belief that art should employ subject matter chosen from real and existing things, immediate experience, and observation, rather than from history, mythology, or imagination.

Realism was used before the nineteenth century, notably in Roman, Flemish, and Dutch painting. In the 1850s, Gustave Courbet extended the concept with new vigor by employing a direct, painterly technique and objective vision to represent images of common life. Courbet's realism broke with the artificial grandeur and exoticism of the popular and academically acceptable styles of his day, and paved the way for a rediscovery of the extraordinary qualities of everyday visual experience.

Courbet's detractors were sure that he was causing an artistic and moral decline by depicting what many considered unpleasant and trivial subjects. The sacred concepts of "Beauty" and

460   Thomas Couture.
ROMANS OF THE DECADENCE. 1847.
Oil on canvas. 15′1″ × 25′4″.
Louvre Museum, Paris.

461 Gustave Courbet.
THE STONE BREAKERS. 1849
(destroyed during World War II).
Oil on canvas. 5′5″ × 7′10″.
Formerly in State Picture Gallery, Dresden, Germany.
Photograph: Gerhard Reinhold,
Leipzig-Molkau, East Germany.

"the Ideal" were seen as under attack by the so-called "cult of ugliness." Realism was perceived as nothing less than the enemy of art, and many believed photography was the source and the sponsor of this disaster.

Actually, the new technique of photography began to be used in the mid-nineteenth century by artist/photographers who insisted upon the importance of objective vision. As both a tool and a way of seeing, photography did influence realism. But photography is not a completely impartial medium; photographs, as well as paintings, reflect the ideas and values of the time, and the attitude and experience of the artist/photographer.

THE STONE BREAKERS shows Courbet's rejection of romantic and neoclassical formulas. Courbet did not idealize the work of breaking stones, or dramatize the struggle for existence. He simply said, "Look at this."

Portable tubes of oil paint became available in 1841. This made it easier for artists to paint outdoors without preliminary drawings or preconceived plans. Courbet was one of the first to complete paintings outdoors directly from nature. Previously, most landscape painting had been done in the artist's studio from memory, sketches, and bits of reference material such as rocks and plants brought in from outside. By working directly from the subject outdoors, painters were able to capture their first clear impressions. This shift in practice opened up whole new ways of seeing and painting.

Courbet's subjects were neither historical nor allegorical, neither religious nor heroic. In THE STONE BREAKERS, they are ordinary road workers, presented almost life-size in a large painting. When the painting was exhibited in Paris in 1850, it was attacked as unartistic, crude, and socialistic. For later expositions, Courbet set up his own exhibits. This laid the

462   Jean Léon Gérôme.
PYGMALIAN AND GALATEA. c. 1860.
Oil on canvas. 35″ × 27″.
Metropolitan Museum of Art, New York.
Gift of Louis Raegner, 1927 (27.200).

463   Thomas Eakins.
WILLIAM RUSH AND HIS MODEL. 1907–1908.
Oil on canvas. 35¼″ × 47¼″.
Honolulu Academy of Arts, Honolulu, Hawaii. Gift of Friends of
the Academy.

groundwork for independent shows organized by artists themselves.

Of his own work, Courbet said,

To know in order to create, that was my idea. To be able to represent the customs, the ideas, the appearance of my own era . . . to create living art; that is my aim.[5]

The realist paintings of American artist Thomas Eakins are remarkable for their humanity and insights into the everyday world. In 1866, Eakins went to Paris, where he studied for three years with the academic painter Jean Léon Gérôme. While in Europe, he was inspired by the work of Rembrandt and Velázquez. On his return to America, Eakins began painting in the powerful realistic style he continued to employ the rest of his life.

Eakins combined artistic and scientific interests. By the 1880s, he was an expert photographer, and used the camera to study the human body at rest and in motion (see page 74). His insistence on realism, including the use of totally nude male and female models in his classes

at the Pennsylvania Academy of Fine Arts, caused a controversy that ended with his resignation from his teaching post. A comparison between paintings by Eakins and his teacher, Gérôme, shows the contrast between officially sanctioned academic art and realism.

The Greek myth of Pygmalion tells of a sculptor who carved a statue of a woman that was so beautiful he fell in love with the sculpture. Pygmalion prayed to Aphrodite, goddess of love, who responded by making the figure actually come to life. Of course, the pair lived happily ever after. In PYGMALION AND GALATEA, a painting illustrating this myth, Gérôme placed the woman on a pedestal, both literally and figuratively. In the painting WILLIAM RUSH AND HIS MODEL, Eakins used his own likeness for Rush, an early-nineteenth-century American sculptor Eakins greatly admired. It was Eakins's last self-portrait. The sculptor is depicted helping his model as she steps down from the stand as if she were a queen being helped from a carriage, yet Eakins's realism shows no hint of flattery.

The attitude Eakins presented is one of great respect for the beauty of the ordinary human being. Gérôme may have been equally interested in ordinary women, yet he created a painting based on classic/academic ideals. Eakins's insistence on painting the way people actually look led him to escape from the bondage of stylization imposed by the rules of the academy, but also led to shock and rejection by the public and much of the art world.

Eakins's influence can be seen in the work of his student and friend Henry Ossawa Tanner. As a boy of thirteen, Tanner watched a landscape painter at work and decided then to become a painter. While studying with Eakins at the Academy of Fine Arts in Philadelphia, Tanner changed his subject matter from landscape to scenes of daily life. In 1891, after an exhibition of his work was largely ignored, Tanner moved to France, where he remained for most of the rest of his life.

The lively realism of THE BANJO LESSON reveals Tanner's considerable insight into the feelings of his subjects, yet avoids the sentimentality that was common in many late-ninteenth-century American paintings. THE BANJO LESSON shows the influence of Eakins in its detail and color, and of the impressionists in its use of light. Through careful attention to supporting details of shape, light, color, line, and texture, Tanner created a strong and memorable mood.

The revolution that occurred in painting in the 1860s and 1870s has sometimes been referred to as the Manet Revolution. Edouard Manet was a student of Couture, but moved away from many of the artistic ideals of his teacher. Compare Couture's ROMANS OF THE DECADENCE (page 352) with Manet's LUNCHEON ON THE GRASS (see next page). Manet's study of the flat shapes of Japanese prints (see page 281) encouraged him to minimize illusionary space, and to make powerful use of value, shape, and color. His painting style and choice of commonplace subjects reflect Courbet's influence. Manet fused Courbet's realism with his own concepts, and sparked the enthusiasm for painterly brushwork and everyday visual experience that led to impressionism.

464 Henry O. Tanner.
THE BANJO LESSON. 1893.
Oil on canvas. 4'½" × 3'11".
Hampton Institute, Hampton, Virginia.

465   Edouard Manet.
LUNCHEON ON THE GRASS. 1863.
Oil on canvas. 84″ X 106″.
Louvre Museum, Paris.

Manet's painting LUNCHEON ON THE GRASS scandalized French critics and the public because of the shocking juxtaposition of a female nude with males dressed in contemporary clothing. It was painted entirely in his studio, though it is an outdoor scene. There is no allegory, history, or mythology, not even a significant title to suggest glorified meaning. Use of nudes and clothed figures in landscape derives from a long tradition of going back to Renaissance and Roman compositions. In fact, Manet based his composition but not his content on the figures on a Renaissance engraving, THE JUDGMENT OF PARIS by Marcantonio Raimondi, who worked from a drawing by Raphael, who in turn was influenced by Roman relief sculpture. What is new, and even revolutionary, about Manet's painting is his emphasis on shapes, like that of the female depicted without chiaroscuro. LUNCHEON ON THE GRASS is painted directly with colors, rather than developed with a monochromatic underpainting in light and shade and then overpainted with colored glazes. Manet's emphasis on the interplay of dark and light shapes and his de-emphasis of both chiaroscuro and perspective cause us to look *at* rather than through or into his paintings.

REVOLUTION IN ARCHITECTURE

New inventions of the industrial age, which led to a revolution in architecture, came at the same time as the rejection of academic styles by realist painters. In September 1850, construction began on Joseph Paxton's CRYSTAL PALACE. The large exposition hall (discussed in chapter 8 under architecture, page 230) was designed to show off the latest mechanical inventions. The building was perfectly suited to the task, because it was the first time that the potential beauty of industrial methods and materials were eloquently presented in architecture. Paxton used the largest piece of glass then available as the module for his revolutionary building. By freeing himself from past styles and masonry construction, Paxton created a whole new architectural vocabulary. The CRYSTAL PALACE, with its unique combination of iron, wood, and glass, was recognized in its day as a highly original expression of the spirit of the new age.

466 Marcantonio Raimondi.
Detail of THE JUDGMENT OF PARIS. c. 1520.
Engraving after Raphael.
Metropolitan Museum of Art, New York. Rogers Fund 1919 (19.74.1).

467 Joseph Paxton.
CRYSTAL PALACE. London. 1850–1851.
Cast-iron and glass. Width 408′; length 1851′.
a. Exterior. (Etching.
Victoria and Albert Museum, London. Crown Copyright.)
b. Interior. (Etching by Lothar Buchar.
Victoria and Albert Museum, London, Crown Copyright.)

IMPRESSIONISM

In 1874, a group of young painters who had been denied the right to show in the Salon of 1873 (the annual exhibition held in Paris) organized an independent exhibition of their work. Landscape and ordinary scenes painted outdoors in varying atmospheric conditions and times of day were their main subjects. Some of them found momentary effects of light particularly interesting. They were dubbed "impressionists" by a critic who objected to the sketchy quality of their paintings. The label, intended to be derogatory, was suggested by Claude Monet's IMPRESSION: SUNRISE.

Although their style came to be known as *impressionism*, they called themselves "illuminists." Impressionism was strongest between 1870 and 1880. After 1880, it was Monet who continued for more than thirty years to advance impressionism's original premise. Instead of painting from sketches, he and most of the others in the group painted outdoors. Monet often returned to the same subject in order to record the mood and qualities of light of each changing hour.

Monet painted with touches of pure color placed next to each other, rather than with colors premixed and then applied to the canvas. This enabled the viewer to experience a form of *optical mixing* (see page 88). A violet area, for example, may be made of blue, violet, and touches of pure red. The viewer does not see the individual colors, but perceives a vibrancy that cannot be achieved with mixed color alone. The effect was startling to eyes accustomed to the muted, continuous tones of academic painting.

Impressionism enthusiastically affirmed modern life. The impressionists saw the beauty of the world as a gift and the forces of nature as friendly aids to human progress. Although misunderstood by their public, the impressionists made visible a widely held optimism about the promise of industrialization.

468 Claude Monet.
IMPRESSION:
SUNRISE.
1872. Oil on canvas.
19½″ × 25½″.
Location unknown. Stolen from the Musée Marmottan, Paris in 1985.

469   Pierre-Auguste Renoir.
THE LUNCHEON OF THE BOATING PARTY. 1881.
Oil on canvas. 51″ × 68″.
The Phillips Collection, Washington, D.C.

Pierre-Auguste Renoir's THE LUNCHEON OF THE BOATING PARTY is a fine example of impressionist themes. A group of friends is seen finishing their lunch at a café situated on the bank of the river Seine a few miles from Paris. By 1881, Renoir had begun to move away from the lighter, more diffuse imagery of the 1870s toward more solid forms and more structured design. His disregard for true linear perspective, as seen in the lines of the railing and table top, reflects the declining interest in naturalistic illusions of depth. As in the works of Monet, pure hues vibrate across the surface in delightfully exuberant brushwork. The young men and women depicted are conversing, sipping wine, and generally enjoying themselves. The Industrial Revolution had created a new leisure for the middle class, and people had more time to gather together for pleasure.

470   Edgar Degas.
THE BALLET CLASS. c. 1878–1880.
Oil on canvas. 32⅛″ × 30⅛″.
Philadelphia Museum of Art. W. P. Wilstach Collection.

Edgar Degas exhibited with the impressionists, although his approach differed from theirs. He shared with the impressionists a directness of expression and an interest in portraying contemporary life, but he combined the immediacy of impressionism with a structured approach to design not found in the work of the impressionists. Degas, along with the impressionists, was strongly influenced by the new ways of seeing and image-making suggested by Japanese prints and by photography. Conventional European compositions placed subjects within a central zone; but Degas used surprising, life-like compositions and effects related to photographs and Japanese prints, which often cut figures at the edge. The tipped-up ground planes and bold asymmetry found in Japanese prints inspired Degas to create paintings filled with intriguing visual tensions, such as those seen in THE BALLET CLASS, in which two diagonal groups of figures are on opposite sides of an empty center.

Degas depicted ballet classes in ways that showed their unglamorous character. Often, as here, he was able to turn his great ability to the task of defining human character and mood in a given situation. The painting builds from the quiet, uninterested woman in the foreground, up to the right, then across to the cluster of dancing girls following the implied line of sight of the ballet master. The stability of the group on the right contrasts with the smaller, irregular shape of the girls before the mirror. Degas managed to balance spatial tensions between near and far, and to create interesting contrasts between stable and unstable, large and small. He emphasized the line in the floor, which he brought together with the top of the woman's newspaper to guide the viewer's eye. The angle of the seated woman's foot brings us back around to begin again.

Painters such as Manet, Monet, Renoir, and Degas rejected the artificial poses and limited color prescribed by the academy. Because they rebelled against acceptable styles, they made few sales in their early years. Many who were considered outsiders, set apart from the acceptable art of their time, we now consider key masters of the nineteenth century and precursors of twentieth-century art.

THE POSTIMPRESSIONIST PERIOD

Postimpressionism refers to the several styles that followed impressionism after 1885. Many painters who tried impressionism early in their careers felt that solidity of form and composition had been sacrificed for the sake of fleeting impressions of light and color. Postimpressionism refers to various reactions to impressionism rather than to a single style. The two dominant tendencies during the period were expressionistic and formalistic. Four painters whose works best exemplify postimpressionist attitudes were Paul Gauguin, Vincent van Gogh, Georges Seurat, and Paul Cézanne.

Gauguin and Van Gogh brought to their work an expressive, emotional intensity and a desire to make their inner thoughts and feelings visible. They used strong color contrasts, shapes with clear contours, bold brushwork, and, in Van Gogh's case, vigorous paint textures. The work of these two painters greatly influenced twentieth-century styles of *expressionism*.

Seurat and Cézanne were more interested in developing significant formal structure in their paintings. Both organized visual form in uniquely personal ways in order to achieve structured clarity of design. (Because of the structural emphasis in his paintings, Degas could be considered one of the formalist postimpressionist painters.)

471   Georges Seurat. SUNDAY AFTERNOON ON THE ISLAND
OF LA GRANDE JATTE. 1884–1886.
Oil on canvas. 81″ × 120⅜″.
Helen Birch Bartlett Memorial Collection (1926.224).

Seurat's large painting SUNDAY AFTERNOON ON THE ISLAND OF LA GRANDE JATTE has the subject matter and the light and color qualities of impressionism, but this painting is not of a fleeting glimpse; it is a structured design worked out with great precision. Seurat set out to systematize the optical color mixing of impressionism and to create a more rigid organization with simplified forms. He called his method *divisionism*, but it is more popularly known as *pointillism*. With it, Seurat tried to develop and apply a "scientific" technique. He arrived at his method by studying the principles of color optics that were being discovered at the time. Through the application of tiny dots of color, Seurat achieved a richly colored surface based on optical color mixture (see page 88).

Seurat made a large number of drawn and painted studies of the subject. With them, he carefully studied the horizontal and vertical relationships, the character of each shape, and the patterns of light, shade, and color.

The final painting shows the total control that Seurat sought through the application of his method. The frozen formality of the figures seems surprising, considering the casual nature of the subject matter; yet it is precisely this calm, formal grandeur that gives the painting its enduring strength and poetic appeal.

Of the many great painters working in France during the last twenty years of the nineteenth century, Cézanne had the most lasting effect on the course of painting. Thus, he is sometimes referred to as the "father of modern art."

Cézanne, like Seurat, was more interested in the structural or formal aspects of painting than in its ability to convey emotions. He sought to achieve lasting strength in the formal structure of his paintings. "My aim," he said, "was to make impressionism into something solid and enduring like the art of the museums."[6]

Both Cézanne and Seurat based their work on observation of nature, and both used visibly separate strokes of color to build their rich surfaces. Cézanne saw the planar surfaces of his subjects in terms of color modulation. He did not use light and shadow in a conventional way, but carefully developed relationships between adjoining strokes of color in order to show the solidity of form and receding space. His paintings are free of atmospheric color effects. Seurat's slow, highly demanding method was not popular

among younger artists. Cézanne's open brush strokes and his concept of a geometric substructure in nature and art offered a whole range of possibilities to those who studied his later paintings.

Landscape was one of Cézanne's main interests. He questioned, then abandoned, linear perspective as defined by Renaissance artists, and went beyond the appearance of nature, to reorganize pictorial form in his own way. In MONT SAINTE-VICTOIRE, we can see how he flattened space somewhat, yet gave an impression of air and depth with some atmospheric perspective and through the use of warm advancing and cool receding colors. The dark edge lines around the distant mountain stop our eyes and return them to the foreground. There is an important interplay between the illusion of depth and the fact of strokes of color on a flat surface. Cézanne simplified the houses and tree masses into

472   Paul Cézanne.
MONT SAINTE-VICTOIRE. 1902–1904.
Oil on canvas. 27½″ × 35¼″.
Philadelphia Museum of Art. George W. Elkins Collection.

473 Mary Cassatt.
THE BOATING PARTY. 1893–1894.
Oil on canvas. 35½″ × 46⅛″.
National Gallery of Art, Washington, D.C.
Chester Dale Collection (1962).

patches of color that suggest almost geometric planes and masses. In a letter to his friend, the young painter Emile Bernard, Cézanne wrote these now-famous words of advice: ". . . treat nature by the cylinder, the sphere, the cone. . . ."[7] Compare this painting with Monet's IMPRESSION: SUNRISE on page 358 to see how far Cézanne had moved from impressionism.

American painter Mary Cassatt went to Paris in the late 1860s to further her artistic development. She was particularly influenced by Manet and Degas, and following an invitation by Degas, she joined and exhibited with the impressionists.

Later, she was among the many European and American artists who were influenced by Japanese prints and "snapshot" composition of late-nineteenth-century do-it-yourself photography.

The depiction of everyday life and the strong sense of design in Japanese prints like Utamaro's REFLECTED BEAUTY on page 281 inspired Western painters to break with the limits of European post-Renaissance styles. The influence of Japanese prints is readily apparent in the simplicity and bold design of Cassatt's THE BOATING PARTY. Cassatt refined her subject in sweeping curves and almost flat shapes.

With Van Gogh, late-nineteenth-century painting moved from an outer impression of what the eye sees to an inner expression of what the heart feels and the mind knows. Vincent van Gogh's intense feeling for life's essential truths and his early interest in literature and religion led him to work as a lay preacher for poverty-stricken coal miners. In this context, he fought against the inhumane conditions of industrial society. Dissatisfied with his inability to correct the social injustice he saw, Van Gogh turned instead to art. With financial support from his brother Theo, the twenty-seven-year-old Van Gogh began working as an artist in 1880 and continued to develop his abilities until his suicide ten years later. During these few years, he overcame an early clumsiness and produced works of great emotional intensity and spiritual strength. His extensive correspondence with Theo provides detailed descriptions of his life and work.

From impressionism, Van Gogh learned the expressive potential of divided brushwork and pure color; but the style did not provide enough freedom to satisfy his desire to express his intuitive feelings. Van Gogh intensified the surfaces of his paintings with textural brushwork that recorded each gesture of his hand and gave an overall rhythmic movement to some of his paintings. He began to use startling color in an effort to express his emotions more clearly. In a letter to Theo he wrote,

. . . instead of trying to reproduce exactly what I have before my eyes, I use color more arbitrarily so as to express myself forcibly. . . .[8] *I am always in hope of making a discovery there to express the love of two lovers by a marriage of two complementary colors, their mingling and their opposition, the mysterious vibrations of kindred tones. To express the thought of a brow by the radiance of a light tone against somber background.*[9]

Like Mary Cassatt and other artists of the period, Van Gogh developed a new sense of design, partly by studying Japanese prints. His copy of a Hiroshige print is quite accurate. In

474 Vincent van Gogh, after Hiroshige.
JAPONAISERIE: FLOWERING PLUM TREE. 1888.
Oil on canvas. 55 cm. × 46 cm.
Vincent van Gogh Foundation/National Museum Vincent van Gogh, Amsterdam.

THE SOWER, Van Gogh demonstrated his newly acquired sense of design featuring bold, simple shapes and flat color areas. The wide band of a tree trunk cuts diagonally across the composition as a major shape, its strength balancing the sun and its energy coming toward us with the movement of the sower.

A strong desire to share personal experience motivated Van Gogh. After tremendous struggle with materials and techniques, he finally reached the point at which he was able to put the intensity of his vision on paper and canvas. He sought to portray not what he saw, but what he wanted others to see:

. . . I should be desperate if my figures were correct, . . . I do not want them to be academically correct. . . . I adore the figures of Michelangelo though the legs are undoubtedly too long, the hips and backsides too large . . . [T]he real artists do not paint things as they are, traced in a dry analytical way, but as they feel them. . . . [M]y greatest longing is to learn to make those very incorrectnesses, those deviations, remodelings, changes in reality, so that they may become, yes, lies if you like—but truer than the literal truth.[10]

In THE STARRY NIGHT, Van Gogh's observation of a town at night becomes the point of departure for a powerful symbolic image. Hills seem to undulate rhythmically to tremendous cosmic forces in the sky. The limited scale of human life is presented in the town nestled into the dark forms of the ground plane. The church's spire reaches toward the heavens, echoed by the larger more dynamic upward thrust of the cypress trees in the left foreground (cypress is traditionally planted beside graveyards in Europe as a symbol of eternal life). All these elements are united by the surging, rhythmic lines that express Van Gogh's passionate spirit and mystic vision. Many know of Van Gogh's bouts of mental illness, but few realize that his paintings were done between seizures, in moments of great clarity.

Paul Gauguin began painting on Sundays, working in an impressionist manner, while making a good living as a stockbroker. Following a crash in the financial world, Gauguin left business—and eventually his family—to devote himself to art. Memories of his childhood in Peru persuaded him that the art of ancient and non-Western cultures had spiritual strength lacking in the European art of his time. Gauguin decided to make his insights clear through an entirely new way of painting. Inspiration came from medieval European art, and from the arts of ancient and non-European cultures that were little known and generally rejected as crude by European society.

Keep the Persians, the Cambodians, and a bit of the Egyptians always in mind. The great error is the Greek, however beautiful it may be.[11]

A great thought system is written in gold in Far Eastern art.[12]

475 Vincent van Gogh.
THE SOWER. 1888.
Oil on canvas. 17⅜″ × 22⅛″.
*Vincent van Gogh Foundation/National
Museum Vincent van Gogh, Amsterdam.*

476 Vincent van Gogh.
THE STARRY NIGHT. 1889.
Oil on canvas. 29″ × 36¼″.
*Collection, The Museum of Modern Art, New
York. Acquired through the Lillie P. Bliss Bequest.*

Gauguin's desire to rejuvenate European art and civilization with insights learned from outside classical Western tradition was shared in the early twentieth century by Picasso, Matisse, and the German expressionists. They adopted Gauguin's vision of the artist as spiritual leader who could select from the past anything capable of releasing the power of self-knowledge and inner life. For Gauguin, art had become above all a means of communicating through symbols—a "synthesis," as he called it, of visual form carrying memory, feelings, and ideas.

In 1888, Gauguin completed THE VISION AFTER THE SERMON, a large, carefully designed painting that was the first major work in his new style. The symbolic representation of unquestioning faith is an image that originated in Gauguin's mind rather than his eye. With it, Gauguin took a major step beyond impressionism. In order to avoid what he considered the distraction of implied deep space, he tipped up the simplified background plane and painted

it an intense "unnatural" vermilion. The entire composition is divided diagonally by the trunk of the apple tree in the manner of Japanese prints. Shapes have been reduced to flat curvilinear areas outlined in black, with shadows minimized or eliminated. Jacob and the angel are shown as they appear to a group of Brittany peasants in a vision inspired by the sermon in their village church.

Gauguin has been associated with the symbolist movement, although he did not think highly of most of the work of the symbolist artists. *Symbolism* was a name given to a movement in literature and the visual arts that developed around 1885 in opposition to what its proponents saw as the false sensibility of objective description and emphasis on the fleeting moment at the expense of enduring significance.

Reacting against realism and impressionism, symbolist poets and painters employed decorative forms and symbols that were vague or open-ended in nature to create imaginative sugges-

477   Paul Gauguin.
THE VISION AFTER THE
SERMON (JACOB
WRESTLING WITH THE
ANGEL). 1888.
Oil on canvas.
28¾″ × 36½″.
*National Gallery of Scotland,
Edinburgh.*

478 Paul Gauguin.
FATATA TE MITI (BY THE SEA). 1892.
Oil on canvas. 26¾″ × 36″.
National Gallery of Art, Washington, D.C.
Chester Dale Collection.

tions. Symbolists sought aesthetic means, filled with emotion and implication, to lift the mind from the mundane and practical. Symbolism was a trend, rather than a specific style, and it provided the ideological background for twentieth-century abstraction. It has been considered a descendent of romanticism and a forerunner of twentieth-century surrealism.

Gauguin's use of color had an important influence on twentieth-century painting. His views on color were prophetic. The subject, as he said, was only a pretext for symphonies of line and color.

In painting, one must search rather for suggestion than for description, as is done in music. . . .
Think of the highly important musical role which colour will play henceforth in modern painting.[13]

Like Van Gogh, Gauguin was highly critical of the materialism of industrial society. This attitude led him to admire the honest life of the Brittany peasants of western France, and then to try to break totally with European civilization by going to Tahiti. In FATATA TE MITI, he combined flat, curvilinear shapes influenced by Japanese prints with tropical and fanciful colors.

479   Henri de Toulouse-Lautrec.
AT THE MOULIN ROUGE. 1892.
Oil on canvas. 48⅜″ × 55¼″.
Helen Birch Bartlett Memorial Collection (1928.610).
© *1988, The Art Institute of Chicago. All rights reserved.*

Henri de Toulouse-Lautrec, another expressionist, painted the gaslit interiors of Parisian nightclubs and brothels, frequently portraying moments of human drama. His quick, long strokes of color define a world of sordid gaiety. Toulouse-Lautrec was influenced by Degas (see pages 125 and 360), whose work he greatly admired. In AT THE MOULIN ROUGE, Toulouse-Lautrec used unusual angles, cropping of images such as the face on the right, and expressive, unnatural color to heighten feelings about the people and the world he painted. His paintings, drawings, and prints of Parisian nightlife influenced twentieth-century expressionists and twentieth-century graphic design.

Edvard Munch traveled to Paris from Norway to study and view the works of his contemporaries, especially Gauguin, Van Gogh, and Toulouse-Lautrec. What he learned from them, particularly from Gauguin's works, enabled him to carry expressionism to a new level of intensity.

In THE SCREAM, Munch takes the viewer far from the pleasant delights of impressionism and extends considerably Van Gogh's emotionalism. It is a powerful image of anxiety. The dominant figure is caught in complete isolation, fear, and loneliness. Despair, carried by continuous linear rhythms, reverberates throughout the picture.

Munch's powerful images explore depths of emotion—grief, loneliness, fear, love (see pages 112–113), sexual passion, jealousy, and death. Munch painted THE SCREAM in 1893, and in 1896 he completed the black-and-white lithograph reproduced here. In the isolated central figure, we may see ourselves; THE SCREAM seems to herald a shared awakening to deeper levels of consciousness. The image has been called the soul-cry of our age.

480 Edvard Munch.
THE SCREAM. 1896.
Lithograph, printed in black. Sheet: 20⅝″ × 15¹³⁄₁₆″.
Collection, The Museum of Modern Art, New York. Matthew T. Mellon Foundation Fund.

481   Henri Rousseau.
THE SLEEPING GYPSY. 1897.
Oil on canvas. 51″ × 79″.
Collection, The Museum of Modern Art, New York.
Gift of Mrs. Simon Guggenheim.

The works of Munch and naive French painter Henri Rousseau show different expressions of the human psyche. Rousseau was an untrained, so-called primitive painter, and not a member of the Paris art community. He did, however, catch the attention of many artists, including Picasso, who were looking for fresh approaches to visual form. Rousseau's naive purity, innate sense of design, imaginative use of color, and his taste for exotic subjects gave his paintings a mysterious, magical quality. THE SLEEPING GYPSY appears to be the visualization of a dream.

The invention and development of photography, with its ability to record appearances, and the rediscovery of non-Western and pre-Renaissance art forms strongly affected the direction of Western art in the second half of the nineteenth century. Artists renewed their perception and sought a deeper reality as they broke away from what they saw as the artificial idealism of officially recognized academic art. The fresh beginning was full of self-assurance, as seen in the optimistic mood of impressionism. Yet the process of seeing the visual world anew brought with it levels of awareness beyond the visible realm. The appearance of things came to be less important than the relationship between viewer and reality. It became, once again, the artist's task to probe and reveal hidden worlds—to make the invisible visible. Artists gave increasing importance to the elements of form and to the formal structure of seen and invented imagery. Nature was internalized and transformed in order to portray a greater reality.

The Early Twentieth Century

The art of our time is the result of a series of revolutions in thinking and seeing. Each new movement rejects what it considers the failures of immediate predecessors, and takes what it needs from the past.

Now that we are approaching the end of the twentieth century, we can identify dominant concerns among early-twentieth-century artists and see characteristics of their work that reveal the unique features of the age. These features include rapid change, diversity, individualism, and exploration followed by abundant discoveries. Leading artists have questioned assumptions of the past and expanded the limits of what we believe to be true and possible. The explosion of new styles during this century has been built upon, yet challenges European art of the late nineteenth century, and has also been strongly influenced by non-Western traditions.

As in earlier chapters, we will look at works of a few of the artists who were part of leading trends. Not all artists of a given period work in styles that are recognized at the time or that later seem historically important. Many continue to work in traditional styles, in their own unique ways, or in ways that do not attract attention.

During the first decade of this century, Western views of reality underwent an irreversible upheaval. In 1903, the Wright brothers flew the first power-driven aircraft. In 1905, Albert Einstein triggered a change in Western concepts of time and space with his theory of relativity. Matter could no longer be considered solid; it was recognized as a field of energy. Simultaneously, great changes occurred in art, and some of them were inspired by scientific discoveries. In 1913, Russian artist Wassily Kandinsky (see page 381) described how deeply he was affected by the discovery of subatomic particles:

A scientific event cleared my way of one of the greatest impediments. This was the further division of the atom. The crumbling of the atom was to my soul like the crumbling of the whole world.[1]

This is not to imply that art follows science. Art is a parallel creative field of exploration and exposition complementary to science. In their working processes, artists investigate, reveal, and extend our perception of "reality." Twentieth-century artists have studied the visible world, and many have gone further to reveal inner worlds seen only in the mind. In so doing, they, like physicists, have challenged preconceptions regarding the nature of reality, and have made new levels of consciousness visible.

The major transition in early-twentieth-century art continued the general shift from naturalistic to abstract and nonrepresentational (nonobjective) art begun in the late nineteenth century. The comparison in chapter 3 of two works of sculpture, both titled THE KISS (pages 42–43), illustrates the transition from nineteenth- to twentieth-century thinking. Rodin, leading sculptor of the nineteenth century, created a naturalistic work. Brancusi, major sculptor of the first half of the twentieth, produced an abstract interpretation.

482   Constantin Brancusi.
SLEEPING MUSE. 1906.
Marble. 6½″ × 12″.
National Museum, Bucharest, Romania.

483   Constantin Brancusi.
SLEEPING MUSE. 1909–1911.
Marble. Height 11½″.
Hirshhorn Museum and Sculpture Garden,
Smithsonian Institution, Washington, D.C.
Gift of Joseph H. Hirschhorn (1966).

484   Constantin Brancusi.
THE NEWBORN. 1915.
Marble. 6″ × 8½″.
Philadelphia Museum of Art.
The Louise and Walter Arensberg Collection.

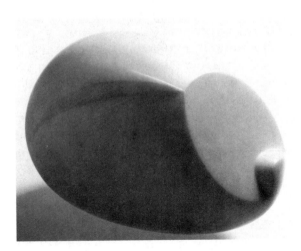

After studying art in his native Romania, and spending time in Germany and Switzerland, Brancusi arrived in Paris in 1904. Following his showing in a Paris exhibition, Brancusi was invited by Rodin to be his assistant. Brancusi is said to have turned him down with the reply, "Nothing grows under the shade of great trees." His early work shows the influence of Rodin, but Brancusi went on to develop his own unique style. He was a superb craftsman, who possessed great sensitivity to the character of his materials —primarily metal, stone, and wood.

Brancusi's early work shows his radical break with the past. His SLEEPING MUSE of 1906 has an appearance similar to Rodin's romantic naturalism. In the 1911 version of SLEEPING MUSE, Brancusi minimized the subject as he moved from naturalism to abstraction. THE NEWBORN of 1915 has the refined simplicity of a powerful conception stripped to its essentials. Brancusi said, "Simplicity is not an end in art, but one arrives at simplicity in spite of oneself, in approaching the real sense of things."[2]

These three works span nine years of Brancusi's evolution toward the elemental form for which he is best known. Seen together, they illustrate the transition from representational to abstract art within the work of one individual. The influence of Cycladic and archaic Greek sculpture is evident in Brancusi's work. Ancient sculpture from the Cycladic islands of the Aegean Sea has a distinctive, highly abstract elegance. Brancusi must have been particularly fascinated by the refined simplicity of these four-thousand-year-old marble sculptures.

In BIRD IN SPACE, Brancusi transformed inert mass into a dramatic thrust. The implied soaring motion of the "bird" embodies the idea of flight. The highly reflective polish given to the bronze surface adds considerably to the form's weightless quality. Brancusi started working on this visual concept about a decade after the Wright brothers initiated the age of human flight, but long before the world was filled with streamlined aircraft, cars, pens, and telephones. Brancusi said, "All my life I have sought the essence of flight. Don't look for mysteries. I give you pure joy."[3]

486 Constantin Brancusi.
BIRD IN SPACE. (1928?).
Bronze (unique cast). 54″ high.
Collection, The Museum of Modern Art, New York.
Given anonymously.

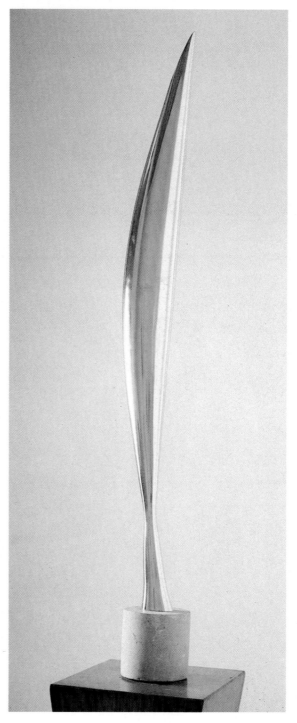

485 CYCLADIC HEAD. 2500–3000 B.C.
Marble. Height 10½″.
Louvre Museum, Paris.

487 Henri Matisse.
JOY OF LIFE. 1905–1906.
Oil on canvas. 68½″ × 93¾″.
The Barnes Foundation, Merion Station, Pennsylvania.
Photograph © 1989 by The Barnes Foundation.

THE FAUVES AND EXPRESSIONISM

Between 1901 and 1904, the works of Van
Gogh, Gauguin, and Cézanne were exhibited
in Paris. Henri Matisse was the leader of a group
of young expressionist artists influenced by these
postimpressionists as well as by the brilliant colors and flattened picture space of Islamic art, and
the primal power of Oceanic and African art.
The paintings that resulted from these influences
shocked the public. A critic of their first show de-
risively called them *les fauves* ("the wild beasts").
Far from being insulted, they enthusiastically
adopted the name.

488 Henri Matisse.
LANDSCAPE. Study for JOY OF LIFE. 1905.
Oil on canvas. 46 cm. × 44 cm.
Royal Museum of Fine Arts, Copenhagen. J. Rump Collection.

489 André Derain. LONDON BRIDGE. 1906. Oil on canvas. 26″ × 39″. *Collection, The Museum of Modern Art, New York. Gift of Mr. and Mrs. Charles Zadok.*

The *fauve* movement lasted little more than two years—from 1905 to 1908—yet it was one of the most influential developments in early-twentieth-century painting. The fauves extended the expressive color of Gauguin and Van Gogh by freeing color from its traditional role of describing the natural appearance of an object. In this way, they led to an increasing use of color as an independent expressive element.

Henri Matisse had early training in the nineteenth-century academic style, as did most leading European painters of his time; but early in his career he began to move away from traditional practice. His painting JOY OF LIFE is a major early work in his long career, and a key masterpiece of fauvism. Pure hues vibrate across the surface; lines, largely freed of their descriptive roles, align with simplified shapes to provide a lively rhythm in the composition.

A black-and-white reproduction of JOY OF LIFE can only suggest the vitality of the original. The painting is owned by the Barnes Foundation, which does not permit color reproductions. But the study Matisse made for JOY OF LIFE indicates the intense color of the final work. Matisse's seemingly careless depiction of the figures is based on his knowledge of human anatomy and of drawing. The intentionally direct, childlike quality of the form serves to heighten the joyful content.

From 1908 until his death in 1954, Matisse alone remained close to the principles of fauvism, yet he continued to transform fauve ideas with his extraordinary sensitivity to the potential of color and shape. His inventive paintings, drawings, and sculptures are among the strongest and most influential works of this century (see also pages 24 to 27).

André Derain's friendship with Matisse led to his association with the fauves. In Derain's LONDON BRIDGE, brilliant, invented color is balanced by some use of traditional composition and perspective. Derain spoke of intentionally using discordant color. It is an indication of today's acceptance of free use of strong color that Derain's painting does not appear disharmonious.

510 Pablo Picasso.
THREE MUSICIANS. 1921.
Oil on canvas. 6'7" × 7'3¾".
Collection, The Museum of Modern Art, New York.
Mrs. Simon Guggenheim Fund.

Picasso painted THREE MUSICIANS in the flat, decorative style of synthetic cubism. Although it is a painting, its form is heavily influenced by the cut-out shapes of cubist collages. Two of the life-size figures are the traditional characters of French comedy—Pierrot, in white, playing a recorder, and brightly costumed Harlequin in the center, playing a guitar. The third figure wears a black monk's habit and a veiled mask, and sings from the sheet of music he holds. Behind the trio a black dog lies with tail raised. Although abstract, the figures have a real presence. The work is solemn and whimsical at the same time.

Many historians find Picasso's work difficult to deal with because he shifted from style to style, using one approach and then another. He painted THREE MUSICIANS at the same time he was reexamining and working with the style and subject matter of ancient Greece, creating figures that had the solid appearance of classical sculpture (see HEAD OF A YOUNG MAN, page 59). As a teenager, Picasso had made detailed drawings of plaster casts of Greek sculpture, as did all art students of the nineteenth and early twentieth centuries, but some were surprised to see the adult artist return to a source rejected by his colleagues. As we look back over his career, we see that the dramatic shifts in style are indicative of Picasso's extraordinary inventive ability. He was by far the most influential artist of the twentieth century.

For sculptor Jacques Lipchitz, "Cubism was essentially a search for a new syntax."[10] He came to Paris from Poland just as cubism was developing. His larger-than-life-size FIGURE of the late 1920s, however, is not simply cubist. The large piece has the awesome presence we might expect to find in a figure from Africa or the South Pacific. Here the power comes in part from Lipchitz's sense of human existence in his own time. FIGURE appears to be a symbol of humanity in the twentieth century. (Compare Lipchitz's sculpture with Munch's print THE SCREAM on page 371.) A viewer asked Lipchitz to explain his work. "It wouldn't help you," the sculptor answered. "If I were to explain it in Chinese, you would tell me you didn't know Chinese, and I would tell you to learn Chinese and you will understand. Art is harder than Chinese. Anyone can look—you have to learn to see."[11]

Cubism brought about the most radical and complete artistic revolution since the Renaissance. Through its indirect influence on architecture and the applied arts, it has become part of our daily lives.

511 Jacques Lipchitz.
FIGURE. 1926–1930.
Bronze. 7'1¼" × 38⅝".
*Kroller-Mueller Rijksmuseum,
Otterlo, Netherlands.*

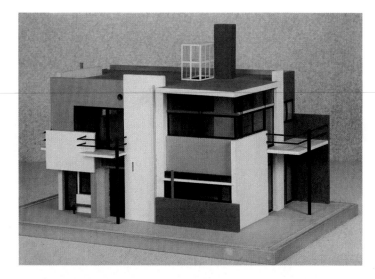

527   Gerrit Rietveld.
MODEL OF THE SCHRÖDER HOUSE. 1923–1934.
Glass and wood. 17⅜" × 28⅜" × 19⅓".
Stedelijk Museum, Amsterdam, Netherlands.
© *Gerrit Rietveld/VAGA New York, 1988*

International Style

After 1910, the search for a new language of form was carried on by architects as well as painters. Ideas about form developed by Frank Lloyd Wright, the cubist painters, and the de Stijl artists were carried further by later architects who were stimulated by the structural possibilities of modern materials including steel, plate glass, and reinforced concrete.

About 1918, a new style of architecture began to emerge simultaneously in Germany, France, and the Netherlands, and thus it came to be called the *international style.* Steel-frame curtain-wall construction methods made it possible to build structures characterized by undecorated rectilinear planes which open up interior space and make us aware of the proportions of each building's design. Extensive use of glass in non-load-bearing exterior walls brings abundant light to interiors. In many international-style buildings, particularly early ones, asymmetrical designs create dynamic balances of voids and solids. In contrast to Frank Lloyd Wright, who blended houses with their natural surroundings, architects working in the international style deliberately created a visual contrast between natural and manufactured forms.

Dutch architect Gerrit Rietveld was associated with Mondrian and de Stijl. His SCHRÖDER HOUSE in Utrecht was an early classic of the international style. Its design of interacting planes and spaces and use of primary color accents is closely related to Mondrian's work.

In France, the principles of the international style of architecture were basic to the early work of leading architect, city planner, and painter Charles Edouard Jeanneret, known by the pseudonym Le Corbusier. His drawing on page 232 represents his philosophy that with a basic structural frame one has complete freedom in terms of flow of space and in the use of interior and exterior walls. His most significant early work

528   Le Corbusier.
VILLA SAVOYE. Poissy, France. 1928–1930.
a. Exterior. *Photograph: Prithwish Neogy.*
b. Interior. *Photograph: Lucien Hervé, Paris.*

is the VILLA SAVOYE at Poissy, France, built between 1928 and 1930. The second floor living area seems to float on slender reinforced-concrete columns above a smaller, deeply recessed entrance and service area on the ground. A private interior terrace opens to the sky on the upper level, joined to the living room by floor-to-ceiling panels of plate glass, a new idea that is now common in contemporary homes. Le Corbusier called the houses he designed "machines for living."

The international style buildings designed by Walter Gropius for the Bauhaus (see page 232) clearly reflect the the concepts of both de Stijl and constructivism. Today, the spare style that Mondrian and the Bauhaus helped to initiate can be seen in the design, not only of buildings, but also of books, interiors, clothing, and many other articles of daily life.

Architect-designer Ludwig Mies van der Rohe was one of the most influential figures associated with the Bauhaus and the international style. His imaginative and highly refined GERMAN PAVILION, built for the International Exposition at Barcelona in 1929, acted as a kind of touchstone for architects working in the international style. Its function as a reception center was simple enough to allow Mies to concentrate on sculpting space with horizontal and vertical planes of polished green tinian marble, travertine, golden onyx, chrome, and glass. In its refinement, simplification, and elegance of proportion, the design exemplifies his ideal, "Less is more." The pavilion was dismantled following the exposition, but it was considered so important to the history of architecture that it was carefully rebuilt in exactly the same location in 1986. Mies designed the BARCELONA CHAIR (page 209) for the original building. In 1938, Mies van der Rohe emigrated to the United States. There, his ideas and works such as the SEAGRAM BUILDING (page 233) strongly influenced the post-World War II development of the rectilinear, metal- and glass-sheathed, steel-frame skyscraper.

529 Ludwig Mies van der Rohe.
GERMAN PAVILION, International Exposition, Barcelona. 1929 (dismantled in 1930, and rebuilt in 1986).
Photographs: Prithwish Neogy.

533 Hannah Höch.
THE MULTI-MILLIONAIRE. 1920.
Photomontage.
Location unknown.

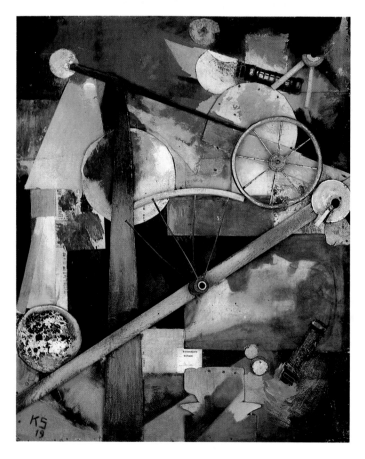

When Picasso and Braque put actual pieces of rope and scraps of newspapers into their work, they began one development in the art of pre-existing things—collages and assemblages (see page 388). Things are not *re*-presented, but are themselves *presented* in a new context. One form which has become familiar is *photomontage*, in which parts of photographs are combined in new ways (see also page 160). In THE MULTI-MILLIONAIRE, by dadaist Hannah Höch, man, the artifact-making industrialist, stands as a fractured giant among the things he has produced.

Kurt Schwitters was a master of dada collage. From 1917 until his death in 1948, he created such images as CONSTRUCTION FOR NOBLE LADIES out of society's discards. By re-presenting, and asking us to look again at these cast-offs, Schwitters helped us to see poetry in the most unlikely places.

I could not, in fact, see any reason why one should not use the old tickets, driftwood, cloakroom numbers, wires and parts of wheels, buttons, and old lumber out of junk rooms and rubbish heaps as materials for paintings as well as the colors that were produced in factories.[5]

The dadaists intended to be anti-aesthetic. Ironically, they created a new aesthetic that has had a continuing impact on art and life throughout the remainder of the twentieth century.

Fantasy in Art

The highly personal and inventive art of Paul Klee provided inspiration for both dadaists and surrealists. Although Klee was not a member of either group, his work paralleled both movements and he exhibited with both groups.

Klee gave up a career as a concert violinist to be an artist. As he worked to develop his art,

534 Kurt Schwitters.
CONSTRUCTION FOR NOBLE LADIES. 1919.
Assemblage-mixed media; wood, metal, paper, cardboard, and paint. 40½″ × 33″.
Los Angeles County Museum of Art.

535 Paul Klee.
BATTLE SCENE FROM THE COMIC OPERA "THE
SEAFARER." 1923.
Colored sheet, watercolor, and oil drawing. 15″ × 20¼″.
Collection Frau T. Durst Haass, Muttenz, Switzerland.

he intentionally freed himself from the accumu-
lation of history in an effort to begin all over
again. In his diary he wrote,

*It is a great difficulty and great necessity to have to
start with the smallest. I want to be as though
new-born, knowing nothing, absolutely nothing,
about Europe; ignoring poets and fashions, to be
almost primitive. Then I want to do something very
modest; to work out by myself a tiny formal [motif],
one that my pencil will be able to hold without any
technique.*[6]

Paul Klee remained an independent artist all
his life. He was able to tap the resources of his
own unconscious, creating fantastic images years
before surrealism became a group style. Klee's

receptivity to inspiration from unconscious
sources was apparent when he said,

*. . . everything vanishes around me and good works
rise from me of their own accord. My hand is
entirely the implement of a distant sphere. It is not
my head that functions but something else, something higher, something more remote. I must have
great friends there, dark as well as bright. . . .
They are all very kind to me.*[7]

In Klee's painting BATTLE SCENE FROM THE
COMIC OPERA "THE SEAFARER," Sinbad the
Sailor fights three monsters in a battle that suggests the universal human struggle against fear
of things both real and imagined. Marvelous line
patterns, distinctive use of color, and an attitude
of innocence are common to Klee's small paintings. Klee maintained a balance between whimsical and mystical elements.

Both whimsy and mystery pervade Klee's THE TWITTERING MACHINE. With subtle suggestion rather than explicit detail, Klee intrigues the viewer. A major part of the intrigue comes from the title and its relationship to the "machine." We participate in the fun as we imagine the twittering sounds that will come forth when the crank is turned. As a machine it is absurd—a kind of useless dada object.

Marc Chagall assimilated the influence of the cubists by blending their use of geometric abstraction with his own personal subject matter. Chagall's fantasy-filled paintings incorporate symbolism drawn from eastern Jewish Hasidism, folklore, and childhood memories of Russian life (see I AND THE VILLAGE, page 53). His work had a major influence on surrealism. Throughout his long life, Chagall continued to create paintings based on fantasy and symbolism, and in this sense his paintings continue to be associated with surrealism.

Shortly before Chagall's marriage to Bella, she brought him flowers on his birthday. In Bella's autobiography, she wrote of their rapture:

536 Paul Klee.
TWITTERING MACHINE. 1922.
Watercolor, pen and ink. 16¼" × 12".
Collection, The Museum of Modern Art, New York, Purchase.

537 Marc Chagall.
THE BIRTHDAY. 1915.
Oil on canvas. 31¾" × 39¼".
Collection, The Museum of Modern Art, New York.

Soon I forget the flowers. You work with your brushes . . . You pour on color . . . Suddenly you jump in the air . . . You float among the rafters. You turn your head and you twist mine too . . . and both together we rise over the clean little room.

"How do you like my picture?" you ask . . . You wait and are afraid of what I may tell you. "It's very good . . . you float away so beautifully. We'll call it the Birthday." [8]

Many of Chagall's paintings show people "flying," or with feet off the ground, as a metaphor for love. Chagall's immense outpouring of work included prints and stained glass as well as paintings. His images are filled with delightfully fantastic combinations of gestures, objects, environments, and figures. The dreamlike fantasies of Klee and Chagall are often joyful, in contrast to the eerie quality of some of the later surrealist works.

Italian metaphysical painter Giorgio de Chirico had a more direct relationship to surrealism than Klee or Chagall. In THE MYSTERY AND MELANCHOLY OF A STREET, De Chirico used distorted linear perspective, with conflicting vanishing points, to create an eerie space peopled by faceless shadows. The painting speaks the symbolic language of dreams and mystery. According to the artist:

Everything has two aspects: the current aspect, which we see nearly always and which ordinary men see, and the ghostly and metaphysical aspect, which only rare individuals may see in moments of clairvoyance and metaphysical abstraction. [9]

Surrealism

In the 1920s, a group of writers and painters gathered to proclaim the omnipotence of the unconscious mind, thought to be a higher reality than the conscious mind. Their goal was to make visible the imagery of the unconscious. This group, the surrealists, was indebted to the shocking irrationality of dadaism and the fantastic creations of Chagall, Klee, and especially the dream images of De Chirico. They also drew heavily on the new psychology of Sigmund Freud.

Surrealism was officially launched in Paris in 1924 by the publication of its first manifesto, written by poet-painter André Breton. In it he defined the movement's purpose as

the future resolution of these two states, dream and reality, which are seemingly so contradictory, into a kind of absolute reality, a surreality, *if one may so speak.* [10]

Among the prominent members of the surrealist group were painters Salvador Dali and Joan Miró. Picasso took part in the first exhibit, but did not remain in the style long.

538 Giorgio de Chirico.
THE MYSTERY AND MELANCHOLY OF A STREET. 1914.
Oil on canvas. 34¼″ × 28⅛″.
Private collection.

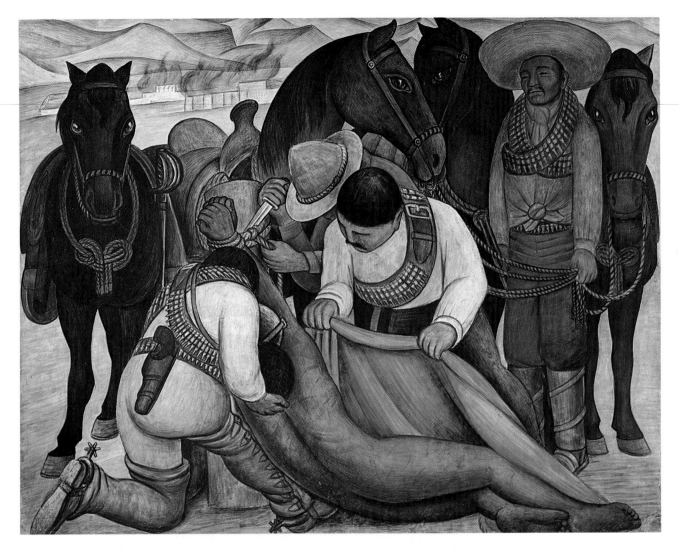

544   Diego Rivera.
THE LIBERATION OF THE PEON. 1931.
Fresco. 74″ × 95″.
Philadelphia Museum of Art. Given by Mr. and Mrs. Herbert C. Morris.

While various schools of abstract art were emerging in Europe, an undercurrent of conservative realism continued to be practiced. Some repressive governments restricted artists to an illustrative, realistic style which they considered politically advantageous. Easily understood realism was seen as a propaganda tool by political leaders in Nazi Germany, Communist Russia, and Communist China. For many decades, prior to recent trends toward modernization and reconciliation, neither Russia nor China would permit any other mode. More sincere forms of social realism came to prominence in Mexico and the United States in the 1920s and 1930s.

545 Dorothea Lange.
A DEPRESSION BREADLINE, SAN FRANCISCO. 1933.
Photograph.
The Oakland Museum. Dorothea Lange Collection.

The Mexican renaissance, led by Diego Rivera with help from José Clemente Orozco (see page 105) and others, influenced artists in both Mexico and the United States. Inspired by Italian Renaissance frescoes he had seen during his first trip to Europe, Rivera envisioned a national art that would glorify the traditional Mexican heritage and also promote the aims and accomplishments of the new, revolutionary government. During the 1920s and 1930s, large frescoes painted on public buildings throughout Mexico and in a few places in the United States emphasized revolutionary themes. Rivera's THE LIBERATION OF THE PEON summarizes agrarian reform. The landlord's house burns in the distance, while revolutionary soldiers free the peon from his servitude and cover his naked body, scarred from repeated lashings. This painting is a variation of a large fresco on a wall of

the Ministry of Education in Mexico City (see also Rivera's SUGAR CANE on page 138).

During the Depression years of the 1930s, the United States government maintained an active program of subsidy for the arts. The Works Progress Administration (WPA) commissioned painters to paint murals in public buildings, and the Farm Security Administration (FSA) hired photographers to record the eroding dustbowl and its work-worn inhabitants. One of these photographers, Dorothea Lange, also documented the helplessness and hopelessness of the urban unemployed. Her sensitive study of A DEPRESSION BREADLINE, SAN FRANCISCO is from this difficult period.

546   Georgia O'Keeffe.
BLACK CROSS, NEW MEXICO. 1929.
Oil on canvas, 39″ × 30″.
The Art Institute Fund (1943.95).

AMERICAN PAINTING

The American public had its first extensive look at leading developments in European art during the Armory Show held in New York in 1913. This show of over sixteen hundred works became the best-known and the most influential art exhibition ever held in the United States. The exhibit brought many important examples of the new European styles to America for the first time. Americans, especially young American artists, were able to see key works by impressionists, postimpressionists, and fauves—particularly Matisse, who was much maligned by the critics. Also shown were paintings by Picasso, Braque, Léger, and Duchamp, and sculpture by Brancusi. As a result, cubism and other forms of abstract art spread to America. Among the Americans who exhibited in the Armory show were John Marin (see page 130), Stuart Davis (see page 430), Charles Sheeler (see pages 126), and Edward Hopper.

547   Georgia O'Keeffe.
ORIENTAL POPPIES. 1928.
Oil on canvas. 30″ × 40⅛″.
University Art Museum, University of Minnesota, Minneapolis. Purchase (37.1).

Americans saw Europe as the center of traditional culture, as well as the source of the modern movement. In the early twentieth century, it was common for American artists to go to Europe to study. Georgia O'Keeffe was an exception. She stayed in New York, yet she was influenced by the revolutionary changes in European art. O'Keeffe's personal style is apparent in her majestic paintings of flowers and her interpretations of the American Southwest. Her art developed during her early years in New York. There she was befriended by, and eventually married, the older, already famous photographer, Alfred Stieglitz (see page 387). O'Keeffe eventually rejected what she saw as the superficial materialism of the city in favor of country life. In 1929, she began spending her summers in Taos, New Mexico, where she continued to find inspiration for her powerful abstractions. In BLACK CROSS, NEW MEXICO, the single dominant shape of the cross pushes forward from the infinite vista of subtle glowing landscape behind it. Here, as in much of O'Keeffe's work, she achieved a powerful simplicity through subtle shading and careful design.

Edward Hopper made several trips to Europe between 1906 and 1910, but his art was largely unaffected by the experience. He remained apart from European avant-garde movements as he portrayed the loneliness that permeated much of American life. NIGHTHAWKS shows Hopper's fascination with the visual mood of a particular place at a particular time. The haunting effect of his paintings comes largely from Hopper's stark, architecturally structured design and his emphasis on controlled use of light and shadow areas. Hopper and the impressionists were both interested in light, but for different purposes: Hopper employed it to define and organize structure, while the impressionists used light in ways that seemed to dissolve structure.

In the 1930s, the spread of the Depression, along with political upheaval, helped motivate artists in America to search for both national and personal identity. American artists were caught between a largely indifferent public at home and a feeling, both at home and abroad, that American art was merely provincial. In this atmosphere of cultural inferiority, a native American regionalism developed, based on the idea that artists in America could find their own identity by focusing attention on subject matter that was uniquely their own. For these artists, subject matter was important as a way of taking pride in their own culture and of making their art relevant to themselves and their audience.

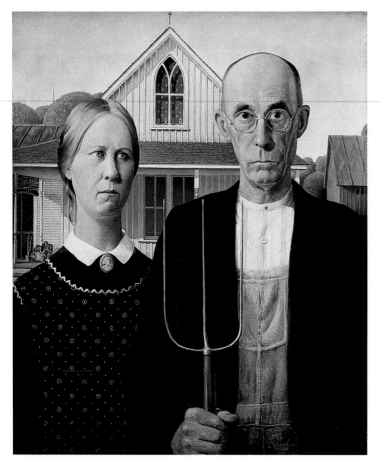

549 Grant Wood.
AMERICAN GOTHIC. 1930.
Oil on beaver board. 29⅞″ × 24⅞″.
Friends of American Art Collection (1930.934).
© 1988 The Art Institute of Chicago. All rights reserved.

Regional painter Grant Wood turned away from urban culture and also revolted against what he and other American regional artists considered the cultural insignificance of modern art. He sought to participate in the reality of American life in order to develop an art with which people could identify, even though the idealized farm life shown in his paintings was derived from a way of life that was fast disappearing.

In the early 1920s, Wood studied art in Paris. Although he never worked with cubist or expressionist ideas, he did identify with the modern trends, and began making freely brushed paintings derived from impressionism. After years of little success, Wood returned to his birthplace in rural midwestern America. There he let go of the widely held attitude that the Midwest was a cultural desert and decided to dedicate himself to memorializing the unique character of the land, the people, and their way of life. Childhood experience as an Iowa farm boy and the perception of his artistic maturity combined to make Grant Wood an astute observer of rural America.

Wood's personal style of crisp realism was inspired by the paintings of the Northern Renaissance masters such as Van Eyck, Dürer, and Holbein. He also drew on American folk painting and the characteristically stiff, long-exposure portraits taken by late-nineteenth-century photographers. Wood, like Van Eyck, calculated every aspect of design and all details of the subject matter to enhance the content of his paintings.

The idea for AMERICAN GOTHIC came to Wood when he saw a modest farmhouse built in Carpenter Gothic style. The restrained color, simplification of round masses such as trees and people, and use of detail are typical of Wood's paintings. The two figures are echoed in the pointed-arch window shapes. Vertical lines and paired elements dominate. For example, the lines of the pitchfork are repeated in the man's overalls and shirt front. The upright tines of the fork seem to symbolize the pair's firm, traditional stance and hard-won virtue. Wood's AMERICAN GOTHIC has become a famous national symbol that speaks clearly to many, yet sparks a wealth of different responses.

By far the most forceful spokesman for the idea of an independent American art was Thomas Hart Benton. In 1908, Benton went to Paris to study European art. His early encounter with cubism and constructivism provided a visual vocabulary based on the new pictorial space that gave strength and clarity to his mature work. But Benton's conservative midwestern background and traditional art training led him to be even more impressed with the work of Italian Renaissance masters than with the French moderns.

After 1918, Benton worked to create an art that was American in both form and content—a realistic style that would be easily understood by all, based on the clear depiction of American themes. Some of the strength for both figures and composition came from the influence of Michelangelo and El Greco. Benton transformed Renaissance and modern influences in a highly personal style in which all forms are conditioned by strong curvilinear rhythms. The push and pull of shapes in shallow space, emphasized by contrasting light and dark edges, shows what Benton learned from cubism. The painting PALISADES exhibits the personal mode of expression Benton employed the rest of his life.

By 1939, the beginning of World War II had caused tremendous disruption of normal life in Europe. The emigration of large numbers of people to the United States brought about a reexamination of art's relationship to modern life. Expatriated European artists brought new ideas and purposes to America. It was in this context that the illustrative styles of painters such as Thomas Hart Benton lost favor as New York became the new center of art activity.

550 Thomas Hart Benton.
PALISADES, from the series AMERICAN HISTORICAL EPIC. 1919–1924.
Oil on canvas. 72″ × 84″.
The Nelson-Atkins Museum of Art, Kansas City, Missouri.
Bequest of Thomas Hart Benton.

CONCEPTUAL ART

If one is engaged in pushing back limits, the next reductive step after minimal art is no art at all—or better yet, an art of ideas rather than objects. Conceptual art, in which an idea takes the place of the art object, was an outgrowth of minimal art and a reaction to pop. The movement was heavily indebted to Marcel Duchamp, the first champion of an art of ideas. Joseph Kosuth was the most rigorous early conceptualist. Motivation came in part from his anger at the materialism of the art market and what he perceived as pop art's embrace of commercialism. In 1965, he produced a work titled "One and Three Chairs," which consisted of a wooden chair, a photograph of the same chair, and a photographic enlargement of a dictionary definition of the word "chair."

Another notable conceptual work was "Ice," by Rafael Ferrer. In 1969, Ferrer put together an assemblage of ice blocks and autumn leaves on the Whitney Museum's entry ramp. When collectors complained about the ephemeral nature of his creation, Ferrer suggested that the iceman's bill might be collected as a kind of "drawing." In the true spirit of conceptualism, we have decided not to illustrate these works.

EARTHWORKS AND SITE WORKS

In recent years, a number of artists, working under the influence of minimalism, have gone beyond the prevailing idea of sculpture as portable precious objects by creating works that are inseparable from the sites for which they were designed. In these *site-specific* works the artist's sensitivity to the whole location determines the composition, scale, medium, and even the content.

Earthworks, sometimes called *earth art*, are sculptural forms made of materials such as earth, rocks, and sometimes plants. They are often very large, and executed in remote locations. Earthworks are usually designed to merge with or complement the landscape. *Site works* are environmental constructions, frequently made of sculptural materials, designed to interact with, but not permanently alter, the environment. While earthworks and site works can be commissioned, they are almost never resold—unless someone buys the land of which they are a part. Some of the works are intended to be temporary; project drawings and photographs, however, can be collected. Conceptual art, earthworks, site works, and performance art share a common concern for preventing art from being a mere commodity. Along with a desire to subvert the

581 Robert Smithson.
SPIRAL JETTY. Great Salt Lake, Utah. 1970.
Earthwork. Length 1500', width 15'.
Photograph: © 1989 Gianfranco Gorgoni/Contact Press Images, Inc.

582   Walter De Maria.
THE LIGHTNING FIELD. New Mexico. 1971–1977.
400 stainless-steel poles, average height 20'7";
land area 1 mile × 1 kilometer.
Photograph: John Cliett, © Dia Art Foundation 1980.

gallery-museum-collector syndrome is a positive interest in ecology and the earth works of ancient America.

Robert Smithson was one of the founders of the earthworks movement. His SPIRAL JETTY, completed at Great Salt Lake, Utah, in 1970, has since been almost lost to view due to the rising water level. Its natural surroundings emphasized its form as willful human design. Although our society has no supportive, agreed-upon symbolism or iconography, we instinctively respond to universal signs like the spiral, which are found in nature and in ancient art.

Walter De Maria's THE LIGHTNING FIELD is a site sculpture designed to be viewed over a twenty-four-hour period. The work consists of four hundred stainless steel poles arranged in a rectangular grid over an area measuring 1 mile by 1 kilometer in west central New Mexico. The sharpened tips of the poles form a level plane, a kind of monumental bed of nails. Each of the poles can act as a lightning conductor during the electrical storms that occur frequently over the desert. Actual strikes are rare, however. Early and late in the day the poles reflect the sun, creating accents of technological precision in sharp contrast to the otherwise natural landscape. Purposely isolated from the art-viewing public, THE LIGHTNING FIELD combines aspects of both conceptual and minimal art. Viewers must arrange their visits through the Dia Foundation, which commissioned the piece; they are left to study the work and come up with their own interpretations.

583   Alan Sonfist.
TIME LANDSCAPE. Laguardia Place and Bleeker Street,
New York City. 1965–1978.

Many contemporary artists address the crucial questions of our time in their work. Environmental artist Alan Sonfist calls attention to the current breakdown in our relationship to nature. During his childhood in the densely populated, violence-prone South Bronx, Sonfist found refuge in a small but heavily wooded remnant of the native forest near his home. A continuing affinity with nature became the basis for his art. Sonfist seeks to provide city dwellers with contact with nature and natural processes. His environmental works vary widely in form, with each designed for its particular site and purpose. TIME LANDSCAPE consists of a piece of expensive real estate in the heart of lower Manhattan which Sonfist replanted with native trees. He based the work on descriptive notes and comments written by the first Dutch colonists. Sonfist believes that the natural environment, which is part of the city's history, should have as much importance and care as the architectural environment to which it provides balance. The replanted forest will grow and change as it continues to fulfill its promise as a cooperative art project between people and nature.

When Bulgarian artist Christo was a student, he was alienated by the narrowness of his country's officially prescribed social realist art. His enthusiasm was aroused, however, by government-sponsored trips to the countryside during which he and other art students covered hay and old farm equipment with tarpaulins in order to improve the appearance of the landscape for foreigners traveling on the *Orient Express*. He later went to Prague to study stage set design. There he discovered paintings by Matisse, Miró, and Kandinsky hidden in the basement of the city's art museum. He immediately decided his artistic future was in the West.

Christo was first known in Europe as a gifted portrait painter. In Paris, he joined artists who were presenting objects as art, rather than painting or sculpting representations of objects. In the late 1950s, he gained notoriety when he closed off a Paris alley with a wall of 50-gallon oil drums. Thus began the work of an artist who makes the world his gallery. After the oil drums, Christo literally wrapped in fabric objects ranging in size and complexity from a motorcycle to a mile of sea cliffs in Australia. One of his most ambitious projects was RUNNING FENCE, a temporary environmental artwork that was as much a process and an event as it was sculpture. The 18-foot-high white nylon fence ran from the ocean at Bodega Bay in Sonoma County, California, through 24½ miles of agricultural and dairy land. RUNNING FENCE was a unique environmental event, ultimately involving thousands of people. The project required political action, the agreement of landowners, and the help of hundreds of volunteers. Christo raised the necessary funds by selling preliminary drawings and collages of the work.

The seemingly endless ribbon of white cloth made the wind visible and caught the changing light as it stretched across the gently rolling hills, appearing and disappearing on the horizon. The simplicity of RUNNING FENCE relates it to minimal art, but the fence itself was not presented as an art object. It was a key part and the focal point for a work that included the interweaving of people, process, object, and place. Christo's works are conceptual in the way they alert viewers to the fact that art is experience before and after it is anything else.

As an idea and a process, RUNNING FENCE may have helped protect not only the land it temporarily graced, but other landscapes as well. Christo's ideas may help people to become more perceptive, particularly of the beauty and character of open countryside. RUNNING FENCE celebrated landscape, light, and vision. A 280-page Environmental Impact Statement required by the Sonoma County Superior Court concluded that "the only large scale irreversible change may very well be in the ideas and attitudes of the people."[4]

Alice Aycock has designed a number of site-specific outdoor and indoor constructions in which she evokes the mysterious, psychologically provocative quality of places encountered in dreams. Her interest in the symbolic and expressive aspects of human constructions—from underground wells and passageways to mazes, stockades, towers, and factory complexes—has led her to build some amazing structures. In the artist's words, COLLECTED GHOST STORIES FROM THE WORKHOUSE "contains the power to conjure spirits and challenge the viewer's intellectual comprehension of material and psychic phenomena."[5] The materials and form of this work relate it to the nearby industrial structures.

The earthworks and site works movements have helped redirect relationships between architecture, sculpture, and the environment. In the 1970s and 1980s, these movements influenced a variety of directions, from public monuments to site-specific sculpture and installations.

584 Christo.
RUNNING FENCE. Sonoma and Marin Counties, California. 1972–1976.
Nylon fabric and steel poles. 18′ × 24½ miles.
Photograph: © Wolfgang Volz.

585 Alice Aycock.
COLLECTED GHOST STORIES FROM THE WORKHOUSE. 1980.
Cable, copper, galvanized steel, glass piping, motors, steel wire, and wood. 30′ × 75′ × 120′.
University of South Florida, Tampa. Temporary installation.
Photograph courtesy of the artist.

589 George Segal.
WALK, DON'T WALK. 1976.
Museum installation, with viewer. Plaster, cement, metal,
painted wood, and electric light. 104″ × 72″ × 72″.
Collection of Whitney Museum of American Art, New York (79.4).

George Segal combines manufactured objects with life-size plaster figures in everyday settings. With works such as WALK, DON'T WALK, Segal leads us to contemplate life today. The expressionless white figures become types of people rather than individuals. Segal often enables viewers to interact with his sculpture by making his figures part of the viewers' space, rather than separated by a pedestal or frame.

RUCKUS MANHATTAN, a refreshing, wildly humorous installation, was created by Red Grooms and a group called the Ruckus Construction Company. Grooms defines "ruckus" as "a beautiful southern word meaning a 'disorderly commotion.'"[8] The elaborate sculptural extravaganza featured caricatures of many of the most famous landmarks in New York City, including a 30-foot high version of the World Trade Center, a subway train, the Woolworth Building, a Times Square porno shop, a Staten Island ferry one could "ride" on, and the Statue of Liberty in red platform shoes, holding a cigar in her raised right hand. The show was a marvelous cartoon mix of theater, circus, carnival, parade, and amusement park. Realistic details were everywhere – including steam puffing out of manholes.

Viewers became part of the work as they mingled with papier-maché and cut-out figures in a complex of walk-in buildings, shops, roads, and bridges – installed first in Manhattan's Marlborough Gallery in the summer of 1976. As live people and papier-maché people blended in the chaos of the mini-city, it seemed like all Manhattan and all the world were really just a giant cartoon.

590 Red Grooms and the Ruckus
Construction Company.
RUCKUS MANHATTAN. 1976.
Mixed media installation.
Photographed at Marlborough Gallery, New York.

EVENTS, HAPPENINGS, AND PERFORMANCE ART

Swiss assemblage sculptor Jean Tinguely makes machines that do just about everything except work in the manner expected of machines. For Tinguely, life is play, movement, perceptual change. Although much kinetic art has celebrated science and technology, Tinguely enjoys a playful, mocking, yet sympathetic relationship to machines and machine fallibility. "I try to distill the frenzy I see in the world, the mechanical frenzy of our joyful, industrial confusion. . . ."[9] Clearly, Tinguely is the artistic grandson of both Duchamp (see BICYCLE WHEEL, page 402) and Klee (see TWITTERING MACHINE, page 406).

591 Jean Tinguely.
HOMAGE TO NEW YORK; A SELF-CONSTRUCTING,
SELF-DESTRUCTING WORK OF ART. 1960.
Photograph: David Gahr.

In 1960, Tinguely built a large piece of mechanized sculpture that he put together from materials gathered from junkyards and stores in the New York City area. The result was a giant assemblage designed to destroy itself at the turn of a switch—which it did in the courtyard of the Museum of Modern Art in New York City on March 17, 1960. The environmental sculpture was appropriately called HOMAGE TO NEW YORK: A SELF-CONSTRUCTING, SELF-DESTRUCTING WORK OF ART. Tinguely's HOMAGE TO NEW YORK was an event, similar in its effect to a happening.

Happenings are cooperative events in which viewers become active participants in partly planned, partly spontaneous performances with loose scenarios and considerable improvisation. Strictly speaking, happenings are drama with "structure but no plot, words but no dialogue, actors but no characters, and above all, nothing

logical or continuous."[10] Unlike dada and surrealist events, the first happenings were frequently nihilistic, without a relieving sense of humor. No help was given the viewer, who was expected to find his or her own answers.

The term happening was first used by Allan Kaprow in the late 1950s. There were no spectators at Kaprow's happening, HOUSEHOLD. At a preliminary meeting, participants were given parts. The action took place at an isolated rural dump, amid smoldering piles of refuse. The men built a wooden tower on a trash pile, while the women constructed a nest on another mound. During the course of a series of interrelated events, the men destroyed the nest, and the women retaliated by pulling down the men's tower. Then the participants licked a car covered with jam. By bringing ordinary things into unexpected relationships, participants gained a new perspective on the theatre of life in our time.

No two happenings were alike. Kenneth Dewey's happening, MUSEUM PIECE, reached a high point when Rose Marie Larsson "married" an automobile. As she walked down the aisle, Ms. Larsson wore an enigmatic 180-foot history-of-the-world-in-rags train.

592 Allan Kaprow.
HOUSEHOLD.
Happening commissioned by
Cornell University,
performed May 1964.
Photograph: Solomon A. Goldberg.

593 Kenneth Dewey.
Detail of MUSEUM PIECE.
Happening performed at the
Modern Art Museum,
Stockholm, April 7, 1964.
*Photograph: © Ingemar Berling,
Pressens Bild AB.*

594   ANTI-AUTO POLLUTION DEMONSTRATION.
New York. 1971.
Photograph: Horst Schafer.

595   Gilbert and George.
THE RED SCULPTURE. First shown in Tokyo in 1975.
Photograph courtesy of Sonnabend Gallery, New York.

596   Laurie Anderson.
From HOME OF THE BRAVE. 1986.
Film.
Photograph courtesy of Original Artists, New York.

Street protests can also work as happenings, as frequently was the case in the late 1960s and early 1970s. If the participants in the event have a sense of symbolic drama, the result can be highly effective, aesthetic communication.

Abstract expressionists emphasized the act of painting by making images that clearly recorded the process. In happenings, the process was everything. The record was in the remembered experience of the participants and in a few photographs. Happenings in turn led to more controlled and focused types of performance activity. British performance artists Gilbert and George present precisely orchestrated works. Their physical presence and their involvement in ordinary, everyday activities is the material of their "living sculpture." They see their performances as part of the continuum of their lives.

Laurie Anderson is a multitalented performance artist whose social commentary makes the familiar seem unfamiliar. Her mastery of electronic equipment has helped her to move from performance to audio recording to video to film. HOME OF THE BRAVE, Anderson's first film, employs the performance/rock video format.

Anderson's performances are filled with stories and anecdotes that seem unrelated, but add up to a strong comment on the love/hate relationship Americans have with technology. As a performance artist and musician, she depends heavily on both body language and spoken language; her trademark is a talking violin. Anderson is a storyteller with a social conscience, zany sense of humor, and incredible energy and imagination. Her performances and videos are thought provoking and technically innovative.

597   Aaron Siskind.
SYMBOLS IN LANDSCAPE (GLAUCESTER 1). 1944.
Gelatin silver print. 9¼″ × 13″.
Courtesy of the artist.

598   Jerry Uelsmann.
UNTITLED. 1969.
Photograph.
Collection of the artist.

PHOTOGRAPHY

Recognition and support for the art of photography has been long in coming. Until recently, photography has been left out of art history due to a bias in favor of older, more traditional media. Many critics, historians, and museums now acknowledge the importance of photography.

In the 1940s, Aaron Siskind used straight photographic technique and direct engagement with the physical world to evolve a body of work more consistently "abstract" than that of any other photographer up to that time. Siskind's photographs show his awareness of abstract surrealism and other midcentury trends. SYMBOLS IN LANDSCAPE of 1944 and his related works of the period are parallel to abstract expressionism in painting.

The manipulated images of Jerry Uelsmann have added new dimensions to the art of photography and have encouraged younger photographers to go beyond classical "straight" photography. Uelsmann was inspired by O. J. Rejlander's mid-nineteenth-century multiple-negative photographs (see page 352). In the darkroom, which is for him "a visual research lab," Uelsmann combines parts of images from several separate negatives in one print. By manipulating the print he achieved a mystical, visionary quality that can be seen as an outgrowth of surrealism. In this untitled print, trees float above the reflected image of a giant seed pod, invoking a mood of timeless generative forces. Uelsmann makes clear his approach to form, content, and subject matter:

I am involved with a kind of reality that transcends surface reality. More than physical reality, it is emotional, irrational, intellectual, and psychological. It is because of the fact that these other forms of reality don't exist as specific, tangible objects that I can honestly say that subject matter is only a minor consideration which proceeds after the fact and not before.[11]

John Pfahl both challenges and affirms the planographic character of the photographic image through carefully placed additions to his chosen subjects. In AUSTRALIAN PINES, the band of blue water between the white sand and the distant horizon appears to be on the same plane as the tree trunks in the foreground due to Pfahl's strategically placed aluminum foil wrappings. The formal composition is enlivened by the eye- and mind-teasing content.

The present generation of photographers has challenged traditions of straight photography in many ways. One of these is to make studio setups and direct live models. Nowhere is the idea of visualizing a desired photograph more apparent than in Sandy Skoglund's humorous REVENGE OF THE GOLDFISH. Skoglund took advantage of the inherent believability of photography to convince the viewer of the truth of her brilliantly created surreal world.

Painting has long been recognized as a major influence on photographers. What has not been so well understood are the ways in which photography has influenced painting since the mid-nineteenth century. One of the most obvious recent examples is photorealist painting.

599 John Pfahl.
AUSTRALIAN PINES (FORT DESOTO, FLORIDA). 1977.
Ektacolor c-print. 8″ × 10″.
Courtesy of the artist.

600 Sandy Skoglund.
REVENGE OF THE GOLDFISH. 1981.
Cibachrome print.
30″ × 40″.
Courtesy of the artist.

603   Duane Hanson.
TOURISTS. 1970.
Fiberglass and polychromed polyester. 64″ × 65″ × 67″.
Scottish National Gallery of Modern Art.

At times during the twentieth century, the human image has all but disappeared from the mainstream of art. Since the 1970s, however, an increasing number of artists have returned to the human figure as a major subject. One explanation may be that many young artists, schooled in the ideas of nonrepresentational art, found these modes to be inadequate to communicate their most urgent feelings and concerns.

A sculptural counterpart to photorealism can be seen in the work of Duane Hanson. His *super-realist* figures, cast in polyester and fiberglass then painted in minute detail, are unsettling when experienced face-to-face. Viewers marvel over the incredible technique; but for Hanson, technique is a means, not an end. Hanson not only imitates reality, he sometimes presents ideas about reality that are unpleasant. He takes a documentary approach to realist sculpture; his figures are

ordinary people, with no trace of idealism. Carefully selected clothing and other props are important parts of each of Hanson's pieces, and he gives considerable thought to relationships among the figure, clothing, and articles.

TOURISTS is a pointed social comment on Americans in general, and American tourists in particular. The overweight figures, encumbered with possessions, look like people we know or have seen many times. Strong and varied content in Hanson's work suggests that he has a love-hate relationship with middle-class America.

In contrast to Hanson's figures are those by John DeAndrea (see page 181), who uses the same materials and similar technique to achieve a different goal. DeAndrea's figures are usually beautiful young adults without clothing or evidence of life experience, while Hanson's are very much a part of the everyday world.

POSTMODERN ARCHITECTURE

By the mid-1960s, international style (also called "modern") architecture was drawing negative responses from architects and critics who felt that the followers of Le Corbusier, Gropius, and Mies van der Rohe had turned the revolutionary ideas of these masters into a movement too impersonal and regimented to meet the needs of a diverse society. Critics maintained that the "styleless" style of "modern" architecture had little relation to site, climate, tradition, or function, and that it had become a hollow formula, guided by mere technological expediency rather than current human concerns and public preferences.

By the 1970s, those who declared modernism "dead" began to rally around a shared attitude of acceptance of modes quite different from the cool formalism of the modernist movement, which had gained popular acceptance by the middle of the twentieth century. The work of those who rejected the limitations and expectations of modernism came to be designated postmodern—literally, "after the present" or "newer than now" (see discussion on page 235). The paradoxical nature of the term "postmodern" is part of its appeal, and makes it a fitting handle for the entire spectrum of diverse departures from modernism in the arts.

Postmodern became the catch-all label of the 1980s, applied in retrospect to much of the art of the 1960s and 1970s. It is the term for an art based on freedom of choice and tolerance. Postmodernists embrace an eclectic mix of historical influences, decorative tendencies, expressionism, symbolism, and the popular styles of architecture and applied arts enjoyed by the general public. They divorce themselves and their work from the accepted meanings of "traditional" and "modern," and do not value either one more than the other. The attitudes associated with postmodernism are very much a part of all the arts, and are particularly recognized in literature. In the visual arts, postmodern is best known and most easily seen in architecture.

Philadelphia architect Robert Venturi is seen as the "father" of postmodern. He was among the first to practice, theorize, and write about the new inclusive aesthetic. In his book *Complexity and Contradiction in Architecture* (1966), Venturi maintained that the insistence of modern establishment architects on a single reductivist style is contradictory to the complexity of modern life. He pointed out that the great architecture of the past was not always classically simple, but often complex and ambiguous. In response to Mies van der Rohe's often-quoted statement, "Less is more," Venturi declared, "Less is a bore."

Venturi believes that the architects of today should study the commercial roadways of Las Vegas, much as their predecessors studied the temples of ancient Greece and Rome. He feels the "strip" is the new urban form, and that architects should either learn to love it as is, or design it well. While his ideas and theories have caused Venturi to be looked upon as architecture's pop artist, most of his buildings are rather conservative.

The GUILD HOUSE, which contains ninety-one apartments for the elderly, combines aspects of ordinary and historical buildings, and blends well with other inner-city urban-renewal projects. (See also the postmodern HUMANA BUILDING by Michael Graves, page 235.)

604 Venturi Ranch and Scott Brown in association with Cope and Lippencott.
GUILD HOUSE. Philadelphia. 1961.
Photograph: William Watkins.

605 Arata Isozaki.
MUSEUM OF CONTEMPORARY ART. Los Angeles. 1982–1986.
Photograph: Prithwish Neogy.

Japanese architect Arata Isozaki brings a Japanese sensibility to shape and color to postmodern architecture. In his MUSEUM OF CONTEMPORARY ART in Los Angeles, completed in 1987, visitors enter through a rooftop complex in which arches and pyramidal forms punctuate an austere, yet playful sequence of spaces.

606   Miriam Schapiro.
WINDOW ON MONTANA. 1972.
Acrylic and fabric. 5' × 4'2''.
Private collection.
Photograph courtesy Bernice Steinbaum Gallery, New York.

FEMINIST ART

The feminist movement became visible in art in the 1970s, largely through the work of Judy Chicago and Miriam Schapiro. The decorative impulse, which had been suppressed during the reign of abstract expressionism, pop, and minimal art, resurfaced. A revival of interest in pattern and decoration was given a boost by feminist artists ready to confront those who sought to maintain a distinction between "high" art and decorative arts. "Feminist art" has more to do with content and the related use of materials and media long associated with women than it has to do with style.

Miriam Schapiro, known for her decorative mixed-media collages, has been a leader in the feminist art movement. Her WINDOW ON MONTANA brings together acrylic paint with a dazzling collection of patterned fabric. When many patterns from diverse sources are combined, the complexity can overwhelm the eye with conflicting sensations. Schapiro manages to avoid such visual overload, yet maximize the variety of rich patterns. She coined the term "femmage" for her highly personal collages, in which she combines such traditionally feminine materials as fabric scraps, lace, sequins, and buttons with paper and paint in compositions of sumptuous color and intricate design.

Schapiro started her artistic career as an abstract expressionist painter, then received recognition as the creator of hard-edge paintings based on designs she worked out on a computer. In the late 1960s, she joined the women's movement and became codirector, with artist Judy Chicago, of the Feminist Art Program of the California Institute of the Arts in Los Angeles. She began to draw upon women's traditional materials and decorative patterns, such as pieced fabrics, laces, and trims.

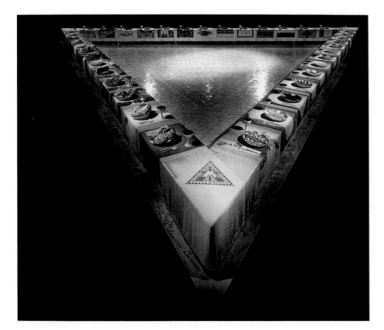

607   Judy Chicago, in cooperation with a working community of 300 women and men.
THE DINNER PARTY. 1979. (Dismantled.)
Mixed media. Triangle, 48' each side.
Photograph courtesy ACA Gallery, New York.

In 1977, Schapiro discussed her work:

The new work was different from anything I had done before. . . . I wanted to explore and express a part of my life I had always dismissed—my home-making, my nesting. I wanted to validate the traditional activities of women, to connect myself to the unknown women artists who made quilts, who had done the invisible "women's work" of civiliza-tion. I wanted to acknowledge them, to honor them. The collagists who came before me were men, who lived in cities. . . . My world, my mother's and grandmother's world was a different one. The fabrics I would use would be beautiful if sewed into clothes or draped against windows, made into pil-lows, or slipped over chairs. My "junk," my fabrics, allude to a particular universe which I wish to make real, to represent.[12]

Judy Chicago was trained as a painter, but is best known for her innovative use of women's crafts in large collaborative projects. The produc-tion of THE DINNER PARTY, which combined fine arts and craft in a visual women's history, involved hundreds of women artisans over a pe-riod of five years. A large triangular table con-tained place settings for thirty-nine women who have made important contributions to world his-tory. Names of 999 additional women of achieve-ment were inscribed on ceramic tiles below the table. Each place setting included a hand-embroidered fabric runner and porcelain plate designed in honor of that woman. Traditional crafts were combined with complex symbolism. Some of the plates are painted with flat designs; others have modeled and painted relief motifs; many are explicitly sexual, embellished with flower-like unfoldings of female genitalia. The project proved as controversial as it was erotic.

DIVERSITY IN RECENT REPRESENTATIONAL ART

The return to representation and the human figure that led some artists into photorealist painting and super-realist sculpture brought overdue recognition to outstanding artists such as Romare Bearden, who had long used figures as subject. The renewed interest in representa-tion also provided stimulus for a variety of new responses, particularly expressionist approaches to figurative painting.

Bearden's subjective visual poetry communi-cates life as he experienced it. As a musician and former songwriter, he said he painted out of the tradition of the blues. He presented life in the rural south and the urban north with vibrant colors and dynamic interacting shapes in a paint and collage technique. Qualities of dream and ritual lend an air of mystery. In ROCKET TO THE MOON, collage fragments portray a scene of quiet despair and stoic perseverance. While

608 Romare Bearden.
ROCKET TO THE MOON. 1967.
Collage. 12½″ × 9″.
Collection of Nanette Rohan Bearden, New York City.

609   Masami Teraoka.
McDONALD'S HAMBURGERS
INVADING JAPAN: GEISHA AND
TATTOOED WOMAN. 1975.
Watercolor. 14½" × 21½".
Private collection.
Photograph courtesy of the artist.

a barely visible rocket heads for the moon, ghetto life remains punctuated by two red stop-lights for each green arrow.

Bearden's formal style ensures that his images are not overly sentimental in spite of their loaded content. Sensitivity to design gives strength and unity to his poignant subject matter. His study of art history led Bearden to admire the paintings of Dutch masters Vermeer and de Hooch (pages 338–339 and 104), as well as cubist paintings and Benin sculpture (pages 386 and 291) — all of which were among the many important influences on his work. His photocollages are alive with references to Bearden's own heritage, yet communicate universal concerns.

Masami Teraoka's art is related to that of Bearden in the use of ethnic heritage as a source of inspiration and identity. When he came to the United States in 1961, Teraoka was fascinated by New York's pop and minimal art. But in the early 1970s he made what he described as a "scary decision" to commit to doing figurative work. It was a bold move at a time when the art establishment showed little interest in narrative work.

The iconographic complexity of modern times is expressed in Teraoka's McDONALD'S HAMBURGERS INVADING JAPAN: GEISHA AND TATTOOED WOMAN. It is the story of cultural crossover, painted by a Japanese-born American citizen. Teraoka's painting style is based on the traditional Ukiyo-e woodblock print style (see page 281), popular in Japan from the seventeenth through nineteenth centuries. Both Ukiyo-e prints and Teraoka's paintings depict worldly pleasures; but Teraoka's, which contain references to products such as hamburgers, ice cream cones, cameras, and computers, are clearly late twentieth century in content. With great wit and skillful design, Teraoka combines the clichés of Eastern tradition and Western subject matter in highly inventive images which play on the irony of contemporary East-West relations. The Japanese writing is a major element in the composition, but also contributes to the humor of the work for those who can read it.

Jennifer Bartlett is a prolific artist who has proven her versatility by working successfully in a variety of styles and media (see also her pencil drawing on page 123). She works in series, exploring many of the infinite possibilities of each subject or theme. In WHITE HOUSE, and other installations of the mid-1980s, Bartlett combined landscape paintings with actual objects such as small boats, fences, or houses. With the actual object and the illusion of the object presented simultaneously, the viewer is brought into the art process in a surprising way.

Neo-expressionist Anselm Kiefer's landscapes are often monumental in size. The West German artist combines the paint application of abstract expressionism with nineteenth-century feelings for history and archetypal mythology. In contrast to the abstract expressionist emphasis on aesthetic issues, Kiefer gives equal attention to moral and cultural issues. His paintings, loaded with symbolism, mythology, and religion, probe the German national conscience and reveal the grim confusion felt by many postwar German artists. Kiefer sees art as having redeeming powers, the ability to provide spiritual catharsis; yet his disturbing work presents more questions than answers.

OSIRIS AND ISIS combines the Egyptian myth of Isis and Osiris with the present reality of nuclear energy and possible nuclear destruction. Osiris symbolized the indestructible creative forces of nature. According to legend, the god was slain and cut into pieces by his evil brother, Set. Isis, sister and wife of Osiris, found and buried the pieces, and made each burial place sacred. In another version of the story, Isis collected the pieces and brought Osiris back to life. In Kiefer's painting, the goddess Isis, in the form of a TV circuit board, sits on top of the pyramid, sending out a network of wires, each attached to a fragment of the dismembered Osiris. The dark, heavily textured surface, made with paint, mud, earth, rock, tar, and bits of ceramic and metal, intensifies the image's disturbing power. Some see Kiefer's enormous, angst-filled, end-of-the-world paintings as dreary and depressing; while others feel Kiefer is awakening his fellow Germans to their tragic heritage, and helping them to move beyond guilt to an era of renewed hope.

610 Jennifer Bartlett. WHITE HOUSE. 1985.
Installation view. Oil on canvas, wood, enamel paint, metal, tar paper. Painting 10′ × 16′; fence 36″ × 12′; and 10¼″ × 5′; house 45″ × 60″ × 58¼″; swimming pool 7″ × 43¾″ × 31½″.
Photograph: Geoffrey Clements. Courtesy of Paula Cooper Gallery, New York.

611 Anselm Kiefer.
OSIRIS AND ISIS. 1985–1987.
Mixed media. 148″ × 281″.
San Francisco Museum of Modern Art.
Purchased through a gift of Jean Stein, by exchange, the Mrs. Paul L. Wattis Fund, and the Doris and Donald Fisher Fund.

612 Gaylen Hansen.
LADY ON TRAPEZE. 1980.
Oil on canvas. 72½″ × 71″.
Monique Knowlton Gallery, Inc. New York.

Gaylen Hansen was an early exponent of the neo-expressionist movement of the late 1970s and early 1980s that reintroduced subject matter with subjective content heightened by expressionist modes of painting. Hansen uses a deliberately naive, folk art style to depict dreamlike encounters between people and other creatures. Danger, mystery, and humor are central to many of his paintings, including LADY ON TRAPEZE.

Two exhibitions held in New York in 1978, "Bad Painting" at the New Museum and "New Image Painting" at the Whitney, were organized to show the works of a highly diverse group of artists who led in the return to representational painting. Joan Brown was included in the "Bad Painting" show. Her DANCERS IN THE CITY challenges academic notions of good and bad drawing and painting. Brown had moved quickly through a brief abstract expressionist phase to develop an intentionally primitive style based on the blunt portrayal of modern life.

The best art of our time enriches and unveils life today, and at the same time shows us our connection to the past. The immediate power and size of Jonathan Borofsky's RUNNING PEOPLE sweeps the viewer into the painting. The running figures are among the many images that

613 Joan Brown.
DANCERS IN THE CITY #3.
1973.
Enamel on canvas. 8′ × 10′.
Collection of Dorothy Goldeen,
Los Angeles.
Photograph courtesy of
Dorothy Goldeen Galley,
Santa Monica.

result from his practice of drawing quickly after dreaming, then enlarging the drawings on wall surfaces.

Compare this 1979 painting with a prehistoric painting of marching figures, painted five to ten thousand years ago. While the sizes of the two images are vastly different (the recent painting is 28 feet long, while the prehistoric one is 9 inches across), each tells us about human experience in its context. The media and content of art have changed considerably since prehistoric times, but the primary fact of being alive and human remains.

As we approach the end of the twentieth century, leading artists continue to augment society's experience. A trend toward greater public involvement with art has been fueled by revolutionary thinking about the nature of art and its role in society.

Recent developments in art, science, and other fields are too close to us in time to be perceived clearly. It usually takes one or two generations for significant patterns, movements, and breakthrough ideas to be assessed in terms of their long-term value for humanity. Even if we are not concerned with historic importance, it is often difficult to look the present in the eye. It is natural to feel more comfortable with the art of the past, which has been around long enough to be sorted out and understood through the perspective of time. Since contemporary art is an integral, if sometimes obscure, part of late twentieth-century life, today's art shares with the rest of experience some of the dominant characteristics of our era: complexity, contradiction, rapid change, and commitment to both the excitement of the avant-garde and the comfort of established traditions.

Artworks of poor quality from long ago have generally not been saved, and are therefore often removed from consideration. In contrast, we have a full array of works—good, bad, and indifferent—from our own time and the recent past. If we are open, some contemporary art will speak to us and provide us with valuable experiences. Marcel Duchamp makes this point well:

614   Jonathan Borofsky.
RUNNING PEOPLE AT 2,661,216. 1979.
Latex paint on two walls and ceiling beams. 14' × 18'.
Installation, Portland Center for Visual Arts, Portland, Oregon.

615   WARRIORS. Gasulla Gorge, Castellon, Spain. c. 8000–3000 B.C. Approx. 9" wide.

The work of art is always based on the two poles of the onlooker and the maker, and the spark that comes from that bipolar action gives birth to something—like electricity. But the onlooker has the last word, and it is always posterity that makes the masterpiece.[13]

Current Issues

ART IN PUBLIC PLACES

As we have seen, today's cultural diversity and rapid change have led to wide variety in both art styles and personal responses to works of art. Because there is no longer general agreement on what constitutes "good" art, selection of a work of art for a public place can be an emotional, and often a political, issue. While most people readily accept the decisions of experts in other areas, many believe they have the right to view or not view art, and to decide for themselves what art they want to see. The placement of an artwork in a public space makes it accessible, but may lead to the feeling that some so-called art experts have decided what the public should learn to like. In the case of government art commissions, people who dislike the "art" may be additionally distressed when they realize that their tax dollars helped to pay for it.

The idea of public art goes back to ancient times. Government and religious leaders have commissioned many of history's best-known artists to execute works for the public. In the United States, however, public art (other than architecture) was largely confined to commemorative statues and monuments in parks until nearly the middle of this century. The short-lived WPA (see page 413) federal art program of the late 1930s and early 1940s provided modest support for the participating artists, who created a great number of public murals, in addition to easel paintings, prints, photographs, and sculpture. However, it is only within recent decades that we have seen a steady stream of commissions given to large numbers of American artists for public art.

During the 1960s, the American economy was strong, and government leaders began to spend money in new areas. Since the arts are considered beneficial for individuals and communities, it seemed appropriate for city, state, and national governments to become involved in bringing the arts to the public. A high percentage of today's public art is now commissioned by government agencies.

Among the largest sponsors of public art is the federal government's General Services Administration (GSA) Art-in-Architecture program, begun in 1962 during John F. Kennedy's presidency. The program requires that 0.05 percent of the cost of each new government building be spent for art to be located in or around the new building. A number of states, cities, and counties subsequently implemented similar programs, with varying percentages designated for the purchase or commissioning of works of art.

The federal government's currently active National Endowment for the Arts (NEA) was created in 1965. Among the NEA's many programs is the Art in Public Places Program, under which communities can request matching funds for commissions of large outdoor artworks.

Corporations have also become involved in supporting the arts. Many have found that by providing more rewarding environments for their own employees and by making cultural contributions to the larger community, they generate good will both within their own companies and with the general public. Corporate support for the arts ranges from buying or commissioning artworks, to sponsoring public television programs and traveling art exhibitions.

Public art programs have had problems and failures as well as notable successes. In some instances, the results have been cosmetic attempts to hide inferior architecture, or simply "decoration" inappropriately applied as an afterthought. To insure effective, integrated results, architects, landscape architects, interior designers, and artists have become increasingly aware of the need to work with each other and with clients, starting in the conceptual and planning stages of projects.

Most art in outdoor public places is in the form of large sculpture or murals, which minimize problems of theft and vandalism by being as durable and immovable as possible. Occasionally, existing works are purchased for outdoor locations, but more often artists are commissioned to design site-specific works. Beginning in the late 1960s and 1970s, local and national government commissions have also become involved in purchasing portable artworks for permanent collections. Such works are displayed in many kinds of public buildings, from airports to universities to government offices, and may be moved from one location to another. Public art programs recognize that contemporary art can make a contribution to the quality of life. People who have little previous experience with today's art are finding that it is becoming part of their daily lives.

The making and managing of public art in Seattle has been particularly successful, due to the effective collaboration between the art agencies of Washington state, Seattle, and King County governments. Seattle's many public art programs have made artists feel well supported, and caused the area to attract artists who enjoy major involvement in planning processes. Since the early 1970s, the arts have come to play an increasing role in the cultural life of Seattle, and have provided the city with an economic as well as aesthetic boost. Seattle residents take pride in their public art programs and other environmentally oriented, voter-supported decisions aimed at rejuvenating the city, which suffered severe economic depression in the early 1970s.

616 Herbert Bayer.
Detail of MILL CREEK CANYON EARTHWORKS.
Kent, Washington. 1979–1982.
Photograph: © John Hoge, Seattle.

Herbert Bayer's EARTHWORK, commissioned by King County, is one of a number of earthworks which have been designed, in part, to deal with environmental problems. Bayer's piece consists of grass mounds and platforms, which created enjoyable park space and also solved a drainage problem.

On local, state, and national levels, artists are generally selected for public commissions by a panel of art experts. As noted above, disputes occasionally result when the tastes and views of such experts are at odds with the preferences of the public. Among the most highly publicized public art controversies in recent times were those surrounding two pieces of minimal sculpture, each in the form of a wall—one by well known sculptor Richard Serra, and the other by architecture student Maya Lin.

617 Richard Serra.
TILTED ARC. New York City. 1981.
Cor-ten steel. 12′ × 120′.

618 Richard Serra.
SPIN OUT. 1973.
Hot-rolled steel. Three plates, each 10′ × 40′ × 1½″.
Kröller-Müeller Rijksmuseum, Otterlo, Netherlands.

In 1979, Richard Serra was selected by a panel of art professionals working with the GSA to submit a proposal for a sculpture to be located in the plaza at the corner of Broadway and Lafayette Street in New York City. The panel subsequently approved the design, and in 1981 TILTED ARC was fabricated and installed. The sculpture is made of Cor-ten steel, which is supposed to develop a thin layer of rust. In time, the surface of TILTED ARC acquired its patina of rust—and also graffiti. The site-specific work is a slightly curved wall weighing 73 tons, measuring 120 feet long by 12 feet high. It was positioned so that it seemed to turn its back on the large fountain that had been the focal point of the plaza. It blocked the view of a tree-filled park from the entrance of the Jacob K. Javits Federal Building, and the view up Broadway from the entrance to the Courthouse.

TILTED ARC was greeted with enormous hostility from people who worked in the buildings facing the plaza. In protest, thirteen hundred government employees signed petitions demanding the removal of the sculpture. The work became the subject of a lengthy, heated battle involving artists, art critics, the press, public hearings, administrative panels, and a United States District Court. Following a GSA panel's recommendation that the work be relocated at an estimated cost of $50,000, Serra filed a lawsuit against the GSA, seeking $30 million in damages. Serra maintained that relocation of the site-specific work would destroy its integrity and therefore destroy the piece itself. The dispute caused a split in the art community, and further divided art professionals from a public already wary of much contemporary art.

Serra saw the intent of TILTED ARC as "a way to dislocate or alter the decorative function of the plaza, and actively bring people into the sculpture's context."[1] The employees and many others didn't like either the "dislocation" or the "sculpture's context." In retrospect, given the confrontational nature of much of Serra's previous work, the GSA took a major risk in selecting Serra in the first place.

For an earlier commission for the Kröller-Müeller Museum's sculpture park, Serra designed a related, minimal sculpture. SPIN OUT consists of hot-rolled steel walls which emerge from wooded slopes around a clearing. Implied convergence of the walls punctuates, rather than disrupts the continuity of the forest clearing.

The highly publicized VIETNAM VETERANS MEMORIAL, located on the Mall in Washington, D.C., sparked a different kind of controversy. The 250-foot-long, V-shaped black granite wall bears the names of the nearly sixty thousand American servicemen and women who

619 Maya Lin.
VIETNAM VETERANS
MEMORIAL. The Mall,
Washington, D.C. 1980–1982.
Black granite.
Each wall 10′1″ × 246′9″.

died or are missing in Southeast Asia. The non-profit Vietnam Veterans Memorial Fund Inc. (VVMF) was formed in 1979 by a group of Vietnam veterans who believed a symbol of recognition of the human cost of the war would help speed the process of national reconciliation. Domestic controversy over American involvement in the war had caused returning veterans to receive less than a hero's welcome.

In 1980, Congress authorized the site, and the VVMF announced a national design competition. The VVMF set design criteria which specified that the memorial be reflective and contemplative in character, harmonize with its surroundings, contain the names of all those who died or remain missing, and that it make no political statement about the war. After examining 1,421 anonymously submitted entries, the jury of internationally recognized artists and designers unanimously selected the design of twenty-one-year-old Maya Ying Lin of Athens, Ohio, then a student at Yale University. Lin had gone to visit the site and decided to create a design that would work with the land rather than dominate it. "I had an impulse to cut open the earth . . . an initial violence that in time would heal. The grass would grow back, but the cut would remain, a pure, flat surface, like a geode when you cut it open and polish the edge. . . .

I chose black granite to make the surface reflective and peaceful."[2]

Initial reaction by the press was favorable, and in spring 1981 the Commission of Fine Arts and other government agencies approved the design. But several months later, a Vietnam veteran appeared before the Commission and called the proposed design a "black gash of shame." He hit a nerve, and subsequent accusations in the press called the design "unheroic," "defeatist," and "death-oriented." Veterans themselves were divided on the issue. It was, indeed, a hard design to "explain." In January 1982, Secretary of the Interior James Watt put the project on hold.

A compromise was reached several months later when it was decided that a figurative sculpture and a flag would be added to the site. Frederick Hart was chosen to create a naturalistic bronze statue to be located in a cluster of small trees near the wall. In time, the compromise seemed to please all sides. The wall was dedicated on Veterans Day 1982, and the Hart statue in 1984. Most of the modernists who were dismayed at the idea of cluttering up the site with yet another bronze commemorative statue were pleasantly surprised by the high quality of the

620   Frederick Hart.
VIETNAM MEMORIAL SCULPTURE.
The Mall, Washington, D.C. 1984.
Bronze. Life-size.

figurative work, and the fact that it complements, rather than detracts from the wall. Yet, despite public clamor for a traditional monument, a large majority of the thousands of tourists who flock to the memorial each day never even see the Hart sculpture; they are drawn right to the wall.

Lin's bold, eloquently simple design creates a memorial park within a larger park. The polished black surface reflects the surrounding trees and lawn, and the tapering segments point

to the Washington Monument in one direction and the Lincoln Memorial in the other. Names are inscribed in chronological order of the date of death, with each name given a place in history. As visitors walk toward the center, the wall gets higher and names pile up inexorably. The monument, visited by more than ten thousand per day, has the power not only to make people cry, but also to console and heal.

The fragmented nature of contemporary American culture presents a dilemma for both artists and sponsors involved with public art. Should the freedom of the creative individual be unquestioned, with the hope that the public audience will follow, or at least accept, the art that results? Or should the public, or some part of the public, have a voice in setting guidelines for selection, and actually selecting art that becomes part of the public environment—particularly when the art is paid for by tax dollars? Just how democratic should the process be? On the one hand, we could rely entirely on "art experts," whose tastes are often very different from that of the public; at the other extreme, with a lot of public input, we might yield to the lowest common denominator of popular taste. Clearly, efforts are being made to find a balance—a middle ground. Recent controversies have caused everyone involved in public art commissions, and many other concerned citizens, to give serious thought to the procedures involved.

Businesses, particularly large corporations, have generally experienced good results from their relatively new role as patron of the arts. Isamu Noguchi's RED CUBE, commissioned by the Marine Midland Bank, has become a popular New York landmark. With its monumental diagonal contours and bright color, the sculpture vitalizes its surroundings. Pedestrians are immediately engaged in the dynamics of balance and shaped space. RED CUBE is more visually active and decorative than other minimal style works to which it is related.

Paintings in public places take a variety of forms, from murals on walls of buildings to paintings on construction fences. They may be made by professional artists, commissioned by a government agency, corporation, or other group, or they may be made by young people or other nonprofessional artists as part of educational or social programs, neighborhood renewal projects, or protests. Among the most intriguing murals in public places are those painted in a *tromp l'oeil* or fool-the-eye realist style, such as the walls painted by Richard Haas.

For painter and printmaker Haas, exteriors of buildings provide large, highly visible surfaces for paintings that cause viewers to "do a double take." Inspired by baroque illusionistic wall paintings he had seen in Italy, and his desire to carry his painting to the streets of the city, Haas conceived the idea of painting architectural illusions on blank exterior walls of older city buildings. The first such project he undertook was a wall at the corner of Prince and Greene Streets in New York. It was commissioned by City Walls, Inc., a nonprofit service organization that promoted and administrated wall-painting projects. After obtaining the many necessary permits and approvals, Haas and his assistants made extensive preliminary scale studies in gouache. The actual painting on the wall was done by professional sign painters under the direction and supervision of Haas.

621 Isamu Noguchi.
RED CUBE. Marine Midland Bank, 140 Broadway, New York. 1969. Painted welded steel and aluminum. Height 28'.

622 Richard Haas.
UNTITLED (WALL PAINTING).
114 Prince St., New York. 1975. 60' × 70'.
a. Before painting.
Photograph courtesy of the Public Art Fund.   b. After painting.

623   KEITH HARING AT WORK.
Photograph: Tseng Kwong Chi, New York.

Street art, which is related to graffiti, is another kind of public art. There is sometimes a fine line between street art and vandalism. Perhaps the best-known works of street art were created not on the street, but in the New York subway stations, by vigilante artist Keith Haring. Solid black paper on empty advertising signboards provides the surface for Haring's line drawings in white chalk. His drawings became so popular that in the mid-1980s, he became commercially successful as an artist.

When he first saw a blank subway panel, Haring immediately went above ground and bought chalk. He began drawing on empty panels as he waited for subway trains to take him to and from work. Occasionally, advertisements on adjacent panels provide inspiration, or create humorous associations. Even when his drawings remain only a short time before they are covered by new advertisements, they are seen and enjoyed by thousands of people – many more than would see them in a gallery or museum. And Haring enjoys the realization that most of those who appreciate his subway drawings are not the people who go to museums and galleries, but are a true cross-section of the residents of the city he loves.

Haring's drawings are simple and quickly made – for easy readability, and so the artist can avoid arrest. Technically, they are graffiti; but because they are made with chalk on temporary coverings of paper, it is hard to think of them as vandalism. The influence of Haring's popular style on graphic and textile designers has further extended the impact of his work.

MUSEUMS AND GALLERIES

Although art in museums is often far removed from the people and cultures of its origin, without museums, much of the art of the past would not have been saved and would not be accessible to the public. As museums improve their abilities to care for and display their holdings, private collectors are increasingly drawn to share their collections by giving or loaning works to museums.

In recent decades, museum directors and curators have expanded the role of museums. Educational programs in many museums are growing to include outreach programs, film series, and a variety of performances.

In addition to providing displays of their permanent collections, most museums now present a wide variety of temporary exhibitions which often feature works not owned by the museum. With financial help in the form of grants from government, corporate, or private sources, museums organize and display traveling exhibitions. Major, large exhibitions as well as smaller shows are well attended cultural events in the cities to which they travel.

Commercial galleries play a key role in providing opportunities for young and unknown artists, in addition to being the primary marketplace for established artists. As businesses, galleries must exhibit and represent artists whose works the dealers think are, or will become, saleable. Much has been said and written on the contemporary gallery system, and the power of a few art dealers and gallery owners to create "stars." In a few instances, dealers and gallery owners have provided what they believed were promising artists with regular incomes—regardless of whether or not their works sold—thus enabling the artists to continue working. Of course, when such an artist does achieve commercial success, the dealer benefits too. As with other kinds of investments, some pay off and some do not.

Do art museums, galleries, and art critics influence or control taste? Some people feel they do. The decision to exhibit or write about certain artists and not others determines what is brought to the attention of the art-viewing public. A museum exhibition, or the efforts of a well-financed gallery owner can make the difference between obscurity and high visibility for a particular artist. However, as with all marketable commodities, advertising and exposure are not enough in the long run; the artist's work has to have genuine merit to achieve lasting acclaim.

The idea of art-as-commodity has been rejected by many of today's artists, who avoid the art market by deliberately creating works such as installations and earthworks that can't be bought and sold. Some artists are concerned that when art is treated as a commodity, it cheapens art's essential nature and purpose. Others, like Keith Haring and Laurie Anderson, have taken to the streets and subways rather than wait to be discovered or supported by museums, galleries and private collectors.

Every profession has a few unscrupulous operators, and art is no exception. While the majority of art dealers and galleries are well-intentioned and honest, a few engage in malpractice. The biggest problems in this area have been with works sold as signed and numbered original prints, when in fact they are simply signed and numbered photomechanical reproductions. Since the early 1970s, there has been an enormous increase in misrepresentation in this area. Cities frequented by tourists have been the favored locations for the few galleries engaged in print fraud, because the customers are usually far away by the time they discover that they have been duped. Lawsuits filed by people who have been sold fake "original" prints by Salvador Dali and others have grown so numerous that international, federal, and state authorities are working hard to enforce existing laws and pass new laws that will help both consumers and honest dealers. The increase in print fraud has made a few collectors wary of fine art prints. This situation is damaging to the whole art community, and doubly unfortunate because prints are generally far more affordable than paintings or sculpture. (See the discussion of prints and reproductions on pages 139–140.)

Reproductions, including posters, have important functions, but they should be identified as photomechanical reproductions, rather than fine art prints, and be sold for low prices. As in other areas, it is important for consumers to be well informed. Art buyers need to know about materials and methods, the practices of the artist, current prices, and the reputation of the dealer.

COLLECTING ART

The collecting of art takes many forms. Some people buy art for their own pleasure, some for prestige, and some for investment. Of course, there is often more than one reason for buying a work of art. People who acquire artworks purely for the pleasure of living with them base each decision to buy (and how much they are willing to spend) on the degree of enjoyment they expect to derive from living with a given piece. Such people are likely to be primarily interested in the form and content of the work, and perhaps in owning work by artists they know. Such collectors generally derive great personal satisfaction from living with art—regardless of whether the works are by friends and relatives, little-known artists, or established masters.

Collectors often find that as their aesthetic sensibilities become more developed, their preferences shift. Some collectors acquire a variety of art, while others limit themselves to a particular style, media, ethnic group, or historical period.

The prestige or anticipated investment value of owning works by famous artists may be a primary factor for some collectors. It is said that when the stock market is shaky, people are more inclined to invest in things they can touch such as real estate, gold, and art. Unless collectors for whom investment is an important consideration are very knowledgeable, they may end up paying high prices for works with little resale value.

The art market received a lot of publicity in the 1980s because some well-publicized record prices were paid for works of art. The fact that a work is expensive, however, does not necessarily mean that it is good art; nor does a low price necessarily indicate poor quality. It is ironic that the two paintings which were sold at record high auction prices in 1987 were made by an artist who died a century ago, after selling only one work in his lifetime. The paintings were by Vincent van Gogh, and they have not improved in the century since his death. In fact, some of the colors have lost brilliance due to his use of unstable pigments. What has changed is public perception and taste.

While enormously high prices are paid at auction for the resold works of a few well-established artists, many more fine works by unknown artists are either not sold at all, or sold for very low prices. Large numbers of high-quality artworks can be purchased for reasonable prices; low budget collectors derive great satisfaction from "finding" and living with such works by young and other "undiscovered" artists.

PRESERVATION AND RESTORATION OF ART

Much of the art of the past that we enjoy today would have perished but for those people in each generation who have made the effort to care for and, when necessary, to restore selected works. Restoration is a difficult, time-consuming, and sometimes impossible task.

Today's trained professional restorers follow scientifically exacting procedures. They are aware that they don't have all the answers, so they are careful to make as few additions as possible, and to use substances that can be easily removed if future technology provides better solutions. It is ironic that the high-tech societies able to support specialized restoration technology are the same societies in which air pollution from industrial production and traffic is rapidly destroying some of the world's finest art.

In the past, restoration was often so ill-conceived that it did more harm than good, either by adding to and altering the original—as was done with Leonardo's LAST SUPPER (see page 327)—or by adding materials that caused new problems, as in the use of iron rods in the Parthenon.

The history of the Parthenon (see page 302) illustrates some of the ways human values and actions have affected creative works of earlier peoples. Since its construction more than 2,400 years ago, the Parthenon has been subjected to the ravages of human history. Conquering Romans used it as a brothel; Christians turned it into a church; the Turks refurbished it as a mosque, then stored explosives in it while they fought the Venetians. In 1687, a Venetian artillery shell exploded the Turks' store of gunpowder, causing major damage to the structure. From 1801 to 1803, while Greece remained under Turkish rule, Lord Elgin, the British ambassador to Turkey, was permitted to remove a large number of Greek sculptures, including many from the friezes of the Parthenon.

Early in this century, would-be restorers inserted iron bars between the remaining stones of the Parthenon's columns as reinforcements. Unfortunately, the sea air soon corroded the iron, causing many stones to split. Nothing in its entire history, however, has been as hard on the Parthenon as twentieth-century air pollution.

The marble of the Parthenon and other buildings on the Acropolis is being eaten away by the sulphur dioxide produced when automobile and other fuel exhaust combines with moisture. Sulphur dioxide converts marble into a soft, chalky substance called gypsum. Driving rain, wind-blown sand, and dirt now cause greater damage to the fragile surfaces of these structures in one year than weathering previously did in a century. Ironically, by being housed in the British Museum, the works removed (some would say stolen) by Lord Elgin have been protected not only from normal weathering, neglect, and the possible ravages of war, but also from the more insidious process of corrosion from air pollution.

The conservation and restoration of old buildings often becomes an issue for public debate. Sometimes buildings are saved and restored for aesthetic and historical, rather than economic reasons. In each case, those involved must determine what the issues are, and whether the building is worth saving. Many old buildings of all kinds have been saved from demolition following their placement on state or national historic registers.

The restoration of well-known artworks sometimes causes controversy among art historians, as in the late-twentieth-century cleaning of the Sistine Chapel ceiling (see page 329). Nonetheless, conservation and restoration are important considerations for artworks of all kinds, from small drawings, to fabrics, to large buildings. Some materials used by artists begin to deteriorate very quickly. Artworks deemed worth preserving must be maintained and handled appropriately. Fortunately, experts using state-of-the-art instruments and materials are now able to clean, mend, reinforce, and partially restore works that may appear to be beyond repair.

THE ROLE OF THE ARTIST TODAY

Many of the roles artists have played throughout history are still with us, and new ones have been added. Historic roles include providing religious, ceremonial, or political support; creating or interpreting beauty; educating the illiterate; providing entertainment; responding to social, environmental, or political issues; designing functional and aesthetically pleasing objects and environments; and organizing visual form in ways that express spiritual, aesthetic, or moral truth. Today's artists also cause us to question assumptions, prejudices, and expectations. Above all, it is the role of the artist to enrich and expand experience—to cause us to see anew.

When we are shocked by some of the new works of literature, music, and the visual arts, it is because they do not match our preconceptions. The discerning person has expectations which can be used as a starting point to new aesthetic experience rather than a barrier to such experience. Artists continue to question assumptions about art and life, and in so doing create vehicles for increased awareness and understanding. A questioning, exploring state of mind is as necessary in art as it is in science.

Any work of art precedes and is more important than theories and explanations that are applied to it, names that classify it, and terms that help analyze it. It often appears that avant-garde artists in all fields wish merely to shock us with their work. Yet it is enlightening to realize that much of what we now accept as standard fare in the arts was at one time thought to be either scandalous, or at least very strange. For example, in the 1870s the paintings of the French impressionists were considered radical and unacceptable by most art critics as well as the public.

People who admire naturalistic works, and even those who enjoy cubist and abstract expressionist painting, may find works such as Frank Stella's LO SCIOCCO SENZO PAURA totally bewildering. Knowledge of recent art movements is helpful in approaching such works, but often the key for the viewer is to be open and receptive rather than threatened. If we can simply be

624   Frank Stella.
LO SCIOCCO SENZO PAURA (#1, 4X). 1984.
Oil, urethane enamel, fluorescent alkyd, acrylic, and printing ink
on canvas, etched magnesium, aluminum, and fiberglass.
130″ × 127″ × 23″.
Collection of Ann and Robert L. Freedman, New York.
Photograph courtesy of M. Knoedler & Company, New York.

illusions. He began by making his images as flat as possible, with the designs dictating the shape of the canvas. The painting became an object in its own right rather than a reference to something else. Next, instead of creating illusions of depth, he began to include actual three-dimensional projections. Stella's huge painted constructions of the 1980s project aggressively toward the viewer. LO SCIOCCO SENZO PAURA may be a caricature of the idea of modernism, as well as a comment on the manufactured madness of our times.

It is not surprising that the often abrasive quality of modern life has found full force in contemporary art. Consciously or unconsciously, artists speak for their age as well as for themselves. Art making is a continual process of give and take, of creative forming and being formed by the quality and values of the present. By "reading" the art of our time we can become aware of the full spectrum of what is happening in the contemporary world.

It often seems as if artists are ahead of their time, but it may be that they are among the few who are truly with their time, as Gertrude Stein observed:

A creator is not in advance of his generation, but he is the first of his contemporaries to be conscious of what is happening to his generation.[3]

aware of the feelings aroused by a work of art, we are likely to perceive the artist's intended message. This doesn't mean we will necessarily appreciate it; sometimes we can understand what an artist is "saying" and still not like the work or its content.

Through three decades, Stella's work has gone through a series of progressive phases, each with its own internal logic, and each a clear, if surprising, outgrowth of the preceding work. The three painted constructions reproduced here and on pages 435 and 136 represent Stella's early and recent phases, and demonstrate the major change in his work. He took painting from "cool," formal, shaped flatness to "hot," highly expressive, three-dimensional projections—pure visual "razzle-dazzle"—all within his own nonrepresentational "abstract" idiom. Stella rejected the idea of painting as a window for three-dimensional

The inventive and unusual environmental designs created by SITE Projects cause people to see anew, and to reconsider habits of applying old solutions to new problems. SITE, which stands for Sculpture-in-the-Environment, is an interdisciplinary architecture and environmental arts firm led by Alison Sky, Michelle Stone, Emilio Souza, and James Wines. SITE draws on sources outside traditional architectural conventions as it seeks to increase the expressive potential of buildings and public spaces.

Highrise of Homes is a SITE research project presented as an exhibit and a book. It is based on the premise that architects are obliged to consider individual housing choices within the highrise context. SITE looked at stacked and clustered housing from a historical perspective, and reviewed recent and former traditions in highrise construction. In drawings such as WATER'S EDGE, Jim Wines explores fantasies and

625 James Wines.
WATER'S EDGE. Drawing for *Highrise of Homes*.
SITE Projects, Inc. 1981.
Ink and charcoal. 24″ × 30″.
Collection of Laura Carpenter, Dallas, Texas.

technological innovations. Wines developed his
concept for both new construction and the reuse
of old industrial buildings. The project stimulates thinking that could lead to breakthroughs
in housing design.

In FOREST SHOWROOM by SITE Projects, an
otherwise ordinary suburban department store
appears to be returning to the surrounding forest. The forest, which remains on two sides of
the store, seems to break through the parking
lot, and even to separate the front of the building from the main showroom. Soil, leaves and
roots of the forest floor show through the store
windows. Rather than destroy over six acres of
woodland, architect Emilio Souza found a way
to preserve much of the forest, and to integrate

626 SITE Projects, Inc.
FOREST SHOWROOM. Richmond, Virginia. 1980.

627   E. Fay Jones & Associates.
THORNCROWN CHAPEL. Eureka Springs, Arkansas. 1981.

it with the building. This and other Best Products Company showrooms designed by SITE symbolize the all-important dialogue between the built environment and the natural world. Dislocated walls, crumbling facades, and other startling disruptions of standard architecture confront unsuspecting shoppers with surprise and humor. SITE's purpose is to question assumptions about architecture through an approach they call *de-architecture*. The FOREST SHOWROOM and other SITE designs are both romantic and postmodern in orientation.

THORNCROWN CHAPEL, designed by E. Fay Jones, challenges architectural assumptions in a very different way. The nondenominational Christian wayfarers' chapel is located in a secluded spot along a wooded trail high in the Ozark Mountains. Jones knew that heavy earth-moving construction equipment would damage the wooded setting; therefore, the entire structure was designed to require only materials that could be carried by two people along a narrow hillside path. The architect points out that the structure is a kind of reverse-Gothic construction. Gothic cathedrals are supported by exterior structures in compression, while THORNCROWN CHAPEL is held together by lightweight interior timbers in tension. The highly creative design provides inspiration on several levels.

For both artists and viewers the personal nature of art is all important. Artists use that which they know best as a way to illuminate universal themes and concerns. In the title of his self-portrait, Harold Tovish alludes to the ways in which we become the measure of our relationship to the universe.

Many artists draw inspiration from personal experience, while others depict things they can imagine, but have not experienced firsthand. By addressing particular issues in their art, some artists hope to bring social, political or environmental problems to the attention of people who might affect change. According to artist Fritz Scholder,

. . . the role of the artist is not to compromise, but to express the truth as he sees it with all the power of which he is capable.[4]

A sense of concern and social responsibility motivates Scholder, who has made many paintings and lithographs about the plight of the Native American. He merges traditional subject matter with his own insights, feelings, and contemporary expressionist style and carefully avoids romanticized stereotypes. Scholder, who is part Native American, treats his subjects with sympathy, compassion, appreciation for their traditions, and occasionally humor and/or satire. In SUPER INDIAN NO. 2, the powerful chief in his rugged buffalo headdress tenderly holds a pink ice cream cone. Scholder's painterly brushwork, sensitive use of shapes, and monumental design heighten the impact and irony of his subject matter. In a statement written to accompany the painting, Scholder described the situation:

He tried to ignore the hoard of ugly tourists as he left the others. In the old days there were few white watchers along with the professional Indian lovers. Now it had turned into a carnival. He stepped up to the red, white, and blue concession stand and ordered an ice cream cone—a double-dip strawberry.[5]

628 Harold Tovish.
UNIT OF MEASURE (SELF PORTRAIT). 1977.
Bronze. Height 12″.
Private Collection. Photograph courtesy of the artist.

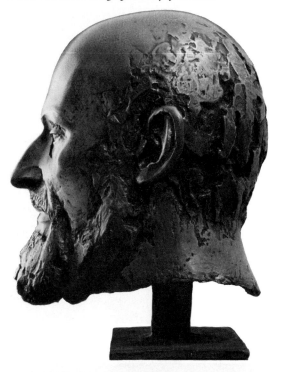

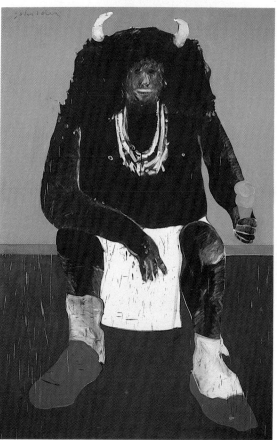

629 Fritz Scholder.
SUPER INDIAN No. 2. 1971.
Oil on canvas. 90″ × 60″.
Photograph courtesy of Aberbach Fine Art, New York.

Ansel Adams, one of America's best-known photographers, used the power of his reputation as an artist to increase public awareness and appreciation for the beauty of the natural environment and the need for its preservation. MOON AND HALF DOME is one image from a lifetime of photographs that have inspired others to cherish the Earth.

Anselm Kiefer (page 457) and Jennifer Bartlett (pages 123 and 457) probe the significance of landscape in ways quite different from Adams and from each other. Kiefer embraces current and ancient chaos and despair and gives them lasting meaning. Bartlett delights in the lyric beauty of interacting natural and human constructs which inspire her recreative powers of perception.

Through their art, artists contribute to the quality of life by awakening the creative impulse in others, by heightening perceptions, and by guiding the process of form-making. Appreciation for the artistic dimension within each individual is as important as the recognition of the roles of art and artists in society at large. If, in the process of strengthening our understanding and appreciation for the art produced by recognized masters, we neglect the art within ourselves, we will be worse off than when we started. To prevent such a dead end it is necessary to give equal care and attention to the development of the art within oneself.

An art-full life may or may not involve the making of "art." One may simply develop awareness and powers of seeing to a degree that everything takes on an aesthetic dimension. A person with heightened perceptive abilities will tend to share observations and insights with others, and will also be open to insights shared by others. Such openness and responsiveness enables us to relate constructively not only to art, but to the whole of the natural and manufactured world.

We can develop our aesthetic awareness and creativity to such an extent that we erase the line between the art of everyday life and the art of museums. When we surround ourselves with the elements of a lifestyle we have consciously chosen as constructive and enjoyable, the best in us is reaffirmed.

Art offers us a way to go beyond mere physical existence. The ideas, values, and approaches that constitute the basis of the visual arts can continue to enrich our lives and surroundings. Art encourages and puts to good use our expanding awareness. We, the creatures with the most advanced consciousness, have been described as nature becoming aware of itself. We form art. Art forms us.

633   Ansel Adams.
MOON AND HALF DOME, YOSEMITE NATIONAL PARK, CALIFORNIA. c. 1960.
Courtesy the Ansel Adams Publishing Rights Trust.

Timeline scale (left to right): 30,000 20,000 10,000 5000 3000 2000 1000 500 250 BC 0 AD 200 400 600 800

AMERICAS

MAYAN
Temple 1   *Man & Woman*

RUSSIA

Female Figure

NORTHERN EUROPE

SCYTHIANS
ANIMAL STYLE

VIKING
Purse Cover   *Dragon's Head*

Head of Neighing Horse

Le Pont du Gard

Book of Kells

SOUTHERN EUROPE

Lascaux Cave Paintings

CHRISTIAN ERA BEGINS

POMPEII BURIED
•

MEDITERRANEAN

CLASSICAL
Parthenon Warrior

ROMAN EMPIRE
Pantheon   Division of Empire   Fall of Western Empire

Head of Constantine

ARCHAIC
Kore Kouros

HELLENISTIC
Laocoon

BYZANTIUM

AFRICA

OLD KINGDOM
Mycerinus Pyramids

NEW KINGDOM
Qennefer Tomb Paintings

Mummy Portrait

IFE

MIDDLE EAST

NEOLITHIC REVOLUTION BEGINS

SUMERIAN CITIES
Bull-headed Harp Ziggurats "GILGAMESH EPIC"

BRONZE AGE BEGINS •

AKKADIANS
Head of Ruler

Luristan bronzes

BIRTH OF CHRIST

BIRTH OF MOHAMMED 570

INDIA

INDUS VALLEY CIVILIZATION
Harappa Torso

BIRTH OF BUDDHA 563

• INDIA VISITED BY ALEXANDER

Great Stupa

Standing Buddha

CHINA

SHANG CHINA
Burial Urn   *Ritual Vessel*

Great Wall

BUDDHISM SPREAD TO CHINA
Flying Horse
• PAPER INVENTED

CHAN (LATER ZEN) BUDDHISM

• PRINTING DEVELOPED

JAPAN

BUDDHISM SPREAD TO JAPAN

Ise Shrine

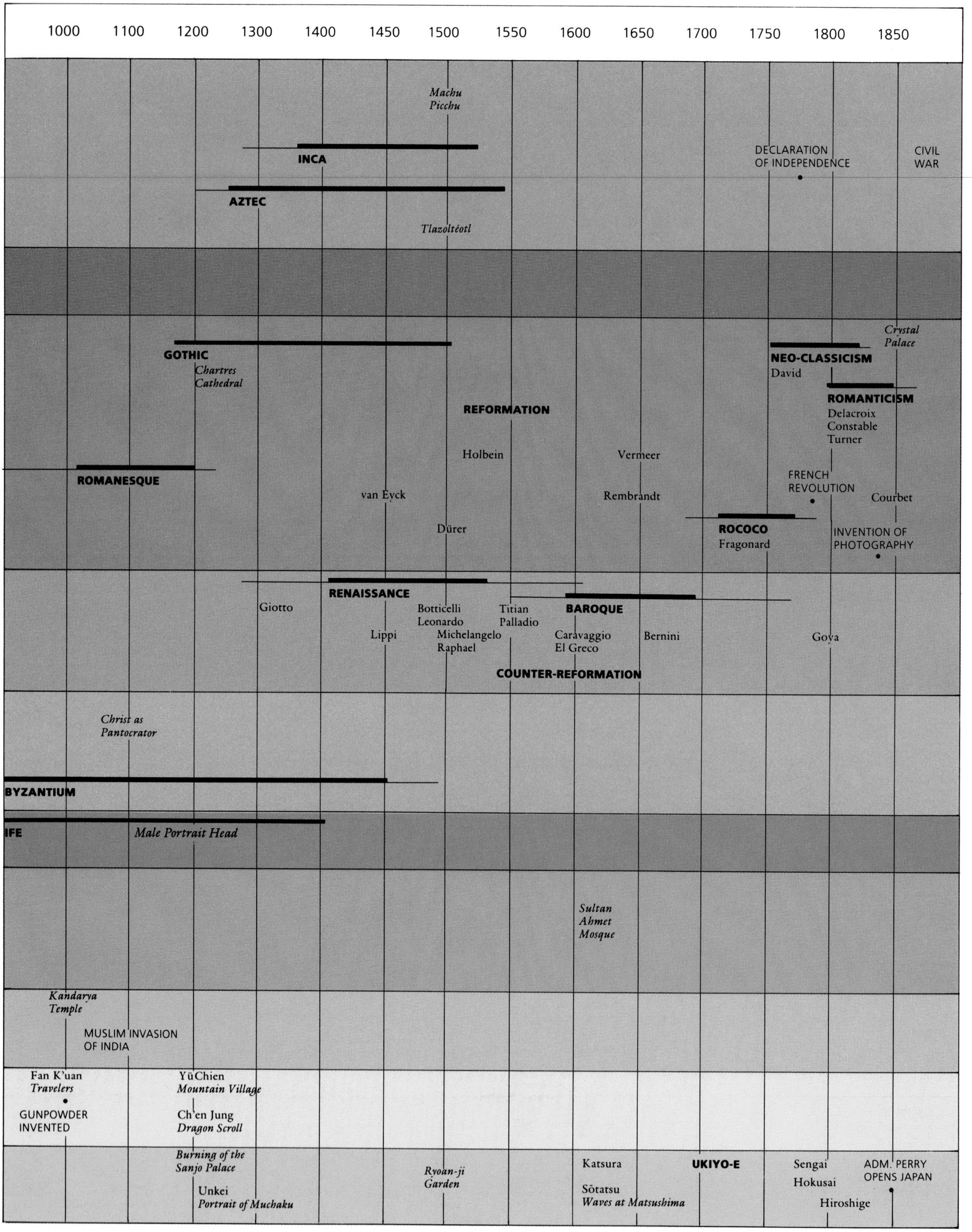

1000	1100	1200	1300	1400	1450	1500	1550	1600	1650	1700	1750	1800	1850

*Machu
Picchu*

INCA

DECLARATION
OF INDEPENDENCE

CIVIL
WAR

AZTEC

Tlazoltéotl

*Crystal
Palace*

GOTHIC

*Chartres
Cathedral*

NEO-CLASSICISM
David

ROMANTICISM
Delacroix
Constable
Turner

REFORMATION

Holbein

Vermeer

FRENCH
REVOLUTION

ROMANESQUE

van Eyck

Rembrandt

Courbet

Dürer

ROCOCO
Fragonard

INVENTION OF
PHOTOGRAPHY

RENAISSANCE

Giotto

Botticelli
Leonardo

Titian
Palladio

BAROQUE

Lippi

Michelangelo
Raphael

Caravaggio
El Greco

Bernini

Goya

COUNTER-REFORMATION

*Christ as
Pantocrator*

BYZANTIUM

IFE

Male Portrait Head

*Sultan
Ahmet
Mosque*

*Kandarya
Temple*

MUSLIM INVASION
OF INDIA

Fan K'uan
Travelers

YüChien
Mountain Village

GUNPOWDER
INVENTED

Ch'en Jung
Dragon Scroll

*Burning of the
Sanjo Palace*

*Ryoan-ji
Garden*

Katsura

UKIYO-E

Sengai

ADM. PERRY
OPENS JAPAN

Unkei
Portrait of Muchaku

Sōtatsu
Waves at Matsushima

Hokusai

Hiroshige

1870	1880	1890	1900	1910	1920	1930	1940	1950	1960	1970	1980	1990	2000

AMERICAS

• FIRST MOON LANDING

ABSTRACT EXPRESSIONISM
Pollock
Kline
de Kooning
Hofmann
Frankenthaler

CONCEPTUAL

WORLD WAR I

WORLD WAR II

POP
Wesselmann
Warhol

PHOTOREALISM
Estes
Eddy

WRIGHT BROTHERS' FIRST FLIGHT

REGIONALISM
Wood

MINIMAL
T. Smith
Held

NEO-EXPRESSIONISM

RUSSIA

CONSTRUCTIVISM
Tatlin
Gabo

NORTHERN EUROPE

Manet

IMPRESSIONISM
Monet
Renoir
Degas
Rodin

Rousseau
Munch

CUBISM
Braque
Picasso

INTERNATIONAL STYLE

BAUHAUS

DE STIJL
Mondrian
Rietveld

POST-IMPRESSIONIST PERIOD
Seurat
Cézanne
Gauguin
van Gogh
Toulouse-Lautrec

FAUVISM
Matisse

Brancusi

DADA
Duchamp
Höch

EINSTEIN'S THEORY OF RELATIVITY
•

GERMAN EXPRESSIONISM
Kirchner
Nolde
Kollwitz

SURREALISM
Miró   Magritte
Dali

SOUTHERN EUROPE

FUTURISM
Balla
Boccioni

MEDITERRANEAN

AFRICA

MIDDLE EAST

NOTE: In presenting the Artforms Time Line, it has been necessary to use several different scales to indicate both long and short spans of years on a few pages. If a ten-year scale were used to cover the entire 32,000-year period presented, the time line would be more than a hundred feet long.

INDIA

CHINA

JAPAN

on design, leadership in art education, and its philosophy of applying design principles to machine technology.

binder The material used in paint that causes *pigment* particles to adhere to one another and to the *support*; for example, linseed oil or acrylic polymer.

buttress A *support*, usually exterior, for a wall, *arch*, or *vault* that opposes the lateral forces of these structures. A flying buttress consists of a strut or segment of an arch carrying the thrust of a vault to a vertical pier positioned away from the main portion of the building. An important element in *Gothic* cathedrals.

Byzantine art Styles of painting, design, and architecture developed from the fifth century A.D. in the Byzantine Empire of ancient eastern Europe. Characterized in architecture by round *arches*, large *domes*, and extensive use of *mosaic*; characterized in painting by formal design, frontal and stylized figures, and rich use of color, especially gold, in generally religious subject matter.

calligraphy The art of beautiful writing. Broadly, a flowing use of line, often varying from thick to thin.

camera A mechanical device for taking photographs. It generally consists of a light-proof enclosure with an *aperture*, which allows a controlled light image to pass through a shuttered *lens* and be focused on a photosensitive material.

camera obscura A dark room (or box) with a small hole in one side through which an inverted image of the view outside is projected onto the opposite wall, screen, or mirror.

cantilever A beam or slab projecting a substantial distance beyond its supporting post or wall; a projection supported only at one end.

capital In architecture, the top part, cap stone, or head of a column or pillar.

caricature A distorted representation in which the subject's distinctive features are exaggerated.

cartoon 1. A humorous or satirical drawing. 2. A drawing completed as a full-scale working drawing, usually for a *fresco* painting, *mural*, or tapestry.

carving A *subtractive* process in which a sculpture is formed by removing material from a block or mass of wood, stone, or other material, using sharpened tools.

casein A white, tasteless, odorless milk protein used in making paint as well as plastics, adhesives, and foods.

casting A process that involves pouring liquid material such as molten metal, clay, wax, or plaster into a mold. When the liquid hardens, the mold is removed, leaving a form in the shape of the mold.

ceramic Made of clay hardened into a relatively permanent material by firing (baking).

chiaroscuro Italian word meaning "light-dark." The gradations of light and dark *values* in *two-dimensional* imagery; especially the illusion of rounded, three-dimensional form created through gradations of light and shade rather than line. Highly developed by *Renaissance* painters.

chroma See *intensity*.

cinematography The art and technique of making motion pictures, especially the work done by motion picture camera operators.

classical 1. The art of ancient Greece and Rome. In particular, the style of Greek art that flourished during the fifth century B.C. 2. Any art based on a clear, rational, and regular structure, emphasizing horizontal and vertical directions, and organizing its parts with special emphasis on balance and proportion. The term classic is also used to indicate recognized excellence.

closed form A self-contained or explicitly limited form; having a resolved balance of tensions, a sense of calm completeness implying a totality within itself.

cluster houses Housing units placed close together in order to maximize usable exterior space in the surrounding area, within the concept of single-family dwellings.

coffer In architecture, a decorative sunken panel on the underside of a ceiling.

collage From the French *papiers colles* or pasted papers. A work made by gluing various materials, such as paper scraps, photographs, and cloth, on a flat surface.

colonnade A row of columns usually spanned or connected by beams.

color field painting A movement that grew out of *abstract expressionism*, in which large stained or painted areas or "fields" of color evoke aesthetic and emotional responses.

color wheel A circular arrangement of contiguous spectral *hues* used in some color systems. Also called a color circle.

complementary colors Two *hues* directly opposite one another on a *color wheel* which, when mixed together in proper proportions, produce a neutral gray. The true complement of a color can be seen in its *afterimage*.

composition The combining of parts or elements to form a whole; the structure, organization, or total form of a work of art. See also *design*.

conceptual art An art form in which the originating idea and the process by which it is presented take precedence over a tangible product. Conceptual works are sometimes produced in visible form, but often exist only as descriptions of mental concepts or ideas. This trend developed in the late 1960s, partially as a way to avoid the commercialization of art.

content Meaning or message contained and communicated by a work of art, including its emotional, intellectual, symbolic, thematic, and narrative connotations.

contour The edge or apparent line that separates one area or mass from another; a line following a surface drawn to suggest volume.

contrapposto Italian for "counterpoise." The counterpositioning of parts of the human figure about a central vertical axis, as when the weight is placed naturally on one foot causing the hip and shoulder lines to counterbalance each other—often in a graceful S-curve.

cool colors Colors whose relative visual temperature makes them seem cool. Cool colors include green, blue-green, blue, blue-violet, and violet. See also *warm colors*.

crosshatching See *hatching*.

cubism The most influential style of the twentieth century, developed in Paris by Picasso and Braque, beginning in 1907. The early mature phase of the style, called analytical cubism, lasted from 1909 through 1911. Based on the simultaneous presentation of multiple views, disintegration, and geometric reconstruction of the subject in flattened, ambiguous pictorial space; figure and ground merge into one interwoven surface of shifting planes. Color was limited to *neutrals*. By 1912, the more decorative phase called synthetic or collage cubism began to appear; it was characterized by fewer, more solid forms, conceptual rather than observed subject matter, and richer color and texture.

curtain wall A non-load-bearing wall.

curvilinear Formed or characterized by curving lines or edges.

dada A movement in art and literature founded in Switzerland in the early twentieth century that ridiculed contemporary culture and conventional art. The dadaists shared an anti-militaristic and anti-aesthetic attitude, generated in part by the horrors of World War I and in part by a rejection of accepted canons of morals and taste. The anarchic spirit of dada can be seen in the works of Duchamp, Man Ray, Höch, Miro, and Picasso. Many dadaists later explored *surrealism*.

design Both the process and the result of structuring the elements of visual form; composition.

de Stijl A Dutch purist art movement begun during World War I by Mondrian and others. It involved painters, sculptors, designers, and architects whose works and ideas were expressed in *De Stijl* magazine. De Stijl, Dutch for "the style," was aimed at creating a universal language of *form* that would be independent of individual emotion. Visual form was pared down to primary colors plus black and white, and rectangular shapes. The movement was influential primarily in architecture.

divisionism See *pointillism*.

dome A generally hemispherical roof or vault. Theoretically, an arch rotated 360 degrees on its vertical axis.

drypoint An *intaglio* printmaking process in which lines are scratched directly into a metal plate with a steel needle. Also, the resulting *print*.

earth art; earthworks Sculptural forms of earth, rocks, or sometimes plants, often on a vast scale and in remote locations. Some are deliberately impermanent.

earthenware Coarse, porous, often reddish ceramic ware, fired in low temperature ranges.

eclecticism The practice of selecting or borrowing from earlier styles and combining the borrowed elements, rather than originating new forms.

edition In printmaking, the total number of *prints* made and approved by the artist, usually numbered consecutively. Also, a limited number of multiple originals of a single design in any medium.

elevation In architecture, a scale drawing of any vertical side of a given structure.

embossing A technique for producing raised designs on paper, metal, or leather. In printmaking, embossed areas are created by pressing a raised, uninked design into the paper with a printing press.

encaustic A painting medium in which *pigment* is suspended in a *binder* of hot wax.

engraving An *intaglio* printmaking process in which grooves are cut into a metal or wood surface with a sharp cutting tool called a burin or graver. Also, the resulting *print*.

entasis In *classical* architecture, the slight swelling or bulge in the center of a column which corrects the illusion of concave tapering produced by parallel straight lines.

etching An *intaglio* printmaking process in which a metal plate is first coated with acid-resistant wax, then scratched to expose the metal to the bite of nitric acid where lines are desired. Also, the resulting *print*.

expressionism The broad term that describes emotional art, most often boldly executed and making free use of distortion and symbolic or invented color. More specifically, expressionism refers to individual and group styles originating in Europe in the late nineteenth and early twentieth centuries. See also *abstract expressionism*.

eye level The height of the viewer's eyes above the ground plane.

facade In architecture, a term used to refer to the front exterior of a building. Also, the other exterior sides when they are emphasized architecturally.

fauvism A style of painting introduced in Paris in the early twentieth century, characterized by areas of brilliant, contrasting color and simplified shapes. The name *les fauves* is French for "the wild beasts."

figure Separate shape(s) distinguishable from a background or *ground*.

flamboyant Any design dominated by flamelike, curvilinear rhythms. In architecture, having complex, flamelike forms characteristic of fifteenth- and sixteenth-century *Gothic* style.

flying buttress See *buttress*.

foreshortening The representation of *forms* on a *two-dimensional* surface by shortening the length in such a way that the long *axis* appears to project toward or recede away from the viewer.

form In the broadest sense, the total physical characteristics of an object, event, or situation.

formalist Having emphasis on highly structured visual relationships rather than subject matter or nonvisual content.

format The shape or proportions of a picture plane.

fresco A painting technique in which *pigments* suspended in water are applied to a damp lime-plaster surface. The pigments dry to become part of the plaster wall or surface.

frontal An adjective describing an object that faces the viewer directly, rather than being set at an angle or *foreshortened*.

futurism A group movement that originated in Italy in 1909. One of several movements to grow out of *cubism*. Futurists added implied motion to the shifting planes and multiple observation points of the cubists; they celebrated natural as well as mechanical motion and speed. Their glorification of danger, war, and the machine age was in keeping with the martial spirit developing in Italy at the time.

geodesic A geometric form basic to structures using short sections of lightweight material joined into interlocking polygons. Also a structural system developed by R. Buckminster Fuller to create *domes* using the above principle.

gesso A mixture of glue and either chalk or plaster of Paris applied as a *ground* or coating to surfaces in order to give them the correct properties to receive paint. Gesso can also be built up or molded into *relief* designs, or carved.

glaze In *ceramics*, a vitreous or glassy coating applied to seal and decorate surfaces. Glaze may be colored, transparent, or opaque. In oil painting, a thin transparent or translucent layer brushed over another layer of paint, allowing the first layer to show through but altering its color slightly.

Gothic Primarily an architectural style that prevailed in western Europe from the twelfth through the fifteenth centuries, characterized by pointed *arches*, ribbed *vaults*, and flying *buttresses*, which enabled buildings to reach great heights.

gouache An opaque, water-soluble paint. *Watercolor* to which opaque white has been added.

green belt A strip or belt of planned or protected open green space, consisting of recreational parks, farm land, or uncultivated land, often used to define and limit the boundaries of a community and prevent urban sprawl.

ground The background in two-dimensional works—the area around and between *figure(s)*. Also, the surface onto which paint is applied.

happening An event conceived by artists and performed by artists and others, usually unrehearsed and without a specific script or stage.

hard-edge A term first used in the 1950s to distinguish styles of paintings in which shapes are precisely defined by sharp edges, in contrast to the usually blurred or soft edges in *abstract expressionist* paintings.

hatching A technique used in drawing and linear forms of printmaking in which lines are placed in parallel series to darken the value of an area. Cross-hatching is drawing one set of hatchings over another in a different direction so the lines cross.

Hellenistic Style of the later phase of ancient Greek art (300–100 B.C.) characterized by emotion, drama, and interaction of sculptural forms with the surrounding space.

hierarchic proportion Use of unnatural *proportions* to show the relative importance of figures.

high key Exclusive use of pale or light *values* within a given area or surface.

horizon line In linear *perspective*, the implied or actual line or edge placed on a *two-dimensional* surface to represent the point in nature where the sky meets the horizontal land or water plane. The horizon line matches the *eye level* on a two-dimensional surface. Lines or edges parallel to the ground plane and moving away from the viewer appear to converge at *vanishing points* on the horizon line.

hue That property of a color identifying a specific, named wavelength of light such as green, red, violet, and so on.

humanism A cultural and intellectual movement during the *Renaissance*, following the rediscovery of the art and literature of ancient Greece and Rome. A philosophy or attitude concerned with the interests, achievements, and capabilities of human beings rather than with the abstract concepts and problems of theology or science.

icon An image or symbolic representation (often with sacred significance).

iconography The symbolic meaning of subjects and signs used to convey ideas important to particular cultures or religions, and the conventions governing the use of such forms.

impasto In painting, thick paint applied to a surface in a heavy manner, having the appearance and consistency of buttery paste.

impressionism A style of painting that originated in France about 1870. (The first impressionist exhibit was held in 1874.) Paintings of casual subjects were executed outdoors using divided brush strokes to capture the light and mood of a particular moment and the transitory effects of natural light and color.

intaglio Any printmaking technique in which lines and areas to be inked and transferred to paper are recessed below the surface of the printing plate. *Etching, engraving, drypoint,* and *aquatint* are all intaglio processes. See also *print*.

intensity The relative purity or saturation of a *hue* on a scale from bright to dull.

intermediate color A *hue* between a primary and a secondary on the color wheel, such as yellow-green, a mixture of yellow and green.

international style An architectural style that emerged in several European countries between 1910 and 1920. Related to purism and *de Stijl* in painting, it joined structure and exterior design into a noneclectic form based on rectangular geometry and growing out of the basic function and structure of the building.

kiln An oven in which pottery or *ceramic* ware is fired (baked).

kinetic art Art that incorporates actual movement as part of the design.

kore Greek for "maiden." An archaic Greek statue of a standing clothed young woman.

kouros Greek for "youth." An archaic Greek statue of a standing nude young male.

lens The part of a *camera* that concentrates light and focuses the image.

linear perspective See *perspective*.

lithography A planographic printmaking technique based on the antipathy of oil and water. The image is drawn with a grease crayon or painted with *tusche* on a stone or grained aluminum plate. The surface is then chemically treated and dampened so that it will accept ink only where the crayon or tusche has been used.

local color The actual color as distinguished from the apparent color of objects and surfaces; true color, without shadows or reflections.

logo Short for "logotype." Sign, name, or trademark of an institution, firm or publication, consisting of letter forms, borne on one printing plate or piece of type.

loom A device for producing cloth by interweaving fibers at right angles.

low key Consistent use of dark *values* within a given area or surface.

lumia The use of actual light as an art *medium*.

mannerism A style that developed in the sixteenth century as a reaction to the classical rationality and balanced harmony of the High *Renaissance*; characterized by dramatic use of space and light, exaggerated color, elongation of figures, and distortions of *perspective*, *scale*, and *proportion*.

mass *Three-dimensional* form having physical bulk. Also, the illusion of such a form on a *two-dimensional* surface.

mat Border of cardboard or similar material placed around a picture as a neutral area between the frame and the picture.

matte A dull finish or surface, especially in painting, photography, and *ceramics*.

medium (pl. media or mediums) 1. A particular material along with its accompanying technique; a specific type of artistic technique or means of expression determined by the use of particular materials.   2. In paint, the fluid in which *pigment* is suspended allowing it to spread and adhere to the surface.

megastructure A very large building complex combining many functions in a single structure.

minimalism A *nonrepresentational* style of sculpture and painting, usually severely restricted in the use of visual elements and often consisting of simple geometric shapes or structures. The style came to prominence in the 1960s.

mixed media Works of art made with more than one *medium*.

mobile A type of sculpture in which parts move, often activated by air currents. See also *kinetic art*.

modeling 1. Working pliable material such as clay or wax into *three-dimensional* forms.   2. In drawing or painting, the effect of light falling on a three-dimensional object so that the illusion of its *mass* is revealed and defined by *value* gradations.

modernism Theory and practice in late nineteenth- and twentieth-century art, which holds that each new generation must build on past styles in new ways or break with the past in order to make the next major historical contribution. Characterized by idealism; seen as "high art," as differentiated from popular art. In painting, most clearly seen in the work of the *postimpressionists*, beginning in 1885; in architecture, most evident in the work of *Bauhaus* and *international style* architects, beginning about 1920.

module A standard unit of measure in architecture. The part of a structure used as a standard by which the rest is proportioned.

monochromatic A color scheme limited to variations of one *hue*; a hue with its *tints* and/or *shades*.

montage 1. A composition made up of pictures or parts of pictures previously drawn, painted, or photographed. 2. In motion pictures, the combining of separate bits of film to portray the character of a single event through multiple views.

mosaic An art *medium* in which small pieces of colored glass, stone, or ceramic tile called *tessera* are embedded in a background material such as plaster or mortar. Also, works made using this technique.

mural A large wall painting, often executed in *fresco*.

naturalism A style of *representational art* that presents a close approximation of optical appearances.

nave The tall central space of a church or cathedral, usually flanked by side aisles.

negative shape A background or *ground* shape seen in relation to foreground or *figure* shape(s).

neoclassicism New classicism. A revival of classical Greek and Roman forms in art, music, and literature, particularly during the eighteenth and nineteenth centuries in Europe and America. It was part of a reaction against the excesses of *baroque* and *rococo*.

neutrals Not associated with any single *hue*. Black, white, grays, and dull gray-browns. A neutral can be made by mixing complementary hues.

nonobjective See *nonrepresentational art*.

nonrepresentational Art without reference to anything outside itself–without representation. Also called "nonobjective"–without objects.

offset printing Planographic printing by indirect image-transfer from photomechanical plates. The plate transfers ink to a rubber-covered cylinder, which "offsets" the ink to the paper. Also called photo-offset and offset lithography.

oil paint Paint in which the *pigment* is held together with a *binder* of oil, usually linseed oil.

opaque Impenetrable by light; not transparent or translucent.

op art Short for "optical art." A style of *two-dimensional* art that uses lines, or shapes of contrasting color to generate optical sensations not actually present in the initial image.

open form A form whose contour is irregular or broken, having a sense of growth, change, or unresolved tension; form in a state of becoming.

optical color mixture Apparent rather than actual color mixture, produced by interspersing brush strokes or dots of the *hues* to be "mixed" instead of physically mixing them. The implied mixing occurs in the eye of the viewer and produces a lively color sensation.

painterly Painting characterized by openness of form in which shapes are defined by loose brushwork in light and dark color areas rather than by outline or contour.

performance art Dramatic presentation by visual artists (as distinguished from theater artists such as actors and dancers) in front of an audience.

perspective A system for creating an illusion of depth or *three-dimensional* space on a *two-dimensional* surface. Usually used to refer to linear perspective, which is based on the fact that parallel lines or edges appear to converge and objects appear smaller as the distance between them and the viewer increases. Atmospheric perspective (aerial perspective) creates the illusion of distance by reducing color saturation, value contrast, and detail in order to imply the hazy effect of atmosphere on distant objects.

perspective rendering A view of an architectural structure drawn in linear *perspective*, usually from a three-quarter view or similar vantage point that shows two sides of the proposed building in detail.

photorealism A style of painting that became prominent in the 1970s, based on the cool objectivity of photographs as records of subjects.

pictorial space Illusionary space in a painting or other *two-dimensional* art which appears to recede backward into depth from the *picture plane*.

picture plane The *two-dimensional* picture surface.

pigment Any coloring agent, made from natural or synthetic substances, used in paints or drawing materials.

plan In architecture, a scale drawing in diagrammatic form showing the basic layout of the interior and exterior spaces of a structure, as if seen in a cutaway view from above.

plastic 1. Pliable; capable of being shaped. Pertaining to the process of shaping or modeling (i.e., the plastic arts). 2. Synthetic polymer substances, such as acrylic.

pointillism A system of painting using tiny dots or "points" of color; developed by French artist Georges Seurat in the 1880s. Seurat systematized the divided brushwork and *optical color mixture* of the *impressionists* and called his technique "divisionism."

polychromatic Having many colors; random or intuitive use of color combinations as opposed to color selection based on a specific color scheme.

pop art A style of painting and sculpture that developed in the late 1950s and early 1960s, primarily in the United States; based on the visual clichés, subject matter, and impersonal style of popular mass-media imagery.

positive shape A *figure* or foreground shape, as opposed to a *negative* ground or background shape.

post-and-beam system (post and lintel) In architecture, a structural system that uses two or more uprights or posts to support a horizontal beam or lintel which spans the space between them.

postimpressionism A general term applied to various personal styles of painting by French artists, or artists living in France, that developed from about 1885 to 1900 in reaction to the formlessness and indifference to subject matter of *impressionism*. Postimpressionist painters were concerned with the significance of form, symbols, expressiveness, and psychological intensity. They can be broadly separated into two groups—*expressionists*, such as Gauguin and Van Gogh, and *formalists*, such as Cézanne and Seurat.

postmodern An attitude or trend of the 1970s and 1980s in which artists and architects accept all that *modernism* rejects. In architecture, the movement away from or beyond what had become cold, boring adaptations of the *international style*, in favor of an imaginative, eclectic approach. In the other visual arts, postmodern is characterized by an acceptance of all periods and styles, including modernism, and a willingness to combine elements of all styles and periods. Although modernism makes distinctions between high art and popular taste, postmodernism makes no such value judgments.

prehistoric art Art created before written history. Often the only record of early cultures.

primary colors Those *hues* that cannot be produced by mixing other hues. *Pigment* primaries are red, yellow, and blue; light primaries are red, green, and blue. Theoretically, primaries can be mixed together to form all the other hues in the spectrum.

prime In painting, a primary layer of paint or sizing applied to a surface that is to be painted.

print (artist's print) A multiple original impression made from a plate, stone, wood block, or screen by an artist or made under the artist's supervision. Prints are usually made in *editions*, with each print numbered and signed by the artist.

proportion The size relationship of parts to a whole and to one another.

realism A type of *representational art* in which the artist depicts as closely as possible what the eye sees. Particularly the mid-nineteenth-century style of Courbet, based on the idea that ordinary people and everyday activities are worthy subjects for art.

registration In color printmaking or machine printing, the process of aligning the impressions of blocks or plates on the same sheet of paper.

reinforced concrete (ferroconcrete) Concrete with steel mesh or bars embedded in it to increase its tensile strength.

relief printing A printing technique in which the parts of the printing surface that carry ink are left raised, while the remaining areas are cut away. Woodcuts and linoleum prints (linocuts) are relief prints.

relief sculpture Sculpture in which *three-dimensional* forms project from the flat background of which they are a part. The degree of projection can vary and is described by the terms high relief or haut relief and low relief or bas relief.

Renaissance Period in Europe from the fourteenth through the early sixteenth centuries that was characterized by a renewed interest in human-centered *classical* art, literature, and learning. See also *humanism*.

representational art Art in which it is the artist's intention to present again or represent a particular subject; especially pertaining to realistic portrayal of subject matter.

reproduction A mechanically produced copy of an original work of art; not to be confused with an original *print* or art print.

rhythm The regular or ordered repetition of elements or units within a design.

ribbed vault See *vault*.

rococo From the French *rocaille* meaning "rock work." This late *baroque* (c. 1715–1775) style used in interior decoration and painting was characteristically playful, pretty, romantic, and visually loose or soft; it used small *scale* and ornate decoration, and was based on the use of pastel colors and asymmetrical arrangement of curves. Rococo was popular in France and southern Germany.

Romanesque A style of European architecture prevalent from the ninth to the twelfth centuries, influenced by

Roman architecture. Seen most clearly in the use of round *arches* and barrel *vaults*.

romanticism 1. A literary and artistic movement of late eighteenth- and nineteenth-century Europe, aimed at asserting the validity of subjective experience as a countermovement to the often cold formulas of *neoclassicism*; characterized by intense emotional excitement, powerful forces in nature, exotic lifestyles, danger, suffering, and nostalgia. 2. Art of any period based on spontaneity, intuition, and emotion rather than carefully organized rational approaches to form.

saturation See *intensity*.

scale The size or apparent size of an object seen in relation to other objects, people, or its environment or *format*. Also used to refer to the quality or monumentality found in some objects regardless of their size. In architectural drawings, the ratio of the measurements in the drawing to the measurements in the building.

screenprinting (serigraphy) A print-making technique in which stencils are applied to fabric stretched across a frame. Paint or ink is forced with a squeegee through the unblocked portions of the screen onto paper or other surface beneath.

secondary colors Pigment secondaries are the *hues* orange, violet, and green, which may be produced in somewhat diluted form by mixing two *primaries*.

section In architecture, a scale drawing of part of a building as seen along an imaginary plane that passes through a building vertically.

serigraphy See *screenprinting*.

setback The legal distance that a building must be from property lines. Early setback requirements often increased with the height of a building, resulting in step-like recessions in the rise of tall buildings.

shade A *hue* with black added.

shape A *two-dimensional* or implied two-dimensional area defined by line or changes in value and/or color.

shutter In photography, the part of the *camera* that controls the length of time the light is allowed to strike the photosensitive film.

silk screen See *screenprinting*.

silverpoint A drawing technique seldom used today, in which a silver-tipped pencil-like tool is used on paper covered with a white or lightly tinted *matte* coating, producing silver-gray indelible lines that darken as the silver tarnishes.

simultaneous contrast An optical effect caused by the tendency of contrasting forms and colors to emphasize their difference when placed together.

site-specific art Any work made for a certain place, which cannot be separated or exhibited apart from its intended environment.

size Any of several substances made from glue, wax, or clay, used as a filler for porous material such as paper, canvas, or other cloth, or wall surfaces. Used to protect the surface from the deteriorating effects of paint, particularly oil paint.

still life A painting or other *two-dimensional* work of art representing inanimate objects such as bottles, fruit, and flowers. Also, the arrangement of these objects from which a drawing, painting, or other work is made.

stoneware Relatively hard, vitreous *ceramic* ware, often gray or tan, fired in medium temperature ranges.

stupa The earliest form of Buddhist architecture, probably derived from Indian funeral mounds.

style A characteristic handling of *media*, techniques, and elements of form, that give a work its identity as the product of a particular person, group, art movement, period, or culture.

stylized Simplified or exaggerated visual *form* which emphasizes particular or contrived design qualities.

subtractive color mixture Mixture of colored *pigments* in the form of paints, inks, pastels, and so on. Called subtractive because reflected light is reduced as pigment colors are combined. See *additive color mixture*.

subtractive sculpture Sculpture made by removing material from a larger block or form.

support The physical material that provides the base for and sustains a *two-dimensional* work of art. Paper is the usual support for drawings and prints; canvas or panels are supports in painting.

suprematism An offshoot of *cubism*; the style was invented by Malevich (c. 1913) as a pure, geometric, non-representational art.

surrealism A style of painting that developed in the 1920s; derived from *dada* and *cubism*. Based upon dreams, the irrational, and the fantastic, surrealism took two directions: *representational* and *abstract*. Magritte's work, with his use of impossible combinations of objects painted in a realistic manner, typifies representational surrealism. Miró's work, with his use of abstract and fantastic shapes and creatures, is typical of abstract surrealism.

symbol A form or image implying or representing something beyond its obvious and immediate meaning.

symmetry A design (or composition) with identical or nearly identical form on opposite sides of a dividing line or central *axis*; formal *balance*.

synthetic cubism See *cubism*.

tempera A water-based paint that uses egg, egg yolk, glue, or *casein* as a *binder*. Many commercially made paints identified as tempera are actually *gouache*.

terra cotta Italian for "baked earth." A porous, reddish ceramic ware fired in low temperature ranges; *earthenware*.

tessera Bit of colored glass, ceramic tile, or stone used in a *mosaic*.

texture The tactile quality of a surface or the representation or invention of the appearance of such a surface quality.

three-dimensional Having height, width, and depth.

throwing The process of forming clay objects on a potter's wheel.

tint A *hue* with white added.

townhouse One of a row of houses connected by common side walls.

trompe l'oeil French for "fool the eye." A *two-dimensional* representation that is so naturalistic that it looks actual or real (*three-dimensional*).

truss In architecture, a structural framework of wood or metal based on a triangular system, used to span, reinforce, or support walls, ceilings, piers, or beams.

tunnel vault (barrel vault) See *vault*.

tusche In *lithography*, a waxy substance used to draw or paint images on a lithographic stone or plate.

two-dimensional Having the dimensions of height and width only.

typography The art and technique of composing printed materials from type.

unity The appearance of similarity, consistency, or oneness. Interrelational factors that cause various elements to appear as part of a single complete form.

value The lightness or darkness of tones or colors. White is the lightest value; black is the darkest. The value halfway between these extremes is called middle gray.

vanishing point In linear *perspective*, the point on the *horizon line* at which lines or edges that are parallel appear to converge.

vantage point The position from which the viewer looks at an object or visual field; also called "observation point" or "viewpoint."

vault A masonry roof or ceiling constructed on the principle of the *arch*. A tunnel or barrel vault is a semicircular arch extended in depth; a continuous series of arches, one behind the other. A groin vault is formed when two barrel vaults intersect. A ribbed vault is a vault reinforced by masonry ribs.

vehicle Liquid emulsion used as a carrier or spreading agent in paints.

video Television. The term "video" emphasizes the visual rather than the audio aspects of the television *medium*. The term is also used to distinguish television used as an art medium from general broadcast television.

visualize To form a mental image or vision; to imagine.

volume 1. Space enclosed by and defined by *mass*. 2. Three-dimensional bulk or mass present in or suggested by a form.

warm colors Colors whose relative visual temperature makes them seem warm. Warm colors or *hues* include red-violet, red, red-orange, orange, yellow-orange, and yellow. See also *cool colors*.

warp In weaving, the threads that run lengthwise in a fabric, crossed at right angles by the *weft*. Also, the process of arranging yarn or thread on a *loom* so as to form a warp.

wash A thin, transparent layer of paint or ink.

watercolor Paint that uses water-soluble gum as the *binder* and water as the *vehicle*. Characterized by transparency. Also, the resulting painting.

weft In weaving, the horizontal threads interlaced through the *warp*. Also called woof.

woodcut A type of *relief print* made from an image that is left raised on a block of wood.

PRONUNCIATION GUIDE

Magdalena Abakanowicz (mahg-dah-*lay*-nuh ah-bah-kah-*no*-vich)

Yaacov Agam (*yah*-kuv ah-*gahm*)

Fra Angelico (frah ahn-*jay*-lee-coe)

Sofanisba Anguissola (so-fah-*niss*-bah ahn-*gwees*-so-la)

Stephan Antonakos (ahn-toh-*nah*-kohs)

Richard Anuszkiewicz (ah-*nuhs*-ke-vich)

Giacomo Balla (*jah*-koh-moh *bahl*-la)

Bambara (bahm-*bar*-uh)

Louis Barbedor (loo-ee bahr-buh-dore)

Ernst Barlach (airnst *bahr*-lahk)

Benin (ben-in)

Gianlorenzo Bernini (jahn-low-*ren*-tsoh ber-*nee*-nee)

Werner Bischof (*bish*-off)

Umberto Boccioni (oom-bair-toh boh-*choh*-nee)

Pierre Bonnard (pee-*air* baw-*nar*)

Lee Bontecou (*bahn*-te-koo)

Borobodur (boh-roh-buh-*door*)

Hieronymous Bosch (heer-*ahn*-ni-mus *bosh*)

Sandro Botticelli (bought-tee-*chel*-lee)

Constantin Brancusi (*kahn*-stuhn-teen *brahn*-koo-see)

Georges Braque (zhorzh brahk)

Pieter Bruegel (*pee*-ter *broy*-guhl)

Michelangelo Buonarotti, see *Michelangelo*

Callicrates (kah-*lik*-rah-teez)

Michelangelo da Caravaggio (my-kel-*an*-jay-loe da car-ah-*vah*-jyoh)

Henri Cartier-Bresson (on-*ree* car-tee-*ay* bruh-*sohn*)

Mary Cassatt (cah-*sat*)

Paul Cézanne (say-*zahn*)

Marc Chagall (shah-*gahl*)

Jean-Baptiste Simeon Chardin (zhon-bah-*teest* say-may-*on* sharr-*dan*)

Chartres (*shahr*-truh)

Chen Rong (Ch'en Jung) (chen yung)

Maria Chino (*chee*-noh)

Giorgio de Chirico (*johr*-jyo de *key*-ree-co)

Christo (*kree*-stoh)

Chryssa (*kriss*-ah)

Constantine (*kahn*-stuhn-teen)

Gustave Courbet (*goos*-tahv koor-*bay*)

Thomas Couture (toh-*mah* koo-*tyoor*)

Louis Jacques Mandé Daguerre (loo-ee zhahk mon-*day* dah-*gair*)

Salvador Dali (sahl-vah-*dore dah*-lee)

Dao Ji (Tao Chi or Shih T'ao) (dow jee)

Honoré Daumier (awn-ohr-*ay* doh-mee-*ay*)

Jacques Louis David (*zhahk* loo-ee dah-*veed*)

John DeAndrea (dee-*ann*-dray-ah)

Edgar Degas (ed-*gahr* duh-gah)

Willem de Kooning (*vill*-em duh *koe*-ning)

Eugène Delacroix (oo-*zhen* duh-lah-*kwah*)

André Derain (on-*dray* duh-*ran*)

Richard Diebenkorn (*dee*-ben-korn)

Henry Dreyfuss (*dray*-fuhs)

Marcel Duchamp (mahr-*sell* doo-*shahm*)

Albrecht Dürer (*ahl*-brekht *duh*-ruhr)

Eugène Durieu (oo-zhen doo-ree-*yuh*)

Thomas Eakins (*ay*-kins)

Charles and Ray Eames (eems)

Sergei Eisenstein (sair-gay *eye*-zen-styn)

El Greco (el *greh*-co)

M. C. Escher (*esh*-uhr)

Fan Kuan (fahn kwahn)

Jean-Honoré Fragonard (zhon-oh-no-*ray* fra-go-*nahr*)

Helen Frankenthaler (frank-en-*thahl*-er)

Naum Gabo (nawm *gah*-boh)

Ganges (*gan*-jeez)

Paul Gauguin (go-*gan*)

Jean Léon Gérôme (zhon *lay*-on zhay-*roam*)

Lorenzo Ghiberti (low-*rent*-soh ghee-*bair*-tee)

Alberto Giacometti (ahl-*bair*-toh jah-ko-*met*-tee)

Giorgione da Castelfranco (jor-joh-nay da cah-stell-*frahn*-koh)

Giotto di Bondone (*joht*-toe dee bone-*doe*-nay)

Giza (*ghee*-zuh)

Francisco Goya (fran-*sis*-coe *go*-yah)

Walter Gropius (*val*-tuhr *grow*-pee-us)

Guan Yin (Kwan Yin) (*gwan* yeen)

Heiji Monogatari (hay-jee mo-no-gah-*tah*-ree)

Hannah Höch (*hahn*-nuh *hohk*)

Hans Hofmann (*hahns hohf*-mahn)

Hokusai (hohk-*sy*)

Hans Holbein (*hahns hohl*-byn)

Pieter de Hooch (*pee*-tuhr duh *hohk*)

Huangshan (hwanhng-shahn)

Remmert W. Huygens (*rem*-muhrt *hoy*-gens)

Ictinus (ick-*tee*-nuhs)

Inca (*eenk*-ah)

Ise (*ee*-say)

Arata Isozaki (ahr-ah-tah ee-so-*zah*-kee)

Luis Jiménez (loo-*ees* hee-*men*-nehs)

Kandarya Mahadeva (gan-dahr-reeah mah-hah-*day*-vuh)

Vasily Kandinsky (vass-*see*-lee can-*din*-skee)

Katsura (kah-*tsoo*-rah)

Kenojuak (ken-*oh*-jew-ak)

Anselm Kiefer (*ahn*-sehlm *kee*-fuhr)

Ernst Ludwig Kirchner (*airnst loot*-vik *keerkh*-ner)

Paul Klee (clay)

Gustav Klimt (*goos*-tahv *kleemt*)

Gerhardt Knodel (gair-hard no-duhl)

Misch Kohn (mish cone)

Käthe Kollwitz (kay-teh *kahl*-wits)

Konarak (*kohn*-ahr-ok) or (kohn-ehr-rek)

Krishna (*krish*-nuh)

Laocoön (lay-*ah*-koh-ahn)

Jacques Henri Lartigue (*zhahk* on-ree lahr-*teek*)

Lascaux (lass-coe)

Le Corbusier (luh core-boo-zee-ay)

Fernand Léger (fair-*non* lay-*zhay*)

Alphonse Legros (luh-*grow*)

Pierre Charles L'Enfant (pee-*air* sharl lon-*fon*)

Roy Lichtenstein (*lick*-ten-steen)

Maya Lin (*my*-uh *lin*)

Jacques Lipchitz (zhahk *lip*-sheets)

Fra Filippo Lippi (frah fill-*leep*-poh *leep*-pee)

Marshall Lomokema (loh-moh-kem-ah)

Claude Lorrain (*klohd* luh-*ran*)

Machu Picchu (*mah*-choo *peek*-choo)

René Magritte (ruh-*nay* muh-*greet*)

Kasimir Malevich (*kah*-sim-eer mahl-*yay*-vitch)

Edouard Manet (ay-*dwahr* mah-*nay*)

Andrea Mantegna (ahn-*dray*-ah mahn-*ten*-yah)

Giacomo Manzu (*jah*-koh-moh mahn-*dzoo*)

Etienne-Jules Marey (ay-tee-*en* zhyool mah-*ray*)

Marisol (mah-ree-*sohl*)

Masaccio (mah-*sach*-chyo)

Henri Matisse (on-ree mah-*tees*)

Mayan (*my*-un)

Michelangelo Buonarotti (my-kel-*an*-jay-loe bwoh-nah-*roe*-tee)

Ludwig Mies van der Rohe (*loot*-vik *mees* vahn dair *roh*-eh)

Mi Fei (mee fay)

Joan Miró (*zhoh*-ahn mee-*roh*)

Issey Miyake (*iss*-ay mee-*yah*-kay)

Paula Modersohn-Becker (*moh*-dur-zohn-*bek*-ur)

László Moholy-Nagy (*lahs*-loh *moh*-hoh-lee-*nahd*-yuh)

Piet Mondrian (*peet* mohn-dree-ahn)

Claude Monet (*klohd* muh-*nay*)

Berthe Morisot (*bairt* moh-ree-*zoh*)

mosque (mahsk)

Mummenschanz (moom-un-shahnts)

Edvard Munch (*ed*-vard *moonk*)

Mu Qi (Mu Ch'i) (moo-kee) or (moo-chee)

Eadweard Muybridge (*ed*-wurd *my*-brij)

Mycerinus (miss-uh-*ree*-nuhs)

Isamu Noguchi (is-*sah*-moo noh-*goo*-chee)

Emil Nolde (*ay*-muhl *nohl*-duh)

Notre Dame de Chartres (*noh*-truh dahm duh *shahr*-truh)

Mayumi Oda (my-*oo*-mee *oh*-duh)

Claes Oldenburg (klahs ol-den- burg)

José Clemente Orozco (ho-*say* cleh-*men*-tay oh-*rohs*-coh)

Hafiz Osman (hah-*fez* ohs-mahn)

Padmapani (*padh*-muh-*pah*-nee)

Nam June Paik (nahm joon pike)

Andrea Palladio (ahn-*dray*-uh pahl-*lah*-dyo)

Giovanni Paolo Panini (jyo-*vahn*-nee *pah-oh*-lo pah-*nee*-nee)

Joachim Patinir (*yoh*-ahk-hihm pah-tih-*neer*)

John Pfahl (fall)

Pablo Picasso (pab-lo pea-*cah*-so)

Marianna Pineda (pin-*ay*-duh)

Michelangelo Pistoletto (my-kel-*an*-jay-loh pee-stoh-*let*-toh)

Jackson Pollock (*pah*-lock)

Polyclitus (pol-ee-*cly*-tus)

Pompeii (pahm-*pay*)

Pierre-Paul Prud'hon (proo-*dohn*)

Angelo Puccinelli (poo-chee-*nell*-lee)

Radha (*rad*-duh)

Marcantonio Raimondi (mark-ahn-*tohn*-yoh ray-*mohn*-dee)

Robert Rauschenberg (*roh*-shen-buhrg)

Ad Reinhardt (add *ryn*-hahrt)

Gerrit Reitveld (*gair*-it *ryt*-velt)

O. G. Rejlander (*ray*-lahn-der)

Rembrandt van Rijn (*rem*-brant van *ryne*)

Pierre August Renoir (pee-*err* oh-*goost* ren-*wahr*)

Diego Rivera (dee-*ay*-goh ree-*vay*-rah)

Sabatino Rodia (roh-*dee*-uh)

Francois August Rodin (frahn-swah oh-*goost* roh-*dan*)

Georges Rouault (*zhorzh* roo-*oh*)

Henri Rousseau (on-ree roo-*soh*)

Ryoan-ji (ryoh-ahn-jee)

Betye Saar (sahr)

Eero Saarinen (eer-oh *sahr*-uh-nen)

Moshe Safdie (*mosh*-uh *sahf*-dee)

Sāñchī (*sahn*-chee)

Raphael Sanzio (ra-fay-el *sahn*-zee-oh)

Hideo Sasaki (hid-ay-oh sah-sah-kee)

Sassetta (suh-*set*-tuh)

Miriam Schapiro (shuh-*peer*-oh)

Oskar Schlemmer (*shlem*-uhr)

Fritz Scholder (*showl*-duhr)

Kurt Schwitters (*koort shvit*-uhrs)

George Segal (*see*-guhl)

Sengai (sen-guy)

Sesshū (seh-shoo)

Georges Seurat (zhorzh sir-*ah*)

Kathryn Sharbaugh (*shahr*-baw)

Shiva Nataraja (*shih*-vuh nah-tah-*rah*-jah)

Paolo Soleri (pah-*oh*-lo soh-*lay*-ree)

Tawaraya Sōtatsu (tah-wa-rah-ya *soh*-taht-soo)

Fausta Squatriti (*fow*-stah skwah-*tree*-tee)

Alfred Stieglitz (*steeg*-lits)

St. Savin-sur-Gartempe (san sah-*van* suhr gahr-*tomp*)

stupa (*stoo*-pah)

Tagasode (ta-ga-so-day)

Kazuaki Tanahashi (ka-zoo-*ah*-kee tahn-ah-*ha*-shee)

Vladimir Tatlin (*vlad*-ih-mir *tat*-lin)

Toshiko Takaezu (tosh-ko tah-kah-ay-zoo)

Kenzo Tange (ken-zo tahn-gay)

Masami Teraoka (ma-sah-mee tair-ah-oh-ka)

Jean Tinguely (zhon tan-*glee*)

Tlingit (*tling*-git)

Vincent Topazio (toh-*pah*-zyo)

Henri de Toulouse-Lautrec (on-*ree* duh too-*looz* low-*trek*)

James Turrell (tuh-*rell*)

Tutankhamen (too-tahn-*kahm*-uhn)

Jerry Uelsmann (*uhlz*-man)

Unkei (ung-kay)

Ur (er)

Kitagawa Utamaro (kit-ah-*gah*-wah ut-ah-*mah*-roh)

Theo van Doesburg (*tay*-oh van dohz-*buhrg*)

Jan van Eyck (*yahn* van *ike*)

Vincent van Gogh (*vin*-sent van goe; also, van *gawk*)

Victor Vaserely (vah-zuh-ray-*lee*)

Diego Velázquez (dee-*aye*-goh bay-*lahth*-kehth; also, vay-las-kes)

Robert Venturi (ven-*tuhr*-ee)

Jan Vermeer (*yahn* ver-*mair*)

Versailles (vair-*sy*)

Leonardo da Vinci (lay-oh-*nahr*-doh dah *veen*-chi)

Peter Voulkos (*vool*-kohs)

Ann Wärff (wahrf)

Andy Warhol (*wohr*-hohl)

Antoine Watteau (an-*twahn* wah-*toe*)

Yu-Jian (Yü-Chien) (yu-jee-en)

Shibata Zeshin (she-bah-tah zeh-sheen)

ziggurat (*zig*-uh-raht)

Francisco de Zurbaran (frahn-*thee*-skoh de thoor-bah-*rahn*; also, frahn-see-skoh de soor-bar-rahn)

NOTES

PART ONE. Why Art?

Chapter 1. The Nature of Art

1. C. L. Barnhart and Jess Stein, eds., *The American College Dictionary* (New York: Random House, 1963), 70.

2. Leo Tolstoy, *What Is Art?* (London: Walter Scott, 1899), 50.

3. Don Fabun, *The Dynamics of Change* (Englewood Cliffs, New Jersey: Prentice Hall, 1968), 9.

4. Carroll Quigley, "Needed: A Revolution in Thinking?" in *The Journal of the National Education Association 57*, no. 5 (May 1968): 9.

5. Henri Matisse, "The Nature of Creative Activity," in *Education and Art*, edited by Edwin Ziegfeld (New York: UNESCO, 1953), 21.

6. Rev. Paul S. Osumi, *Honolulu Advertiser,* November 26, 1976, F-11.

7. Edward Weston, *The Daybooks of Edward Weston*, 2 vols., edited by Nancy Newhall (Millerton, New York: Aperture, 1973), vol. 2, 181.

8. Ibid., 154.

9. Douglas Davis, "New Architecture: Building for Man," in *Newsweek 77*, no. 16 (April 19, 1971): 80.

10. Betty Burroughs, ed., *Vasari's Lives of the Artists* (New York: Simon & Schuster, 1946), 191.

Chapter 2. Art as Experience

1. Erich Fromm, "The Creative Attitude," in *Creativity and Its Cultivation*, edited by Harold H. Anderson (New York: Harper & Brothers, 1959), 44.

2. Bergen Evans, *Dictionary of Quotations* (New York: Delacorte Press, 1968), 340.

3. John Holt, *How Children Fail* (New York: Pitman, 1964), 167.

4. Courtesy of the Committee for Simon Rodia's Towers in Watts.

5. Henri Matisse, "Notes of a Painter," translated by Alfred H. Barr, Jr., in *Problems of Aesthetics*, edited by Eliseo Vivas and Murray Krieger (New York: Holt, Rinehart & Winston, 1953), 256; originally printed as "Notes d'un peintre," in *La Grande Revue* (Paris, 1908).

6. Ibid., 260.

7. Ibid., 259–260.

8. "Louise Nevelson: a Conversation with Barbara Diamonstein" in *Nevelson: Maquettes for Monumental Sculpture.* [catalog] (New York: Pace Gallery, 1980), 2.

9. *Louise Nevelson: Atmospheres and Environments.* [catalog] (New York: Whitney Museum of American Art, 1980), 55.

10. *Nevelson: Maquettes*, 7.

PART TWO. The Language of Visual Experience

1. Jean Schuster, "Marcel Duchamp, vite," in *le surrealisme* (Paris), no. 2 (Spring 1957): 143.

Chapter 3. Visual Communication

1. Gyorgy Kepes, *The Language of Vision* (Chicago: Paul Theobald and Co., 1944), 9.

2. From "Notes d'un pientre sur son dessin," in *Le Point IV*, XXI (1939): 14.

3. "Interview with Roger Reynolds" [December 1961] in *John Cage* [catalogue] (New York: Henmar Press, 1962), 47.

Chapter 4. Visual Elements

1. Maurice Denis, *Theories 1870–1910* (Paris: Hermann, 1964), 13.

2. Interview with Jean vanden Huevel, "Straight from the Hand and Mouth of Steinberg," in *Life 59*, no. 24 (December 10, 1965): 59.

3. D. T. Suzuki, "Sengai, Zen and Art," in *Art News Annual 27*, pt. 2, no. 7 (November 1957): 118.

4. Ray Bethers, *Composition in Pictures* (New York: Pitman, 1949), 163; originally printed in the *Manifesto of the Futurist Painters*, Italy, 1910.

5. Faber Birren, *Color Psychology and Color Theory* (New Hyde Park, New York: University Books, 1961), 20.

6. Albert E. Elsen, *Purposes of Art* (New York: Holt, Rinehart & Winston, 1967), 437.

Chapter 5. Principles of Design

1. R. G. Swenson, "What is Pop Art," in *Art News* (November 1963): 62.

2. Elizabeth McCausland, "Jacob Lawrence," in *Magazine of Art*, (November 1945): 254.

3. Ragna Thiis Stang, *Edvard Munch* (New York: Abbeville Press, 1979), 74.

PART THREE. The Visual Arts

1. Vernon Blake, *Art and Craft of Drawing* (London: Oxford University Press, 1927), 234.

Chapter 6. Two-dimensional Media

1. Frederick Franck, *The Zen of Seeing: Seeing/Drawing as Meditation*

(New York: Vintage Books, 1973), 6.

2. Betty Edwards, *Drawing on the Right Side of the Brain* (Los Angeles: J. P. Tarcher, Inc., 1979).

3. Anthony Blunt, *Picasso's Guernica* (New York: Oxford University Press, 1969), 28.

4. Ichitaro Kondo and Elsie Grilli, *Katsushika Hokusai* (Rutland, Vermont: Charles E. Tuttle, 1955), 13.

5. André Malraux, *Museum Without Walls*, translated by Stuart Gilbert and Francis Price (Garden City, New York: Doubleday & Co., 1967), 12.

6. Editors of Time-Life Books, *The Art of Photography* (New York: Time-Life, 1981), 12.

7. "Edwin Land," in *Time* (June 26, 1972): 84.

8. Henri Cartier-Bresson, *The Decisive Moment* (New York: Simon & Schuster, 1952), 1.

9. Ibid., 14.

10. Andrew Sarris, ed., *Interviews with Film Directors*, translated by Alice Turner (New York: Avon Books, 1969), 35.

11. "Ring Lardner, Jr.," in *American Film* (June 1985): 81.

Chapter 7.   Three-dimensional Media

1. Betty Burroughs, ed., *Vasari's Lives of the Artists* (New York: Simon & Schuster, 1946), 62.

2. *Fausta Squatriti* (Genoa: Center for Cultural Initiative, 1980), 15.

3. Fausta Squatriti, lecture at the University of Hawaii, March 1987.

4. Glenn Collins, "Mummenschanz Is Back, with a New Bag of Tricks," in *The New York Times* (April 20, 1986): H-8.

5. Henry Hopkins, *Fifty West Coast Artists* (San Francisco: Chronicle Books, 1981), 25.

6. John Coyne, "Handcrafts," in *Today's Education* (November–December 1976): 75.

7. Otto B. Rigan, *New Glass* (San Francisco: San Francisco Book Co., 1976), 105.

8. *Abakanowicz* (New York: Abbeville Press, 1982), 127.

Chapter 8.   Design Principles

1. Henry Dreyfuss, *Designing for People* (New York: Paragraphic Books, 1967), iii.

2. Louis Sullivan, "The Tall Office Building Artistically Considered," in *Lippincott Monthly Magazine* (March 1896): 408.

3. Michael Demarest, "He Digs Downtown," in *Time* (August 24, 1981): 46.

4. Peter Blake, "The Ugly American," in *Horizon 3*, no. 5 (May 1961): 6.

PART FOUR.   Art of The Past

1. "Picasso Speaks" in *The Arts* (May 1923): 319.

2. Jacob Bronowski, *The Ascent of Man* (Boston: Little, Brown, 1973), 42.

3. Carl G. Jung *et al.*, *Man and His Symbols* (New York: Doubleday, 1964), 232.

4. From the film *The Eye of Picasso*, written and produced by Nelly Kaplan, Cythere Films, Paris, 1969.

Chapter 10.   Beyond the Western World

1. James Cooke, *A Voyage to the Pacific Ocean* (Dublin: Printed for H. Chamberlaine and others, 1784), vol. 2, 206.

Chapter 11.   Ancient through Medieval

1. Erwin Panofsky, *Meaning in the Visual Arts* (Garden City, New York: Doubleday, 1955), 128.

Chapter 12.   Renaissance and Baroque

1. Leonardo da Vinci, *The Notebooks of Leonardo Da Vinci*, translated and arranged by Edward McCurdy (New York: Reynal & Hitchcock, 1938), vol. 1, 242–243.

2. Jonathan Brown, "El Greco and Toledo," in *El Greco of Toledo* (Boston: Little, Brown, 1982), 131.

3. Saint Teresa of Jesus, *The Life of Saint Teresa of Jesus,* translated by David Lewis; edited by Benedict Zimmerman, O. C. D. (Westminster, Maryland: The Newman Book Shop, 1947), 266.

PART FIVE.   The Modern World

1. Jacob Bronowski, *The Ascent of Man* (Boston: Little, Brown, 1973), 20.

Chapter 13.   The Late Eighteenth and Nineteenth Centuries

1. C. R. Leslie, *Memoirs of the Life of John Constable* (London: J. M. Dent & Sons, 1913), 274.

2. Ibid., 178.

3. Eugène Delacroix, *The Journal of Eugène Delacroix*, translated by Walter Pach (New York: Covici-Friede Publishers, 1973), 314.

4. Beaumont Newhall, "Delacroix and Photography," in *Magazine of Art 45*, no. 7 (November 1952): 300.

5. Margaretta Salinger, *Gustave Courbet, 1819–1877*, Miniature Album XH (New York: Metropolitan Museum of Art, 1955), 24.

6. *Cézanne and the Post-Impressionists*, McCall's Collection of Modern Art (New York: McCall Books, 1970), 5.

7. Paul Cézanne, *Letters*, edited by John Rewald (Oxford: Bruno Cassier, 1946), 234.

8. Vincent van Gogh, *Further Letters of Vincent van Gogh to His Brother, 1886–1889* (London: Constable & Company, 1929), 139.

9. Ibid., 166.

10. Vincent van Gogh, *Complete Letters* (Greenwich, Connecticut: New York Graphic Society, 1959), vol. 2, 401.

11. Paul Gauguin, *Lettres de Paul Gauguin à Georges-Daniel de Monfried* (Paris: Ediciones Georges Cres, 1918), 89.

12. John Russell, *The Meanings of Modern Art* (New York: Harper & Row, 1974), 35.

13. Ronald Alley, *Gauguin*, The Color Library of Art (Middlesex, England: Hamlyn Publishing Group, 1968), 8.

Chapter 14.   The Early Twentieth Century

1. Wassily Kandinsky, "Reminiscences," in *Modern Artists on Art*, edited by Robert L. Herbert (Englewood Cliffs, New Jersey: Prentice-Hall, 1964), 27.

2. Alfred H. Barr, Jr., ed., *Masters of Modern Art* (New York: The Museum of Modern Art, 1955), 124.

3. H. H. Arnason, *History of Modern Art*, rev. ed. (New York: Abrams, 1977), 146.

4. William Fleming, *Art, Music and Ideas* (New York: Holt, Rinehart & Winston, 1970), 342.

5. Ibid., 342.

6. Ibid.

7. Georges Braque in Roland Penrose, *Picasso: His Life and Work* (New York: Schocken Books, 1966), 125.

8. Nathan Lyons, ed., *Photographers on Photography* (Englewood Cliffs,

New Jersey: Prentice-Hall, Inc., 1966), 133.

9. Beaumont Newhall, *The History of Photography* (New York: The Museum of Modern Art, 1964), 111.

10. Barr, *Masters of Modern Art*, 86.

11. "Venerable Giant of Modern Sculpture Bares Views," in *Honolulu Star-Bulletin*, August 24, 1971, F-2.

12. Joshua C. Taylor, *Futurism* (New York: The Museum of Modern Art, 1961), 124.

13. Jasper Johns, "Marcel Duchamp (1887–1968)," in *Artforum 7* no. 3 (November 1968): 6.

14. Barr, *Masters of Modern Art*, 121.

15. *Gabo: Constructions, Sculpture, Paintings, Drawings, Engravings*. With introductory essays by Herbert Read and Leslie Martin. (London: Lund Humphries, 1957), 151.

16. Piet Mondrian, "Plastic Art and Pure Plastic Art," in *Circle*, edited by J. L. Martin, Ben Nicholson, and N. Gabo (New York: Praeger, 1971), 53.

17. Piet Mondrian, "Neo-Plasticism" in *Abstraction-creation*, no. 1. (1932): 25.

Chapter 15.   Between World Wars

1. Alfred H. Barr, Jr., *Masters of Modern Art* (New York: The Museum of Modern Art, 1955), 137.

2. Hans Richter, *Dada 1916–1966* (Munich: Goethe Institut, 1966), 22.

3. Barr, *Masters of Modern Art*, 137.

4. Hans Arp in Paride Accetti, Raffaele De Grada, and Arturo Schwarz, *Cinquant'annia Dada–Dada in Italia 1916–1966* (Milano: Galleria Schwarz, 1966), 39.

5. Kurt Schwitters in Accetti *et al.*, *Cinquant'annia Dada*, 25.

6. Leopold Zahn, *Paul Klee* (Potsdam: Gustav Kiepenheuer Verlag, 1920), 26.

7. Barr, *Masters of Modern Art*, 131.

8. Ibid., 133.

9. William Fleming, *Art, Music and Ideas* (New York: Holt, Rinehart & Winston, 1970), 346.

10. André Breton, *Manifestos of Surrealism*, translated from the French by Richard Seaver and Helen R. Lane (Ann Arbor, Michigan: University of Michigan Press, 1972), 14.

11. Lael Wertenbaker, *The World of Picasso*, editors of Time-Life Books (New York: Time, Inc., 1967), 130.

12. Herbert Read, *A Concise History of Modern Painting* (New York: Praeger, 1959), 160.

Chapter 16.   Accelerated Change: Art Since World War II

1. *Richard Hamilton: Catalogue of an exhibition at the Tate Gallery*, 12 March–19 April 1970 (London: Tate Gallery, 1970), 31.

2. R. G. Swenson, "What Is Pop Art?" in *Art News* (November 1963): 25.

3. Donald Judd, "Specific Objects," in *Arts Yearbook 8* (1965): 78.

4. Werner Spies, *The Running Fence Project, Christo* (New York: Harry N. Abrams, 1977), unpaged.

5. Margaret A. Miller, "Alice Aycock at USF," in *Alice Aycock Projects, 1979–81* (Tampa: University of South Florida, 1981): 47.

6. Julia Brown, *Occluded Front: James Turrell* (Los Angeles: Fellows of Contemporary Art and the Lapis Press, 1985), 15.

7. Patricia Failing, "James Turrell's New Light on the Universe," in *Art News* (April 1985): 71.

8. Grace Glueck, "Odd Man Out: Red Grooms, the Ruckus Kid," in *Art News* (December 1973): 27.

9. Edward Lucie-Smith, *Sculpture Since 1945* (London: Phaidon, 1987), 77.

10. Calvin Tomkins and the editors of Time-Life Books, *The World of*

Marcel Duchamp (New York: Time, Inc., 1966), 162.

11. James L. Enyeart, *Jerry N. Uelsmann, Twenty-Five Years: A Retrospective* (Boston: Little Brown, 1982), 37.

12. Miriam Schapiro, "Notes from a Conversation on Art, Feminism, and Work," in *Working It Out*, edited by Sara Ruddick and Pamela Daniels (New York: Pantheon, 1977), 296–297.

13. Tomkins, *Marcel Duchamp*, 171.

Chapter 17. Current Issues

1. Clara Weyergraf, ed., *Richard Serra: Interviews, Etc.* (Yonkers: Hudson River Museum, 1980), 168.

2. Joel L. Swerdlow, "To Heal a Nation," in *National Geographic* (May 1985): 557.

3. Gertrude Stein, *Picasso* (Boston: Beacon Press, 1959), 30.

4. Fritz Scholder, *Scholder/Indians* (Flagstaff, Arizona: Northland Press, 1972), 56.

5. Ibid., 14.

CREDITS

The authors and publisher wish to thank artists, owners, museums, galleries, and others for supplying photographs and permission to reproduce them. In addition to those named in the captions, we would like to acknowledge the following:

SUGGESTED READING

GENERAL REFERENCE

Gowing, Sir Lawrence, ed. *Encyclopedia of Visual Art*. Danbury, Connecticut: Grolier Educational Corp., 1983.

Jones, Lois Swan. *Research Methods and Resources: A Guide to Finding Art Information*. Dubuque, Iowa: Kendall/Hunt, 1985

Panofsky, Erwin. *Meaning in the Visual Arts*. Chicago: University of Chicago Press, 1983.

PART ONE. Why Art?

Canaday, John. *What is Art? An Introduction to Painting, Sculpture & Architecture*. New York: Knopf, 1980.

Cole, Natalie Robinson. *The Arts in the Classroom*. New York: John Day, 1940.

Edwards, Betty. *Drawing on the Artist Within: A Guide to Innovation, Invention and Creativity*. New York: Simon and Schuster, 1986.

Flack, Audrey. *Art and Soul: Notes on Creating*. New York: Dutton, 1986.

Johnson, Jay. *American Folk Art of the Twentieth Century*. New York: Rizzoli, 1983.

Lowenfeld, Viktor. *Creative and Mental Growth*, 8th ed. New York: Macmillan, 1987.

May, Rollo. *The Courage to Create*. New York: W. W. Norton, 1975.

McKim, Robert. *Experiences in Visual Thinking*, 2d ed. Monterey, California: Brooks/Cole, 1980.

Samuels, Mike, M.D., and Nancy Samuels. *Seeing with the Mind's Eye: The History, Techniques and Uses of Visualization*. New York: Random House, 1975.

Steichen, Edward. *The Family of Man*. New York: Simon & Schuster, 1967.

PART TWO. The Language of Visual Experience

Anderson, Donald M. *The Art of Written Forms*. New York: Holt, Rinehart & Winston, 1969.

Arnheim, Rudolf. *Art and Visual Perception*. Berkeley: University of California Press, 1969.

Berger, John. *Ways of Seeing*. New York: Penguin, 1977.

Dosczi, Gyorgy. *The Power of Limits: Proportional Harmonies in Nature, Art and Architecture*. Boulder, Colorado: Shambhala, 1981.

Kepes, Gyorgy. *Language of Vision*. Chicago: Paul Theobald, 1949.

Lauer, David A. *Design Basics,* 2d ed. New York: Holt, Rinehart & Winston, 1985.

Nelson, George. *How to See*. Boston: Little, Brown, 1977.

Shahn, Ben. *The Shape of Content*. New York: Random House, 1957.

Varley, Helen, ed. *Colour*. London: Mitchell Beazley, 1980.

Zelanski, Paul, and Mary Pat Fisher. *Shaping Space: The Dynamics of Three-dimensional Design*. New York: Holt, Rinehart & Winston, 1987.

PART THREE. The Visual Arts

Bacon, Edmund N. *The Design of Cities*, rev. ed. New York: Penguin, 1976.

Blake, Peter. *Form Follows Fiasco: Why Modern Architecture Hasn't Worked*. Boston: Little, Brown, 1988.

Cartier-Bresson, Henri. *The Decisive Moment*. New York: Simon & Schuster, 1952.

Castleman, Riva. *Prints of the Twentieth Century: A History*. New York: Oxford University Press, 1976.

Constantine, Mildred, and Jack Lenor Larson. *Beyond Craft: The Art Fabric*. New York: Van Nostrand Reinhold, 1980.

Dreyfuss, Henry. *The Measure of Man*. New York: Whitney, 1967.

Edwards, Betty. *Drawing on the Right Side of the Brain*. Los Angeles: J. P. Tarcher, 1979.

Franck, Frederick. *The Zen of Seeing: Drawing as Meditation*. New York: Random House, 1973.

Frings, Gini S. *Fashion: From Concept to Consumer*. Englewood Cliffs, New Jersey: Prentice-Hall, 1982.

Fuller, R. Buckminster. *Operating Manual for Spaceship Earth*. Carbondale, Illinois: Southern Illinois University Press, 1969.

Gardiner, Stephen. *Introduction to Architecture*. Oxford: Equinox, 1983.

Goldstein, Nathan. *The Art of Responsive Drawing*, 3d ed. Englewood Cliffs, New Jersey: Prentice-Hall, 1984.

Heller, Steven, ed. *Innovators of American Illustration*, New York: Van Nostrand Reinhold, 1986.

Ivins, William M. *Prints and Visual Communication*. New York: Plenum, 1969.

Knight, Arthur. *A Panoramic History of the Movies,* rev. ed. New York: Macmillan, 1978.

Le Normand-Romain, Antoinette, et al. *Sculpture: The Adventure of Modern Sculpture in the Nineteenth and Twentieth Centuries*. New York: Rizzoli, 1986.

Lucie-Smith, Edward. *The Story of Craft: The Craftsman's Role in Society*. Ithaca, New York: Cornell University Press, 1981.

Macaulay, David. *Cathedral: The*

Story of Its Construction. Boston: Houghton Mifflin, 1973.

Mast, Gerald. *A Short History of the Movies.* New York: Macmillan, 1986.

Mayer, A. Hyatt. *Prints and People: A Social History of Printed Pictures.* Princeton: Princeton University Press, 1980.

Mayer, Barbara. *Contemporary American Craft Art.* Salt Lake City: Gibbs M. Smith, 1988.

Mayer, Ralph. *Artists Handbook of Materials and Techniques.* New York: Viking, 1981.

Nelson, Glenn C. *Ceramics, A Potter's Handbook,* 5th ed. New York: Holt, Rinehart & Winston, 1985.

Nicolaides, Kimon. *The Natural Way to Draw.* Boston: Houghton Mifflin, 1975.

Piper, David. *Looking at Art: An Introduction to Enjoying Great Paintings of the World.* New York: Random House, 1984.

Rudofsky, Bernard. *Architecture without Architects: A Short Introduction to Non-pedigreed Architecture.* New York: Doubleday, 1964.

Sachs, Paul. J. *Modern Prints and Drawings.* New York: Knopf, 1954.

Salvadori, Mario. *Why Buildings Stand Up.* New York: W. W. Norton, 1980.

Scully, Vincent, Jr.. *Modern Architecture: The Architecture of Democracy.* New York: Braziller, 1977.

Smith, Paul J., and Edward Lucie-Smith. *Craft Today: Poetry of the Physical.* New York: American Craft Council, 1986.

Smith, Stan, and Friso Ten Holt, eds. *The Artist's Manual: Equipment, Materials, Techniques.* New York: Mayflower Books, 1980.

Thomas, Michel, Cristine Mainguy, and Sophie Pommier. *Textile Art.* New York: Rizzoli, 1985.

Upton, Barbara London with John Upton. *Photography,* 3d ed. Boston: Little Brown, 1984.

Watkin, David A. *A History of Western Architecture.* London: Barrie & Jenkins, 1986.

Wines, James. *De-Architecture.* New York: Rizzoli, 1987.

PART FOUR. Art of the Past

Bronowski, Jacob. *The Ascent of Man.* Boston: Little, Brown, 1974.

Broude, Norma, and Mary D. Garrad. *Feminism and Art History: Questioning the Litany.* New York: Harper & Row, 1982.

Clark, Kenneth. *Civilisation: A Personal View.* New York: Harper & Row, 1969.

Coe, Ralph T. *Lost and Found Traditions: Native American Art 1965–1985.* New York: American Federation of the Arts. 1986.

De la Croix, Horst, and Richard Tansey. *Gardner's Art through the Ages,* 8th ed., 2 vols. New York: Harcourt, Brace, Jovanovich, 1986.

Dwyer, Jane P., and Edward B. Dwyer. *Traditional Arts of Africa, Oceania and the Americas.* San Francisco: The Fine Arts Museums of San Francisco, 1973.

Fine, Elsa H. *Women and Art: A History of Women Painters and Sculptors from the Renaissance to the 20th Century.* Montclair, New Jersey: Allanheld & Schram, 1978.

Fleming, William. *Art and Ideas,* 7th ed. New York: Holt, Rinehart & Winston, 1986.

Gillon, Werner. *A Short History of African Art.* New York: Facts on File, 1984.

Goldwater, Robert, and Marco Treves, eds. *Artists on Art.* New York: Pantheon, 1958.

Gombrich, E. H. *The Story of Art,* 14 ed. Englewood Cliffs, New Jersey: Prentice-Hall, 1985.

Hauser, Arnold. *The Social History of Art,* 4 vols. New York: Random House, 1957–1958.

Heller, Nancy G. *Women Artists: An Illustrated History.* New York: Abbeville, 1987.

Herbert, Robert L., ed. *Modern Artists on Art.* Englewood Cliffs, New Jersey: Prentice-Hall, 1964.

Janson, H. W. *History of Art,* 3d ed., revised by Anthony Janson. Englewood Cliffs, New Jersey: Prentice-Hall, 1987.

Lee, Sherman. *A History of Far Eastern Art,* 4th ed. Englewood Cliffs, New Jersey: Prentice-Hall, 1982; New York: Abrams, 1982.

Malraux, Andre, trans. Stuart Gilbert and Francis Price. *Museums without Walls.* Garden City, New York: Doubleday, 1967.

Mead, S. M. *Exploring the Visual Arts of Oceania.* Honolulu: University Press of Hawaii, 1979.

Newhall, Beaumont. *The History of Photography,* rev. ed. New York: The Museum of Modern Art, 1982.

Peterson, Karen, and J. J. Wilson. *Women Artists: Recognition and Reappraisal from the Early Middle Ages to the Twentieth Century.* New York: New York University Press, 1976.

Pfeiffer, John E. *The Creative Explosion: An Inquiry into the Origins of Art and Religion.* New York: Harper & Row, 1982.

Reti, Ladislao, ed. *The Unknown Leonardo.* New York: McGraw Hill, 1974.

Ruspoli, Mario. *The Cave of Lascaux: The Final Photographic Record.* Paris: Bordas, S.A., 1986. London: Thames & Hudson, 1987.

Stanley-Baker, Joan. *Japanese Art.* New York: Thames & Hudson, 1984.

Sullivan, Michael. *The Arts of China,* 3d ed. Berkeley: University of California Press, 1984.

PART FIVE. The Modern World

Arnason, H. H. *History of Modern*

Art: Painting, Sculpture, Architecture, Photography. New York: Abrams, 1986.

Ashton, Dore. *The New York School: A Cultural Reckoning.* New York: Penguin, 1980.

———. *Twenthieth-Century Artists on Art.* New York: Pantheon, 1985.

Banfield, Edward C. *The Democratic Muse: Visual Arts and the Public Interest.* New York: Basic Books, 1984.

Beardsley, John. *Earthworks and Beyond.* New York: Abbeville, 1984.

Blake, Peter. *God's Own Junkyard: The Planned Deterioration of America's Landscape.* New York: Holt, Rinehart & Winston, 1979.

Brown, Milton Wolf. *The Story of the Armory Show,* 2d ed. New York: Abbeville, 1988.

Bruckner, D. J. R., Seymour Chwast, and Steven Heller. *Art Against War.* New York: Abbeville, 1984.

Canaday, John. *Mainstreams of Modern Art,* 2d ed. New York: Henry Holt, 1981.

Chase, Judith Wragg. *Afro-American Art and Craft.* New York: Van Nostrand Reinhold, 1971.

Cockcroft, Eva, John Weber, and James C. Cockcroft. *Toward a People's Art: A Contemporary Mural Movement.* New York: Dutton, 1977.

Felshin, Nina. *Disarming Images: Art for Nuclear Disarmament.* New York: Adama Books, 1984.

Fleming, Ronald Lee, and Renata von Tscharner. *Place Makers: Creating Public Art That Tells You Where You Are.* New York: Harcourt, Brace, Jovanovich, 1986.

Gablik, Suzi. *Has Modernism Failed?* New York: Thames and Hudson, 1984.

Harris, Ann Sutherland, and Linda Nochlin. *Women Artists: 1550–1950.* New York: Knopf, 1977.

Henri, Adrian. *Total Art: Environ-ment, Happenings, and Performance.* New York: Praeger, 1974.

Hughes, Robert. *The Shock of the New.* New York: Knopf, 1981.

Hunter, Sam, and John Jacobus. *Modern Art,* New York: Abrams, 1985.

Jencks, Charles. *Post-Modernism: The New Classicism in Art and Architecture.* London: Academy Editions, 1987.

Johnson, Ellen H. *American Artists on Art from 1940 to 1980.* New York: Harper & Row, 1982.

Jordan, Sherrill, et al., eds. *Public Art, Public Controversy: Tilted Arc on Trial.* New York: American Council for the Arts, 1987.

Kaprow, Allan. *Assemblage, Environments, and Happenings.* New York: Abrams, 1966.

Klotz, Heinrich. *The History of Postmodern Architecture.* Cambridge: MIT Press, 1988.

Lancaster, Clay. *The Japanese Influence in America.* New York: Abbeville, 1985.

Neff, Terry Ann R. *In the Mind's Eye: Dada and Surrealism.* New York: Abbeville, 1985.

Pelfrey, Robert H. with Mary Hall-Pelfrey. *Art and the Mass Media.* New York: Harper & Row, 1984.

Quirarte, Jacinto. *Mexican American Artists.* Austin: University of Texas Press, 1973.

Richter, Hans. *Dada: Art and Anti-Art.* New York: Abrams, 1970.

Rickey, George. *Constructivism: Origins and Evolution.* New York: Braziller, 1967.

Robbins, Corrine. *The Pluralist Era: American Art, 1968–1981.* New York: Harper & Row, 1984.

Rose, Barbara. *American Art Since 1900,* rev. ed. New York: Praeger, 1975.

Rubin, William, and Kirk Varnadoe, eds. *Primitivism in 20th Century Art: Affinity of the Tribal and the Modern,* 2 vols. New York: The Museum of Modern Art, 1984.

Sandler, Irving. *American Art of the 1960s.* New York: Harper & Row, 1988.

Scully, Vincent. *Modern Architecture: The Architecture of Democracy.* New York: Braziller, 1977.

Seitz, William. *Abstract Expressionist Painting in America.* Cambridge: Harvard University Press, 1983.

Selz, Peter. *Art in Our Times: A Pictorial History, 1890–1980.* New York: Abrams, 1981.

Smagula, H. J. *Currents: Contemporary Directions in the Visual Arts.* Englewood Cliffs, New Jersey: Prentice-Hall, 1983.

Stern, Robert A. M. *American Architecture: Innovation and Tradition.* New York: Rizzoli, 1985.

Tuchman, Maurice, *The Spiritual in Art: Abstract Painting 1890–1985.* New York: Abbeville, 1986.

INDEX

ABOUT THE AUTHORS

Duane and Sarah Preble live at the edge of a tropical forest overlooking Honolulu and the Pacific Ocean. They have taken active roles in their community. Duane has served on boards of governmental, environmental, and arts organizations. He is on the Board of Trustees of Hawaii's major art museum, the Honolulu Academy of Arts, and is a frequent consultant to art, environmental, and educational organizations.

Extensive travel has given the Prebles global perspective. Duane taught on two round-the-world Semester at Sea voyages with the Institute for Shipboard Education, and he has led study tours in the United States, Europe, and Japan for the University of Hawaii.

After completing his BA in painting, graphics, and sculpture at UCLA, Duane received his Master of Fine Arts degree from the University of Hawaii. Since 1961 he has been a member of the art faculty at the University of Hawaii as well as an exhibiting artist. He has taught a wide variety of courses, including introduction to the visual arts, art history, photography, drawing, and design. In 1975, Duane was selected for listing in *Outstanding Educators of America*.

Sarah studied art and psychology at St. Lawrence University and the University of Hawaii. After receiving her BA in psychology and Master of Library Science degree from the University of Hawaii, she became a reference librarian.

They continue to pursue their individual interests in the visual arts—Sarah in ceramics and research, and Duane in painting and photography.